The Book of Job

Judaism in the 2nd Century BCE:
An Intertextual Reading

Leslie S. Wilson

Studies in Judaism

University Press of America,® Inc.
Lanham · Boulder · New York · Toronto · Oxford

University Press of America,® Inc.
4501 Forbes Boulevard
Suite 200
Lanham, Maryland 20706
UPA Acquisitions Department (301) 459-3366

PO Box 317
Oxford
OX2 9RU, UK

Printed in the United States of America
British Library Cataloging in Publication Information Available

Library of Congress Control Number: 2006922582
ISBN-13: 978-0-7618-3462-5 (paperback : alk. paper)
ISBN-10: 0-7618-3462-1 (paperback : alk. paper)

The paper used in this publication meets the minimum requirements of American National Standard for Information Sciences—Permanence of Paper for Printed Library Materials, ANSI Z39.48—1984

Studies in Judaism

TABLE OF CONTENTS

PREFACE AND ACKNOWLEDGEMENTS

My interest in the book of Job began several years ago as the simple (*sic*) exercise of reading the first two chapters of one of the most often cited and least understood books of the Hebrew Bible. I was, I thought, familiar with its plot and cognizant of the theological *cruces* or pillars that it contained. Little did I understand the extent of my ignorance—less still the brilliance and polymathy of its author.

My original intent was to confine the scope of this book to the Prologue alone. However, it became clear to me quite early that the Prologue is prefatory to the Book of Job in general and to the Final Epilogue in particular. Thus the scope expanded to include the entire work.

This book is not intended as a commentary, rather as an attempt at a working solution to a puzzle. Any views set forth are not intended as exegesis; they are an attempt to systematically articulate the product of the author's mind.

All Hebrew citations are to be assumed to be unvocalized and are so represented in the transliterations except where I have supplied vocalization. This is done in order to allow the reader to work on a "level playing field" without the preconceived direction that vocalization provides. Except where noted, all translations are my own. I alone am responsible for such errors that I may have made in either translation or interpretive extrapolation.

I realize that this work takes to task some of the doyens of modern Joban scholarship. This in no way lessens my deep respect for their work without which I might never have had the opportunity to study this magnificent treasure. *Poenitet me si male scripsi.*

I wish to express my sincere gratitude to Professor William Hallo, my teacher and mentor; Rabbi Benjamin Scolnic, for his friendship and unwavering confidence in the validity of this project; Rabbi James Ponet, of whose gifted insights I am a beneficiary; David Berg, whose analytical and keen intellect helped me climb out of some crucial quagmires; and last but not least my wife Kathy, for her endless patience, tolerance, and constant support.

L.S.W.
Hanukkah 5766
December, 2005

INTRODUCTION

> Persecution cannot prevent even public expression of the heterodox truth, for a man of independent thought can utter his views in public and remain unharmed, provided he moves with circumspection...Persecution, then, gives rise to a peculiar technique of writing, and therewith to a peculiar type of literature, in which the truth about all crucial things is presented exclusively between the lines.
>
> *Leo Strauss*

These words of Leo Strauss[1] may be interpreted as applying strictly to physical persecution; however, the same words may be invoked in other circumstances. While in many cases the brutality of physical corporal persecution is indeed the consequence of non-conformism and heterodoxy, there exists another persecution, which, while causing its own anguish, may be differently defined. That persecution entails social and religious consequences that might take the form of ostracism or exile.

This chapter is a simplified overview of a work whose complex nature resembles the tentacles of an octopus. To the greatest extent possible, the general statements will be addressed as their particular relevance occurs within our investigation of the Book of Job. These general statements are not intended to ask the reader to make unsubstantiated "leaps of faith"; rather they serve to prepare the reader for a non-establishment approach to and treatment of this difficult work.

What is this book all about? With what is the author taking issue? When did our author write the Book of Job? We will tackle these questions in sequence.

The Book of Job deals with a variety of issues, both superficial and profound. Most people, if they have any familiarity with the Book of Job, know it as paradigm for "why bad things happen to good people." Scholars and theologians see the book as somewhat more problematic, assigning various theories in an effort to morally justify the actions of the Divine towards humanity.

---

[1] Strauss (1952, 24-25)

Our reading will suggest a far wider-ranging scope of inquiry. The interaction of the Divine and humanity is a *datum*. It is the quality of this interaction, examined under a philosophic microscope and extended out to the end of time, that provides the focus.

As to when the book was written, we shall demonstrate, based on technical literary and philological evidence, that it dates to the first half or the mid-point of the 2nd century BCE. In fact, the author provides a snapshot of the political and religious issues of the day, making the Book of Job a primary source of information along with the Book of Maccabees, the works of Josephus and the Dead Sea Scrolls.

What was going on in the world of the author in his own day? It may not have been a time of outright physical or religious repression emanating from external sources such as the Seleucids; however the encroachment of Hellenism almost certainly inspired a movement or movements within the general sphere of "Judaism" that were agitating for or against change. The priesthood was not Aaronide but "Zadokite" and at that perhaps not the original Zadokites that traced their lineage back to the Zadok who was King David's High Priest. We know that within another hundred years, Jewish schismatic sects would abound, each in search of the magic formula that would restore the Jews to the innocence of the days of "Creation." Of course, each sect possessed its own vision of that idyllic time. What these sects did seem to have in common was the vehicle by which this restoration would be accomplished, namely a "messiah" whose righteousness and purity would be absolute and whose lineage would be unimpeachable. The Dead Sea Scrolls bear eloquent witness to the articulations of a number of these groups of people, even though we cannot necessarily identify them by name. While sectarianism seemed to abound in southern Judah, perhaps for its abundance of hiding-places, the Samaritans of Shechem and Mount Gerizim in northern Israel had developed their own Messianic system that dated back to the 5th century BCE and possibly before the "return" of the exiles from Babylon.

Jewish "messiahs" have come in many forms throughout history; however, they generally fall into two categories, namely, the "Kingly Messiah" and the "Priestly Messiah." If we look to the origins of these two "types" we must look to the Levitical "anointed priest" and the "anointed king" of the Books of Samuel and Kings. The "anointed priest" was a descendant of Aaron and the "anointed king" was of the lineage of David. Prior to King David, king and priest were combined in a single person as in the case of King Saul. The latter had the kingship wrested from him by the prophet Samuel in a particularly unpleasant manner. Nonetheless, contemporary late 3rd and early 2nd century BCE sects made use of one of these two paradigms. The "anointed priest" paradigm was clearly more popular since there was no monarchy either in Samaria or Judah at the time.

We have all heard about "false Messiahs," be they charlatans or hapless, "misguided," well-meaning people. Each segment of the religiously split populace was anxious to be known as the promoter of the "real Messiah," so there was doubtless a number of candidates campaigning at any given time.

Enter our author, skeptical of eschatology and especially disdainful of its promulgators. Proceeding counter to contemporary wisdom, he embarks upon his own investigation of the principles of the *eschaton* and finds them failing. His purpose is to debunk the Messianic notion in its entirety; however, to do so explicitly is risky. Thus he constructs an elaborate encryption system for his work. The combination of encoding and underlying polemics belies a powerful indictment of the Messianic movements. So he wrote the Book of Job in a way that it could be read on two levels.

First, the general reader could extract a politically and religiously correct story of a man whose perfect piety and righteousness enabled him to overcome the worst of adversities. Second, the informed reader would decipher the code and engage in a discourse based on the philosophic knowledge of his day.

The author bases his premises on the philosophic principles of Aristotle and is immediately faced with his first contradiction. The deity has created humanity in his own image; therefore, humanity possesses all the attributes of the deity. How does one reconcile the "perfection" of the deity with the "imperfections" of humanity? The deity must also be somehow flawed.

The Author's Message

The Jews and "Judaisms" of the author's times are in turmoil. With widespread religious and political unrest, the Jewish nation is splintered into sects, each in search of a quick "fix." The "fix" is in the form of a "messiah," for whom each sect claims a different pedigree. Our author identifies two Messianic sources.

First, he uses the Pentateuchal verse about "sword and scepter" using language from the story of Bilʿam in Num. 24. Second, he uses the story of "the righteous branch" from Jer. 23[5] and Zech. chapters 3 and 6 when he identifies Job by the Messianic attributes of those sources.

In addition, the author is directing his argument against those who identify with the concept of the "Priestly Messiah." The Hebrew root that conveys the meaning of "righteousness" is the same as that of the name of the contemporary High Priestly family of Zadok and the name of one or more splinter sects. These included the Samaritans who practiced their religion outside the pale of such normative Judaism as might have been described for the times.

The concept of "righteousness" derived from the same root is explicitly defined by the prophet Ezekiel (Chapter 18). Ezekiel does not necessarily espouse Messianism; however, he specifies "righteousness" as the criterion for surviving the day of the Apocalypse.

Given all of these pre-conditions, the author now adds the layer of Aristotelian logic that was becoming current with the rapid spread of Hellenism. Using these tools, he describes a paradox, the enigmatic conundrum articulated above. A "messiah" is simply a logical impossibility and all who seek Messianic salvation are destined to fail in their search. Salvation at the hands of Yahweh will be apocalyptic; for all intents and purposes the world will come to an end.

The author's answer uses the principle of "Occam's Razor."2 For humanity and indeed the deity to survive, there must be a truce, an acceptance of two mutually incompatible sets of attributes. Neither of these two sets can exist by itself and their incompatibility will forever engender a tension between humanity and the Divine. This is however, the solution for universal survival.

Methodology

The roots of this study of the Book of Job lie in the recognition in the Prologue of a pattern of words and phrases that seemed to frequently originate from the book of Genesis. Upon close reading and investigation, it became clear that these occurrences might each be unique and deliberate rather than accidental. An empirical test of this hypothesis led to the discovery that this was indeed a method to which the author of the book of Job strictly adhered. Upon further research, it became apparent that this method was self-predictive throughout those portions of the book that the author intended the knowing reader to recognize and interpolate.

There are two criteria that define this study. First is the absence of theological motivation; that is to say that there is no predetermined necessary outcome. Second, the methodology employed is valid since it can be tested at any point. The resulting outcome rises to the surface by itself as a result of the method employed.

The author was intimately familiar with all of *BH*,[3] drawing upon turns of phrase that occur but twice in the Hebrew Bible (and, as we shall see, the Dead

---

[2] *Pluralitas non est ponenda sine neccesitate* – "entities should not be multiplied unnecessarily."

[3] We shall use the abbreviation *BH* in referring to the Hebrew Bible in order to avoid the anachronistic names such as "Old Testament" or "Masoretic Text." *BH* refers to no edition of the Hebrew Bible in particular.

Sea Scrolls), once in the Book of Job and once elsewhere in *BH*.[4] By our empirical approach and in our critical readings we will identify this unique source material and use it alone to describe the real intent of the author. It is just as our opening quotation from Leo Strauss articulates.

The methodology may be described as "intertextual" with the strict *caveat* that the intertextuality is exact and not approximate. Pyeon describes two levels of intertextuality, which he describes as "synchronic" and "diachronic."[5] "Synchronicity" involves the multiple uses of words and expressions within the body of the subject text. "Diachronicity" involves the uses of words and expressions within the body of the subject text as compared with their occurrences in other bodies of literature. At first glance, one may question if there is any difference between Pyeon's methodology and that employed here. There is a difference that is both subtle and defining. Pyeon's "intertextuality" allows him the freedom to make loose comparisons and citations. It is this looseness that forces Pyeon, even at the end of his work, to refer to "the problem of Job's justice or his righteousness."[6] The "intertextuality" that has been described above requires an exact equivalence such that there can be no doubt as to its meaning.

---

[4] As we shall see, the author on occasions fashions a phrase, which is a composite. By that I mean that he combines not one but two *BH* antecedents to form a single phrase. If there are three elements to the phrase, each *BH* antecedent will contain one unique element and one common element.

[5] Pyeon (2003, 67)

[6] Pyeon (2003, 202)

LITERARY BEGINNINGS

The Prologue

The Prologue serves to introduce the reader to the purpose of the material—both substantive and thematic—that the author wishes to present. We will accomplish this introduction in two steps before we proceed to the main poetic body of the Book of Job. First, we need to recreate the story recounted in the Prologue according to our critical readings. Second, we need to discern the details of the author's intended *agenda*.

Our author takes pains to portray a priestly patriarchal Job in terms of the attributes of Abraham and Isaac. He deliberately excludes Jacob from the character of Job; it is the character of יהוה (YHWH) that is portrayed through the attributes of Jacob. However, while there is none of Jacob in Job, Job conducts his daily life in terms of יהוה (YHWH) as seen in Jacob.[1] This definition is critically important to the reader because it provides the framework for all of the background information that follows.

"Piety" and "integrity"[2] find their expression in Job's slavish practice of apotropaic ritual. His believes that his daily sacrifices serve to ward off the consequences of sin,[3] which is specifically defined as "blasphemy." His wealth is not the gift of a grateful, benevolent deity; rather, it is the result of his own efforts along with the protection afforded him by the deity by dint of his ritual faith.

The deity is a triad about which Job knows very little. He stands in awe of אלהים (*ʾelohîm*), the monolithic, perpetual, and immutable institution of justice. The laws of אלהים (*ʾelohîm*) dictate the morals and ethics of Job's life; however, there is no communication between Job and אלהים (*ʾelohîm*). Were there to be communication, the immutable institution would no longer be immutable.

Job knows יהוה (YHWH) as the recipient of his daily sacrifice, the god who would guarantee his security as long as Job ritually worshiped him. In Job's

---

[1] Our author has a very low opinion of Jacob and his ethics. See the discussion of $1^{8,9}$.

[2] Which we have just described as צדק (*ṣdq*), צדיק (*ṣdyq*) and צדקה (*ṣdqh*) – "relative wholeness."

[3] We are here describing חטא (*ḥṭʾ*)—"unintentional sin" described in 1^{5}.

world there was no mishap or accident that יהוה (YHWH) would or could not avert. That is not to say that Job was necessarily happy; his pre-occupation with the "care and feeding"[4] of יהוה (YHWH) along with a constant worry about the "piety" and "integrity" of his children, left him little time to savor happiness. Job knew nothing of the mercurial nature of יהוה (YHWH), namely, that he could be insecure, cruel, vengeful, deceitful, and whimsical in addition to being compassionate, merciful, kind, and loyal. The author takes the reader into the inmost machinations of יהוה (YHWH)'s mind, providing a vivid depiction of the insecurity of יהוה (YHWH). That insecurity is reflected in Deut.13[4]:

כי מנסה יהוה אלהים אתכם לדעת הישכם אהבים את יהוה אלהיכם
בכל לבבכם ובכל נפשכם

ky mnsh yhwh ʾlhykm ʾtkm ldʿt hyškm ʾhbym ʾt yhwh ʾlhykm
bkl lbbkm wbkl npškm

...for YHWH your God is testing you to determine if you love YHWH your God with all your heart and with all your soul.

along with the numerous commandments to the Israelites "to love YHWH your God."

Job apparently enjoys a harmonious relationship with his deity(ies). He lives in a utopian, albeit fool's, paradise, blissfully unaware of the existence of השטן (*haśśaṭan*). It is important to note here that nowhere is the reader given the impression that השטן (*haśśaṭan*) either was or ever represented evil. He was simply the "representation" of יהוה (YHWH)'s insecurity, the executor of יהוה (YHWH)'s will; his guarantee of distance from unpleasantness and his assurance of love and popularity. השטן (*haśśaṭan*) existed only in the consciousness of יהוה (YHWH). Were Job possessed of השטן (*haśśaṭan*), our author might have named him "blasphemy." When *haśśaṭan*/YHWH strikes, Job is blindsided.

In the blink of an eye, Job's world is turned upside-down. The impossible happens, an accident, an event against which his god has provided no protection. In four consecutive strokes Job's belief system crumbles before him and is nullified. Job's shocked reaction is not one of sorrow but one of anger and frustration. He defies ritual and convention by ripping his "priestly"[5] robe, shearing his hair, and falling flat on his face. He curses יהוה YHWH for failing to protect him, realizing for the first time that all of his "care and feeding" of

---

[4] Oppenheim (1964:183-198).

[5] We shall discuss this in detail in our treatment of 1^{20} below.

יהוה (YHWH) was for naught and that his wealth was never really protected. Our author is careful to remind us that it is יהוה (YHWH) who is the object of Job's outburst and not אלהים (*ʾelohîm*).[6] At least אלהים (*ʾelohîm*) has not betrayed him; Job does not know of Jacob's deal with אלהים (*ʾelohîm*) in Gen.28[20] in which he declared that יהוה (YHWH) would become his אלהים (*ʾelohîm*). It is not difficult to understand the confusion of identities both in the mind of Job and the reader.

As we shall see, this is part of the deliberate ploy of the author to cast doubt on at least the efficacy if not the very existence of a single deity.

Our author uses Chapter Two to concentrate further on the insecurity of יהוה (YHWH). Has Job really cursed him? After all, he did not use the "C" word, rather its opposite as a euphemism. יהוה (YHWH) is torn between his intuitive belief in Job's fidelity and his *alter ego*'s taunts to the contrary. Can יהוה (YHWH) be so *naïve* in his intuition? יהוה (YHWH) experiences the equivalent of a nervous breakdown in 2[3] when he loses his ability to distinguish himself from his *doppelgänger*. Thus blinded, יהוה (YHWH) sends השטן (*haśśaṭan*), armed with more weaponry, to resolve his doubts. Job, already emotionally disengaged from יהוה (YHWH), takes his beating and makes no effort to either resist or surrender.

Job is physically livid but emotionally paralyzed to all but his wife. She has suffered through these ordeals at her husband's side and shared in his feelings of anger and frustration. She however, seems to have made peace with her suffering and rationalizes that life is a day-to-day experience that brooks no foresight. Having seen Job curse יהוה (YHWH) and survive, she now challenges him to curse אלהים (*ʾelohîm*). She knows that he will not die; however, all this is just too much for Job. She has attacked his sole source of security, the belief that justice will prevail. She bears the brunt of his enraged response in which he dismisses her summarily. Her rational existentialism is not an acceptable solution for our author and she does not appear again directly.[7]

There now appear three "friends" who have come ostensibly to "comfort" Job but both the text and their actions tell another story. Tearing their robes and throwing dust skyward in an effort to be sympathetically stricken with sores is hardly comforting.[8] The action that speaks loudest is their silence. Were they truly trying to console Job, they would have spoken words of comfort. They

---

[6] Or השטן (*haśśaṭan*) for that matter.

[7] Her presence is assumed in the 3rd Epilogue as the mother of Job's new set of children.

[8] Moses accomplished this feat in Ex.9[8-10]. See below 2[12]. The contrast of Moses' success and the failure of the "friends" in these actions serves to delegitimize them *ab initio*.

recognize that Job is not in mourning; he is raging inside. One does not try to speak to a person at the height of their rage, rather, one sits patiently waiting for the anger to become quiet. Finally, Job can no longer keep his anger and frustration under wraps and it boils over as he prepares to speak. It is the screaming of a man outraged, extended far beyond reasonable human emotional limits.

The Poetic Section of the Book of Job

The Prologue and 3rd Epilogue bracket a select anthology of mixed *genre* literature. The form of this literature is classic poetry of the Ancient Near East, being distinguished by parallelism, both simple and complex. This poetry is enhanced further by the use of assonance, and alliteration—features that point perhaps to original oral sources.[9] There is no evidence that this anthology is not the work of a single author, yet many scholars use this reasoning in their exegetical effort—heterogeneity is a convenient excuse for including or excluding text when it does not fit a particular theory. The text may also be declared corrupt and emended to suit the interpretive context.

Some of the aforementioned may certainly be true, especially if we accept the idea of an original oral transmission. However, we do not grant the license to emend the text as a legitimate approach to the understanding of this corpus. While its original sources are perhaps heterogeneous, we will demonstrate that this poetic body of the Book of Job is the assembled product of the author of the Prologue and 3rd Epilogue. The formulaic rubrics that divide the chapters into the speeches that are politely described as a "debate" are part of a *schema* that incorporates the subject of Messianism into the author's investigation. We shall treat the subject of Messianism in the Book of Job in a separate chapter.

As previously stated, the poetic chapters are filled with philological and lexical problems to an extent found nowhere else in *BH*. However, the contextual meaning and intent are quite clear. The sections are assembled by the author in a manner consistent with the Prologue and 3rd Epilogue, namely as a *pastiche*. While he remains true to his methodology of invoking unique *BH* antecedents, he now utilizes poetic pieces that are constructed for the most part of couplets and triplets. The author has occasionally inserted explicative language in the style of the surrounding material. It is the identification of these patches of the quilt that is the principle that guides the reader. We will comment only on verses or phrases that are of particular interest within the context of our methodology.

---

[9] While cases have been made for the existence of meter in the poetry of the Ancient Near East, there is no definitive pattern discernible.

From the very beginning of Chapter 4, the author presents the reader with a battleground scene. ʾEliphaz cannot wait to rip into Job at both very personal and theological levels. We use the term "theological" advisedly because it describes "belief systems," primitive though they may be. While Chapters 4-25 have been most commonly depicted as "dialogue," "debate," or "disputation," none of these terms really apply. What is taking place can only be described as a "gang assault" on Job, who parries while still clearly affected by his earlier outbreak.

As Job defends himself, we begin to observe a subtle shift in his position, which is in diametric contradistinction with the intransigence of his attackers. In this movement, the author is working out the core of his argument. The analysis of the speeches by dividing them into strophes or sections and identifying so-called "nodal" verses is not new.[10] It is almost certainly the mechanical key to unlocking the author's true *agendum*. However, there has until now been no evidence of any effort to connect these "nodal" verses mainly because no connection has been identified. It is the identification and connection of these "nodal" verses that give shape to seemingly amorphous snippets of "wisdom" literature. Traditional scholarship regards each section of the "anthology" as a position statement of the speaker with respect to a permutative combination consisting of the speaker himself, the Deity, or Job. The substance of the positions appears to consist, either in part or as a whole, of cosmology, teleology, and the human condition. On the surface, these elements appear to combine to form the basis of a theology, a reconciliation of the relationship between humanity and deity.

An examination of the poetic section of the book makes it increasingly apparent that part of the author's true purpose, hidden beneath a superficially correct story, was the articulation of a postulate that revolved around the words **צדק**(*ṣdq*), **צדיק** (*ṣdyq*) and **צדקה** (*ṣdqh*), whose conventional meaning is accepted as depicting the multi-faceted concept of "righteousness." This identification poses further challenges, since the author seems to have had a clearly Aristotelian vision of logic; that is to say that one word has one and only one meaning. Any violation of this cardinal rule would admit of invalid syllogisms, which were anathema to Aristotelian logic. There is an absence of relativity in the Aristotelian system; "righteousness" is an absolute and there is no such thing as "more or less righteous." This definition is crucial to the understanding of the Book of Job.

What this meant was that **צדק** (*ṣdq*), **צדיק** (*ṣdyq*) and **צדקה** (*ṣdqh*) could no longer fall under the umbrella definition of "righteousness." However, as we

---

[10] See Clines (1989, 75) for a comprehensive bibliography.

shall see, our author had the distinct advantage of being able to use the full semantic range of √צדק (*ṣdq*) without fear of multiple definitions or descriptions, theological, political, psychological or otherwise. That is to say that the range of meanings of √צדק (*ṣdq*) might refer to innocence in the face of the law, "righteousness," the High Priestly proper name Zadok, the politico-religious Sadducees or the splinter group Sadduceans. The author of the Book of Job exploits many if not all of these possibilities. The translator must find a word of appropriate transparency in his or her own language in order to preserve not only the author's integrity, but to also enable him/her to construct the author's postulate and comprehend his intent.

Our identification of צדק (*ṣdq*), צדיק (*ṣdyq*) and צדקה (*ṣdqh*) – "relative wholeness" as the "nodal" words of the poetic section will remove the screen behind which our author has concealed his *agenda*.[11]

√צדק (*ṣdq*) as "Whole" and "Wholeness"

Thus, for better or for worse, we shall use the term "to be whole," along with its adjective "whole," and its denominative "wholeness," as our respective paradigms for √צדק (*ṣdq*). The shortcomings of the use of the word "righteous" to describe √צדק (*ṣdq*) will become easily and quickly apparent as we examine both the text itself and the scholarship of others as they tackle this magnificent yet difficult work. It is in fact the issue that is the main objective of the author's search.

Why have we settled on the term "whole?" The notion of using a single word form to depict an equivalent original term is not original. This methodology has however become the bane of translators' tasks as they have dealt with the pitfalls of idiom, colloquialism and indeed the tendency of the "translating" term to carry linguistic and psychological baggage in its own vernacular. Thus "translation," the very action of first order of removal from the original, performs an immediate disservice to both scholar and educated reader. Within linguistic groups such as Semitic and Indo-European, the disservice is somewhat mitigated by common features of semantics, psychology, and structure; however, when the "translation" crosses the border between linguistic groups, the separation becomes quite stark. When an author is employing a cipher whose key is the unique meaning of a word in a given context, the very concept of "translation" is virtually precluded. The reader is required to be fully conversant with the language of the author if he or she is to comprehend the message.

---

[11] Pyeon (2003, 202) deals with צדק (*ṣdq*), צדיק (*ṣdyq*) and צדקה (*ṣdqh*) as synchronically intertextual; thus he precludes the author's intended method of examination, which was to attempt to reconcile the entire semantic range of √צדק (*ṣdq*).

All of this leaves us with a formidable challenge if we are to be successful in remaining true to the author's *agenda* while attempting represent it in another language. This brings us to the choice of "whole" for √צדק (*ṣdq*). The conventional English translations of √צדק (*ṣdq*) are "righteous," "just," "innocent," "pious," and even "perfect." These words carry their own baggage even before they are loaded with theological flavor. As we shall see, more than one translator of the Book of Job has staked his work to one of the meanings enumerated above.

The English word "whole" connotes "entirety" in an almost neutral sense. When substituted for any of the synonyms that we have mentioned, the word "whole" manages to convey a meaning "in context" without bias either psychological or theological. This would appear to come closest to representing the author's use of √צדק (*ṣdq*).

Both the Prologue and 3rd Epilogue adhere to a strict code of using unique Hebrew *BH* words and phrases with which to direct the reader to the intended meaning. Our author has devised a similar code for the poetic body. In addition to focusing on each individual word of the text, he turns now to the conceptual thread that permeates the substantive meaning.

The thread that connects these sections is the concept of √צדק (*ṣdq*) – "wholeness," as it applies, separately but equally, to Job and יהוה (YHWH). Job's assertions that his own level of צדק (*ṣdq*), צדיק (*ṣdyq*) and צדקה (*ṣdqh*) is higher than that of יהוה (YHWH) are portrayed in a series of monologues and dialogues that feature the contrast of transition and intransigence. We witness the transition of Job from rage to self-pity and depression and thence to self-realization. The three "friends" are intransigent in their position. They never depart from their opening assumption that the צדק (*ṣdq*), צדיק (*ṣdyq*) and צדקה (*ṣdqh*) of the deity is paramount and that the deity never acts without just cause; *ergo* Job must somehow be at fault.

The Literary Structure of the Book of Job

As can be seen from the schematic below, we differ from traditional literary analysis in that we include Job's diatribe in the Prologue. As stated earlier, we also identify and postulate the existence of not one but three epilogues.

For our purposes, the schematic structure of the Book of Job may be described thus:

- 1^{1}-2^{10} —**Prologue**
- $2^{11\text{-}13}$ —Introduction of the "three friends"
- $3^{1\text{-}2}$ —*Segue* to Job's Diatribe
- $3^{3\text{-}26}$ —Job's Diatribe—**End of Prologue**
- 4^{1}-26^{14} —**The Interaction of Job and the "three friends"**
- 27^{1}-31^{40} —**Job's Last Monologue**
- 32^{1}-37^{24} —**First Epilogue**—'Elihu's Rebuttal of both Job and the "three friends" (4^{1}-26^{14})
- 38^{1}-42^{6} —**Second Epilogue**
  1. 38^{1}-39^{30}—YHWH's First Response to Job
  2. $40^{1\text{-}5}$—Job's First Rejection of YHWH
  3. 40^{6}-41^{26}—YHWH's Second Response to Job
  4. $42^{1\text{-}6}$—Job's Final Rejection of YHWH
- $42^{7\text{-}17}$ —**Third Epilogue**
  The Reconciliation of Job and YHWH

A Literary Guide to the Dating of the Book of Job

The dating of the most frequently debated issues among scholars of the Book of Job. The disagreements are as numerous as the scholars; however, we can draw some persuasive inferences from the author's use of language. We shall present these clues in historical order beginning with the chronologically earliest.

The author uses Chapters 14 and 18 of the Book of Ezekiel as the spine of his superficial plot. The span of Ezekiel's *floruit* was 593-571 BCE.

The author's insinuates usage that is unique to the Book of the prophet Zechariah whose work spanned the years 520-518 BCE. He uses the word **צניף** (*ṣnyp*) in 29^{14}, which occurs elsewhere only in Zech.$3^{3,5}$, to describe the headpiece of the High Priest.[12] Had the author wished to point to the original *BH* reference, he would have used the term **מצנפת** (*mṣnpt*).[13]

The use of √זכה (*zkh*) in a legal context with the meaning of "to be innocent" is certainly Mishnaic and has pre-Mishnaic antecedents. This is evidenced by the language of the Dead Sea Scrolls.

In the Prologue we find use of √קבל (*qbl*). We have no evidence for the usage of √קבל (*qbl*) with the meaning of "acceptance" or "receipt" until

---

[12] Two other occurrences in Isa.50^{23} and 62^{3} only serve to emphasize further the lateness of this usage.

[13] See Ex.28^{4} and seven other occurrences in Exodus, three in Leviticus and one in Ezek.21^{31}.

Mishnaic or immediately pre-Mishnaic times in approximately the 2nd-1st century BCE.[14]

Last, and perhaps most important, is the remarkable stylistic similarity between certain of the Dead Sea Scrolls, particularly the *Florilegium* and the *Hodayot*, and the Book of Job. We find expressions such as ילוד אשה (*ylwd ʾšh*),[15] סתר עמל מעני (*str ʿml mʿny*),[16] שוך בעד (*śwk bʿd*)[17] and מחמר קרצתי (*mḥmr qrṣty*)[18] that are unique in *BH* to the Book of Job yet occur in the Dead Sea Scrolls. We find evidence in the Scrolls of contextual familiarity of language, for example in 4^{17}, where the breakout question of ʾEliphaz finds its complement.[19] Other vocabulary, such as אבדון (*ʾbdwn*)[20] and פלצות (*plṣwt*)[21] that occur in *BH* on only two or three other occasions respectively along with Job, are used relatively freely throughout the Dead Sea Scrolls

An Overview of the Author's *Agenda*

It has already become clear that the underlying subtexts of the Prologue and the "poetic body" that describes the perorations of Job and the three "friends" have little or nothing to do with "guiltless victims," "patience," "suffering," and the "compassion" of the deity.

The author of the Book of Job had his own *agenda*, namely, the redefinition of √צדק (*ṣdq*) in the context of Genesis, Ezekiel, the prophets of the post-exilic period, and the Dead sea Scrolls. To this end he has devised a contemporary re-interpretation of the Genesis stories, and an attempt to redefine the nature of the Divine entity, its interactive relationship with humanity and the delivery of Messianic salvation by the hand of a human being. He denies any direct reciprocity in this relationship, yet the messianic event will require divine participation. This is one of the traditional *cruces* of the Prologue—*do ut des*[22] and *cui bono*[23]—that we will encounter in 1^{9}.

---

[14] See 2^{10} below.

[15] Job 14^{1}; 15^{14}; 25^{4}; *1QH^a* Col.xxi l.1, 8-9, Col.xxiii ll.12-13; *4Q264* 8.

[16] Job 3^{10}; *1QH^a* Col.xix l.19.

[17] Job 1^{10}, 3^{23};*1QS* Col.x. ll.24-25, *1QH^a* Col.x l.21, *1QH^a* Col.xiii l.33, *1QH^a* Col.xvi l.11; 4Q426 1ii 8.

[18] Job 33^{6}; *4Q511* Frags. 28-29, 4.

[19] See below in discussion of 4^{17}.

[20] $\psi 88^{12}$, Prov. 15^{11}, Job 26^{7}, 28^{22}, 31^{12}; *1QM* Col.xiv l.17,18, 1*QH^a* Col.xi ll.16, 19, 32.

[21] Isa.21^{4}, Ezek.7^{18}, $\psi 55^{6}$, Job 21^{6}, *1QH^a* Col.xi ll.11,12.

[22] Lit. "I give so that you may give [in return]"

[23] Lit. "who benefits?"

In order to simplify an already complex structure, we will state the author's purpose in writing the Book of Job. Our author's logical train of thought runs as follows:

The "deity" אלהים (*'elohîm*) created "humanity" האדם (*h'dm*) in the "image of the deity" בצלם אלהים (*bṣlm 'lhym*); therefore, the attributes of both "humanity" האדם (*h'dm*) and the "deity" אלהים (*'elohîm*) are identical. It is a *datum* that humanity האדם (*h'dm*) is neither perfect nor absolutely good; therefore the "deity" אלהים (*'elohîm*) must likewise be neither perfect nor absolutely good. The preceding statement prevailing, if the "deity" אלהים (*'elohîm*) can be better or worse than "humanity" האדם (*h'dm*), the converse must also be true. We recognize the imperfections and flaws of "humanity" האדם (*h'dm*); where are the imperfections and flaws of the "deity" אלהים (*'elohîm*)?

Given the validity of this argument, then the socio-religious history portrayed by the Book of Genesis is not accurate. The patriarchal stories are an apology rather than a thematic statement of position. The author in a sense rewrites the Book of Genesis, recasting its central patriarchal characters in a manner consistent with his main argument. In a counter-intuitive move, he also recasts the nature of the Genesis deity, adhering closely to the *BH* definitions of אלהים (*'elohîm*) and יהוה (YHWH).

In addition, the concept of the delivering of salvation by a "human messiah" is not compatible with the postulate that both deity and human are flawed and not "perfect." How can the world be restored to its original pristine state so long as such action is at the hand of an entity that is less than totally "whole?" Thus the concept of the "messiah" is not possible by the author's system of logic. Since he is the promulgator of the Messianic salvation, the deity must surely know that it cannot possibly succeed.

The object of the author's inquiry is the paradox of divine and human "wholeness" – √צדק (*ṣdq*) with the additional requirement that a "messiah" be "whole."[24] While logic dictates that the nature of "wholeness" – √צדק (*ṣdq*) be the same for both, it becomes clear that in this respect they are quite different. "Divine wholeness" is distinct from "human wholeness" and the two are mutually exclusive. By the same token "divine imperfection" differs from "human imperfection." The Aristotelian system of syllogisms and unique semantics breaks down in the face of this realization.

---

[24] See Jer.23[5] and 33[14].

The Epilogues

The author has taken his argument as far as he can within the bounds of his philosophical system. He now has to conclude but no single conclusion lends itself to preference. His unique solution is to offer the reader three separate, mutually exclusive possibilities.

The First Epilogue – ʾElihu

The speech of ʾElihu has been generally regarded as the interpolation of a later author or editor. Its inclusion in this volume is dictated by our conviction that it is an integral part of the Book of Job, written by a single author. The clever name-play of the opening verses of Chapter 32 and the internal intertextuality of its content lend support to this position.

ʾElihu's monologue is the first of the three possible endings of the Book of Job. Chapter $32^{1\text{-}5}$ sets the scene for ʾElihu's appearance. ʾElihu substantively berates both Job, for making himself "more whole" than אלהים (*ʾelohîm*)," and the "three friends" for pillorying Job while not being able to answer Job's arguments. In a strange aside in 32^{5}, ʾElihu pays lip service to Job as his senior, yet he has no tolerance for either Job or the vapid stance of the "three friends."

However, 32^{6}-37^{24} is a monologue, a statement of position that is final and brooks no challenge. The Deity reigns supreme and is beyond question, let alone criticism. "Wholeness," צדק (*ṣdq*), צדיק (*ṣdyq*) and צדקה (*ṣdqh*), belongs to the Deity alone—no human may ever aspire to it. More than that, the deity brooks no direct human approach; only an intercessor or intermediary can effect communication. The author gives the impression that ʾElihu thinks of himself as qualified for the job.[25] Does he too think that he is perhaps a "messiah"? How can that be since man is inherently flawed, a state not within the Messianic realm?

This first conclusion writes off the "wholeness" of any one individual. There is no effort that is great enough in order for a human to achieve standing before the divinity other than as a humble servant and supplicant.

The Second Epilogue "From the Whirlwind"

The Second Epilogue is generally regarded as a "divine harangue" in which יהוה (YHWH) mounts a full frontal attack on Job. He asserts his supremacy, cosmic and terrestrial, at the same time forcing Job to admit his own inferiority and insignificance.

Nothing could be further from the truth. It is the author's response through Job's mouth at the end of each of the two monologues from the whirlwind that

---

[25] See 33^{23}.

defines their content. Granted, יהוה (YHWH) begins assertively; however, Job's response is not a retreat into abjectness or inferiority rather it is an outright rejection. Job tells יהוה (YHWH) that he has cursed him explicitly. He tells him that he has nothing more to say.

יהוה (YHWH) responds in a much softer tone. He in effect implores Job to sympathize with all the problems that he has faced in the creation of the cosmos and its population. There is an air of pathos as יהוה (YHWH) interacts with Job at his own level as a human being.

Job will have none of it. Having heard יהוה (YHWH) and seen him "eye to eye," as it were, Job refuses him even more emphatically. "And so I reject (you)", he says, "and I feel sorry for all humanity."

To our author, this conclusion is not satisfactory either. From Job's standpoint, humanity without a deity is a rudderless ship. Mutiny against the captain because his skills are less than perfect will leave the ship without any chance of reaching safe haven. From יהוה (YHWH)'s view, a world full of "zombies" constitutes a failure in the act of creation, an affirmation of Job's earlier desire to annihilate his creation.

The Third Epilogue

The third and final Epilogue is a set of compromises. Both Job and יהוה (YHWH) concede ground to one another. There is a mutual realization of the necessity for co-existence. There is also the realization that neither humanity nor the deity is "perfect." "Divine wholeness" and "human wholeness" are two mutually exclusive qualities that have only one thing in common, namely, the words צדק (*ṣdq*), צדיק (*ṣdyq*) and צדקה (*ṣdqh*). The wait for a "messiah" will be long.

The Deity in the Poetic Section of the Book of job

The author has written the Prologue, 3rd Epilogue, and rubrics in the classical Hebrew of *BH*. This is no accident, for we will see that his *agendum* requires a stark contrast for him to pursue his investigation. It is no accident either, that the author in the poetic section refers to the deity by almost every name other than יהוה (YHWH)[26] and אלהים (*ʾelohîm*)[27]. The author shows a preference for invoking the deity in terms of the neutral ground of ancient polytheism. In this

---

[26] Once in 12^9.

[27] Twice, in 20^{29} and 28^{23}. We find most commonly אלוה (*ʾlwh*), אל (*ʾl*), שדי (*šdy*), and perhaps even פחד (*pḥd*). We do not count the reference to בני אלהים (*bny ʾlhym*) in 38^7, since we shall identify this category separately in 1^6. See Appendix 4.

way, he can work out his heterodox thoughts without referencing the Jewish deity and the "religious baggage" that is associated with it. However, if we probe a little, we find that the term **אלוה** (*'lwh*) performs a double function. We read in Hab.1^3:

אלוה מתימן יבא וקדוש מהר פארן סלה
'lwh mtymn yb' wqdwš mhr p'rn slh
'eloah comes from Teman, the holy one from Pa'ran (Selah).

and in Deut.33^2:

יהוה מסיני בא וזרח משעיר למו
הופיע מהר פארן ואתה מרבבת קדש
yhwh msyny b' wzrḥ mś'yr lmw
hwpy' mhr p'rn w'th mrbbt qdš
YHWH came from Sinai, dawned from Se'ir;
He shone forth from the mountains of Pa'ran and came from Ribebot Qodeš

Once again, the citation is fraught with lexical issues, which can give rise to a multitude of explanations. The salient point, however, is the commonality of the origin of **אלוה** (*'lwh*) and **יהוה** (YHWH). Our author seems to be telling us that we are to understand **יהוה** (YHWH) wherever the text reads **אלוה** (*'lwh*). We shall learn the true identification of **יהוה** (YHWH) in 40^2.

The contrasts presented by our author are consistent with the methodology that we have identified in our critical reading. The author is in dangerous territory and cannot present his argument at face. As we have uncovered the method for "reading between the lines" of the Prologue and 3rd Epilogue, we will do the same for the incorporated poetic corpus.

Ascribing philological or thematic parallels to known ancient texts has become a scholarly end unto itself, as though the origins of the words and phrases will cast light on the belief systems of Job and his "friends." While this pursuit is certainly valid as an exercise in comparative literature, it is not necessarily relevant with respect to the substantive objective of the text.

Introduction to the Prologue

Since earliest times, the peculiarities of the Book of Job have piqued the interest of a diverse range of scholars. The list includes Bible commentators, text critics, theologians, historians, philologists, and scholars of comparative literature, and there are many in each of these fields. There exist numerous pat theories that are trotted out by rote, each espousing the particular specialty of its proponent. While there exists a host of commentaries on the Book of Job, most of which pay a small *modicum* of attention to the Prologue (Job 1^{1} – 3^{1}) and the 3rd Epilogue (Job 42^{7} – 42^{17}), there are only a few scholars who have undertaken studies that limit themselves, albeit generally to the Prologue alone.

The common methodological thread that runs through the scholarly works on the Book of Job is the principle that "exegesis begets analysis." Since there is an apparent logical or ideological disconnect between the Prologue, the 3rd Epilogue, and the poetic body of the book, all the effort goes into the construction of plausible theories that ostensibly address a majority of the problems posed by such a daunting challenge. The focus of the majority of studies is that theology that can be extracted from the "debates" of Job and his friends. However, these pursuits are only worthwhile if the premises on which they are based are valid.

Meir Weiss[1] has written a profoundly perceptive study devoted to the literary structure of the Prologue of Job using his "total interpretive method." His observation that "Job's differing reactions to disaster reflect fluctuation in the soul of Job, a wavering of faith…," comes tangentially close to our own; however, he nonetheless sets out with the usual set of preconceptions. Some examples are:

- Job's "wholeness" was perfect and complete, hence his reward had to be perfect and complete...He was blessed with happiness and wealth…[2]

---

[1] Weiss (1983)
[2] Weiss (1983, 21)

- …making a point of Job's absence from [his children's] feasts not only emphasizes his tact, but indicates his confidence that his children will do no wrong…[3]
- The scene before us is that of a divine assembly, a concept that was widespread in the ancient Near East.[4]
- It is clear from the story that Satan is one of the "sons of God." He is, therefore, subordinate to God.[5]

What differentiates Weiss from the pack is that he actually investigates the heterodox possibilities that the text presents. In the end, however, he reaches his position by extensive exegesis and inference rather than through an exact reading. This is perhaps because he is held captive by his religious views, which exercise *force majeure* on his ability to follow the logical course.

Similarly, Tsevat introduces Job as "the pious man, the one on whom God's blessing rests."[6] At no point in the Prologue does the author of the Book of Job assert such a claim. Tsevat's initial description of Job colors the entirety of his essay and leads him astray when his own train of thought ultimately brings him so close to understanding the author's "real" *agenda*.

Perhaps the best example of this retrograde thinking can be found in the work of Yaïr Hoffman who suggests that, "there are some elements whose existence in the prologue is intelligible only if the following speeches are taken into consideration."[7] There is no shortage of definitions of a prologue:

> [The Prologue] provides a sample of the subject, in order that the hearers may know beforehand what it is about, and that the mind may not be kept in suspense, for that which is undefined leads astray; so then he who puts the beginning into the hearer's hand enables him, if he holds fast to it, to follow the story.[8]

Or

---

[3] Weiss (1983, 29)
[4] Weiss (1983, 32)
[5] Weiss (1983, 37)
[6] Tsevat (1966, 2). Any notion of Job's being blessed is, in fact, introduced by השטן (*haśśaṭan*) in response to יהוה (YHWH)'s question in $1^{8\text{-}10}$.
[7] Hoffman (1981, 165)
[8] Aristotle, *Rhetoric* 3.14.6.

> The sole purpose of the Prologue is to prepare our audience in such a way that they will be disposed to lend a ready ear to the rest of our speech.[9]

To suggest that one can understand the introduction only if one is intimately familiar with the body proper is absurd. Hoffman never extricates himself from his basic premise, yet states in his concluding remarks:

> Irony is a device for discovering the truth, which is not always unequivocal...This irony, the author's wink from between the lines, which breaks the literary illusion, is clearly an alien element, and one might deny the relevance of such a modern approach to an ancient piece of literature like the Book of Job. Yet I think such a denial is to be rejected...

Hoffman cannot recognize his own glimpse of the author's agenda; his faulty methodology acts as a screen and he presents himself as totally uncomprehending and conflicted.

Habel opens the introduction to his commentary with the following statement of methodology:

> The *translation*...is conservative, avoiding emendation or paraphrase wherever possible...we seek to capture the nuances of Hebrew literary style within the limitations of the English language and to enable the vivid imagery of the original to emerge without resorting to the prosaic leveling typical of some translations....Wherever possible we have also tried to capture the force of verbal allusion and thematic development by rendering key terms with the same English equivalent....The several names of God found in the original have been reflected in the translation so as to give the reader a sense of the diversity of ancient titles associated with God...[10]

Habel betrays his noble intention in the very first verse of the very first chapter when he renders אלהים (*ʾelohîm*) as "God."[11] Despite his intentions, he must resort to exegesis to make sense of his literal translation. In addition, Habel's stated method denies the semantic range of the Semitic verb root system. The root may contain a broad spectrum of physical and psychological attributes that cannot be reflected by the use of a slavish "literal" system of

---

[9] Quintilian, *Institutio Oratorica* 4.1. Both of these quotations are cited in Cooper (1990).
[10] Habel (1985, 21-22)
[11] Habel (1985, 74)

translation, which only contributes further to the confusion and subsequent need for exegesis.

Tsevat begins his essay on "The Meaning of the Book of Job" as follows:

> The opening of the Book of Job is a case of the rule that a great author can be recognized by the way he fashions the opening of his work. As the prologue (chapter 1 f.) tells the events on earth and in heaven, it provides the reader with the factual background of what is to come and introduces him with equal clarity to the problem of the book.[12]

This comprises the entire text of the first page of Tsevat's essay; the remainder of the page is given to two footnotes that server as "modifiers" of the grand statement. It is as though Tsevat knew the purpose and definition of a prologue but simply could not apply them to this Prologue.

It is our position that the premise of the author of the Book of Job is articulated in the Prologue and stands or falls based on the integrity of the reading of these two chapters. We have presented the premises based on which scholars have elicited various themes based on a superficial reading of the texts. We have observed that all of these themes rely on a substantial amount of exegesis in order to get over the rough spots. Some examples are the reconciliation of Chapters 1 and 2, questions of the separation of the authorship of the two chapters, and the roles of השטן (*haśśaṭan*) and Job's wife. It is the exegesis that is the foundation of the premise; the subtleties and *nuances* of the exegesis steer the different theological emphases that are the supposed substance of the work.[13] In the interests of time and space, we will generally not cite individual scholars unless the citation sheds an important new light on a particular word or phrase. As Clines so aptly remarks:

> Scholars quote scholars and create their own canon of approved literature on the Book of Job. Those writings that are not soon cited by commentators do not generally get cited by subsequent commentators.[14]

Greenberg provides the most articulate observation and criticism of current biblical scholarship:

---

[12] Tsevat (1966, 1)

[13] Notable among these are the work of Tsevat (1966), Pope (1973), Hoffman (1981), Weiss (1983), Clines (1985), Habel (1985), Cooper (1990), Handy (1993).

[14] Clines (1989, xxx)

> A translation of and commentary on a biblical text should bridge the gap that separates the present-day reader—with his culture and tradition-bound range of knowledge, assumptions and conventions—from the ancient Israelite who encountered the text with different knowledge, assumptions and conventions conditioned by his circumstances. There is no way of ascertaining how the ancient Israelite was informed, but since biblical literature in general, and prophecy in particular, aimed at edifying the people, there is every reason to assert that it composed in accord with the understanding of the people. Idioms, figures, and forms of expression and composition familiar to his audience must be reflected in, must indeed have determined, the formulation of a biblical author's creations. Knowledge of these elements of communication, never articulated in antiquity but implicitly shared by author and audience, has now to be gathered from the texts themselves. It is a precondition for a correct translation and a proper commentary.
>
> The linguistic gap between the ancient Israelite and the modern reader is obvious and suffices to justify and, to a large extent, define the task of translation. Present day ignorance of ancient persons, places, and things likewise defines an aspect of the work of a commentator. Less obvious, and less understood, is the gap in assumptions and conventions governing audience expectations that separates the modern man from the ancient Israelite. Even a cursory perusal of scholarly Bible commentaries will attest to this gap in the amount of rewriting, reshaping, and reordering of text that every commentator feels is necessary for bringing the biblical writing up to his standards.
>
> Most scholarly commentaries...reflect not only text-critical but historical decisions regarding what is authentic; their interpretation of any given passage depends not only on how they reconstruct it but on systematic alteration or elimination of related passages....[15]

The approach of this study is unique in that it requires no exegetical suppositions prior to reading. The Prologue and 3rd Epilogue are an elegant *pastiche* of words and phrases that have unique *BH* antecedents. We shall see that the poetic section (which includes the first two Epilogues) deals explicitly with the nature of √צדק (*ṣdq*),[16] the meanings of which are the object of the author's quest. We shall also see that chapters 32 – 42^6 comprise two additional epilogues. It is remarkable that a literary work could be thus composed,

[15] Greenberg (1983, 18)

[16] These are the verbal, adjectival and nominal forms of √צדק (*ṣdq*), generally rendered as "righteous." For reasons that will be explained later, we will translate √צדק (*ṣdq*) as "to be whole" throughout our study.

conventional enough on its face, yet concealing an articulate anti-orthodox message. Cooper unknowingly comes close to uncovering the author's methodology when he states:

> The Book of Job is actually a refutation of precisely those notions of divine justice and providence that the 'happy ending' seems to affirm. There is an exoteric level of meaning that champions conventional piety, and an esoteric level of meaning that challenges it. The latter, accessible to only the most sophisticated reader, conveys the true message of the book.[17]

The two chapters that form the Prologue to the Book of Job are of essentially prose composition, as is the 3rd Epilogue in $42^{7\text{-}17}$.[18] They, and the rubrics that introduce each speaker, bracket a number of poetic compositions that may be of ancient provenance, some of which reflect "wisdom" poetic literature that may have been in circulation since ancient times.[19]

The question of the religious status of Job, namely, whether he was a Jew or not is generally regarded as open.[20] We will provide evidence that strongly supports a proposition that Job was indeed Jewish.[21] We will encounter suggestions in the text that the author was almost certainly *au fait* with *BH* laws and realize that he is telling us about himself and Job.

Using a careful critical reading of the text, we will eliminate many of the "inconsistencies" of plot, grammar and syntax, and literary and historical devices that are applied to *BH* texts. The Prologue of the Book of Job is a programmatic reconstruction by our author of the Genesis stories of the Garden of Eden, Adam (**האדם** *ha'adam*), Eve (**האשה** *ha'išah*), and the Serpent (**הנחש** *hannaḥaš*), God's evaluation of the human condition, the "Sons of *'elohîm*," Abraham, the "sacrifice" of Isaac, Sarah, and the other Patriarchs/Matriarchs.

The other, equally important source texts are Numbers 22-24 (the story of Bil'am), Ezekiel 14 and 18 (which describe Job, the events of the "Apocalypse," and the definition of **צדיק** (*ṣdyq*) – "whole), Zech.1-6, Haggai, Nahum and

---

[17] Cooper (1990, 74)

[18] References to citations from the Book of Job are identified only by chapter and verse. The label "Job" is to be understood.

[19] We will postulate that there is more than one epilogue. The Epilogue proper continues from 42^7 to the end of the book.

[20] Ezekiel $14^{14,20}$ refers to Job and two other ancients as classical examples of men who will survive the apocalypse by dint of their **צדקה** (*ṣdqh*). There is no indication that these men were of the Israelite cult or Jewish faith.

[21] See our discussion below of the names of the three "friends" in 2^{11}.

Habakkuk. It is the combination of unique *BH* sources and these texts,[22] which form the backbone of the author's methodology.

As we recognize each patch of this brilliantly constructed quilt, we put into proper perspective the traditional myths of the "Patience of Job" and "The Suffering Servant" as essential to the understanding of the Book of Job. We will comprehend Job as the author really intended, namely, as a stubborn human being with human foibles and human emotion but also a man of whom the impossible was expected. The author uses the theme of these ancient Near East myths as a very credible cover beneath which he can pursue his *agenda.*[23]

Traditional scholarship does not consider even the possibility of an author's *agenda.* It rather ties the meaning of the Book of Job very closely to the narrative, be it prose or poetry. It would be fair to state that the views of traditional scholarship are reflected in the writings of Pope, Habel, and Clines and we will cite them *verbatim* where appropriate:

> ...the purpose of the book is to give an answer to...the problem of divine justice or theodicy. This question is raised inevitably by any and every instance of seemingly unmerited or purposeless suffering, and especially the suffering of a righteous man....A man of exemplary rectitude and piety is suddenly overwhelmed with disasters and loathsome disease. How can such a situation be reconciled with divine justice and benevolent providence?...The Book of Job fails to give a clear and definitive answer to this question...The problem of theodicy continues to thwart all attempts at rational solution.[24]

> We suggest that the model for the Book of Job is the traditional Biblical narrative. This model has been modified with the expansion of the dialogue into speeches, which both retard and complicate the plot....I would argue that the artist who created the Book of Job has constructed the dialogue as a feature of the plot rather than as an independent theological disputation.[25]

---

[22] This, in effect, is a subset of *BH* references in general and falls into the category of "unique."

[23] This is not to invalidate the ancient Near Eastern myths that contain themes or literary forms that are partially reflected in the Book of Job. Examples of this thematic proximity are: "The Dispute between a Man and His *Ba* (Egyptian *COS* 3.146), "The Eloquent Peasant" (Egyptian: *COS* 1.43), "Man and His God (Sumerian: *COS* 1.179), *ludlul bēl nēmeqi*—"I Will Praise the Lord of Wisdom" (Akkadian: *COS* 1.153), "The Babylonian Theodicy" (Akkadian: *COS* 1.154), "The *Kirta* Epic" (Ugaritic *COS* 1.102).

[24] Pope (1974, *LXX*III)

[25] Habel (1985, 26)

> The Book of Job is a brilliant tapestry of literary art and theological dispute. Ambiguous images of the world are interwoven with conflicting perspectives about the world. The quest of the wise to interpret reality, suffering and the order of things is integrated with a struggle to understand the quest itself and the God who launched them on that quest.[26]

> We have distinguished between the narrative of the framework of Job and the argument of the poetry that forms the core of the book (exposition, complication, and resolution). But this distinction is not wholly valid. For we have been able to speak of...a narrative that does not only *frame* the book, but which runs *through* it. And we can speak of the argument not just of the *speeches* in which the characters are obviously arguing with one another, but of *the book as a whole*, narrative and speeches included...
> What is the argument of the book? It is the view the book takes of the principal issues it is addressing. We may either suppose...that the major question in it is the problem of suffering. Or ...the chief issue is the problem of the moral order of the world, of the principles on which it is governed.[27]

It is indeed interesting how the same text can spawn three so distinct avenues of approach, each of which requires extensive exegesis. Pope takes his stance based simply on the Prologue. Habel dances closest to the flame, but cannot, in the final analysis, tear himself away from traditional exegesis. Clines cannot find a premise without considering the book in its entirety and, even then, leaves himself room for two possible treatments. Clines' approach renders a Prologue completely unnecessary since a Prologue is written specifically to inform the reader of the subject matter under discussion.

Hoffer sees the Prologue as a series of allusions and indeed identifies many of the *BH* sources that are the author's code. She is absolutely correct when she says:

> By following the story from its beginning, it will be possible to see how pervasively inter- and intra-textual connections, wordplay, and considered word choice are used to create rich and polyvalent images and meanings.

Unfortunately, her reading of these "rich and polyvalent images and meanings" never achieves coherence and she becomes mired in a tangle of

---

[26] Habel (1985, 60)
[27] Clines (1989, xxxix)

exegesis and superficial attempts at interpretation. No consistent methodology is ever achieved. This is perhaps best exemplified in her attempts to understand two of the *cruces* of the Prologue, ויקדשם (*wyqdšm*) and the use of √ברך (*brk*).[28] In the case of the former, she defers to the Masoretic "accents" to bolster her interpretation, an anachronism since the text predates the Masoretic "accents" by many centuries. In the case of the latter, in deriving √ברך (*brk*)

> "from the root for 'knee'...a verb in the qal, a bodily position of subjugation. It sets up a relationship of the supplicant to God." To do the opposite would mean to repudiate one's relative lowliness in that relationship.

She then attempts to apply this "technique" to Job's children, Job's wife and then Job himself. Each instance must carry a slightly different *nuance* in order to fit the context.

Conclusion

In summary, we have attempted to demonstrate the methodologies of Joban scholarship and the characteristic constraints that they share.[29] Most, if not all, of the circuitous approaches are made necessary by the theological and exegetical inconsistencies of the author's superficial "story." The Prologue is indeed the introduction to the Book of Job. The critical reading that follows lays out the true *agenda* that are being pursued and confirm the unity of the composition of this work.

---

[28] Hoffer (2001, 91-94)

[29] Extensive bibliographies of Joban scholarship may be constructed from the work of most of the scholars cited. However, since the path that we are taking is so different from that of traditional scholars, it would be prolix to list them all here. Those whose works are cited directly are appropriately recognized in our bibliography.

The Prologue
Part 1

Chapter One

1:1

1[1a]

איש היה בארץ עוץ איוב שמו
'yš hyh b'rṣ 'wṣ 'ywb šmw
There was a man in the land of Uz; Job was his name;

איש היה (*'yš hyh*) is an unusual construction[1] that occurs here and similarly in Gen.6[9]:

נח איש צדיק תמים היה בדרתיו את האלהים התהלך נח
nḥ 'yš ṣdyq tmym hyh bdrtyw 't h'lhym hthlk nḥ
Noah was a whole, honest man in his time; Noah roamed with *ha'elohîm*[2]

The construction **איש...היה** (*'yš... hyh*) appears here as the Pentateuchal *BH* antecedent to the first phrase of 1[1]. Second, the phrase **צדיק תמים** (*ṣdyq tmym*)[3]

---

[1] Hoffer (2001, 87ff.) recognizes the unusual construction; however, she does not understand the importance of exact wording in *BH* antecedents when she cites 2Sam.12[1]: **שני אנשים היו** (*šny 'nšym hyw*), which reflects the same construction but in the plural form and provides no contextual information. We have also the instance of Esth.2[5], in which this construction occurs with reference to Mordechai (**איש יהודי היה** – *'yš yhwdy hyh*); however, (a) one may question the author's knowledge of the existence of the Book of Esther and (b) the concept of **צדק** (*ṣdq*), **צדיק** (*ṣdyq*) and **צדקה** (*ṣdqh*) is not present either explicitly or implicitly.

[2] See 1Kings 18[39] – **יהוה הוא האלהים** (*yhwh hw' h'lhym*). This is the *locus classicus* for the statement of the equivalence of **האלהים** (*h'lhym*) with **יהוה** (YHWH), although there are three other occurrences of this phrase. See Deut.4[35],4[39] and 1Kings 8[39]. **האלהים** (*h'lhym*) is not to be confused with **אלהים** (*'lhym*) or **בני האלהים** (*bny h'lhym*). (See 1[6]).

[3] Which is not in accord with the Masoretic cantillation marks.

subliminally introduces the element צדק (*ṣdq*), צדיק (*ṣdyq*) and צדקה (*ṣdqh*) that is ultimately the main focus of the book and the author's true *agenda*.

Our author is trying to tell us specifically about Noah;[4] he is placing the narrative in ancient time. He is specifically pointing at Ezekiel $14^{14,20}$, where Job and Noah are named as two of the three men in history who would survive the apocalypse on account of their צדקה (*ṣdqh*).[5] Chapter 14 of the Book of Ezekiel will feature prominently as we work our way through the Prologue.

Unlike Gen.6^9, the איש (*ʾyš*) of 1^1 is unqualified. This is intended to make the reader aware that that emphasis is elsewhere, namely on the verb היה (*hyh*), which is the root of the Tetragrammaton יהוה (YHWH), and reflective of the term used by YHWH to describe himself in Ex.3^{14}, אהיה אשר אהיה (*ʾhyh ʾšr ʾhyh*). As has just been shown, האלהים (*hʾlhym*) is synonymous with יהוה (YHWH). This notion is further reinforced with the use of והיה (*whyh*) to introduce the second clause of the verse:

והיה האיש ההוא תם וישר וירא אלהים וסר מרע
whyh hʾyš hhwʿ tm wyšr wyrʾ ʾlhym wsr mrʾ
And that man was honest and upright, revering *ʾelohîm* and shunning evil.

The usage of the *waw* as a simple conjunction rather than the customary tense converter from perfect to future is intended to attract the readers attention away from the plain meaning of the verb "to be" and toward the association with יהוה (YHWH). We will see that the author intends to make a definitional statement of identity when using יהוה (YHWH) as opposed to אלהים (*ʾelohîm*).

בארץ עוץ (*bʾrṣ ʿwṣ*) "in the land of ʿUz." There is a great deal of scholarly material on בארץ עוץ "in the land of ʿUz" (*bʾrṣ ʿwṣ*).[6] Discussions and arguments range from the geographic location of ʿUz to interpretational inferences to be derived from its lexical roots. While עוץ (*ʿwṣ*) occurs as a personal name,[7] it is mentioned as a place name only once in *BH* in Lam.4^{21}:

---

4 For the author's denial of Noah as patriarch, see p.7.

5 The name of Job appears in Ezek.14^{14} in the company of Daniʾel and Noah as examples of pious non-Jews whose righteousness would save them from annihilation by יהוה (YHWH). Scholars generally agree that Daniʾel is not that of *BH* but *Dan ʾilu*, the hero of the ancient Ugaritic *Aqhat* epic. We cannot be sure that this Job is the same as that of Ezekiel. There is a likelihood that our Job is anachronistically named as is probably the case with Jonah, whose name first appears in 2Kings 14^{25}.

6 Pope (1974, 3-4)

7 Gen.10^{23}, 22^{21}, 36^{28}

שישי ושמחי בת אדום יושבת בארץ עוץ
śyśy wśmḥy ywšbt b'rṣ ʿwṣ
Rejoice and be glad, O daughter of Edom,
Who dwells in the land of ʿUz.

where עוץ (*ʿwṣ*) is parallel with "the daughter of Edom." Associations of עוץ (*ʿwṣ*) with wisdom (עצה *ʿṣh*) are a stretch of the imagination, although Weiss makes this a cornerstone of his analysis:

> "...viewed from this perspective, several details that are formally organic but thematically superfluous, including the mention of "the Land of Uz" itself, take on a significance that is organically consonant with the theme of the story and even complements it. The following examples give a clear illustration:
> The Land of Uz...is the home of Edom...Both the name and genealogy of 'Eliphaz the Temanite...are associated with Edom. Edom and Teman are considered centers of wisdom." ...The conceptual starting point of the story (and of the entire book) is the world of Wisdom literature. The story's (and the book's) purpose is to dispute the conventional claims of Wisdom, and specifically that outlook whose basic principle is expressed in the sentence *ṣaddîq vᵉṭôv lô* (צדיק וטוב לו),[8] the righteous man is blessed with good—material good, first and foremost."[9]

Like most commentators and critics, Weiss seems intent on fitting the Book of Job into a *genre* such as "Wisdom Literature." His realization of the importance of the term צדיק (*ṣaddîq*) brings him tantalizingly close to identifying the *crux* of the work. Unfortunately, he is constrained by the bounds of convention and he, like others, is compelled to make homiletical assumptions that have no basis in the text.

It is likely that עוץ (*ʿwṣ*) is geographically Edom to the east, as is inferred from the phrase גדול מכל בני קדם (*gdwl mkl bny qdm*) – "greater than all the people of the East," which occurs at the end of 1[3].[10]

איוב שמו (*'ywb šmw*)—"Job was his name." There are many ways to describe a person's name in the *BH*; however this construction, predicate followed by subject, serves to highlight the predicate, in this case the name. We

[8] This expression appears first in T. Bavli *Berachot* 7a and cannot possibly be retrojected as a thematic motive for the Book of Job.
[9] Weiss (1983, 24)
[10] See below

find this construction six other times in the *BH* referring once to **יהוה** (YHWH), most famously in Ex.15³,[11] also to Goliath,[12] Nabal,[13] Sheba ben Bichri,[14] King Josiah,[15] and Ṣemaḥ[16]. We can be fairly certain that the author wished to emphasize the name, mostly because of an ensuing word-play. In the case of Ex.15³:

יהוה איש מלחמה יהוה שמו
yhwh ʾyš mlḥmh yhwh šmw
YHWH is a man of war; YHWH is his name.

the author both accents the name of God as **יהוה** (YHWH) and the root √**היה** (*hyh*) to remind the reader of both **יהוה** (YHWH) in general and in particular Ex.3¹⁴ **אהיה אשר אהיה** (*ʾhyh ʾšr ʾhyh*).[17]

However, the exact *BH* antecedent is a complex parallel between the descriptions of Job and Ṣemaḥ. Job is referred to in 1¹ as:

איש...איוב שמו
ʾyš... ʾywb šmw
A man…Job (was) his name

and in 42⁷ as:

עבדי איוב
ʿbdy ʾywb
my servant Job

---

[11] See also Jer.33², Amos 5⁸, 9⁶

[12] In 1Sam.17⁴, the expression is **איש...גלית שמו** (*ʾyš... glyt šmw*); the second part of the equivalence is absent.

[13] Likewise, in 1Sam.25²⁵, we find **איש...נבל שמו** (*ʾyš... nbl šmw*) alone.

[14] The expression **איש...שבע בן בכרי שמו** (*ʾyš... šbʿ bn bkry šmw*) is found in 2Sam.20²¹; however Sheba ben Bichri is never described as **עבדי** (*ʿbdy*)—"my servant."

[15] In 1Kings 13², Josiah is not called **איש** (*ʾyš*) or **עבדי** (*ʿbdy*).

[16] Described more fully below.

[17] If there is a criticism that we are mixing citations from prose and poetry, we affirm that the author was concerned with the empirical accuracy of the citation to support his point, and did not discriminate between literary *genres*.

Ṣemaḥ is referred to in Zech.6[12] as:

איש צמח שמו
ʾyš ṣmḥ šmw
A man, Ṣemaḥ (is) his name

and in Zech.3[8] as:

עבדי צמח
ʿbdy ṣmh
My servant Ṣemaḥ[18]

Our author goes to great lengths to make a seemingly esoteric *nexus*, namely, the connection of Job with Ṣemaḥ. The latter name is laced with Messianic and eschatological inferences. The name Ṣemaḥ literally means "sprout" or "offshoot" with the explicit understanding of "future wholeness" as articulated in Jer.23[5,6]:[19]

והקמתי לדוד צמח צדיק ומלך מלך והשכיל ועשה משפט וצדקה בארץ
...וזה שמו אשר יקראו יהוה צדקנו
whqmty ldwd ṣmḥ ṣdyq wmlk mlk whśkyl wʿśh mšpṭ wṣdqh bʾrṣ
... wzh šmw ʾšry qrʾw yhwh ṣdqnw
And I shall establish a whole Ṣemaḥ for David
And he shall reign as king
And he shall be discerning, practicing justice and wholeness in the land.
...And this is the name by which he shall call him, YHWH, our wholeness.

Not only does the above citation make the eschatological connection, it affirms the significance of √**צדק** (*ṣdq*) as the most important component of the *eschaton*. It is as though the author is adding another layer to the already complex character of Job. In embedding the "messiah" into the *persona* of Job, the author is ascribing the characteristics of a "messiah" to the attributes of Job, which we ascertain from Job's very name.

---

[18] Moses is called **האיש משה** (*hʾyš mšh*)—"Moses, the man" in Num.12[3], which is not an exact parallel to the Job and Zechariah citations, he is referred to as **עבדי משה** (*ʿbdy mšh*)—"my servant Moses" in Num.12[7]. The references to David as **עבדי** (*ʿbdy*) in 2Sam.7[5,8] and 1Kings 11[13,32,34,37,38] are entirely consistent as antecedents for Zechariah.
[19] See also Jer.33[14]. See Isa.4[2] for the earliest association of **יהוה** (YHWH) and **צמח** (*ṣmh*).

והשכיל (*whśkyl*) – "And he shall be discerning" may be a precursor to the משכיל (*mśkyl*) of the Dead Sea Scrolls. We shall return to this at 19[25,26].

In addition, we observe in Zech.3[1-2] the introduction of השטן (*haśśaṭan*) and his coarse interaction with יהוה (YHWH). The interaction is direct and without intermediary and has great bearing on the characterization of השטן (*haśśaṭan*) in the Book of Job.[20]

BH vocalizes איוב (*ʾywb*) as *ʾîyyôb.* It has been suggested that the name איוב (*ʾywb*) means "hated," being of the *qiṭṭôl* construction as in the word ילוד (*yillôd*), meaning "born."[21] This appears problematic since the other two examples of the *qiṭṭôl* construction, namely גבור (*gibbôr*), "mighty" and שכור (*šikkôr*) "drunkard," are intensive active forms.[22] Thus rendered, the connotation of the name איוב (*ʾywb*) is "hater," either habitual or intensive. Our author recognizes this duality and takes the opportunity to make a subliminal suggestion to which the alert reader is receptive. There are aspects of Job's character that render him as both "the hated one" and "the hater."

In all the other so-called "Job stories" of the ancient Near Eastern traditions, it is the theme of the story that sparks comparison—none of the characters is named Job.[23]

Thus, in a mere six words, the author has set the scene in time and place, complete with characters whose traits are conventionally both divine and human. The author nails his point down in 1[1b]:

והיה האיש ההוא תם וישר וירא אלהים וסר מרע

whyh hʾyš hhwʿ tm wyšr wyrʾ ʾlhym wsr mrʾ

And that man was of integrity and upright, revering *ʾelohîm* and shunning evil.

Again the author wants us to recognize the connection between (or opposition of) the man and יהוה YHWH by using the perfect tense of √היה (*hyh*),

---

[20] The characterization of השטן (*haśśaṭan*) as the agent of יהוה (YHWH) in Numbers 22[22]ff. and Zech.3[1,2] is crucially relevant to his portrayal in the Book of Job and will be more fully discussed below.

[21] Weiss (1983, 20) ילוד (*yillôd*) has a passive connotation.

[22] Both of these forms occur in the Book of Job, see

[23] See Pope (1974, 5-6) for an exhaustive treatment of the origins of the name איוב (*ʾywb*) from comparative sources. *COS* 1.58, which may be a Hittite precursor to the *BH* story of Joseph, also contains some narrative that may pertain to the story of Job. One of the two brothers who are central to the story is *Appu*, which name has been suggested as a possible source for the name איוב (*ʾywb*).

this time with the conjunctive *waw*.[24] While the initial היה (*hyh*) prepares the reader for the association with יהוה (YHWH), this combination of consonants (והיה – *whyh*) is an anagram of the Tetragrammaton יהוה (YHWH).

תם וישר (*tm wyšr*) occurs elsewhere only in $\psi 25^{21}$ where it is vocalized *tôm wᵉyôšer*. The context of the Psalms quotation will shed some light on why this phrase was selected in a revocalized form. $\psi 25^{19\text{-}21}$ reads:

ראה אויבי כי רבו ושנאת חמס שנאוני
שמרה נפשי והצילני אל אבוש כי חסיתי בך
תם וישר יצרוני כי קויתיך
r'h 'wyby ky rbw wśn't ḥms śn'wny
šmrh npšy whṣylny 'l 'bwš ky ḥsyty bk
tm wyšr yṣrwny ky qwytyk
See how many are my enemies, and the violent hatred (with which) they hate me.
Preserve my life, and deliver me; do not let be ashamed, for I take refuge in you.
May integrity and uprightness preserve me, for I hope for you.

All the elements are present here—enmity, hate, violence, integrity, uprightness, and hope.[25] There is also the expectation of salvation in return for honesty and uprightness. This becomes a central element later in the chapter. We recall that the author has indirectly termed Job as צדיק תמים (*ṣdyq tmym*) by associating him with Noah. Our author's cynicism is evident even at this early stage since *DSS* expresses the central stark reality when we read:[26]

ואני ידעתי כי לא לאנוש צדקה ולוא לבן אדם תום דרך
לאל עליון כול מעשי צדקה ודרך אנוש לא תכון כי אם ברוח יצר אל לו
w'ny yd'ty ky lw' l'nwš ṣdqh wlw' lbn 'dm twm drk
l'l 'lywn kwl m'śy ṣdqh wdrk 'nwš lw' tkwn ky 'm brwḥ yṣr 'l lw
For I know that "wholeness" does not belong to man
Nor a perfect way to the son of man.
To *'el 'elyôn* belong all deeds of "wholeness,"
And the path of man is not secure
But for the spirit that *'el* created for him.

---

[24] As opposed to the *waw* consecutive.
[25] See also Prov.11^{8} and 14^{16}
[26] *1QHᵃ* col.xii ll.30-31.

He is also aware of the paradox of Eccles.7[20]:

כי אדם אין צדיק בארץ אשר יעשה טוב ולא יחטא
ky ʾdm ʾyn ṣdyq bʾrṣ ʾšr yʿśh ṭwb wlʾ yḥṭʾ
For there is no *ṣaddîq* in the world,
Who does good and does not sin.

The author uses the tension between צדיק תמים (*ṣdyq tmym*) and both *DSS* and Eccles.7[20] to demonstrate that neither the archetypes Abraham and Noah nor Job was able to maintain "perfect wholeness" throughout his life. This runs counter to the basic presumption that Job was indeed perfect, wealthy, and happy. We shall discuss this in greater detail later.

וירא אלהים (*wyrʾ ʾlhym*)—This attribute is specifically applied to Abraham in Gen.22[12] in the context of the sacrifice of Isaac:"[27]

עתה ידעתי כי ירא אלהים אתה
(*ʿth ydʿty ky yrʾ ʾlhym ʾth*)
Now I know that you revere *ʾelohîm*

In Gen.42[18] Joseph asserts:

את האלהים אני ירא
ʾt hʾlhym ʾny yrʾ
"it is *haʾelohîm* whom I revere."[28]

The latter citation, while superficially appearing relevant, is in fact a reference to יהוה (YHWH). As we have already remarked, our author is very clear in his use of the names of the deity.

√ירא (*yrʾ*) does indeed carry the meaning of "pathological fear," as in the case of Gen.3[10], in which *haʾadam* gives *ʾelohîm* the excuse that "I was afraid because I was naked and I hid."[29] The term ירא אלהים (*yrʾ ʾlhym*) carries more of a connotation of "unquestioning reverential awe." This distinction is important since it describes the progress of sophistication in human social

[27] Jonah describes himself (Jon.1[9]) as את יהוה אלהי השמים אני ירא (*ʾt yhwh ʾlhy hšmym ʾny yrʾ*)—"It is YHWH, the god of the heavens whom I revere." This does not fit our criterion of "exact matching"; however, see the Appendix 2 on Job and Jonah for a more detailed examination of the relationship between the two works.

[28] Our author understands יהוה (YHWH). We have already explained the distinction between אלהים (*ʾlhym*) and האלהים (*hʾlhym*) above.

[29] ואירא כי עירם אנכי ואחבא (*wʾyʾ ky ʿyrm ʾnky wʾḥbʾ*)

development. Thus also האדם (*h'dm*), "the man of the earth" in Gen.3[22] has become איש (*'yš*) "the societal man" in Gen.4[1].[30]

וסר מרע (*wsr mr'*) occurs only in Isa.59[15] and Prov.14[16] and it is the latter citation that piques our interest. The full verse reads:

חכם ירא וסר מרע וכסיל מתעבר ובוטח
ḥkm yr' wsr m' wksyl mt'br wbwṭḥ
A wise man is reverential and turns away from evil
But a fool becomes angry and careless[31]

We see here use of very specific language to describe Job's moral character. The author had a very fine rôle model at his disposal in the form of Noah. As we have shown previously, Noah is described in Gen.6[9]:

נח איש צדיק תמים היה בדרתיו את האלהים התהלך נח
nḥ 'yš ṣdyq tmym hyh bdrtyw 't h'lhym hthlk nḥ
Noah was a whole, honest man; Noah roamed with *'elohîm*

Thus we have seen that *ab initio* the author knew this text and was extremely careful in his choice of vocabulary; therefore, we must ask the question of why he did not use the Genesis citation as the archetype for Job's character. Gen.6[9] seems to say most of the things that the author expresses in 1[1]; the attributes are positive, direct, and not circumlocutory or negative.

Noah does not fit our author's patriarchal prototype. Of all the characters in Genesis, in fact in the Pentateuch as a whole, Noah is the only one who influences יהוה (YHWH) directly by his action. Having survived the flood unharmed and without loss; his first expression of gratitude was to make an animal sacrifice (עולה (*'wlh*) which involved killing) to יהוה (YHWH), who is pleased enough by "the aroma" of the sacrifice to regret ever having had the intent of totally annihilating all that was alive in the world. Since our author postulates that יהוה (YHWH) acts independent of human input, he cannot describe Job in terms of Noah alone. He needs to connect Job to the "Jewish" or

---

30 In which Eve declares: קניתי איש את יהוה (*qnyty 'yš 't yhwh*)—"I have created a man with YHWH." We use the rendering "create" for √קנה (*qnh*) since that is its original meaning.

31 The conventional translation of √בטח (*bṭḥ*) is "to trust"; however, in this context, it neither makes sense nor parallels וסר מרע (*wsr mr'*). The cognate Arabic √بطح a (*baṭaḥa*) means "to flatten, throw down, fell" indicating brashness, overconfidence. For this usage in *BH* compare Isa.32[9].

"Israelite" patriarchs, Abraham and Isaac, and this he accomplishes very cleverly. In Gen.6^{9}, **יהוה** (YHWH) does not tell Noah to be **צדיק** (*ṣdyq*) nor does he tell him to "walk with him." In the case of Abraham, **יהוה** (YHWH)'s instruction is very explicit, as we read in Gen.13^{19}:

וירא יהוה אל אברם ויאמר אליו אני אל שדי התהלך לפני והיה תמים
wyr' yhwh 'l 'brm wy'mr 'lyw 'ny 'l šdy hthlk lpny whyh tmym
And YHWH appeared to Abram and said to him, "I am *'el shadday*,
Walk before me and be perfect."

Abraham is nowhere directly described as being inherently **צדיק** (*ṣdyq*) and our author confers this status upon him by the use of the word **תמים** (*tmym*) – "perfect" which occurs adjacent to the word **צדיק** (*ṣdyq*) in Gen.6^{9}. Thus, when we read the cryptic verse in Gen.15^{6}:

והאמן ביהוה ויחשבה לו צדקה
wh'mn byhwh wyhšbh lw ṣdqh
And he believed in YHWH and he [YHWH] credited him with *ṣdqh.*

we can understand it in terms of Gen.13^{19}.[32]

Gen.6^{9} and 13^{19} address another potential problem which would appear to lie with the word **התהלך** (*hthlk*) – "he roamed."[33] The author has employed the *hithpaʿel* (reflexive) use of the √**הלך** (*hlk*) – "to walk" for the interaction of **יהוה** (YHWH) and **השטן** (*haśśaṭan*) in Job 1^{7}. Gen.6^{9} and 13^{19} demonstrate that **התהלך** (*hthlk*) was **יהוה** (YHWH)'s preferred method of interaction with both humanity and **השטן** (*haśśaṭan*).

וסר מרע (*wsr mr'*)—If, as is apparent, this citation from Prov.14^{16} is the author's *BH* antecedent text, we may infer indeed that Job was a very wise man; however, that is not the main objective of the author. He is setting the scene for the action to come, hinting at the diametric polar opposition of the possibilities of human nature. We see in Gen.3^{22} that this polarity is inherited from the divine. Man is created not simply in the physical image of God but also the psychological:

---

[32] The proof text for the equivalence of **צדקה** (*ṣdqh*) and **אמונה** (*'mnh*) is Deut.32^{4}.

[33] See also Gen.13^{17} in which Abraham is instructed to walk "the length and breadth of the land."

ויאמר יהוה אלהים הן האדם היה כאחד ממנו לדעת טוב ורע
ועתה פן ישלח ידו ולקח גם מעץ החיים ואכל וחי לעלם
wy'mr yhwh 'lhym hn h'dm hyh k'ḥd mmnw ld't ṭwb wr'
w'th pn yšlḥ ydw wlqḥ gm m'ṣ hḥyym w'kl wḥy l'lm
And YHWH *'elohîm* said:
Behold the Man has become like one of us, knowing good and evil;
And now (what would happen) lest he stretch forth his hand
and take also of the Tree of Life, eat and live forever.

In this one short verse, the scene has been set and the characters and traits of Job and יהוה (YHWH) have been sketched out. The following five verses flesh out the sketch of Job to the point that Job's perception of his own *raison d'être* (or lack thereof) is discernable. All of Job's subsequent actions find their roots in $1^{1\text{-}5}$.

1:2-3

ויולדו לו שבעה בנים ושלוש בנות
ויהי מקנהו שבעת אלפי צאן ושלשת אלפי גמלים
וחמש מאות צמד בקר וחמש מאות אתונות ועבדה רבה מאד
ויהי האיש ההוא גדול מכל בני קדם
wywldw lw šb'h bnym wšlwš bnwt
wyhy mqnhw šb't 'lpy ṣ'n wšlšt 'lpy gmlym
wḥmš m'wt ṣmd bqr wḥmš m'wt 'twnwt w'bdh rbh m'd
wyhy h'yš hhw' gdwl mkl bny qdm
And there were born to him seven sons and three daughters.
And his possessions were seven thousand sheep, three thousand camels,
five thousand yoke of oxen, five thousand she-asses,
and a very large household.[34]
And that man was the greatest of all the people of the East.

Much has been made of the significance of the numbers of the various components of Job's material wealth Whether there is any significance to these specific numbers is not relevant here. The author makes use of the word עבדה (*'bdh*), a word that occurs only here and in Gen.26^{14}, where it is used to describe Isaac's wealth. We would do well to include Gen.26^{13} in our deliberation:

---

[34] *NJPS* gently paraphrases עבדה (*'bdh*) as "household" although some type of indentured servant is clearly indicated by the √עבד.

ויגדל האיש וילך הלוך וגדל עד כי גדל מאד
ויהי לו מקנה צאן ומקנה בקר ועבדה רבה...
wygdl h’yš wylk hlwk wgdl ‘d ky gdl m’d
wyhy lw mqnh ṣ’n wmqnh bqr w’bdh rbh...
And the man became great, greater and greater until he was very great
And his acquisitions included sheep and cattle and a large household...

It is clear once again that the author is using vocabulary that is evocative of the patriarch Isaac. The greatness √גדל (*gdl*) referred to both in our passage and in Genesis is without doubt "material wealth" and does not refer to wisdom as was earlier suggested. The words used to describe Isaac's material wealth are the same as those used in the case of Job. This text also clearly identifies Job with Isaac who, of the patriarchs, was the only one who did not have some issue with his God. Abraham passed off his wife Sarah as his sister[35] and asked יהוה (YHWH) for proof that he would actually be the beneficiary of all the promised largesse.[36] Jacob made a ten percent deal with אלהים (*’elohîm*) for protection of his assets and acceptance of יהוה (YHWH) as his deity.[37] Isaac's sole deviation from the moral high ground occurred when he passed off his wife Rebekah as his sister in a situation that strongly resembled that of Abraham and Sarah.[38] The implicit comparison of Job with Isaac is to suggest that Job was indeed susceptible to "unwhole" thoughts, as we shall see. As Weiss so aptly puts it, "Job was innocent but he was not naïve."[39] It is important to note that *BH* is in no way critical of Isaac (or of Abraham, for that matter, when he passed Sarah off as his sister).[40] Our author's agenda is not to pass judgment on *BH*, rather to lay the foundation for his character portrait of Job.

The idiosyncratic phrase בני קדם (*bny qdm*) occurs six other times in *BH*;[41] Weiss elects to use the 1Kings citation (regarding King Solomon's wisdom) to fit his "Wisdom Literature" thesis. This "proof text" does not stand the test of scrutiny, since in our text Job is described as "the greatest of all the people of the east" and we are told in 1Kings 5^{10} that it was Solomon's "**wisdom** (that) was the greatest of all the people of the east." If we examine the six other citations of בני קדם (*bny qdm*), it becomes quickly apparent that קדם (*qdm*), as a geographic term, may vary in location from Edom to Mesopotamia. If we shift

---

35 See Gen.$12^{11\text{-}20}$.
36 See Gen.$15^{1\text{-}8}$.
37 Gen.28^{22}
38 See Gen.26^{7}
39 Weiss (1983, 30)
40 Genesis 20. In fact, both Abraham and Isaac end up the wealthier for the experience.
41 Gen.29^{1}, Jud.7^{12}, 8^{10}, 1Kings 5^{10}, Isa.11^{14}, and Jer.49^{28}.

our focus to קדם (*qdm*) alone from the term בני קדם (*bny qdm*), we find that קדם (*qdm*) assumes a dual meaning of "east" and "ancient.". Now we find in Gen.2[8] and Gen.3[24] respectively:

Gen.2[8]

ויטע יהוה אלהים גן בעדן מקדם

wyṭʿ yhwh ʾlhm gn bʿdn mqdm

And YHWH *ʾelohîm* planted a garden in Eden from ancient time

Gen.3[24]

ויגרש את האדם וישכן מקדם לגן עדן את הכרבים

wygrš ʾt hʾdm wyškn mqdm lgn ʿdn ʾt hkrbym

And He expelled the Man

And He installed the cherubim to the east of the Garden of Eden

In order to round out our understanding of all of the subtleties of קדם (*qdm*), we find in Gen.29[1]:

וישא יעקב רגליו וילך ארצה בני קדם

wysʾ yʿqb rglyw wylk ʾrṣh bny qdm

And Jacob set forth and went to the land of the people of the east

If we accept עוץ (*ʿwṣ*) as Edom[42] and קדם (*qdm*) as meaning both "east" and "ancient,"[43] we see the picture of a man living in a time of early antiquity in a place that Genesis refers to both as Eden and the place whence יהוה (YHWH) originated. So we read in Jud.5[4]

יהוה בצאתך משעיר בצעדך משדה אדום

yhwh bṣʾtk msʿyr bṣʿdk msdh ʾdwm

YHWH, when you went forth from Seʿir,

when you stepped out from the field of Edom

and Deut.33[2]

יהוה מסיני בא וזרח משעיר למו

yhwh msyny bʾ wzrḥ msʿr lmw

YHWH came from Sinai,

And shone from Seʿir

---

[42] From Lam.4[21] cited above.

[43] See also Habel (1985, 39-40).

1:4

והלכו בניו ועשו משתה בית איש יומו
ושלחו וקראו לשלשת אחיתיהם לאכל ולשתות עמהם
whlkw bnyw wʿsw mšth byt ʾyš ywmw
whlkw wqrʾw lšlšt ʾḥytyhm lʾkl wlštwt ʿmhm
And his sons would go and make a feast, each in his home
And they would send invitations to their three sisters to eat and drink with them.

At first blush, this verse seems innocuous enough—nothing could be further from the truth. It is perhaps the *crux*—the focal point around which the author builds his entire work. Job's sons celebrate their birthdays in their own homes and invite their sisters. The clear implication is that the sisters live at home with Job. We will have to wait until the end of the 3rd Epilogue[44] for the resolution of this proposition. At the heart of the issue is the immutability of **אלהים** (*ʾelohîm*)—the unmoving perpetual institution of justice.

The author continues to weave intertextual "patriarchal" themes with subliminal references that leave the reader in awe of his brilliance. In fact, we cannot appreciate verses 4-5 unless we surgically dissect them, making sure that we do not inadvertently discard a word or phrase because, as we have already seen, it may be the *nexus* between themes. With that in mind, we proceed with caution starting not necessarily at the physical beginning of the passage.

ועשו משתה (*wʿsw mšth*) – "and [they would] make a feast." In Gen.26[27], Isaac disingenuously says to Abimelech and his general Pikol after he had deceived them regarding Rebekah: [45]

מדוע באתם אלי ואתם שנאתם אתי ותשלחוני מאתכם
mdwʿ bʾtm ʾly wʾtm snʾtm ʾty wtšlḥwny mʾtkm
Why have you come to me, since you hate me and sent me away?

Abimelech does not want any more trouble from Isaac's God; they make peace and Abimelech declares Isaac to be **ברוך יהוה** (*brwk yhwh*) – "Blessed by **יהוה** (YHWH)." Here we encounter for the first time the controversial √**ברך** (*brk*), already with strong hint of the euphemistic usage that is one of the *cruces* of the entire Prologue. Did Abimelech really mean "Blessed by **יהוה** (YHWH)?

---

[44] Job 42[14-15]

[45] In the incident that was recounted above.

Perhaps he really intended to say “cursed of יהוה (YHWH)”.[46] Then we read in Gen.26[30-31]:

ויעש להם משתה ויאכלו וישתו. וישכימו בבקר...
wy‘s lhm mšth wy’klw wyštw wyškymw bbqr
And he (Isaac) made a feast for them and they ate and drank.
And they arose early in the morning...

This is precisely the same construction as we see here in 1[4-5]. Job is being modeled after Isaac for we read in Gen.22[3]:

וישכם אברהם בבקר ויחבש את חמרו
ויקח את שני נעריו אתו ואת יצחק בנו ויבקע עצי עלה...
wyškm ’brhm bbqr wyḥbš ’t ḥmrw
wyqḥ ’t šny n‘ryw ’tw w’t yṣḥq bnw wybq‘ ‘ṣy ’lh
And Abraham arose early in the morning and saddled his ass;
And he took his two youngsters with him along with his son Isaac;
And he split the wood for the burnt offering...

What is it about Abraham and Isaac and not about Jacob that our author wants us to know? Jacob merits only a passing inference in the בני קדם (*bny qdm*) word play of 1[3]. Abraham, and Isaac especially, are the role models after which Job is fashioned. Jacob represents explicit deviousness and a constant need for *quid pro quo*. He has two strikes against him on character[47] and his very name יעקב (*y‘qb*) derives from √עקב (*‘qb*), which implies “treachery.”[48] These are clearly not the character traits that the author wishes to ascribe to Job. Abraham accepted יהוה (YHWH) and remained faithful even after a series of hurtful experiences;[49] Isaac lived a “simple life” although not without moral imperfections. Job is a composite archetypal patriarch—a combination of Isaac and Abraham—a “good” person but very human. The author of Job subtly subverts the Genesis *agenda*, replacing it with his own.

---

[46] In the same way we read in Jud.17[2] the exclamation of Micah’s mother after she learns that Micah has stolen her money: ברוך בני ליהוה (*brwk bny lyhwh*)—"Blessed (cursed?) is my son of YHWH."
[47] The thefts of Esau’s “birthright” and “patriarchal Blessing.”
[48] The term וישכם יעקב בבקר (*wyškm y‘qb bbqr*) occurs in Gen.28[18]; however, the setting is quite different from Abraham and Isaac. Jacob acts in his own interest, while Abraham acts out of faith and Isaac out of a desire to make peace.
[49] The circumcision of Abraham and Isaac, the near-sacrifice of Isaac, and the episode with Sarah regarding Hagar and Ishmael.

Fishbane recognizes the entire issue of the shaping and reshaping of the patriarchal archetype, separating Jacob from Abraham much the same way as we do here. He demonstrates how Deutero-Isaiah (Isaiah 40-55), Hosea, Jeremiah, Micah, Nahum Habakkuk, Zechariah, and Malachi all contribute to this re-portrayal for then contemporary Israel; however, he does not make the connection with the Book of Job. His chapter is illustrative of the point that we have established here and deals with the topic comprehensively. [50]

1:5

ויהי כי הקיפו ימי המשתה וישלח איוב ויקדשם
והשכים בבקר והעלה עלות מספר כלם
כי אמר איוב אולי חטאו בני וברכו אלהים בלבבם
ככה יעשה איוב כל הימים

wyhy ky hqypw ymy hmšth wyšlḥ ʾywb wyqdšm
whškym bbqr whʿlh ʿlwt mspr klm
ky ʾmr ʾywb ʾwly ḥṭʾw bny wbrkw ʾlhm blbbm
kkh yʿsh ʾywb kl hymym

And when the days of feasting had come full cycle,
Job would send (word) and bless[51] them;
and he would arise early in the morning
and offer burnt offerings for all of them,
for Job said: "perhaps my sons have sinned
and cursed *ʾelohîm* in their hearts."
Job did this all of (his) days.[52]

ויהי כי הקיפו ימי המשתה (*wyhy ky hqypw ymy hmšth*) "And when the days of feasting had come full cycle." We have treated the choice of **המשתה** (*hmšth*) above[53].

The question remains; what does **הקיפו** (*hqypw*) really mean? The answer may not be forthcoming from within the constraints of our investigation. It is certain that this is the only intransitive use of the √**נקף** found in *BH*. The context surely suggests a calendric or seasonal cycle but then the author could have used the idiom of 1Sam.1[20]:

---

[50] Fishbane (1985, 372ff.)
[51] Lit. "sanctify"
[52] Words in parentheses are mine.
[53] As the celebration of a ceremonial event such as the treaty between Isaac and Abimelech in Gen.26.[30].

ויהי לתקפות הימים

wyhy ltqpwt hymym

And so it was at the turning of the year[54]

However, this idiom has problems of its own. First the implicit root is *קוף (*qwp*), which exists only in the nominal form תק(ו)פה (*tq[w]ph*) which appears four times in *BH*.[55] Second, the word is applied to both "year" and "day." Third, *קוף (*qwp*) is not √נקף (*nqp*)[56]; indeed, paradoxically, there is the Ugaritic *nqpt*, "meaning (circuit of the) year," which would indicate a root *nqp*.[57]

Thus הקיפו (*hqypw*) is a philological anomaly. The context does not give us any further aid should we be inclined to accept one of the previously mentioned suggestions. Job had seven sons and three daughters. The sons alone celebrated their birthdays in the company of their sisters. Job was notably absent from these occasions. The number seven has no calendric significance other than constituting the number of days in the week. The occurrences of תק(ו)פה (*tq[w]ph*) are happy occasions—this occasion was not a happy one for Job. Perhaps Job equated "feasting and drinking" with "blasphemy" or even just the thought of "blasphemy." It is a time of suspicion and foreboding, the cloud without a silver lining. It is the reinforcement of Job's morbid psychological makeup and our author perhaps had no other way to convey this but to coin a unique phrase. In any case, הקיפו (*hqypw*) is strongly indicative of a cycle, with Job making sacrifices every appropriate cyclical day; the basis of the cycle would be the rotation of the sun just as with the other occurrences of תק(ו)פה (*tq[w]ph*). We might further speculate that the author wishes the reader to know that he follows a solar calendar. This is not inconsistent with the evidence that the sect(s) of the Dead Sea Scrolls based their calendar on the orbit of the sun. We read in *1Q27 Mysteries* 1 ll.6-7:

והצדק יגלה כשמש תכון תבל

whṣdq yglh kšmš tkwn tbl

And wholeness shall be revealed as the sun that sets [the course of] the world.

---

[54] See *HALOT*, 1784 for a detailed exposition that offers no resolution for the meaning of this word other than to indicate some sort of cycle. The term *nqpt* occurs in the Ugaritic story of the birth of the "double deity" *Šaḥru-wa-Šalimu* – "Dawn and Dusk," where it is parallel to *šnt* – "years." (*CTA* 23:67-68; *COS* 1.87).

[55] See Ex.4[22], 2Chron.24[23] for annual cycle, ψ19[7] for diurnal cycle.

[56] Although there may be a case for associating ע"ו and פ"נ roots.

[57] Aistleitner, 1847; Gordon, *Textbook* § 19:1700

Added value and relevance are to be derived from the appearance of צדק (*ṣdq*)—"wholeness." The context of this citation is the disappearance of evil and folly and the emergence of "wholeness" and knowledge.

וישלח איוב ויקדשם (*wyšlḥ ʾywb wyqdšm*) – "Job would send (word) and bless[58] them." The author is making us work hard to keep up with him. He is using the terseness of the Pentateuchal language to its fullest advantage. Interwoven with the fabric of the verse, is the author's first encounter with an internal contradiction. He knows that whenever he uses the √ברך (*brk*), he intends to turn it on end and make "curse" the principal meaning and "bless" the subtext (as we have previously pointed out in the case of Isaac and Abimelech). Now he really wants Job to bless his sons (for that was the divine and patriarchal rite)[59] and he conjures a brilliant *finesse*.

The author needs to find a synonym for √ברך (*brk*) but only one is available in a Genesis setting and it is appropriately attributed to *ʾelohîm* in Gen.2³:[60]

ויברך אלהים את יום השביעי ויקדש אתו...
wybrk ʾlhym ʾt ywm hšbyʿy wyqdš ʾtw...
And *ʾelohîm* blessed the seventh day and sanctified it...

When we read ויקדשם *wyqdšm* "and he sanctified them" we can only bring to mind Gen.2³ since the pairing of √ברך (*brk*) and √קדש (*qdš*) occurs only there and once again in the Decalogue (Ex.20¹¹) in the same context (that of Sabbath observance). The parallel structure dictates a meaning of "and he blessed them." In the Book of Job, only God can bless with √ברך (*brk*).[61] The author uses √ברך (*brk*) solely as a euphemism when performed by a human; thus from very early on, we are aware of the reality of human pathos and divine antipathy.

והשכים בבקר והעלה עלות (*whškym bbqr whʿlh ʿlwt*) – "and he would arise early in the morning and offer burnt offerings." We see here more than a vestige of Gen.22³ in which Abraham prepares to sacrifice Isaac:

---

[58] Lit. "sanctify"

[59] Oddly enough, it was not Abraham but YHWH who blessed Isaac (Gen.25¹¹). Isaac blessed Jacob with the blessing that he intended for Esau (Gen.27²⁷) and Jacob blessed only Joseph's children Manasseh and Ephraim (Gen.48⁹). The blessings of the patriarchs by YHWH and *ʾelohîm* are liberally strewn throughout the Book of Genesis.

[60] In the context of the "seventh day"—the day of rest at the end of the Creation.

[61] As we shall see later in 42⁸.

וישכם אברהם בבקר...ויבקע עצי עלה
wyškm ʾbrhm bbqr... wybqʿ ʿṣy ʿlh
And Abraham arose early in the morning...and split the wood for the burnt offering

In just four words, our author has painted Job in the colors of the patriarchs Abraham and Isaac, which we maintain is his intention. He has also evoked strong notions of a priestly role for Job, something that will become important later.

אולי חטאו בני וברכו אלהים בלבבם (*ʾwly ḥṭʾw bny wbrkw ʾlhm blbbm*) – "Perhaps my sons have sinned and cursed *ʾelohîm* in their hearts." Here we see Job worrying about what covert moral wrong that his sons may have committed, especially the possibility that they have "cursed **אלהים** (*ʾelohîm*) in their hearts."

Newsom waxes eloquent on √ברך (*brk*) when she says:

> The euphemistic use of "bless" for "curse" in verse 5 and elsewhere in the prose tale is a puzzling feature. Although attested in other Hebrew narratives (1Kgs 21:13), it is not a universal scribal convention (see Ex.22[27]). Since *bērēk* is used both literally and euphemistically in the narrative, the reader must negotiate the contextually proper meaning in each occurrence, heightening its thematic significance. Moreover, the use of the euphemism gives the narrator something of the hyperscrupulous character Job displays. Perhaps most important is the performative significance of barring the word "curse" from the diction of the text. Cursing God quite literally has no place in the linguistic or moral world of the prose tale, for its presence would threaten the harmony upon which its vision is based. The possibility of such cursing is raised (1:5, 11; 2:5) only to be defused (1:5) and rejected (1:22; 2:10), but even in this act of exclusion the word itself is already overwritten, its linguistic place occupied by its opposite.[62]

Not only has Newsom failed to acknowledge the simple symmetry of the attribution of √ברך (*brk*) to divine and human action, she provides a rationale that is based on the exegetical, traditional reading. The last sentence of the citation demonstrates clearly the complexity of the gymnastics required to produce a meaning, if indeed such meaning is ever really produced.

The notion of anticipatory surrogate atonement is unprecedented in patriarchal or even divine history. Indeed, Moses attempted a collective atonement after the incident of the "Golden Calf" as we read in Ex. 32[30-33]:

---

[62] Newsom (2003, 55)

ויאמר משה אל העם אתם חטאתם חטאה גדלה
ועתה אעלה אל יהוה אולי אכפרה בעד חטאתכם
וישב משה אל יהוה ויאמר
אנא חטא העם הזה חטאה גדלה ויעשו להם אלהי זהב
ועתה אם תשא חטאתם ואם אין מחני נא מספרך אשר כתבת

wyʼmr mšh ʼl hʻm ʼtm ḥṭʼtm ḥṭʼh gdlh
wʻth ʼʻlh ʼl yhwh ʼwly ʼkprh bʻd ḥṭʼtkm
wyšb mšh ʼl yhwh wyʼmr
ʼnʼ ḥṭʼ hʻm hzh ḥṭʼh gdlh wyʻśw lhm ʼlhy zhb
wʻth ʼm tśʼ ḥṭʼtm wʼm ʼyn mḥny nʼ msprk ʼšr ktbt

And Moses said to the people, "You have committed a great sin,
Now I will go up to YHWH, perhaps I may atone for your sin."
And Moses returned to YHWH and said,
"This people have committed a great sin, and made a golden god;
And now, please forgive their sin.
If not, then erase me from the book that you have written."

Moses put his own life on the line as expiation of a known sin. The Book of Leviticus[63] clearly recognizes and even mandates the priests to atone on behalf of the sins of the community, sins that are known to have been committed by both individuals and the community as a whole. If Job was as perfect as 1^{1} suggests, why would he even have to suspect his sons and need to pre-empt their sins with atonement? The answer is that there is only one sin that his sons might commit that they could conceal from God, namely, the mere thought of blasphemy and Job knows all about that because he has had that thought before. There are only two citations in the entire *BH* that between them combine √**חטא** (*ḥṭʼ*), √לבב (*lbb*), and √ברך (*brk*) and they are $\psi 4^{5}$ and Deut.29^{18}:[64]

First, $\psi 4^{5}$:

רגזו ואל תחטאו אמרו בלבבכם על משכבכם ודמו

rgzw wʼl tḥṭʼw ʼmrw blbbkm ʻl mškbkm wdmw

Be enraged but do not sin, Say (it) in your heart upon your resting place and be silent.

which includes a combination of √**חטא** (*ḥṭʼ*) and √לבב (*lbb*), and Deut.29^{18}:

---

[63] Lev.16^{1-17}

[64] This is one of the composite phrases that have more than one *BH* antecedent.

והיה בשמעו את דברי האלה הזאת
והתברך בלבבו לאמר שלום יהיה לי כי בשררות לבי אלך
whyh bšmʿw ʾt dbry hʾlh hzʾt
whtbrk blbbw lʾmr šlwm yhyh ly ky bšrrwt lby ʾlk
And when he hears the words of this curse,
He will bless himself in his heart saying:
I will have peace because I will follow my obstinate heart.

which combines √לבב (*lbb*), and √ברך (*brk*). Both verses can support multiple interpretations; however, one is inclined to believe that the author wants us to have the Psalms citation in mind. It is a "wisdom" admonition, discouraging the whole man from overt sin, yet encouraging him to keep his (sinful) thoughts to himself. Job's sacrifices are not a reflection on his sons, they are pre-emptive of Job himself. The citation from Deuteronomy is useful in that it describes the crime of the sinner, namely, the worship of other (false) gods. It is not unreasonable to suspect that this was the weakness that Job feared concerning his sons.

We are still not through with this verse. There is yet another internal word play that is taking place in an almost a:c – b:d chiastic parallelism. That is to say that:

Job would send (word) and bless them…
"perhaps my sons have sinned
and cursed *ʾelohîm* in their hearts."

runs parallel with

And he would arise early in the morning
and offer burnt offerings for all of them …
Job did this all of (his) days[65]

The author wants us to know that Job, while apparently a model patriarch, did not just go through the motions. When he "would arise early in the morning and offer burnt offerings for all of them," he knew the priestly Biblical laws concerning these rites. As we mentioned earlier, perhaps it was not Job who

---

65 **וישלח איוב ויקדשם...אולי חטאו בני וברכו אלהים בלבבם**
והשכים בבקר והעלה עלות מספר כלם...ככה יעשה איוב כל הימים
wyšlḥ ʾywb wyqdšm... ʾwly ḥṭʾw bny wbrkw ʾlhm blbbm
whškym bbqr whʿlh ʿlwt mspr klm... kkh yʿsh ʾywb kl hymym

knew the laws but the author himself.[66] Consider for a moment this passage from Num.15$^{8-12}$:

וכי תעשה בן בקר עלה או זבח לפלא נדר או שלמים ליהוה
והקריב על בן הבקר מנחה סלת שלשה עשרנים בלול בשמן חצי ההין
ויין תקריב לנסך חצי ההין אשה ריח ניחח ליהוה
ככה יעשה לשור האחד או לאיל האחד או לשה בכבשים או בעזים
כמספר אשר תעשו ככה תעשו לאחד כמספרם

wky tʿśh bn bqr ʿlh ʾw zbḥ lplʾ ndr ʾw šlmym lyhwh
whqryb ʿl bn hbqr mnḥh slt šlšh ʿśrnym blwl bšmn ḥṣy hhyn
wyy ntqryb lnsk ḥṣy hhyn ʾšh ryḥ nyḥḥ lyhwh
kkh yʿśh lšwr hʾḥd ʾw lʾyl hʾḥd ʾw lśh bkbsym ʾw bʿzym
kmspr ʾšr tʿśw kkh tʿśw lʾḥd kmsprm

When you prepare a bullock as a burnt offering or sacrifice
To fulfill a vow or a peace offering to YHWH
He (*sic*) shall sacrifice upon the bullock a peace offering
of 3/10 (of an *'ephah*) of flour mixed with ½ a *hin* of oil.
And you shall make a sacrifice of ½ a *hin* of wine as a drink offering;
an aromatic fire offering to YHWH.
Thus shall you do to the ox, the ram the lamb or the kid.
According to the number that you offer,
so shall do to each one according to their number.

These are the detailed laws of sacrifice; our author compresses this entire corpus with his use of the words עלה (*ʿlh*), ככה יעשה (*kkh yʿśh*), and מספר כלם (*mspr klm*). This is no co-incidence—this is the only place in the entire *BH* that these words are used together in the same context. Unless this and the other Jewish-specific references are an act of *braggadocio* on the part of the author, this would support the notion that the author of the Book of Job was a Jew.

Owens falls prey to his theological requirement when he reinvents the translation of the phrase אולי חטאו בני וברכו אלהים בלבבם (*ʾwly ḥṭʾw bny wbrkw ʾlhm blbbm*). He understands as follows:

> And Job proceeded to send and to sanctify them and that being so he rose early in the morning and offered burnt offerings according to the number of all of them, for Job said, "Perhaps my sons have sinned, and that being so, blessed God in their hearts."

---

[66] We will pursue this notion further when we analyze the non-Genesis citations.

Owens continues:

> This interpretation portrays Job as a man who was effective in religion as well as in business. Job's spiritual influence was so effective that his children were by their own character ("in their hearts") in proper relation with God. In a context in which Job is being acclaimed, it would be much more in keeping for him to be shown as effective in leading his children to have their own spiritual identity than for him to be an isolated individual taking a sacrificial "shot in the dark."[67]

Owens' attempt at an apologetic translation is virtually incomprehensible, pockmarked with the phrase "and being so." His subsequent remarks are a perfect example of the preconception dictating the exegesis.

Pope summarizes 1^{1-5} as follows:

> The PROLOGUE introduces the hero as a man of exemplary rectitude and piety, blessed with wealth and a happy family for whom he is particularly solicitous.[68]

This description is based on a superficial reading of the text, which is accepted by most scholars. However, as we have demonstrated above, the text is anything but superficial and demands a scrupulous and careful examination.

While pious and wealthy, Job was hardly happy. In fact, we are not told anything of his social activities or standing. His family may have been happy; however, we know that he did not attend family celebrations for fear that these gatherings might include some act of moral or "religious" impropriety. He was judgmental to the point of making pre-emptive atonement assuming that such acts actually did occur. Thus, one might question whether suspicion and prejudice constitute "particular solicitude." To say that Job was "blessed" is to introduce a notion that is not to be explicitly expressed until the end of the 3rd Epilogue in 42^{12}.

As to Job's being a "hero,"[69] we are once again not convinced. He is simply one of several characters of equal standing around whom the narrative as a whole revolves.

In summary, the first five verses of the Chapter 1 describe the life, times, and highly complex character of Job. He is physically created in the primordial

---

[67] Owens (1971, 461)

[68] Pope (1974, xvi)

[69] In the Western literary sense.

image of the divine. The makeup of his personality and character is described in attributes of Abraham and Isaac as they are set forth in the cited passages of the Book of Genesis.[70] The author is painstakingly meticulous in his choice of language, so much so that in the first six words of 1^{1} lies the key to his methodology and the decipherment of the real drama. By the end of 1^{5}, we have what amounts to a full profile of Job.

1:6

ויהי היום ויבאו בני האלהים להתיצב על יהוה ויבא גם השטן בתוכם

wyhy hywm wyb'w bny h'lhym lhtyṣb ʿl yhwh wyb' gm hśṭn btwkm

And so it was on the appointed day
that the "sons of the gods" came to conspire[71] against YHWH,
and *haśśaṭan* came also amongst them.

ויהי היום (*wyhy hywm*) is an expression that occurs only five times elsewhere in *BH*.[72]. The common translation is "one day" as though in a fairy tale. If we examine the occurrences of **ויהי היום** (*wyhy hywm*), we find that not only was "the day" not random at all but that "the day" was specific in both historical and legendary contexts. In 1Sam.1^{4}, the day was on the occasion of 'Elkanah's family visit to Shiloh to offer sacrifice. In 1Sam.14^{1}, the day was the day after the Philistines moved their garrison to the pass of Michmash. In 2Kings 4, the three occurrences of **ויהי היום** (*wyhy hywm*) were the days that Elisha, the **איש האלהים** (*'yš h'lhym*), made his rounds at Shunem.[73] In our case, the day is that of the appointed meeting, something that took place on some regularly scheduled basis. This explanation is further borne out in the usage of the phrase in 1^{13}.

בני האלהים (*bny h'lhym*) occurs only here and in Gen.$6^{2,4}$. Traditional scholarship would interpret **בני האלהים** (*bny h'lhym*) as actual "gods" themselves, much the same way as **בני ישראל** (*bny yśr'l*) are "Israelites."[74] Pope refers to them as "lesser members of the ancient pagan pantheon who are retained in later monotheistic theology as angels," citing ψ29^{1} and ψ89^{7}.[75] However, the expression used in these verses is **בני אלים** (*bny 'lym*), which is

---

[70] Gen.20 *passim*;22 *passim*, particularly 22^{12};26^{7};$26^{13,14}$;26^{27};28^{22}.

[71] See explanation below.

[72] Besides the Prologue to the Book of Job (1^{13}; 2^{1}). See 1Sam.1^{4},14^{1}; 2Kings $4^{8\ 11,14}$.

[73] In a story that parallels Gen.18ff.

[74] Scholars might even argue that they are "gods" since Gen.1^{26} states **נעשה אדם** (*nʿśh 'dm*) "let us make man." Of course the plural of that declaration is the "royal we."

[75] Pope (1974, 9)

not the same expression and does not meet our author's criterion for an exact *BH* antecedent. Tsevat would have us imagine that this gathering of **בני האלהים** (*bny h'lhym*) is actually the divine court over which **אלהים** (*'lhym*) presides,[76] citing ψ82[1] where we find:

אלהים נצב בעדת אל
'lhym nṣb b'dt 'l
'elohîm stands in the divine assembly

We must render the expression **עדת אל** (*'dt 'l*) as "divine assembly" since **אל** (*'l*) is singular and thus may be a collective term. Any other rendition would require that **אל** (*'l*) be a proper name and therefore redundant.[77]

Our author had these expressions at his disposal had he intended either of their meanings. In using the term **בני האלהים** (*bny h'lhym*), he directs the reader specifically to Gen.6[2,4] and its context, wherein they are described as:

המה הגברים אשר מעולם אנשי השם
hmh hgbrym 'šr m'wlm 'nšy hšm
They are the heroes, who were the famous people of old.[78]

The interaction of **בני האלהים** (*bny h'lhym*) with humans gave them the status equivalent to what Hesiod described as "heroes (ἥρωες)" created by Zeus, son of Kronos:

> αὐτὰρ ἐπεὶ καὶ τοῦτο γένος κατὰ γαῖ' ἐκάλυψεν, αὖτις ἔτ' ἄλλο τέταρτον ἐπὶ χθονὶ πουλυβοτείρῃ Ζεὺς Κρονίδης ποίησε, δικαιότερον καὶ ἄρειον, ἀνδρῶν ἡρώων θεῖον γένος, οἳ καλέονται ἡμίθεοι, προτέρη γενεὴ κατ' ἀπείρονα γαῖαν.
> But when earth had covered this generation also, Zeus the son of Cronos made yet another, the fourth, upon the fruitful earth, which was nobler and more righteous, a god-like race of hero-men who are called demi-gods, the race before our own, throughout the boundless earth.[79]

---

[76] Tsevat (1966, 135)
[77] " *'elohîm* stands in the assembly of *'el.*" As Pope also points out, the concept of a "divine court" is not uncommon in the Ugaritic mythological texts.
[78] Gen.6[4].
[79] Hesiod *Works and Days* 156ff.

These were the "righteous"[80] products of the unions of god and human, thus neither divine nor human, who lived "apart from men…at the ends of the earth."[81]

Genesis 6 picks up the story "when humans began to multiply upon the face of the earth and bore daughters." These then are the "sons of the gods" who were taking up with female humans. The outcome of these unions became the humankind of our times, mostly human, with an increasingly diluted divine component. The first generation בני האלהים (*bny h'lhym*) were all males who lived in "blissful isolation."

השטן (*haśśaṭan*) is generally understood to be one of the בני האלהים (*bny h'lhym*),[82] although this is nowhere explicitly stated in the text. In fact, by singling him out, our author wishes us to know that השטן (*haśśaṭan*) is not one of the בני האלהים (*bny h'lhym*). He was not confined but wandered all over the world—alone. His freedom was from physical confinement, his burden was the fact that he lived and worked alone—like יהוה (YHWH).[83]

להתיצב על יהוה (*lhtyṣb ʿl yhwh*) is commonly translated "to present themselves before יהוה (YHWH)";[84] however, there is no sound reason for this rendition. The occurrence of this idiom in Num.23[3,15] does not have this meaning since it is unlikely that Bilʿam told Balak to "present himself to his sacrifice[85] while he (Bilʿam) went in search of other possibilities for cursing Israel.[86] The major lexicons[87] fail to provide a consistent rendition for התיצב על (*htyṣb ʿl*). If we look at all the occurrences of this idiom in *BH*,[88] the sense is

---

[80] Note the use of the word δικαιότερον "more righteous," which is the Greek equivalent of the key word צדיק (*ṣdyq*).

[81] Hesiod *Works and Days* 169 … κατένασσε πατὴρ ἐς πείρατα γαίης.

[82] Clines (1989, 19ff.), Pope (1974, 10).

[83] We will discuss השטן (*haśśaṭan*) in detail below.

[84] Clines (1989, 19), Pope (1974, 9).

[85] Although its occurrence in the Bilʿam story is unlikely to be coincidental as we shall see below.

[86] It is also hardly co-incidental that Bilʿam encountered a "messenger of יהוה (YHWH)" acting in the capacity of שטן (*śṭn*) on his way to curse Israel for Balak (Num.22[22]). By the same token, the יהוה (YHWH) of 2Sam.24[1] is replaced by שטן (*śaṭan*) in the corresponding passage in 1Chron.21[1]. The story of Bilʿam will resurface at Chapter 27 and at the final *crux* of the 3rd Prologue.

[87] *BDB*, 426 and *HALOT*, 427

[88] The usage of התיצב על (*htyṣb ʿl*) in Zech.6[5] and ψ2[2] is identical in meaning "plotting." Its usage in Num.23[3,15] and. ψ36[5] meaning "stand by" is likewise identical. The author

clearly one of "having negative thoughts, plotting or communing." We see this most clearly in ψ2[1-4], which, because of its context, is most likely our author's immediate subtext:

למה רגשו גוים ולאמים יהגו ריק
יתיצבו מלכי ארץ ורוזנים נוסדו יחד על יהוה ועל משיחו
ננתקה את מוסרותימו ונשליכה ממנו עבתימו
יהוה בשמים ישחק יהוה ילעג למו
lmh rgšw gwym wl'mym yhgw ryq
ytyṣbw mlky 'rṣ wrwznym nwsdw yḥd ʿl yhwh wʿl mšyḥw
nntqh 't mwsrwtymw wnšlykh mmnw ʿbtymw
yhwh bšmym yśḥq yhwh ylʿg lmw
Why do the nations thunder and peoples plot in vain?
The kings of the world conspire
and the princes make secret plans against YHWH and against his anointed.
Let us break their fetters and cast off their ropes
YHWH will laugh in the heavens, YHWH will surely ridicule them.

We see here that התיצב על (*htyṣb ʿl*) can have no meaning other than "plotting, conspiring" as we have suggested above. The parallel is to נוסדו יחד (*nwsdw yḥd*) and violence is quite clearly in the air. This would suggest that the *cadre* had come for their ritual cosmic power struggle." There is a palpable tension between the "sons of the gods" and יהוה (YHWH). יהוה (YHWH) is always triumphant and not at all magnanimous in his victory. There is an almost Sisyphean surrender on the part of בני האלהים (*bny h'lhym*) the "sons of the gods," They are silent and play no part in the story other than to appear as a party in opposition to יהוה (YHWH). Their subordination is almost taken for granted.

ויבא גם השטן בתוכם (*wyb' gm hśṭn btwkm*) Now enters השטן (*haśśaṭan*) who, as we have posited above, is not like one of the בני האלהים (*bny h'lhym*), is not party to their council or their fate. יהוה (YHWH) has always known the whereabouts of בני האלהים (*bny h'lhym*), the "sons of the gods" as we have learned from Hesiod; however that is not the case with השטן (*haśśaṭan*), as we are about to see.

---

cleverly combines both meanings of the phrase, preserving the image of the failed conspiracy of בני האלהים (*bny h'lhym*) and the frustrated intentions of Balak.

We must make a short *excursus* to deal with the morphological issues[89] raised by השטן (*haśśaṭan*) and האלהים (*h'lhym*)[90] mentioned above. We maintain that השטן (*hsṭn*)[91] and האלהים (*h'lhym*), along with הנחש (*hnḥš*),[92] הבעל (*hb'l*),[93] האשרה (*h'šrh*),[94] are specific cultic nomenclatures distinct from those that are generic.

We have defined a cardinal rule that the author of the Prologue to the Book of Job chose each word meticulously and that the understanding of these passages lies in uncovering the intertextual subtext of every word and phrase. Consistent with this methodology, we have made distinctions between יהוה (YHWH), אלהים (*'lhym*), and האלהים (*h'lhym*). The resolution of these distinctions will become apparent as we proceed.

1:7

ויאמר יהוה אל השטן מאין תבא ויען השטן את יהוה ויאמר משוט בארץ ומהתהלך בה

wy'mr yhwh 'l hśṭn m'yn tb' w y'n hśṭn 't yhwh wy'mr mšwṭ b'rṣ wmhthlk bh

And YHWH said to *haśśaṭan*, "Whence do you come?"

And *haśśaṭan* answered YHWH, "From wandering around the world and roaming in it."

Of course this is a woefully inadequate translation since the verse is replete with *nuance*. *NJPS* renders the verse in a weak paraphrase:

> The LORD said to the Adversary, "Where have you been?"
> The Adversary answered the LORD, "I have been roaming all over the earth."

This is the first occasion on which יהוה (YHWH) speaks. He ignores the בני האלהים (*bny h'lhym*) and addresses השטן (*haśśaṭan*) with the "welcoming"

---

[89] Halpern (1993: 121 *passim*) regards the form as a collective. However, he does not adduce the examples cited below, which would appear to obviate his argument.

[90] Perhaps most significant of all the examples, which occurs some 366 times in the *BH*. This is perhaps the subject of another paper, but a cursory glance reveals the distinction between האלהים (*ha'elohîm*), אלהים (*'elohîm*) as God of Israel, the generic אלהים (*'elohîm*), and אלהים אחרים (*'elohîm 'aḥerîm*). It is difficult to see how Halpern's argument stands up, especially in the light of 1Kings 18^{39} – יהוה הוא האלהים (*yhwh hw' h'lhym*).

[91] See Zech.3^{2}(twice), Job 1^{7}(twice),^{8,9,12}(twice); $2^{1,2}$(twice),^{3,4,6,7}.

[92] See Gen.$3^{1,2,4,14}$; Num.$21^{6,7,9}$; 2 Kings 18^{4}; Jer.46^{22}; Amos 5^{20};9^{3}; Micah 7^{17}; Eccles.10^{11}.

[93] Also הבעלים (*hb'lym*).

[94] See Jud.$6^{25,26,30}$; 1Kings 15^{33} 16^{33},18^{19}; 2Kings 13^{7};18^{4};21^{7};$23^{4,6,7}$.

words מאין תבא (*m'yn tb'*), an aggressive opening similar to that found in Jonah 1^8 when he is grilled by the sailors with מאין תבא (*m'yn tb'*) after being the unlucky winner of the lottery, in Jud.17^9 where Micah similarly crudely greets the wandering Levite, and in Gen.42^7 when Joseph gruffly greets his brothers with מאין באתם (*m'yn b'tm*) on their first encounter subsequent to his having been sold to the caravan of Ishmaelites.

The author gives us our first inkling of the identity of השטן (*haśśaṭan*) when he has him respond to יהוה (YHWH)'s question with משוט בארץ ומתהלך בה (*mšwṭ b'rṣ wmthlk bh*)—"From wandering around the world and roaming in it." The response is that of an equal, a peer, something יהוה (YHWH) himself might have said if asked the question by an equal.

משוט בארץ (*mšwṭ b'rṣ*)—"from wandering around the world." This construction occurs only in Zech.4^{10}, which explains אבן הבדיל (*'bn hbdyl*) the faceted stone of Zerubbabel as the seven eyes of יהוה (YHWH) that are משוטטים בכל הארץ (*mšwṭṭym bkl h'rṣ*) – "roaming all over the earth." The verse is filled with irregularities; however, there can be no doubt that our author had this in mind when he crafted השטן (*haśśaṭan*)'s response.

Parallelism and contrast are the major literary devices in Biblical Hebrew and here the contrast between בני האלהים (*bny h'lhym*) and השטן (*haśśaṭan*) comes into sharp focus. Returning to Hesiod's definition for a moment, we remember that the "heroes"—our בני האלהים (*bny h'lhym*)—lived a blissful life albeit geographically confined to the ends of the earth; on the other hand, השטן (*haśśaṭan*) is fated to wander the world, perhaps as the scourge.[95] השטן (*haśśaṭan*) is the distaff side of יהוה (YHWH), who travels the world showering blessings and prosperity on its inhabitants. As the *doppelgänger* of יהוה (YHWH), השטן (*haśśaṭan*) is also his peer.[96] The author has transfixed us again with a brilliant word play—now, in his inimitable way, he nails his point with ומהתהלך בה (*wmhthlk bh*).

ומהתהלך בה (*wmhthlk bh*) is a key expression and is the final piece of the puzzle in the description of the personality of השטן (*haśśaṭan*). Our author endows him with both the divine and human attributes of being מתהלך (*mthlk*),

---

[95] A second √שוט (*šwṭ*) has a meaning of "scourge, punish" and fits our context perfectly. The root occurs only in a nominal form. See 1Kings $12^{11,14}$; Isa.10^{26} in particular.

[96] In the speech in Zech.$3^{1\text{-}2}$, Zechariah has already demonstrated the uneasy relationship between יהוה (YHWH) and השטן (*haśśaṭan*) that our author is about to exploit.

"roaming."[97] We now recall our discussion of ירא אלהים (*yr' 'lhym*) in which the man (האדם – *ha'adam*) gives אלהים (*'elohîm*) the excuse that "I was afraid because I was naked and I hid." We did not say what caused האדם (*ha'adam*) to be afraid in the first place, so we now recall the motivating verse:[98]

וישמעו את קול יהוה אלהים מתהלך בגן לרוח היום ויתחבא האדם ואשתו בתוך עץ הגן
wyšm'w 't qwl yhwh 'lhym mthlk bgn lrwḥ hywm wytḥb' h'dm w'štw btwk 'ṣ hgn
And they heard the voice(?) of YHWH *'elohîm*
roaming in the garden at the breezy time of the day,
And *ha'adam* and his woman hid in the midst of the tree of the garden.

We will ignore the awkwardness of the translation and concentrate on the relevant section:

וישמעו את קול יהוה אלהים מתהלך בגן
wyšm'w 't qwl yhwh 'lhym mthlk bgn
And they heard the voice(?) of YHWH *'elohîm* roaming in the garden

"Roaming" is a "godly" thing to do; "roaming" with the deity may be humanity's closest state to the "divine." We see it on other occasions in *BH*;[99] however, it is the Genesis quotation that is the exact match; the only instance in *BH* where the word מתהלך (*mthlk*) describes both יהוה (YHWH) and אלהים (*'elohîm*). By enticing us with the comparative and contrasting attributes of יהוה (YHWH) and השטן (*haśśaṭan*), the author leads us to a *crux*. Are יהוה (YHWH) and השטן (*haśśaṭan*) one and the same, or is one the divine protagonist and the other the contrarian divine antagonist as we suggested above? The answer to this question is critical to the understanding of the Prologue.

Weiss calls השטן (*haśśaṭan*) a "hypostasis,"[100] which he defines as the "perception of a particular characteristic or emanation of the Divine as a divinity itself, as an independent entity, or as a personification of one of God's attributes." He recognizes the intimate association of the two and their parity but cannot bring himself at this point to identify the two as one entity.

---

[97] See Habel (1985, 89). Habel sees the connection between שוט (*šwṭ*) and מתהלך (*mthlk*) as parallel descriptors of the activities of יהוה (YHWH) and השטן (*haśśaṭan*); however he gets no further than calling השטן (*haśśaṭan*) "Yahweh's suspicious one, his spy." The divine-human connection of מתהלך (*mthlk*) is not acknowledged.
[98] Gen.3^8
[99] See Lev.26^{12}; Deut.23^{15}; 2Sam.$7^{6,7}$; $\psi 43^2$; For a fuller discussion of מתהלך (*mthlk*), see 1^1 above.
[100] Weiss (1983, 39)

יהוה (YHWH) and השטן (*haśśaṭan*) are indeed one and the same, the original psychological mold from which all of humanity was cast. It is only with this understanding that the Prologue can be perceived as a unity, free from criticisms of multiple authorship or prejudiced conceptions of characters whose personalities run counter to common knowledge. That understood, it is important to contrast Clines' understanding of the relationship between יהוה (YHWH) and השטן (*haśśaṭan*):

> For him (the author), there are two heavenly personalities in uneasy confrontation; two personalities who are able to converse freely, who are neither enemies nor conspirators, neither friends nor rivals. The tension of these two personalities can be simply accepted as a datum of the narrative, or it can be probed theologically for its hidden resonances.[101]

One gets the impression that Clines would agree with us were he not shackled by the theological premise that requires him to preserve the separation of יהוה (YHWH) and השטן (*haśśaṭan*). Everything that he says, even as an exegete, begs the combination of יהוה (YHWH) and השטן (*haśśaṭan*) into a single consciousness. Traditional scholarship perceives השטן (*haśśaṭan*) as subordinate to יהוה (YHWH) since his range of activities is restricted by יהוה (YHWH). However, upon closer examination, we find that this may be true only with respect to Job. השטן (*haśśaṭan*) is otherwise unfettered; were he truly governed by יהוה (YHWH) there would be no reason for יהוה (YHWH) to inquire as to his whereabouts and the nature of his activities.

Handy attempts to identify השטן (*haśśaṭan*) from within the context of the Ugaritic pantheon. Unfortunately, he falls almost immediately into the trap of preconception:

> The manner in which a pantheon was seen to be organized in ancient Syria-Palestine needs to be understood in the scenes presented in this narrative frame, especially the questions of how subordinate deities attained and then maintained their position in such a divine hierarchy. It can be demonstrated that the Satan of the Book of Job in a recognizable pattern for members of the *b^enê ^elohîm* confronted by the head of the pantheon.[102]

---

[101] Clines (1989, 22)
[102] Handy (1993, 108)

He has taken for granted suppositions that are not supported by the text. First, it is nowhere stated that השטן (*haśśaṭan*) was one of בני האלהים (*bny h'lhym*) Second, nowhere are בני האלהים (*bny h'lhym*) described as deities at all. Finally, we have no basis for ranking השטן (*haśśaṭan*) subordinate to יהוה (YHWH). Consequently, the rest of Handy's work loses any relevance with respect to the subject at hand.

We must pause to recapitulate what we have established in order for us to proceed further. Job is a human being "cast in the image of אלהים (*'elohîm*)." He is wealthy beyond imagination and appears to be perfect and whole; however, that is an illusion. Job silently suspects his sons of sinning and feels compelled to pre-emptively atone for them. He does not know whether they have blasphemed אלהים (*'elohîm*), even covertly. There is an inherent tension, if not a contradiction, in the notion of a man of such absolute wholeness and piety as Job thinking anything but the best of humanity. We know that his suspicions sadden him and that his atonements do not bring him relief. His suspicion of the presence of evil in his sons is reflected in the mute conspiratorial nature of the "sons of the gods" with respect to יהוה (YHWH). For his part, יהוה (YHWH) has placed a "mole" in the camp of בני האלהים (*bny h'lhym*) "the sons of the gods" in the form of השטן (*haśśaṭan*), who, being יהוה (YHWH) himself, speaks their mind. To put it simply, יהוה (YHWH) is indecisive and is wrestling with his conflicting consciences.

Our author is very careful to separate the identities of אלהים (*'elohîm*) and יהוה (YHWH). The attributes of אלהים (*'elohîm*) are institutional justice, right and wrong, and black and white. אלהים (*'elohîm*) does not speak—he does not have to, everyone knows the expectations of אלהים (*'elohîm*).[103] יהוה (YHWH), on the other hand, is good and evil, compassion, love, loneliness, and idealism, but also vacillation and ambivalence. השטן (*haśśaṭan*) is the *alter ego* of יהוה (YHWH), with cynicism, scathing criticism, brutal realism and the absence of emotion; he is everything that יהוה (YHWH) abhors but of whom he cannot be rid. When the time comes for dealing with distasteful tasks or thoughts, יהוה (YHWH) has his השטן (*haśśaṭan*)[104]—in fact he himself becomes השטן

---

[103] If we accept the muteness of אלהים (*'elohîm*), then we must consider the possibility that the phrase בני האלהים (*bny h'lhym*) might be rendered as "the sons of אלהים (*'elohîm*) in a judicial sense, making their "presence before יהוה (YHWH)" a court of law. This opens up another avenue of exploration, which we will pursue at another time.

[104] See Zech.3[1]ff.

(*haśśaṭan*).[105] On the other hand, **אלהים** (*ʾelohîm*) is a constant value. Job is caught up in the internal struggle of **יהוה** (YHWH) and **השטן** (*haśśaṭan*).[106]

Cooper condenses his "basic ways of reading the Book of Job" as follows:

> One reading concludes that there is, after all, predictable causality in God's dealings with humanity; one finds causality but no predictability; and one finds neither causality nor predictability.
> Each of these readings…is rooted in the reader's empathy (whether conscious or not) with the point of view of one of the three main characters in the prologue: Satan (predictable causality); Job (causality but no predictability); or God (neither causality nor predictability [*ḥinnâm]*). All three readings are flawed, but none can be ruled out unequivocally…the point…is…that the prologue to Job is, *by design*, the introduction of all three.[107]

Once again we observe the consequence of an interpretive methodology that is based on a preconceived notion. While Cooper's points are well taken, his *caveat* that "all three readings are flawed" demonstrates his inability to comprehend the totality of the Prologue and the 3rd Epilogue (which he completely ignores). He has an insight that, if pursued, might have provided him with the key. He discards "the Straussian approach" as failing to "do justice to the richness and openness of the text." He digs his hole further when he asserts that "Even if there is an esoteric level of meaning, there is no reason to assume that it is privileged—that it represents the 'real meaning' of the text just because [it] (*sic*) is obscure or, perhaps heterodox."[108] Had he gone down "the road not taken," he would have found that, in fact, all three statements are true and complementary.

1:8-9

ויאמר יהוה אל השטן השמת לבך על עבדי איוב
כי אין כמהו בארץ איש תם וישר ירא אלהים וסר מרע.
ויען השטן את יהוה ויאמר החנם ירא איוב אלהים.
wyʾmr yhwh ʾl hśṭn hśmt lbk ʿl ʿbdy ʾywb
ky ʾyn kmhw ʾyš tm wyšr yrʾ ʾlhym wsr mrʿ
wyʿn hśṭn ʾt yhwh wyʾmr hḥnm yrʾ ʾywb ʾlhym

---

[105] We will see that a synonym for **השטן** (*haśśaṭan*) is **מלאך יהוה** (*mlʾk yhwh*).

[106] This is not to suggest that our author intends to convey the dualism that is characteristic of Manichaeism and Zoroastrianism. Our scenario is far more complex than a simple juxtaposition of "good and evil" or "light and darkness."

[107] Cooper (1990, 73)

[108] Cooper (1990, 74)

And YHWH said to *haśśaṭan,* "have you considered my servant Job,
for there is no man like him on earth,
an honest and upright man who reveres *ʾelohîm* and shuns evil?"
And *haśśaṭan* answered YHWH and said: "is it *gratis* that Job reveres *ʾelohîm*?"

Here begins in earnest the internal dialogue. This is the place where Weiss asks:

> Does this not indicate that questioner and questioned, answered and answerer are in fact one and the same? That the dialogue between God and Satan is in truth a monologue, a discussion between God and Himself, God's own internal conflict?[109]

We have already come to this conclusion earlier. Perhaps the best way to describe this narrative is as a monologue set in the form of a dialogue. All of the action is in the consciousness of **יהוה** YHWH and the dialogue is a literary device designed to separate the opposing consciences existent within **יהוה** YHWH. The dialogue sets up **יהוה** YHWH as the aggressive antagonist with **ויאמר יהוה אל השטן** (*wyʾmr yhwh ʾl hśṭn*). The response of the defensive but equal protagonist is **ויען השטן את יהוה** (*wyʿn hśṭn ʾt yhwh*). This is a "thrust" and "parry" interchange.

Scholars have generally agreed with the traditional depiction of **השטן** (*haśśaṭan*) as "the prosecutor" or "adversary." There is not a single shred of evidence anywhere in the *BH* to suggest this picture. The depiction of **השטן** (*haśśaṭan*) in Zech.3[1-2] is not explicit at all. It is just as in Gen.3[4], where **הנחש** (*hnḥš*), the serpent, is depicted as evil incarnate without any support from the text. **הנחש** (*hnḥš*) simply told the woman (**האשה** *haʾišhah*), **לא מות תמתון** *(lʾ mwt tmtwn)*—"you shall surely not die" in response to the dictum of **יהוה אלהים** (YHWH *ʾlhym*) in Gen.2[17] **מות תמות** (*mwt tmt*) "you shall surely die" (on the day that you eat of the fruit of the tree of the knowledge of good and evil). Both **הנחש** (*hnḥš*) and **השטן** (*haśśaṭan*) are the foils to the "dark side" of **יהוה** (YHWH). The only variation in theme is that **הנחש** (*hnḥš*) receives "punishment" for what amounts to telling the truth, while **השטן** (*haśśaṭan*) is only "rebuked.". Of course, our author wishes to use this contrast to make a point. **יהוה** (YHWH) has "grown up" in the time between the "Creation" and Job—"reason" or "wisdom" has developed in his consciousness. No longer is the world unquestioningly subservient to its master's capriciousness. No longer

[109] Weiss (1983, 42)

are "good" and "bad" and "right" and "wrong" clearly delineated in black and white. "Good" can be "bad" and "bad" can be "good"; the whole universe is turned topsy-turvy. This notion will become abundantly clear as Chapter One resolves itself.

It is with the aforementioned in mind that we go on with the text:

השמת לבך על עבדי איוב
hśmt lbk ʿl ʿbdy ʾywb
Have you considered my servant Job?

The construction שום לב על (*śwm lb ʿl*) occurs only in Haggai 1[5,7]:

שימו לבבכם על דרכיכם
śymw lbbkm ʿl drkykm
Consider your ways.

Once again the author has chosen his words carefully. The context of Haggai 1[5,7] is: Thus says the LORD of Hosts, "Consider your (evil) ways." Here also, יהוה (YHWH) is asking השטן (*haśśaṭan*)—that is to say, himself—"have you (I) considered Job with evil intent.? This is a semi-rhetorical question; יהוה (YHWH) would have to answer in the affirmative while we would have to infer from the response of his *alter ego* השטן (*haśśaṭan*) that he clearly has not considered Job in an evil light. However, השטן (*haśśaṭan*)'s response has another dimension for it is set in the form of a question. Before we can explore this thought further we must deal with the rest of יהוה (YHWH)'s description of Job.

יהוה (YHWH) calls Job:

עבדי...כי אין כמהו בארץ
ʿbdy... ky ʾyn kmhw bʾrṣ
"My servant...like whom there is none upon the earth."

If, as we suspect, the author drew his character source material from Genesis, then he is comparing Job to the patriarch Abraham who is called עבדי (*ʿbdy*) in Gen.26[24].[110] With the phrase כי אין כמהו בארץ (*ky ʾyn kmhw bʾrṣ*), Job is

---

[110] See discussion of 1[1] above.

endowed with an epithet that יהוה (YHWH) bestows only upon himself in Ex.9^{14}:[111]

בעבור תדע כי אין כמני בכל הארץ
b'bwr td' ky 'yn kmny bkl h'rṣ
So that you should know that there is none like me in all the earth.

We should not be surprised at this equation since we suggested a close association of Job and יהוה (YHWH) in 1^1. The difference between 1^1 and 1^8 is our identification of השטן (*haśśaṭan*) as יהוה (YHWH)'s *alter ego*. The author now makes Job himself a part of the psychological makeup of יהוה (YHWH).

Given the aforementioned, let us now reconsider יהוה (YHWH)'s question. It is no longer simply an interrogative concerning the human Job. יהוה (YHWH) is now effectively asking השטן (*haśśaṭan*), "What do you think of me?" The epithets תם וישר ירא אלהים וסר מרע (*tm wyšr yr' 'lhym wsr mr'*) – "an honest and upright man who reveres *'elohîm* and shuns evil" now redound also to יהוה (YHWH) himself. The only degree of separation between יהוה (YHWH) and Job is the word איש (*'yš*), the human component that we touched upon at the beginning of 1^1. Note the distinction between יהוה (YHWH) and אלהים (*'elohîm*); Job is the servant of יהוה (YHWH) and reverent of אלהים (*'elohîm*). This distinction is continued in השטן (*haśśaṭan*)'s response.

Having recast יהוה (YHWH)'s question, we must do the same with השטן (*haśśaṭan*)'s answer:

החנם ירא איוב אלהים
hḥnm yr' 'ywb 'lhym
"Is it *gratis* that Job reveres *'elohîm*?"

The response is in the form of a question—and a specific question at that. השטן (*haśśaṭan*) grants as a *datum* all of Job's attributes with the exception of one—the reverence of *'elohîm*. השטן (*haśśaṭan*) has seen that יהוה (YHWH) is generous to his followers. Not so the case with אלהים (*'elohîm*). He doubts Job's unquestioning, unwavering reverence of אלהים (*'elohîm*), whom we have earlier defined as "institutional justice, right and wrong, and black and white." How can

---

111 Clines (1989, 24) uses the phrase from 1Sam.10^{24} כי אין כמהו בכל העם (*ky 'yn kmhw bkl h'm*) as his parallel. This is precisely the kind of loose reading that steers the reader off course.

he know? אלהים (*ʾelohîm*) does not speak, and therefore cannot have told him? We know that אלהים (*ʾelohîm*) is not a part of the gathering of בני האלהים (*bny hʾlhym*), "the sons of the gods" otherwise he might have known from them, although that is not likely since they are confined to "the ends of the earth." Thus השטן (*haśśaṭan*)'s response is a *crux*—a question to which יהוה (YHWH) must respond.[112]

We have described these two verses (1^{8-9}) as the beginning of יהוה (YHWH)'s internal dialogue. יהוה (YHWH), whom we similarly defined earlier as compassion, love, loneliness, and idealism, thinks the best of Job; however, his *alter ego*, השטן (*haśśaṭan*), has cast a doubt, which exploits יהוה (YHWH)'s "vacillation and ambivalence." Our author understands the subtlety of השטן (*haśśaṭan*); he already knows that יהוה (YHWH) cannot escape his own words. We read in Gen.6^5:

וירא יהוה כי רבה האדם בארץ וכל יצר מחשבת לבו רק רע כל היום
וינחם יהוה כי עשה את האדם בארץ ויתעצב אל לבו
wyrʾ yhwh ky rbh hʾdm bʾrṣ wkl yṣr mḥšbt lbw rq rʿ kl hywm
wynḥm yhwh ky ʿśh ʾt hʾdm wytʿṣb ʾl lbw
And YHWH saw that *haʾadam*'s wickedness on earth was great,
And that the nature of all his thoughts was ever only evil.
And YHWH regretted that he had made *haʾadam* in the world
And he was pained to his heart.

and the opposite in Gen.8^{20} after Noah had offered his post-diluvian sacrifice:

ויאמר יהוה אל לבו לא אסף לקלל עוד את האדמה בעבור האדם
כי יצר לב האדם רע מנעריו ולא אסף עוד להכות את כל חי כאשר עשיתי
wyʾmr yhwh ʾl lbw lʾ ʾsp lqll ʿwd ʾt hʾdmh bʿbwr hʾdm
ky yšr lb hʾdm rʿ mnʿryw wlʾ ʾsp ʿwd lhkwt ʾt kl ḥy kʾšr ʿśyty
And YHWH said to himself,
"I shall no longer continue to curse the earth on account of *haʾadam*,
For the nature of *haʾadam*'s thoughts is evil from youth;
And I will no longer continue to smite all life as I have done."

---

[112] Clines (1989, 25) misses the point of השטן (*haśśaṭan*)'s answer because he does not distinguish between יהוה (YHWH) and אלהים (*ʾelohîm*). Therefore he is forced to describe השטן (*haśśaṭan*) as *advocatus diaboli* – "the Devil's Advocate"- whose task is to raise objections to the canonization of a saint…The Satan in Job speaks more dramatically and rhetorically than a canon lawyer…but his function may be no different.

In order to preserve the integrity of the *dramatis personae*, we must make a change in nomenclature. Whenever **יהוה** (YHWH) is the speaker, we shall henceforth refer to him as YHWH/*haśśaṭan*. Similarly, whenever **השטן** (*haśśaṭan*) is the speaker, we shall henceforth refer to him as *haśśaṭan*/YHWH. **אלהים** (*ʾelohîm*) remains a separate entity.

Our author further confounds an already rattled YHWH/*haśśaṭan* by inserting the word **החנם** (*hḥnm*)—"Is it *gratis*?"—into the mouth of *haśśaṭan*/YHWH. This evokes the exchange between Laban and Jacob about working for nothing as we read in Gen.29[15]:

ויאמר לבן ליעקב הכי אחי אתה ועבדתני חנם הגידה לי מה משכרתך
wyʾmr lbn lyʿqb hky ʾḥy ʾth wʿbdtny ḥnm hgydh ly mh mśkrtk
And Laban said to Jacob,
"Just because you are my brother, should you work for me *gratis*?
Tell me your pay."

Second, and even more to the point, it is Jacob, the patriarch whom the author excludes from the character makeup of Job, who makes the deal with **אלהים** (*ʾelohîm*). Now it is the heretofore unassailable integrity of **אלהים** (*ʾelohîm*) that is being called into question and it is the "rogue patriarch" who is the vehicle in Gen.28[20-22]:

וידר יעקב נדר לאמר אם יהיה אלהים עמדי ושמרני בדרך הזה אשר אנכי הולך
ונתן לי לחם לאכל ובגד ללבש ושבתי בשלום אל בית אבי והיה יהוה לי לאלהים
והאבן הזאת אשר שמתי מצבה יהיה בית אלהים וכל אשר תתן לי עשר אעשרנו לך
wydr yʿqb ndr lʾmr ʾm yhyh ʾlhym ʿmdy wšmrny bdrk hzh ʾšr ʾnky hwlk
wntn ly lḥm lʾkl wbgd llbš wšbty bšlwm ʾl byt ʾby whyh yhwh ly lʾlhym
whʾbn hzʾt ʾšr śmty mṣbh yhyh byt ʾlhym wkl ʾšr ttn ly ʿśr ʾʿśrnw lk.
And Jacob made a vow, saying,
"If *ʾelohîm* will be with me and watch over me while I go on my way
and gives me bread to eat and clothing to wear—
and if I return safely to my father's house; Then shall YHWH be my *ʾelohîm*.
And this stone, which I have set as a *maṣṣebah*,[113] shall be the house of *ʾelohîm*,
And of all that you give me, I will give a tenth to you."

Now we understand why our author decided to exclude Jacob as a piece of Job's patriarchal *persona*. With his amazing egocentric bargain, Jacob has compromised both **אלהים** (*ʾelohîm*) and **יהוה** (YHWH). He (our author) can deny Jacob with respect to Job, but Jacob is indelibly etched in the essences of **אלהים**

---

113 A large rock or stone pillar used in early Israelite cultic rituals.

(*ʾelohîm*) and יהוה (YHWH). With one questioning word, החנם (*hḥnm*) – "Is it *gratis*?"—*haśśaṭan*/YHWH has destroyed any notion of divine absolutes. Job is the only character in this drama who until now is unaware and naïve. He has not made any conscious connection between his "ritually whole" behavior and the good fortune that has befallen him. Job is about to come face to face with reality.

We have examined חנם (*ḥnm*) at the plot level. At the substrate level, it is also a *crux* as we read in Ezek.14[23]:

ונחמו אתכם כי תראו את דרכם ואת עלילותם
וידעתם כי לא חנם עשיתי את כל אשר עשיתי בה נאם אדני יהוה...
wnḥmw ʾtkm ky trʾw ʾt drkm wʾt ʿlylwtm
wydʿtm ky lʾ ḥnm ʿśyty ʾt kl ʾšr ʿśyty bh nʾm ʾdny yhwh
And they shall comfort you, when you see their ways and their deeds;
And you shall know that it was not *gratis*
That I did all that I have done against it, says Adonai YHWH.....

Our author has dissected Chapter 14 for his own purposes. יהוה (YHWH) is speaking through Ezekiel about the four punishments that he will inflict upon Jerusalem, how the annihilation will be complete with the exception of a small group of survivors. There can never be a total annihilation of Israel by יהוה (YHWH) who needs humanity in order to validate his own existence and purpose. Thus the destruction is limited to Jerusalem in 14[21], so that a remnant of Israel will survive. In the case of Job, the tests follow the question of motivation, whereas in Ezekiel, the reverse applies.

He explains that the punishments have not been inflicted חנם (*ḥnm*) *gratis* or "without cause" and that the example set by the surviving remnant of Jerusalem will be the people's consolation. Thus in Ezekiel, יהוה (YHWH) asserts that he does nothing *gratis*. In the case of Job, YHWH/*haśśaṭan* implicitly asserts Job's gratuitous piety, it is *haśśaṭan*/YHWH who similarly questions Job's motivation. Since we know from Gen.1[26] that man was created in the image of God, it should follow that both human and divine attributes be the same.

1:10

הלא את(ה) שכת בעדו ובעד ביתו ובעד כל אשר לו מסביב
מעשה ידיו ברכת ומקנהו פרץ בארץ
hlʾ ʾt(h) śkt bʿdw wbʿd bytw wbʿd kl ʾšr lw msbyb
mʿśh ydyw brkt wmqnhw prṣ bʾrṣ
Have you yourself not set a fence around him, his house, and all that he owns?
You have blessed the work of his hands and his possessions are spread all over the land.

haśśaṭan/YHWH has answered his own question. While a superficial reading yields an elaboration of the "non-*gratis*" motivation of Job, our methodology demands some *BH* antecedent. The expression **שׂוך בעד** (*śwk bʿd*)[114] occurs only once elsewhere in *BH* and that is in the Book of Job itself where the variant form √**סוך** (*swk*) is used. We read in Job 3^{23}:

לגבר אשר דרכו נסתרה ויסך אלוה בעדו
lgbr ʾšr drkw nstrh wysk ʾlwh bʿdw
Why does he give light to) the man whose path is concealed,
whom *ʾlwh* has fenced all around?

This passage is in the midst of Job's visceral roar of deep despair. He is questioning God's motive in providing any help for those for whom hope has dried up. Perhaps *haśśaṭan*/YHWH is taunting YHWH/*haśśaṭan*, knowing that the fence is illusory. For added irony, *haśśaṭan*/YHWH throws in **מסביב** (*msbyb*), evoking the passage in Deut.12^{10}:

והניח לכם מכל איביכם מסביב וישבתם בטח
whnyḥ lkm mkl ʾybykm msbyb wyšbtm bṭḥ
And He will give you rest from your enemies all around and you dwell in security.

haśśaṭan/YHWH knows full well that the notions of "giving rest from enemies all around" **איביכם מסביב** (*ʾybykm msbyb*)" and "dwelling in security" is about to end. The author knows the lexical relationship between **איוב** (*ʾiyyôb*) "the Hater" and **אויב** (*ʾowyêb*) "the Enemy."[115]

מעשה ידיו ברכת (*mʿśh ydyw brkt*) is another unique construction appearing only in Deut.28^{12}:

---

[114] The construction **שׂוך בעד** (*śwk bʿd*) occurs in the Dead Sea Scrolls, see p.8 above.
[115] Then again there is another, perhaps simpler antecedent. We take note in *BH* that the words **את(ה) שכת** (*ʾt*[*h*] *śkt*) contain a Masoretic correction, a *Qere* and *Ketib*. The word **את** (*ʾt*) meaning "you" (2nd person masc. singular) is written without the final letter **ה** (*h*). Without the final letter **ה** (*h*), the word would be read as 2nd person feminine singular. The word **שכת** (*śkt*) is *hapax legomenon* as it stands. It is possible that the scribal error that was recognized for **את** (*ʾt*) extended to the word **שכת** (*śkt*) where the initial letter **ה** (*h*) was also dropped. If the letter **ה** (*h*) were added to **שכת** (*śkt*), we would read **השכת** (*hśkt*) "you have set fence)." This would then be the *hipʿil* of √**שׂוך** (*swk*), which appears also in Job 3^{23} as cited above.

יפתח יהוה לך אוצרו הטוב את השמים
לתת מטר ארצך בעתו ולברך את כל מעשה ידך
ypth yhwh lk ʾt ʾwṣrw hṭwb ʾt hšmym
ltt mṭr ʾrṣk bʿtw wlbrk ʾt kl mʿśh ydk
YHWH will open for you his rich storehouse, the heavens;
to give the rain of your land in its season and to bless all your undertakings.

This would seem to be only use of √ברך (*brk*) meaning "to bless" in the entire Prologue[116] and is YHWH/*haśśaṭan* who does the "blessing." This is once again in keeping with the superficial context of the verse. It is more likely, however, that *haśśaṭan*/YHWH is piling on the irony and that we should keep in mind the curse that he is about to place on Job.

ומקנהו פרץ בארץ (*wmqnhw prṣ bʾrṣ*) "and his possessions are spread all over the land" is *hapax legomenon* as a phrase; that is to say that there is no *BH* antecedent. We cannot accept that this is the insertion of a later author, we must delve further to understand the meaning of this phrase. If we examine each component of the phrase, we discover that the words מקנה (*mqnh*) and בארץ (*bʾrṣ*) are already known to us from earlier verses. It is the word פרץ (*prṣ*) that requires elucidation and we find our proof text in Gen.30[28-30], where Laban and Jacob are still at loggerheads over compensation:

ויאמר נקבה שכרך עלי ואתנה
ויאמר אליו אתה ידעת את אשר עבדתיך ואת אשר היה מקנך אתי
כי מעט אשר היה לך לפני ויפרץ לרב ויברך יהוה אתך לרגלי ועתה מה אעשה אנכי לביתי
wyʾmr nqbh śkrk ʿly wʾtnh
wyʾmr ʾlyw ʾth ydʿt ʾt ʾšr ʿbdtyk wʾt ʾšr hyh mqnk ʾty
ky mʿṭ ʾšr hyh lk lpny wyprṣ lrb wybrk yhwh ʾtk lrgly wʿth mh ʾʿśh ʾnky lbyty
And he (Laban) said, "Tell me what I owe you and I will pay it."[117]
And (Jacob) said, "You know how I have served you
and how your possessions have fared with me."
For the few that you had before me have burst forth as many,
and YHWH blessed me at my every step;[118]
And now, what am I to do with my household?"

---

[116] It appears once again in the 3rd Epilogue (42[12]) with יהוה (YHWH) doing the "blessing."
[117] Or "establish by piercing." This is probably an idiom for "name your price"; however, since this is the only occurrence, we cannot establish its meaning with certainty.
[118] לרגלי (*lrgly*) another idiomatic expression found only here.

Our author, through *haśśaṭan*/YHWH, compares the enrichment of Job by YHWH/*haśśaṭan* with the enrichment of Laban by Jacob. We already know from Gen.30[31-34] that Jacob proceeds to cheat Laban out of his wealth. We have already established that our author is no admirer of Jacob and excludes him from the patriarchal profile of Job. Thus when *haśśaṭan*/YHWH says **ומקנהו פרץ בארץ** (*wmqnhw prṣ b'rṣ*), he skeptically implies that Job's wealth has been ill-gotten, even though YHWH/*haśśaṭan* has been instrumental in bestowing it upon him.

At this point, YHWH/*haśśaṭan* is no longer sure of anything. His *alter ego* has pierced the illusion of his paternal grace. *haśśaṭan*/YHWH is not through yet; he is not satisfied to allow YHWH/*haśśaṭan* to stew in his frustration. He will challenge him to prove the validity of what he has said about Job.

1:11

ואולם שלח נא ידך וגע בכל אשר לו אם לא על פניך יברכך
w'wlm šlḥ n' ydk wg' bkl 'šr lw 'm l' 'l pnyk ybrkk
Indeed, if you stretch out your hand and touch all that he has,
he will surely curse you in your presence.

haśśaṭan/YHWH makes the no-win proposition to YHWH/*haśśaṭan*. In order to refute his *alter ego*, YHWH/*haśśaṭan* must ruin all that he believes he has accomplished with Job and the entire world; failure to meet the challenge will expose the weakness and lack of confidence that dogs YHWH/*haśśaṭan*.

ואולם (*w'wlm*) is a common term meaning "indeed." In this instance, our author wishes to tell us that this "indeed" carries the full force of an oath. The expressions he recalls are those of 1Sam.20[3], where David makes an oath invoking the name of **יהוה** (YHWH):

ואולם חי יהוה וחי נפשך
w'wlm ḥy yhwh wḥy npšk
I swear by the life of YHWH and by your life

and again in 1Sam.25[34], David swears to Abigail:

ואולם חי יהוה אלהי ישראל
w'wlm ḥy yhwh 'lhy yśr'l
I swear by the life of YHWH the god of Israel

and, most powerful of all, in Num.14[21] where **יהוה** (YHWH) takes the oath "as I live":

ואולם חי אני
w'wlm ḥy'ny
"I swear by my life"[119]

We have established that this is no mere wager—*haśśaṭan*/YHWH, perhaps in a show of *hubris*, has staked his own "life" on his words. Now we can examine his words more closely.

שלח נא ידך (*šlḥ n' ydk*) "stretch forth your hand" takes us back to Gen.22[10,12]. The occasion is the *ʿaqedah*, the sacrificial binding of Isaac by his father Abraham. In 22[10], Abraham "stretched forth his hand" to reach for the knife. In 22[12], it is the messenger of **יהוה** (YHWH) who calls out to Abraham "do not stretch forth your hand." The characters are Abraham, Isaac, and **יהוה** (YHWH), whom we have identified as central figures of the Prologue. Abraham and Isaac are the primary constituents of Job's character, while **יהוה** (YHWH) is both YHWH/*haśśaṭan* and *haśśaṭan*/YHWH. The oath gains weight the further we read.

ונגע בכל אשר לו (*wgʿ bkl 'šr lw*) "and touch all that he has" takes us back to the Gen.3[3] and the Garden of Eden, where the woman (**האשה** – *ha'išhah*) tells the serpent (**הנחש** – *hnhš*) what **אלהים** (*'elohîm*) has commanded:

לא תאכלו ממנו ולא תגעו בו פן תמתון
l' t'klw mmnw wl' tgʿw bw pn tmtwn
"Do neither eat of it nor touch it, lest you surely die."

This is the re-statement of Gen.2[17], in which **יהוה** (YHWH) had instructed the man (**האדם** – *ha'adam*) that "on the day that you eat of it (the tree of the knowledge of good and evil), you shall surely die." The woman (**האשה** – *ha'išhah*) has taken heed, "not eating" includes "not touching," and the consequence of either is death. Now we understand the full force of *haśśaṭan*/YHWH's suggestion; "touching" implies "killing."

אם לא על פניך יברכך (*'m l' ʿl pnyk ybrkk*) "he will surely curse You to your face." The idiom **ואולם...אם לא** (*w'wlm... 'm l'*)[120] constitutes a very strong double negative, a construction found only in 1Kings 20[23], where the context is again a challenge to the very existence of **יהוה** (YHWH). We quote from 1Kings 20[23] and 1Kings 20[28]:

---

[119] These are the only occasions that this construction occurs in *BH*.

[120] Chapter 2[6] reprises this phrase with the exception that the word **אל** (*'l*) is substituted for **על** (*ʿl*).

ועבדי מלך ארם אמרו אליו אלהי הרים אלהיהם על כן חזקו ממנו
ואולם נלחם אתם במישור אם לא נחזק מהם...
...כה אמר יהוה יען אשר אמרו ארם אלהי הרים יהוה ולא אלהי עמקים הוא
ונתתי את כל ההמון הגדול הזה בידך וידעתם כי אני יהוה
wʿbdy mlk ʾrm ʾmrw ʾlyw ʾlhy hrym ʾlhyhm ʿl kn ḥzqw mmnw
wʾwlm nlḥm ʾtm bmyšwr ʾm lʾ nḥzq mhm...
...kh ʾmr yhwh yʿn ʾšr ʾmrw ʾrm ʾlhy hrym yhwh wlʾ ʾlhy ʿmqym hwʾ
wntty ʾt kl hhmwn hgdwl hzh bydk wydʿtm ky ʾny yhwh
And the servants of the King of Aram said to him,
"Their god is the god of the mountains, that is why they are stronger than us;
However, if we go to war with them on the plain,
we [guarantee that we] will surely be stronger than them."...
Thus says YHWH, "Because the Arameans have said
that YHWH is the god of the mountains and not of the valleys;
I will turn that whole great horde over to you,
And you will know that I am YHWH."

יהוה (YHWH) has met the full challenge of the oath and prevailed. What is interesting is his motive, namely, the establishment of his identity. In our text, *haśśaṭan*/YHWH asserts that Job will challenge the very existence of יהוה (YHWH) by cursing him "to his face."

The phrase על פניך יברכך (*ʿl pnyk ybrkk*) "he will curse You in Your presence" evokes the second commandment of the Decalogue (Ex.20^{3}; Deut.5^{7}):

לא יהיה לך אלהים אחרים על פני
lʾ yhyh lk ʾlhym ʾḥrym ʿl pny
"You have no other gods in my presence."

We remember that Job's suspicions of his sons' sins (in 1^{5}) revolved around either covert blasphemy or idol-worship. *haśśaṭan*/YHWH, as the *alter ego*, possesses the same prescience and foresight as YHWH/*haśśaṭan*.

This is *haśśaṭan*/YHWH at the peak of his brutal and cynical realism. YHWH/*haśśaṭan* has seemingly been cornered, confronted with the backlash of his own values and with every avenue of escape apparently blocked. However, the best defense is a good offense and our author provides YHWH/*haśśaṭan* with a strategy worthy only of Jacob. It is not perfect by any means, but it gives him some temporary relief. YHWH/*haśśaṭan* turns the tables and assigns the task to *haśśaṭan*/YHWH as we see in the next verse.

1:12

ויאמר יהוה אל השטן הנה כל אשר לו בידך רק אליו אל תשלח ידך
ויצא השטן מעם פני יהוה

wy'mr yhwh 'l hśṭn hnh kl 'šr lw bydk rq 'lyw 'l tšlḥ ydk
wyṣ' hśṭn m'm pny yhwh

And YHWH said to *haśśaṭan*, "behold all that he has is in your hand,
but do not stretch forth your hand against him.
And *haśśaṭan* departed the presence of YHWH.

Our author demonstrates that YHWH/*haśśaṭan* will use any tactics to assure his survival; after all, Jacob did the very same thing in Gen.32[8]:

ויירא יעקב מאד ויצר לו ויחץ את העם אשר אתו
ואת הצאן ואת הבקר והגמלים לשני מחנות
ויאמר אם יבוא עשו אל המחנה האחת והכהו והיה המחנה הנשאר לפליטה

wyyr' y'qb m'd wyṣr lw wyḥṣ 't h'm 'šr 'tw
w't hṣ'n w't hbqr whgmlym lšny mḥnwt
wy'mr 'm yb' 'św 'l hmḥnh h'ḥt whkhw whyh hmḥnh hnš'r lplyṭh

And Jacob was very afraid and distressed,
And he divided the people who were with him,
Along with the sheep, cattle and camels, into two camps.
And he said, "should Esau come to the first camp and smite it,
then the second shall be an escape."

Jacob will not trust his brother Esau and only shows him half of his family and wealth. Similarly, YHWH/*haśśaṭan* finds an avenue of escape; he challenges *haśśaṭan*/YHWH to do that of which he himself is afraid to do—with the *proviso* that he not touch the physical person of Job. YHWH/*haśśaṭan* does not wish to risk everything in a single action; however, the consequence of his strategy is to concede his prescience and foresight to *haśśaṭan*/YHWH. In this struggle, it becomes clear that *haśśaṭan*/YHWH is indeed the peer of YHWH/*haśśaṭan*.

כל אשר לו בידך (*kl 'šr lw bydk*) "all that he has is in your hand" is a common idiom; however the *nuance* of ביד (*byd*) "in the hand of..." occurs only once in *BH* in Gen.39[6] in the story of Joseph:

ויעזב את כל אשר לו ביד יוסף

wy'zb 't 'šr lw byd ywsp

And he left all that he had in the hand of Joseph...

in which Potiphar gave Joseph complete managerial responsibility for all of his assets. In giving *haśśaṭan*/YHWH complete and total responsibility for investigating the integrity of Job's faith, YHWH/*haśśaṭan* distances himself from the outcome. YHWH/*haśśaṭan* is now beset with ambivalence and self-doubt, a condition that will worsen as he becomes increasingly mired in his own psychosis.

רק אליו אל... (*rq ʾlyw ʾl...*), an expression made up of two common words occurs only in Deut.2[37] where it is applied to the interdiction of making war against the land of the Ammonites.[121] It is best described as a "negative imperative," a strong prohibition.

אל תשלח ידך (*ʾl tšlḥ ydk*) – We have dealt with this expression in the preceding verse.

ויצא השטן מעם פני יהוה (*wyṣʾ hśṭn mʿm pny yhwh*) "And *haśśaṭan* departed the presence of YHWH." The author would appear to be intent on confirming that this "conversation" is "face to face" and not conducted through an intermediary. The only occurrence of this idiom is in Gen.44[29]:

ולקחתם גם את זה מעם פני וקרהו אסון
wlqḥtm gm ʾt zh mʿm pny wqrhw ʾswn
And (now) you are taking this one from before me also,
and danger shall befall him.[122]

where Jacob bemoans Judah's request to take Benjamin to see Joseph in Egypt. The phrase **מעם פני** (*mʿm pny*) clearly indicates physical presence. One can almost imagine YHWH/*haśśaṭan* bemoaning the departure of *haśśaṭan*/YHWH with woeful foreboding.

Since we maintain that the two parties involved in this exchange are in fact a single entity, we have been made witness to the psychological processes of the Divine. The "give and take" exchange is disturbingly human-like; Job alone, in his pious ignorance, cannot entertain this possibility until he is left with no other choice.

1:13

ויהי היום ובניו ובנתיו אכלים ושתים יין בבית אחיהם הבכור
wyhy hywm wbnyw wbntyw ʾklym wštym yyn bbyt ʾḥyhm hbkwr
And so it was on the (appointed) day
that his sons and daughters were eating and drinking wine
at the house of their first-born brother.

---

121 **רק אל ארץ בני עמון לא קרבת** (*rq ʾl ʾrṣ bny ʿmwn lʾ qrbt*)—"You shall not make war against the land of the Ammonites.

122 Chapter 2[7] reprises this phrase with the exception that the word **את** (*ʾt*) is substituted for **עם** (*ʿm*).

ויהי היום (*wyhy hywm*) is “the appointed day,” as we have demonstrated in 1^{6}.

אכלים ושתים יין (*ʾklym wštym yyn*) deviates slightly from 1^{4} in that it specifies what they were drinking, namely, wine. Again this is not prolixity on the part of the author. He wishes to tell us something. He is directing our attention to the relevant passage in Isa.22^{13}:

והנה ששון ושמחה הרג בקר ושחט צאן
אכל בשר ושתות יין אכול ושתו כי מחר נמות
whnh śśwn wśḥh hrg bqr wšḥṭ ṣʾn
ʾkl bśr wštwt yyn ʾkwl wštw ky mḥr nmwt
And behold there was rejoicing and merriment,
Killing of cattle and slaughtering of sheep,
Eating of meat and drinking of wine:
“Eat and drink, for tomorrow we die.”

He wants us to understand that Job’s sons and daughters were feasting and drinking with blissful abandon, unaware that their fate was about to be sealed. It is precisely this kind of activity that motivated Job to make pre-emptive atonement for them.

We are once again supplied with an important piece of information in the phrase בבית אחיהם הבכור (*bbyt ʾḥyhm hbkwr*) “at the house of their first-born brother.” The status of the first-born in *BH* is rife with a variety of misfortunes as is reflected in the Genesis stories of Cain,[123] Isaac,[124] Esau and Jacob,[125] Manasseh and Ephraim.[126] Then there are others such as the death of the first-born in Egypt,[127] the dedication of the first-born to יהוה (YHWH) by sacrifice,[128] the levirate law,[129] the fearful first-born,[130] Amnon, son of David,[131] the first born of the king of Moab,[132] and Micah’s sacrificial first-born.[133] Now עוץ (*ʿwṣ*),

[123] Gen. 4.
[124] Gen. 22.
[125] Gen. 25.
[126] Gen. 48.
[127] Ex. 11 and 12.
[128] Ex.13; Num.8^{17}.
[129] Deut.25^{6}.
[130] Jud.8^{20}.
[131] 2Sam.3^{2}.
[132] 2Kings 3^{27}.
[133] Micah 6^{7}.

which we encountered as a place name in 1[1], was also the name of the first-born of Naḥor, brother of Abraham.[134]

Thus, once again, the author sets the scene in a manner that leaves the reader in no doubt as to what is about to take place.

1:14

ומלאך בא אל איוב ויאמר הבקר היו חרשות והאתנות רעות על ידיהם

wml'k b' 'l 'ywb wy'mr hbqr hyw ḥršwt wh'tnwt r'wt 'l ydyhm

And a messenger came to Job and said,

"the oxen were plowing and the she-asses were grazing by their side."

ומלאך בא (*wml'k b'*) occurs only here and in 1Sam.23[27], where the context is that of a messenger coming to Saul to report the invasion of the Philistines:

ומלאך בא אל שאול לאמר מהרה ולכה

wml'k b' 'l š'wl l'mr mhrh wlkh

And a messenger came to Saul saying, "Come quickly."

Thus the phrase **ומלאך בא** (*wml'k b'*) alone conveys a sense of impending bad news and urgency.

There are two oddities about the colon **הבקר היו חרשות והאתנות רעות על ידיהם** (*hbqr hyw ḥršwt wh'tnwt r'wt 'l ydyhm*). First it is only here and in Gen.33[13] that **בקר** (*bqr*) is used as a feminine; second, we have no other instance in *BH* of "grazing she-asses." However, the **בקר** (*bqr*) and the **אתנות** (*'tnwt*) are also paired in 1[3].

1:15

ותפל שבא ותקחם ואת הנערים הכו לפי חרב ואמלטה רק אני לבדי להגיד לך

wtpl šb' wtqḥm w't hn'rym kw lpy ḥrb w'mlṭh rq 'ny lbdy lhgyd lk

And the Saba came down and took them and killed the young men with the sword;

And I alone escaped to tell you.

This verse contains words and constructions that are unusual and best dealt with individually prior to analyzing the whole.

ותפל (*wtpl*) – this is the only use of √**נפל** (*npl*)in the absolute, that is to say neither transitively nor intransitively. *KB*[135] renders it as "to make a raid," which

---

[134] Gen.22[21]. There may be an underlying suggestion that **יהוה** (YHWH), along with his pedigree from **ארץ עוץ** (*'rṣ 'wṣ*) "the Land of Uz," is also a first-born.

[135] *HALOT*, 710; *BDB*, 657.

is likely correct given the context. The identity of **שבא** (*šbʾ*) is a matter of pure speculation. The lexicons[136] can agree only that the context would dictate that Saba were marauders. It is interesting to note that **שבא** (*šbʾ*) also appears in Gen.10[7,28] once as a descendant of Ham (Gen.10[7]), and once along with **עוץ** (*ʿwṣ*) as a descendant of Shem (Gen.10[28]).

ותקחם ואת הנערים הכו לפי חרב (*wtqḥm wʾt hnʿrym kw lpy ḥrb*) is evocative of Gen.34[26,28,29]:

ואת חמור ואת שכם בנו הרגו לפי חרב ויקחו את דינה מבית שכם ויצאו...
את צאנם ואת בקרם ואת חמריהם ואת אשר בעיר ואת אשר בשדה לקחו.
ואת כל חילם ואת כל טפם ואת נשיהם שבו ויבזו ואת כל אשר בבית.
wʾt ḥmwr wʾt škm bnw hrgw lpy ḥrb wyqḥw ʾt dynh mbyt škm...
ʾt ṣʾnm wʾt bqrm wʾt ḥmryhm wʾt ʾšr bʿyr wʾt ʾšr bśdh lqḥw
wʾt kl ḥylm wʾt kl ṭpm wʾt nšyhm šbw[137] *wybzw wʾt klʾšr bbyt*
And they slaughtered Hamor and his son Shechem with the sword,
And they took their sister Dinah from the house of Shechem and they went out…
They took their flocks, herds, and asses and all that was in the city and in the field.
They took captive and plundered all their wealth,
Their children, their wives, and all that was in the house.

This passage captures the flavor of 1[14-19] not only contextually, but also lexically. The major difference in the two accounts is that Hamor dies and Job survives. In addition, our author has left Job's immediate reaction to his misfortune unspoken, and when he finally reacts, it is with actions in contrast with the words of Jacob in Gen.34[30]:

ויאמר יעקב אל שמעון ואל לוי עכרתם אתי להבאישני בישב הארץ בכנעני ובפרזי
ואני מתי מספר ונאספו עלי והכוני ונשמדתי אני וביתי
wyʾmr yʿqb ʾl šmʿwn wʾl lwy ʿkrtm ʾtyl hbʾyšny byšb hʾrṣ bknʿny wbprzy
wʾny mty mspr wnʾspw ʿly whkwny wnšmdty ʾny wbyty
And Jacob said to Simeon and Levi, "You have brought disaster upon me,
bringing me into disrepute[138] with the inhabitants of the land,
the Canaanites and the Perizzites;
I am few in number and they will gather together against me and strike me,
And I and my family will be destroyed."

---

[136] *HALOT*, 1381; *BDB*, 985. **שבא** (*šbʾ*) is treated extensively in *HALOT*.

[137] We have made it a rule not to try to find meaning in the text through emendation. However, since there is no satisfactory explanation for the word **שבא** (*šbʾ*), we make a suggestion that we read **שביה** (*šbyh*)—"captivity," based on the almost parallel reading in this passage. One might also take note that this word reappears in 42[10].

[138] Lit. "to make me stink."

Jacob's response to his sons' crime of murder was not to rebuke them for this horrendous crime or to punish them; rather he was concerned about his own reputation and what might become of him. Once again, the character trait of Jacob is attributed to YHWH/*haśśaṭan*—the crime against Job is of no significance—what matters is how he appears to his *alter ego*.

ואמלטה (*w'mlṭh*) would not normally draw attention since it is a normal *niph'al* conjugation of the √**מלט** (*mlṭ*); however, in a verse of several irregularities, it bears scrutiny. Once again the context is one of carrying bad news. This time it is David who is the recipient of the news that Saul and Jonathan had been killed in battle—David slays the messenger. We read in 2Sam.1[3,5]:

ויאמר לו דוד אי מזה תבוא ויאמר אליו ממחנה ישראל נמלטתי...
ויאמר דוד אל הנער המגיד לו...
wy'mr lw dwd 'y mzh tbw' wy'mr 'lyw mmḥnh yśr'l nmlṭty
wy'mr dwd 'l hn'r hmgyd lw
And David said to him, "Whence have you come?"
And he said to him, "I have escaped from the camp of Israel..."
And David said to the lad who was telling him...

The conjugation of √**מלט** (*mlṭ*) is the same; however, the perfect tense is used rather than the imperfect with *waw* consecutive of our verse. The messenger has escaped and he is **המגיד** (*hmgyd*) "telling" or "informing" and it is this unique combination of √**מלט** (*mlṭ*) and √**נגד** (*ngd*) in tense and person[139] that connects this citation with our verse.

1:16

עוד זה מדבר וזה בא ויאמר אש אלהים נפלה מן השמים
ותבער בצאן ובנערים ותאכלם ואמלטה רק אני לבדי להגיד לך
'wd zh mdbr wzh b' wy'mr 'š 'lhym nplh mn hšmym
wtb'r bṣ'n wbn'rym wt'klm w'mlṭh rq 'ny lbdy lhgyd lk
This (messenger) was still speaking when another came and said,
The fire of *'elohîm* fell from the heavens
and burned the sheep and the youngsters and consumed them;
And I alone escaped to tell you.

This verse is an apparent *mélange* of common phrases and idioms that can be translated comprehensibly at face.

---

139 The combination occurs also in 2Sam. 1[18], where it is David himself who is the messenger; however it is set in the third person.

עוד זה מדבר וזה בא (*ʿwd zh mdbr wzh bʾ*), while unique to Job 1, is well attested in similarly worded narratives.[140]

ותבער ב... (*wtbʿr b...*) occurs in ψ106^{18}, where we read:

ותבער אש בעדתם להבה תלהט רשעים
wtbʿr ʾš bʿdtm lhbh tlhṭ ršʿym
And a fire burned in their assembly; flame set ablaze the wicked.

The Psalmist is referring to the revolt of Dathan and Abiram in Num.16^{1}. It was not fire that put an end to them; rather the earth "opened and swallowed them." It was only afterwards that "a fire emanated from **יהוה** (YHWH) and consumed the remaining two hundred and fifty offerors of incense."[141] Our author wishes to imply that the fire was the result of an act that was at the very least divisive.

ובנערים (*wbnʿrym*) may be referred to in Gen.48^{16}, where Jacob gives his blessing to Joseph's sons, Manasseh and Ephraim. The irony of Gen.48^{16} lies in its context, in which Jacob asks the messenger **המלאך** (*hmlʾk*) to "bless the youngsters" **יברך את הנערים** (*ybrk ʾt hnʿrym*). We have already posited the equivalence of **המלאך** (*hmlʾk*) and **השטן** (*haśśaṭan*) both in name and in function. One might pause to reflect whether the author intended the reader to recognize this dimension in addition to the explanation that follows.

The troublesome phrase is **אש אלהים נפלה מן השמים** (*ʾš ʾlhym nplh mn hšmym*). The only connection of **אש** (*ʾš*) and **אלהים** (*ʾlhym*) occurs in Genesis 22 from which we quote extensively:

Gen.22$^{5\text{-}8}$:

ויאמר אברהם אל נעריו שבו לכם פה אם החמור
ואני והנער נלכה עד כה ונשתחוה ונשובה אליכם.
ויקח אברהם את עצי העלה וישם על יצחק בנו
ויקח בידו את האש ואת המאכלת וילכו שניהם יחדו.
ויאמר יצחק אל אברהם אביו ויאמר אבי ויאמר הנני בני
ויאמר הנה האש והעצים ואיה השה לעלה.
ויאמר אברהם אלהים יראה לו השה לעלה וילכו שניהם יחדו.

---

140 See Gen.29^{9}, 1 Kings 1^{14,22}, 2Kings 6^{33}.

141 Who had participated in the uprising of Koraḥ.

wy'mr 'brhm 'l n'ryw šbw lkm ph 'm hḥmwr
w'ny whn'r nlkh 'd kh wnštḥwh wvnšwbh 'lykm
wyqḥ 'brhm 't'ṣy h'lh wyśm 'l yṣḥq bnw
wyqḥ bydw 't h'š w't hm'klt wylkw šnyhm yḥdw
wy'mr yṣḥq 'l 'brhm 'byw wy'mr'by wy'mr hnny bny
wy'mr hnh h'š wh'ṣym w'yh hśh l'lh
wy'mr 'brhm 'lhym yr'h lw hśh l'lh bny wylkw šnyhm yḥdw
And Abraham said to his youngsters, "Stay here with the ass
While I and the lad go yonder, And we will worship and return to you.
And Abraham took the timbers for the burnt offering and set them on his son Isaac,
And he took the fire and the sacrificial knife and the two of them went off together.
And Isaac said to his father Abraham "My father."
And Abraham answered, "I am here, my son."
And (Isaac) said, "Here are the fire and the timbers,
But where is the lamb for the burnt offering?"
And Abraham said, " *'elohîm* will provide the lamb for the burnt offering."
And the two of them went off together.

And then we read a little further on in Gen.22[10-12]:

וישלח אברהם את ידו ויקח את המאכלת לשחט את בנו
ויקרא אליו מלאך יהוה מן השמים ויאמר אברהם אברהם ויאמר הנני
ויאמר אל תשלח ידך אל הנער ואל תעש לו מאומה
כי עתה ידעתי כי ירא אלהים אתה ולא חשכת את בנך את יחידך ממני
wyšlḥ 'brhm 't ydw wyqḥ 't hm'klt lšḥṭ 't bnw
wyqr' 'lyw ml'k yhwh mn hšmym wy'mr 'brhm 'brhm wy'mr hnny
wy'mr 'l tšlḥ ydk 'l hn'r w'l t'ś lw m'wmh
ky 'th yd'ty ky yr' 'lhym 'th wl' ḥśkt 't bnk 't yḥydk mmny
And Abraham stretched forth his hand and took the sacrificial knife to slaughter his son.
And a messenger of YHWH called to him from the heavens and said,
"Abraham, Abraham," and he said, "Here I am."
And (the messenger) said,
"Do not stretch forth your hand toward the lad nor do him any harm,
For now I know that you revere *'elohîm*,
And you have not withheld your only son from me."

Out of the preceding narrative, we extract the essential parts of the story. Abraham tells his youngsters **נעריו** (*n'ryw*) to stay put while he and Isaac go to worship. Abraham takes the fire **האש** (*h'š*) and the sacrificial knife **המאכלת** (*hm'klt*)[142] and prepares for ritual sacrifice. When Isaac asks about the lamb, Abraham answers that " *'elohîm* will provide it." As Abraham was about to

142 **מאכלת** (*m'klt*) is an anagram of **תאכלם** (*t'klm*).

deliver the death stroke, the "messenger of YHWH" – מלאך יהוה (*haśśaṭan*/YHWH) calls the whole thing off, satisfied that Abraham is ירא אלהים (*yr' 'lhym*)[143] in not withholding ולא חשכת (*wl' ḥśkt*)[144] his only child.

This passage establishes that the fire was from *'elohîm*;[145] the cruel twist in our verse is that YHWH/*haśśaṭan* is nowhere to be found. In giving *haśśaṭan*/YHWH almost completely free hand with Job, YHWH/*haśśaṭan* has by his own *force majeure* taken himself out of the action. He can only look on and observe.

We are faced here with another scathing indictment of YHWH/*haśśaṭan*. In this instance, YHWH/*haśśaṭan* is confronted by his own inadequacy *vis-à-vis* his other peer, namely, *'elohîm*. Our author has performed the *coupe de grâce* and turned the story of Abraham's near-sacrifice of his son Isaac on its head. Instead of being a story about Abraham's unquestioning piety and יהוה (YHWH)'s compassion, it becomes a tale of the harsh justice of אלהים (*'elohîm*) who brooks no mercy.

1:17

עוד זה מדבר וזה בא ויאמר כשדים שמו שלשה ראשים ויפשטו על הגמלים ויקחום
ואת הנערים הכו לפי חרב ואמלטה רק אני לבדי להגיד לך
'wd zh mdbr wzh b' wy'mr kśdym śmw šlšh r'šym wypšṭw 'l hgmlym wyqḥwm
w't hn'rym kw lpy ḥrb w'mlṭh rq 'ny lbdy lhgyd lk
This [messenger] was still speaking when another came and said,
"Chaldeans formed three fronts, swooped down on the camels and took them,
and killed the young men with the sword;
And I alone escaped to tell you.

The formulation of this disaster is the same as that in the previous verse. We have already dealt with the opening and closing portions and are left with:

כשדים שמו שלשה ראשים ויפשטו על הגמלים ויקחום
kśdym śmw šlšh r'šym wypšṭw 'l hgmlym wyqḥwm
Chaldeans set [themselves into] three fronts,
Swooped down on the camels and took them.

There are two keys to the interpretation of this colon; one is the name Abimelech, which we encountered in our treatment of 1^4 in the context of the character portraiture of Abraham and Isaac.

---

143 See 1^1.
144 See 1^{10}.
145 This is the only other occurrence in *BH* of "fire from *'elohîm*."

This Abimelech was one of the sons of Yerubaʿal (who was also known as Gideon)[146] and the relevant passage is Judges Chapter 9. Abimelech was an extraordinarily ambitious and cruel man, who purchased his kingship with funds provided by the people of Shechem. With this money, he hired a band of rogues and returned to his home town and slaughtered his own brothers. It is a story filled with conspiracy, deception, intrigue, murder, and violence. Abimelech turns on the people of Shechem who have supported him and goes on a rampage of murder and destruction. He meets his own end at the hands of a woman who dropped a millstone on his head from the tower of Shechem, which he was trying to burn down along with all the people who were holed up in it.[147]

Abimelech was not killed instantly and he begged for death exactly as did Saul.[148] The relevant passage is Jud.9[43,44]:

ויקח את העם ויחצם לשלשה ראשים ויארב בשדה
וירא והנה העם יצא מן העיר ויקם עליהם ויכם
ואבימלך והראשים אשר עמו פשטו ויעמדו פתח שער העיר
ושני הראשים פשטו על כל אשר בשדה ויכום.

wyqḥ ʾt hʿm wyḥṣm lšlšh rʾšym wyʾrb bśdh
wyrʾ whnh hʿm yṣʾ mn hʿyr wyqm ʿlyhm wykm
wʾbymlk whtʾšym ʾšr ʿmw pšṭw wyʿmdw ptḥ šʿr hʿyr
wšny hrʾšym pšṭw ʿl kl ʾšr bśdh wykwm

And he divided (his) people into three columns and lay in wait in the field,
And when he saw the people (of Shechem) coming out of the city,
He swooped down on them and struck them (dead).
And Abimelech and the columns that were with him
Swooped down and stood at the city gate,
And the two other columns swooped down on all who were in the field
And struck them (dead).

This is the only passage in *BH* that combines a reference to שלשה ראשים (*šlšh rʾšym*), "three columns," and the √פשט (*pšṭ*) – "to swoop down" in the same context.[149]

---

[146] Jud.8[35]

[147] The Gideon story re-appears as a source in the 3rd Epilogue (42[11]).

[148] 2Sam.1[9] ומותתני (*wmwttny*)

[149] The term שלשה ראשים (*šlšh rʾšym*) occurs alone in Jud.7[16], where we find Gideon preparing to fight the Midianites under the "guidance" of יהוה YHWH. A case could be made that this is the underlying source since it reflects an action that has been instigated by יהוה YHWH; however, this is a far less likely fit.

The combination of √שום (*śwm*) – "to set, put" and שלשה ראשים (*šlšh r'šym*) occurs in 1Sam.11[11]. As we have just noted, the demises of Abimelech and Saul are similarly described. The other thing that they share in common is the three-column formation. 1Samuel 11 recounts the surrender of the people of Jabesh-Gilead to Naḥash, the king of Ammon. The price of surrender was the blinding of the right eye of all the inhabitants of Jabesh-Gilead (as a symbol of shame for all Israel). The inhabitants of Jabesh-Gilead asked for a week in which to consider this proposal. The essence of the story is that when Saul heard of their predicament, he forbade the surrender, united the Israelite people into a fighting force and defeated the Ammonites. Saul's battle strategy is recounted as follows:

ויהי ממחרת וישם שאול את העם שלשה ראשים
ויבאו בתוך המחנה באשמרת הבקר ויכו את עמון עד חם היום
ויהי הנשארים ויפצו ולא נשארו בם שנים יחד
wyhy mmḥrt wyśm š'wl 't h'm šlšh r'šym
wyb'w btwk hmḥnh b'šmrt hbqr wykw 't 'mwn 'd ḥm hywm
wyhy hnš'rym wypṣw wl' nš'rw bm šnym yḥd
And so it was on the next day that Saul set the people into three columns
And they entered the camp at the morning watch
And smote the Ammonites until the heat of the day;
The survivors scattered; not a pair was left together.

This passage uniquely combines שלשה ראשים (*šlšh r'šym*) with √שום (*śwm*) – "to set." 1Sam.11[14] concludes the episode with Saul's declaration:

...כי היום עשה יהוה תשועה בישראל
...*ky hywm 'śh yhwh tšw'h byśr'l*
...for today YHWH has saved Israel.

This seemingly simple language of the disaster that befell Job has all the undertones of cruelty, violence, and the involvement of יהוה YHWH. The word תשועה (*tšw'h*) has all the connotations of a "Messianic" salvation that, in the long run, failed to succeed.

As we noted above,[150] עוץ (*'wṣ*) is both a place and personal name.[151] It is interesting to note that one of the brothers of עוץ (*'wṣ*) was כשד (*kśd*),[152] the

[150] See 1[1] above.
[151] We have noted above (1[15]) the difficulties posed by the word שבא (*šb'*).
[152] Gen.22[22].

apparent ancestor of כשדים (*kśdym*) – "Chaldeans, which in *BH* refers to the Babylonians of the time of Nebuchadnezzar and later. This might be a clue to the dating of the Prologue no earlier than the 6th century BCE. The poetic body of the Book of Job almost certainly antedates this period.[153]

The גמלים (*gmlym*) – "camels" remain unexplained other than to account for their having been among Job's possessions in 1^2.

The story of Judges 9 is yet another disaster, painfully analogous to the story in Genesis 38, which has already been mentioned with reference to 1^{15}. Once again, it is *ʾelohîm* who repairs the damage.[154] *haśśaṭan*/YHWH is giving YHWH/*haśśaṭan* an object lesson in dispassionate brutality. Both Job and YHWH/*haśśaṭan* are psychologically traumatized; however, both are apparently lacking in any emotional reaction. The rapid-fire pace of the action might explain Job's immediate numbness that surely conceals a well of anger and sorrow; YHWH/*haśśaṭan* can only watch powerlessly.

Now comes the fourth and final disaster.

1:18-19

עד זה מדבר וזה בא ויאמר בניך ובנותיך אכלים ושתים יין בבית אחיהם הבכור
והנה רוח גדולה באה מעבר המדבר ויגע בארבע פנות הבית ויפל על הנערים וימותו
ואמלטה רק אני לבדי להגיד לך

ʿd zh mdbr wzh bʾ wyʾmr bnyk wbnwtyk ʾklym wštym yyn bbyt ʾḥyhm hbkwr
whnh rwḥ gdwlh bʾh mʿbr hmdbr wygʿ bʾrbʿ pnwt hbyt wypl ʿl hnʿrym wymwtw
wʾmlṭh rq ʾny lbdy lhgyd lk

This (messenger) was still speaking when another came and said,
"Your sons and daughters were eating and drinking wine
At the house of their first-born brother.
And behold, a great wind arose from across the wilderness,
And touched the four corners of the house,
And it (the house) fell upon the youngsters and they died;
And I alone escaped to tell you.

Once again the message is formulaically structured.[155] The portion that concerns us at this point is:

---

[153] Both Clines (1989, 32) and Pope (1974, 14), in an effort to push back the authorship of the Prologue, makes an argument that Chaldeans are known from Assyrian annals as early as the 10th century BC.

[154] Jud.$9^{56,57}$.

[155] With the exception of the opening word עד (*ʿd*), which *BH* vocalizes as *ʿad* (but which could just as well read *ʿôd*, thus preserving the formula intact) and the exact wording of the deaths of the "youngsters.".

והנה רוח גדולה באה מעבר המדבר ויגע בארבע פנות הבית
whnh rwḥ gdwlh b'h m'br hmdbr wyg' b'rb' pnwt hbyt
And behold, a great wind arose from across the wilderness,
touched the four corners of the house

רוח גדולה (*rwḥ gdwlh*) occurs only here and in Jonah 1[4]:

ויהוה הטיל רוח גדולה אל הים
wywh hṭyl *rwḥ gdwlh 'l hym*
And YHWH hurled a great wind toward the sea

Once again, יהוה (YHWH) is the causative agent. Thus *haśśaṭan*/YHWH allows himself once again the privilege of acting *in loco* YHWH/*haśśaṭan*. This is a clumsy rendition of the phrase אל הים (*'l hym*), which should probably be interpreted as "toward the west," i.e. "from the east."

באה מעבר המדבר (*b'h m'br hmdbr*) – The construction באה מעבר (*b'h m'br*) again occurs only here and in Num.32[19], where באה מעבר (*b'h m'br*) occurs with the following prefix ל (*l*).

כי באה נחלתנו אלינו מעבר לירדן קדמה מזרחה
ky b'h nḥltnw 'lynw m'br lyrdn qdmh mzrḥh
For our inheritance has come to us from across the Jordan to the east

ויגע (*wyg'*) poses questions of the identity of the subject of the verb, which cannot be רוח (*rwḥ*) since רוח (*rwḥ*) is a feminine noun.[156] The only other possible subject is *haśśaṭan*/YHWH who had suggested ונגע בו (*wg' bw*) back in his original challenge in 1[11].

בארבע פנות הבית (*b'rb' pnwt hbyt*) is *hapax legomenon* as a phrase and seems to do no more than to inform us that residences of that period and locale were either square or rectangular.

Our author wishes us to know that the four disasters and the survival of Job are not without precedent. We read in Ezekiel 14[13-20] what is likely the source passage for the surface plot of the fate of Job.[157]

The common thread running through the four disasters in the Job passage is the reflection of YHWH/*haśśaṭan*'s apparent indifference and vacillation when faced with human crisis. *haśśaṭan*/YHWH successfully crafts his strikes to cast

---

[156] רוח (*rwḥ*) does occur as a masculine noun, see Num.11[31]. It is unlikely that רוח (*rwḥ*) would be treated both as masculine and feminine in the same verse.

[157] See Appendix 2 for the full passage.

YHWH/*haśśaṭan* in the worst possible light. The passage from Ezekiel is notable not just for the similarity in the number and nature of the disasters described but also for its description of Job's ability to be saved and survive by dint of his צדקה (*ṣdqh*).

Clines has this to say about the literary form of the disasters:

> The naivety of the style is apparent in the simplicity of the narrative and especially in its repetitiveness, the same device of the messenger being used four times, each of the reports ending with the same formula, all but the first of the reports beginning with the same formula, and the first and the last report balancing one another in contrasting a scene of tranquility with a moment of disaster. The "falseness" of the naivety lies in the dramatic impact that is only heightened by the formality of the narrative.
> Conspicuous by their absence from this catalogue of disasters are both God and the Satan.[158]

The entire impact and import of the disasters has passed Clines by.

1:20

ויקם איוב ויקרע את מעלו ויגז את ראשו ויפל ארצה וישתחו

wyqm ʾywb wyqrʿ ʾt mʿlw wygz ʾt rʾšw wypl ʾrṣh wyštḥw

And Job arose and tore his robe, cut off his hair, and fell to the ground prostrate.

To this point, Job has been involved in the drama only as a background character. Our author has painted a clear portrait of him; however his role has been purely passive. He has neither spoken nor performed any action. Without warning, he finds his world shaken to its foundation. He has been stripped of all of his material wealth and his children have perished. Only he and his wife remain. The expected reaction might have been something akin to Jacob's (Gen.37[34]) when he learned of Joseph's "death," namely:

ויקרע יעקב שמלתיו וישם שק במתניו ויתאבל על בנו ימים רבים

wyqrʿ yʿqb śmltyw wyśm sq bmtnyw wytʾbl ʿl bnw ymym rbym

And Jacob tore his garments and put a sackcloth around his loins,
and mourned his son for many days.

The first thing that Jacob did was to tear his clothes and go into instant mourning mode. We note particularly the conjugation of the √אבל in the

[158] Clines (1989, 30)

hithpaʿel, giving it a sense of "feeling sorry for oneself." This would be consistent for the egotistical Jacob whom the author has portrayed.

Job's reaction could not have been more different. He got up, which presumes that he had assumed some other posture while his world was crumbling around him, and tore his מעל (*mʿl*).[159] Our author chose this word to describe Job's attire for a special reason. We read in Ex.28 [31,32] and also 39 [22,23]:

ועשית (ויעש) את מעיל האפד מעשה ארג כליל תכלת
ופי המעיל בתוכו כפי תחרא שפה לפיו סביב לא יקרע
wʿśyt (wyʿś) ʾt mʿyl hʾpd mʿśh ʾrg klyl tklt
wpy hmʿyl btwkw kpy tḥrʾ lʾ yqrʿ
And you shall make (and he made) the robe of the ephod of woven work, of pure blue.
The opening of the robe, in its center,
Shall be (was) like the opening of a suit of armor[160]
That cannot (could not) be torn.

Our author had many idioms from which to choose to express the rending of garments in mourning. His choice of words is deliberate. First, the מעל (*mʿl*) was the robe of the High Priest, second he would understand לא יקרע (*lʾ yqrʿ*), the stand-alone phrase at the end of the verse, as an imperative "it shall not be torn." We have already hinted in 1[5] that Job assumed a priestly role when he offered sacrifices. By tearing his מעל (*mʿl*) Job defies the divine order to keep his robe intact. Thus Job's first reaction to his calamity was an intuitive act of anger and defiance. The idiom is used similarly in 1Sam.15[27] where Saul tears the corner of Samuel's מעיל (*mʿyl*) as a symbolic termination of Saul's kingship (and thus his priesthood). The passage reads as follows:

ויסב שמואל ללכת ויחזק בכנף מעילו ויקרע
ויאמר אליו שמואל קרע יהוה את ממלכות ישראל מעליך היום ונתנה לרעך הטוב ממך
wysb šmwʾl llkt wyḥzq bknp mʿylw wyqrʿ
wyʾmr ʾlyw šmwʾl qrʿ yhwh ʾt mmlkwt yśrʾl mʿlyk hywm wntnh lrʿk hṭwb mmk
And Samuel turned to leave and he [Saul] grasped the corner of his [Samuel's] cloak
And it became torn.
And Samuel said to him [Saul],
YHWH has today torn the kingship of Israel from upon you
And has given it to your fellow man that is better than you.

---

[159] Defective spelling of מעיל (*mʿyl*).

[160] תחרא (*tḥrʾ*) occurs only here and Ex.28[32] and is translated following *Targum Onkelos*. See *HALOT*, 1720 for full discussion.

Samuel's declaration is the stripping of the divinely originated authority assumed by Saul as King and (would-be) High Priest. The author, who has painted a portrait of Job as a man whose life revolved around his ritual interaction with YHWH, uses language that is entirely consistent with his picture.

As an interesting aside, we note that Samuel declares that "YHWH has today torn the kingship of Israel from upon you." The Hebrew text for "from upon you" is מעליך (*mʿlyk*), which is a subtle word play on the key word מעיל (*mʿyl*) – the priestly cloak.

ויגז את ראשו ויפל ארצה וישתחו (*wygz ʾt rʾšw wypl ʾrṣh wyštḥw*) – Job's next acts appear to be clear and deliberate—he cuts off his hair, and falls to the ground and worships. Our author does not let us off so lightly. That would be too simple.

The word ויגז (*wygz*) appears only here and in Num.11[31] where we read:

ורוח נסע מאת יהוה ויגז שלוים מן הים

wrwḥ nsʿ mʾt yhwh wygz šlwym mn hym

And a wind emanated from YHWH and brought over quail from the sea.

The conventional wisdom is that our instance of ויגז (*wygz*) is from √גזז (*gzz*) "to shear" as in fleece and that the occurrence in Num.11[31] is from √גוז (*gwz*) "to pass over." Be that as it may, the common verb for cutting one's hair is √גלח (*glḥ*), which occurs 23 times in *BH*. This is the only instance in *BH* of √גזז (*gzz*) being applied to a human being. Job did not simply cut his hair; he hacked away, shearing it in anger and frustration. His actions were not planned or controlled; they were born of instinct.

The same is true of the phrase **ויפל ארצה וישתחו** (*wypl ʾrṣh wyštḥw*). The conventional rendering of "he fell to the ground and worshipped" is inconsistent with the context. The proof lies in the way the author sets the phrase. Of all the approximately 80 times in *BH* that the term **וישתחו** (*wyštḥw*) lit. "and he prostrated himself" occurs, it always precedes the direction in which the protagonist lies, namely, **עַל אפיו ארצה** (*ʿl ʾpyw ʾrṣh*) lit. "on his face towards the ground." Second, the term **וישתחו** (*wyštḥw*) has a meaning other than to "worship a deity" in almost half of its occurrences—it merely signifies respect or homage. The word order that our author has chosen is unique. Job falls to the ground prostrate.[161] He is certainly not worshipping nor is he giving homage; these would be planned ceremonial ritual actions. Job may be committing a breach of protocol; however, it is more likely, that he is acting spontaneously out of anger and frustration. He has still not spoken or given any verbal indication of the state of his emotions. His actions speak as loudly as the highly charged and controversial words that follow.

Once again Clines loses ground when he says, "Job's actions in response to the news have been few: there has been no gashing of the body, no donning sackcloth, no scattering dust, no lamentation, no weeping, no fasting. Is this simply the economy of the "naïve" narrative style, or does it signal a disproportionate restraint that will be burst open in the passion of the dialogue?"[162]

1:21

ויאמר ערם יצתי מבטן אמי וערם אשוב שמה
יהוה נתן ויהוה לקח יהי שם יהוה מברך
wy'mr ʿrm yṣty mbṭn 'my wʿrm 'šwb šmh
yhwh ntn wyhwh lqḥ yhy šm yhwh mbrk
And he [Job] said, "Naked did I come out of my mother's belly
And naked shall I return there,
YHWH has given and YHWH has taken; Cursed be the name of YHWH."

This verse is traditionally construed as the ultimate archetypal expression of the "stoic" Job,[163] however, as we have seen from the preceding verse, he is anything but stoic. He is in a state of deep frustration. On its face, the statement "Naked did I come out of my mother's belly and naked shall I return there" suggests that Job is ready to die and that the following "YHWH has given and YHWH has taken; blessed be the name of YHWH" is a deathbed confession. However, our author is cleverly following the mood that he has set. Since Job does not feel that he is about to die, he grows skeptical and becomes even angrier. When he says:

[161] A similar construction occurs in 2Sam.9[6] where we find Mephibosheth, Jonathan's son, giving homage to David- ויפל על פניו וישתחו (*wypl ʿl pnyw wyštḥw*) "and he fell on his face prostrate" omitting the word ארצה (*'rṣh*) "to the ground."
[162] Clines (1989, 35).
[163] This verse has indeed become a pillar of Christian theology.

ערם יצתי מבטן אמי וערם אשוב שמה
ʿrm yṣʾty mbṭn ʾmy wʿrm ʾšwb šmh
Naked did I come out of my mother's belly and naked shall I return there[164]

he is reflecting the "wisdom" of Ecclesiastes 5^{14}:

כאשר יצא מבטן אמו ערום ישוב ללכת כשבא
ומאומה לא ישא בעמלו שילך בידו
kʾšr yṣʾ mbṭn ʾmw ʿrwm yšwb llkt kšbʾ
wmʾwmh lʾ yśʾ bʿmlw šylk bydw
As he comes forth from his mother's womb, Naked shall he return (going as he came)
And he cannot carry in his hand any (of the product) of his toil.

If there is any evidence that our author was guided by "wisdom" literature, it is this connection that provides it. Job's intellectual reasoning (that follows his physical reaction) is to question the purpose of human existence. He has performed all of the required ritual and worked hard all of his life only to see it destroyed in a few moments. He realizes that ritual and the rewards of hard work are entirely without connection. He cannot comprehend either the purpose or the reward of his worship of his god, **יהוה** (YHWH). He realizes (as have we) that his entire life is at the pleasure or displeasure, whim and caprice of **יהוה** (YHWH) when he says:

יהוה נתן ויהוה לקח יהי שם יהוה מברך
yhwh ntn wyhwh lqḥ yhy šm yhwh mbrk
YHWH has given and YHWH has taken;
Cursed be the name of YHWH."

When we read this last phrase, we must remember that we have stated that it is axiomatic to our author that √**ברך** (*brk*), when articulated by humans, is meant only in its euphemistic sense.[165] We therefore must understand Job's statement as "YHWH has given and YHWH has taken; **cursed** be the name of YHWH."[166]

---

[164] *BH* has a *Qere/Kethib* correction of **יצאתי** (*yṣʾty*)—"I came forth" for **יצתי** (*yṣty*). Job reconnects with this theme in $3^{11,16}$. Compare also Jonah $4^{3,8}$.

[165] See next ψ103^2 in which the phrase occurs in its literal sense. Also, see 1^{5a}.

[166] The question of "blessing" and "cursing" is at the center of the Bilʿam story, which occurs in Num.23^{20}:

הנה ברך לקחתי וברך ולא אשיבנה
hnh brk lqḥty wbrk wlʾ ʾšybnh
Behold, I took a curse (with me); But he (Yahweh) has blessed and I will not answer (it).

The phrase יהי שם יהוה מברך (*yhy šm yhwh mbrk*) has a *BH* antecedent in ψ103^2:

יהי שם יהוה מברך מעתה ועד עולם
yhy šm yhwh mbrk mʿth wʿd ʿwlm
May the name of YHWH be **blessed** from now to eternity.

The setting is an exhortatory psalm extolling יהוה (YHWH) and the irony could not be more stark. Job's words shock the reader into the reality of his situation. The author's use of a familiar rallying cry with a dark twist has a gut-wrenching effect.

This is his Job's final thought on the matter. He has recognized יהוה (YHWH) for what he is and apparently wants nothing more to do with him. Our author emphasizes this when he remarks in the following verse:

1:22

בכל זאת לא חטא איוב ולא נתן תפלה לאלהים
bkl zʾt lʾ ḥṭʾ ʾywb wlʾ ntn tplh lʾlhym
In all of his, Job did not sin,
Nor was he offensive to *ʾelohîm*.

The word תפלה (*tplh*), which is vocalized *tip̱lâh* in *BH*, occurs only twice elsewhere in *BH* and that is in Job 24^{12} and Jer.23^{13}. The former citation is consistent with this occurrence, while the citation from Jer.23^{13} would seem to require a different interpretation.[167] Whatever the case, the word as vocalized is of unknown origin and its meaning is taken purely from the context.

Of course there is always the possibility that תפלה (*tplh*) may bear the alternate vocalization *tᵉp̱illah*, meaning "prayer." We have already asserted that אלהים (*ʾelohîm*) (the institution of justice) does not respond to prayer and that Job does not recognize אלהים (*ʾelohîm*) as an alternative to יהוה (YHWH). This might then help explain the use of the term יתפלל עליכם (*ytpll ʿlykm*) – "[Job] will pray for you" in 42^8.

The *NRSV* rendition of this verse is, "See, I received a command to bless; he has blessed, and I cannot revoke it." Nowhere in the entire Bilʿam story is there any suggestion that Bilʿam is in competition with יהוה (YHWH). Our rendition conforms with our rule regarding √ברך (*brk*), which is stated above. We will treat the subject of √ברך (*brk*) more fully in when we deal with the story of Bilʿam.

[167] It is probably not coincidental that the citation from Jer.23^{13} is in such close proximity to Jer.23^5 – the reference to the "royal" Messiah צמח צדיק (*ṣmh ṣdyq*).

Job has subtly cursed יהוה (YHWH) although he does not know whether יהוה (YHWH) has understood the "blessing" as a "curse." However, he has neither offended nor sinned against אלהים (*ʾelohîm*) (the institution of justice), and we recall 1[1,5] in which reverence for אלהים (*ʾelohîm*) was Job's prime concern.

Clines has this to say concerning the *mise en scène*:[168]

> The purely conventional acts of mourning have been performed, and narrated, first because the real issue of whether Job will curse God, must for the sake of dramatic tension be postponed as long as possible. In the event, the Satan is proved both right and wrong…Job indeed "blesses" God; verbally the Satan has been proved right, though on the level of intention he has been proved wrong…have we met once more with the "false naivety" of the narrator in this tiny narrative thread that is not tied up in the narrative itself but cries out for further resolution in the book as a whole?

Clines again demonstrates how his thinking leads him to the brink of a breakthrough only to be stifled by his preconception of the story and its meaning. He needs to contort the sequence of events in order to fit his theology. He recognizes the "curse" but must back away from articulating it explicitly. He retreats to the position of the Talmudic sages:

אמר רבא בשפתיו לא חטא בלבו חטא

ʾmr rbʾ bśptyw lʾ ḥṭʾ blbw ḥṭʾ

Rava said: "He did not sin with his lips, he sinned with his heart."[169]

We have demonstrated clearly that the author is not naïve, he is abundantly sophisticated as he sews each patch of the quilt.

---

[168] Clines (1989, 36)

[169] T. Bavli *B. Bathra* 16a; also *Midrash Rabbah, Bereshith* 19:12.

The Prologue
Part 2

Chapter Two

The opening verses of Chapter Two closely resemble those of the previous chapter. For this reason, many scholars have regarded this chapter as being either of different authorship or, perhaps, an alternate scenario of Chapter One.[1] It is our position that the two chapters are in fact form a single unit and will so demonstrate. We shall see deliberate deviations from the text of Chapter One in the form of small prepositional changes.

2:1

ויהי היום ויבאו בני האלהים להתיצב על יהוה
ויבא גם השטן בתוכם להתיצב על יהוה
wyhy hywm wyb'w bny h'lhym lhtyṣb ʿl yhwh
wyb' gm hśṭn btwkm lhtyṣb ʿl yhwh
And so it was on the (appointed) day
That the "sons of the gods" came to stand before YHWH,
And *haśśaṭan*came also amongst them to stand before YHWH.

In 1^{6}, it was clear that **השטן** (*haśśaṭan*), while present, was not part of the *cadre* of **בני האלהים** (*bny h'lhym*). In this instance, his purpose for being there is stated, thereby implying that he is included in the activities of **בני האלהים** (*bny h'lhym*). This is quite consistent since we have already established that **השטן** (*haśśaṭan*) is the "mole" in the camp of **בני האלהים** (*bny h'lhym*).[2]

2:2

ויאמר יהוה אל השטן אי מזה תבא
ויען השטן את יהוה ויאמר משט בארץ ומתהלך בה
wy'mr yhwh 'l hśṭn 'y mzh tb'
w y'n hśṭn 't yhwh wy'mr mšṭ b'rṣ wmhthlk bh
And YHWH said to *haśśaṭan,* "Whence do you come?"
And *haśśaṭan* answered YHWH, "From wandering around the world and roaming in it."

---

[1] A similar scholarly debate exists concerning the Book of Hosea.
[2] See p.32 above

Once again the text is identical with 1^7, with one very notable exception. In 1^7, יהוה (YHWH) asks השטן (*haśśaṭan*) where he has been using the words מאין תבא (*mʾyn tbʾ*), which we characterized in 1^7 as an aggressive opening. Here, יהוה (YHWH) uses the words אי מזה תבא (*ʾy mzh tbʾ*), which have the same superficial meaning as the phrase used in 1^7 but convey a completely opposite mood. This is a much softer, more polite greeting as was used by David to set at ease the messenger who bore the news of the death of Saul and Jonathan.[3] Here, יהוה (YHWH) is attempting to ingratiate himself with השטן (*haśśaṭan*), who does not take the bait and answers יהוה (YHWH) just as he did the first time.

2:3

ויאמר יהוה אל השטן השמת לבך אל עבדי איוב
כי אין כמהו בארץ איש תם וישר ירא אלהים וסר מרע
ועדנו מחזיק בתמתו ותסיתני לבלעו חנם

wyʾmr yhwh ʾl hśṭn hśmt lbk ʾl ʿbdy ʾywb
ky ʾyn kmhw ʾyš tm wyšr yrʾ ʾlhym wsr mrʿ
wʿdnw mḥzyq btmtw wtsytny lblʿw ḥnm

And YHWH said to *haśśaṭan*, "have you considered my servant Job,
for there is no man like him on earth,
An honest and upright man who reveres *ʾelohîm* and shuns evil?"
Yet he still holds on to his integrity
—and you have incited me to destroy him *gratis*.[4]

This verse is identical to 1^8 with two exceptions, one orthographic[5] and the other in the form of a *cauda* that is pivotal to the entire drama. יהוה (YHWH) is

---

[3] The politeness was an effort to put the messenger at ease; David would murder him as soon as he had extracted the information that he needed. See 2Sam.1^3 and page 29 above. In Gen.15^8, we find the phrase used similarly in the case of Hagar. The messenger of יהוה (YHWH) uses the phrase אי מזה באת ואנה תלכי (*ʾy mzh bʾt wʾnh tlky*)—"where have you come from and where are you going?" He proceeds to tell Hagar to return to Sarah and take her lumps.

[4] The word used here is בתמתו (*btmtw*), a word of uncertain etymology (see *HALOT*, 1745). Most scholars agree that this is a denominative form of √תמם (*tmm*)—"to be innocent, perfect"; however, since these words are absolute in their meaning, they cannot apply here. Job is certainly neither "innocent" nor "perfect." We agree with *NJPS* and *NRSV* on the compromise word "integrity."

[5] The use of the word אל (*ʾl*) for על (*ʿl*) does not change the meaning or intent of the text. The substitutions both here and in 2^5 are perhaps intended to inform the reader that these are two separate encounters and not a simple rerun.

once again transformed into YHWH/*haśśaṭan* and flies into a rage with *haśśaṭan*/YHWH. We must understand the *cauda* as follows:

["I YHWH/*haśśaṭan* sent you *haśśaṭan*/YHWH out to do the dirty work
that I did not have the intestinal fortitude to undertake].
Job is still an honest man [I was right and he did not explicitly curse me, **יהוה** (YHWH),
Even though I, **יהוה** (YHWH), can see through the euphemism
and Job does not know anything about my personal problems]
(now the psychotic episode)
And you, *haśśaṭan*/YHWH, incited me, YHWH/*haśśaṭan*,
[with your challenges to my statements about Job,
which I, YHWH/*haśśaṭan*, had to meet
because I, YHWH/*haśśaṭan*, was not quite as certain as I was at first.
But I was right all along
And now look what you, *haśśaṭan*/YHWH, have made me, YHWH/*haśśaṭan*, do;]
I, YHWH/*haśśaṭan*, have senselessly destroyed the life [of one of my devotees.
AND IT IS ALL YOUR (*haśśaṭan*/YHWH's) FAULT!][6]

While YHWH/*haśśaṭan* has seemingly won the day; he will pay dearly. Any sense of order or control is gone. YHWH/*haśśaṭan* has experienced something akin to a human "nervous breakdown."

To make things worse, his *doppelgänger*, *haśśaṭan*/YHWH cries foul because YHWH/*haśśaṭan* placed a restriction on him in 1[12] by limiting the scope of *haśśaṭan*/YHWH's attacks to Job's family and possessions. *haśśaṭan*/YHWH now goads YHWH/*haśśaṭan* into going all the way.

2:4-5

ויען השטן את יהוה ויאמר
עור בעד עור וכל אשר לאיש יתן בעד נפשו
שלח נא ידך וגע אל עצמו ואל בשרו אם לא אל פניך יברכך
wy'n hśṭn 't yhwh wy'mr
'wr b'd 'wr wkl 'šr l'yš ytn b'd npšw
šlḥ n' ydk wg' 'l 'ṣmw w'l bśrw 'm l' 'l pnyk ybrkk
And *haśśaṭan* answered YHWH and said:
"Skin for skin—a man will give all that he has for his life."[7]
Indeed, if you stretch out your hand and touch his bones and his flesh,
he will surely curse you in your presence.

---

[6] The words inside the square brackets are intended but unspoken.
[7] Apparently an adage of unknown origin that occurs only here in *BH*.

YHWH/*haśśaṭan* cannot deny *haśśaṭan*/YHWH's suggestion. His omniscience and foresight have failed him. Now he yields to his vengeful need to vanquish *haśśaṭan*/YHWH. Uncertainty grips him again and he grants *haśśaṭan*/YHWH his final concession.

2:6

ויאמר יהוה אל השטן הנו בידך אך את נפשו שמר

wy'mr yhwh 'l hśṭn hnw bydk 'k't npšw šmr

And YHWH said to *haśśaṭan*, "behold he is in your hand, just preserve his life.

It is everything that *haśśaṭan*/YHWH needs. Even though **אך את נפשו שמר** (*'k't npšw šmr*) – "just preserve his life" is a constraint, it satisfies the totality of **יהוה** (YHWH). *haśśaṭan*/YHWH does not want to kill Job because he needs Job to be alive to make the explicit curse. YHWH/*haśśaṭan* needs Job to be kept alive for two reasons. First, Job's death at the hand of *haśśaṭan*/YHWH would be the ultimate defeat. It would validate *haśśaṭan*/YHWH's contention that the service to YHWH/*haśśaṭan* is not *gratis*; its price is in fact the heaviest that a person can pay. Second, YHWH/*haśśaṭan* needs Job to be kept alive so that he can fulfill the requirement of Deut.4[9]:

השמר לך ושמר נפשך מאד פן תשכח הדברים אשר ראו עינך
ופן יסורו מלבבך כל ימי חייך והודעתם לבניך ולבני בניך

hšmr lk wšmr npšk m'd pn tškḥ 't hdbrym 'šr r'w ʿynyk
wpn yswrw mlbbk kl ymy ḥyyk whwdʿtm lbnyk wlbny bnyk

Beware and guard your life, lest you forget the things that your eyes have seen
And lest they stray from your heart all the days of your life;
And you shall teach them to your children and to your children's children.

Job must be kept alive so that each party can meet the other's challenge. Thus the constraint **אך את נפשו שמר** (*'k't npšw šmr*) is more a plea than an order. YHWH/*haśśaṭan* realizes that the price of perfect service will result in his own irrelevance. He selfishly needs humanity with all of its flaws to survive in order to ensure his own survival. His struggle with *haśśaṭan*/YHWH defines his own flaws.

2:7-8

ויצא השטן מאת פני יהוה ויך את איוב בשחין רע מכף רגלו עד קדקדו
ויקח לו חרש להתגרד בו והוא ישב בתוך האפר

wyṣ᾽ hśṭn m᾽t pny yhwh wyk ᾽t ᾽ywb bšḥyn r῾ mkp rglw ῾d qdqdw
wyqḥ lw ḥrś lhtgrd bw whw᾽ yšb btwk h᾽pr

And *haśśaṭan* departed the presence of YHWH
And struck Job with wicked ulcers from the sole of his foot to the crown of his head.
And he selected a scab to pick, while he sat among the ashes.

Once again, *haśśaṭan*/YHWH strikes Job with a curse that YHWH/*haśśaṭan* himself has prescribed for those who have not heeded his words and commandments. This language appears only here and in Deut.28[27,35].

יכבה יהוה בשחין מצרים ובעפלים ובגרב ובחרס
אשר לא תוכל להרפא
יכבה יהוה בשחין רע על הברכים ועל השקים
אשר לא תוכל להרפא מכף רגלך ועד קדקדך

ykkh yhwh bšḥyn mṣrym wb῾plym wbgrb wbḥrs ᾽šr l᾽ twkl lhrp᾽
ykkh yhwh bšḥyn r῾ ῾l hbrkym w῾l hšqym ᾽šr l᾽ twkl lhrp᾽ mkp rglk w῾d qdqdk

May YHWH strike you with the incurable ulcers of Egypt,
with hemorrhoids,[8] scabs and with sores.
May YHWH strike you with incurable wicked ulcers on your knees and thighs
From the sole of your foot to the crown of your head.

We digress for a moment to consider these passages, which are almost identical with one another and clearly the source for this, the fifth disaster. First, שחין רע (*šḥyn r῾*) is clearly the same as שחין מצרים (*šḥyn mṣrym*)[9] and the former should be rendered as "the ulcers of Ra῾."[10] Second, חרס (*ḥrs*) probably means some type of sore or scab. This word is spelled in *BH* either with the letter ס (*s*) or the letter שׂ (*ś*); therefore its meaning in 2[8] is unlikely to be "pottery" or "potsherd" but rather "sore." Third, the word להתגרד (*lhtgrd*) is *hapax legomenon* in *BH* and the meaning "to scratch" is no more than conjecture. Scholars agree that there is an Arabic cognate √جرد (*garada*) which, in

---

[8] The *BH Qere* and *Keṯib* of ובטחרים (*wbṭḥrym*) "dysentery" is not useful in our context.

[9] שחין מצרים (*šḥyn mṣrym*) is also the sixth plague wrought upon Egypt by YHWH. See Ex.9[9-10].

[10] The head of the Egyptian pantheon. We interpret Ex.10[11] as Pharaoh threatening the Israelites with the power of Ra`. The *BH* text reads רעה (*r῾h*), which is conventionally translated as "evil."

its various conjugations, spans all the *nuances* of "stripping" or "peeling." The meaning of "to scratch" is extracted to fit the apparent context. However, if חרס (*ḥrs*) or חרש (*ḥrś*) means "sore," then להתגרד (*lhtgrd*) takes on a meaning of "picking off" or "peeling." Fourth, this שחין רע (*šḥyn r'*) is described as being "incurable"—אשר לא תוכל להרפא (*'šr l' twkl lhrp'*). This might explain Job's failure to try to treat it as his ultimate surrender; however, there is another known case of שחין (*šḥyn*) in *BH* and that is the case of King Hezekiah[11] who, after being told that he is to die from the ulcers, is cured by the application of a "cake of figs"[12] to the affected areas. Our author would surely have known of the reference to the cure; however, he needs to preserve the "incurability" in order to make his point.

This is a metaphor for bringing a human being as close to the brink of death as possible—perhaps leaving him to ponder his mortality in agony. For Job, however, this fifth disaster comes as an anticlimax. Losing his children and his possessions have already erased his trust in יהוה (YHWH). There would be no more emotional component to his pain. Thus Job dealt with his physical discomfort with an air of silent yet defiant resignation, sitting pathetically amongst the ashes of what had been his oldest son's house, and making no attempt to cure his ailment: All he has left is his wife, whose own reaction bears some reflection.

2:9

ותאמר לו אשתו עדך מחזיק בתמתך
ברך אלהים ומת
wt'mr lw 'štw 'dk mḥzyq btmtk
brk 'lhym wmt
And his wife said to him,
"Do you still hold on to your integrity?
Curse *'elohîm* and die."

This verse is strange for several reasons. It marks the first appearance of Job's wife whose very existence has only been assumed until now, since she is the putative mother of his children. As we shall demonstrate, if she was not beforehand, she is now an atheist and has no theocentrically constructive reaction of her own to the disasters that have befallen her and her husband jointly. She has given up any notion of purpose in life. Instead, she mocks Job

---

[11] Reported in 2Kings 20^7 and mirrored in Isa.38^{21}.

[12] דבלת תאנים (*dblt t'nym*). On "fig cakes" as a remedy (albeit for an unknown equine medical condition), see *COS* 1.106 (Hippiatric Texts from Ugarit).

and his ritual-based piety, perhaps because she sees that "integrity" with respect to a deity is a sham. After all, Job is still alive after having already cursed **יהוה** (YHWH) when he declared in 1^{21}:

יהוה נתן ויהוה לקח יהי שם יהוה מברך
yhwh ntn wyhwh lqḥ yhy šm yhwh mbrk
YHWH has given and YHWH has taken;
Cursed [blessed] be the name of YHWH."

Job's wife has understood the intentional euphemism and sees that Job is still alive. All the ritual, worship, faith, trust, and emotional dependence on an invisible god have been a sham. She is an existentialist; for her, life is a concatenation of accidents. Job is not to blame.[13] She knows that she must get over this with or without her husband. Thus she eggs Job on to treat his great god, namely **אלהים** (*ʾelohîm*), in a similar manner. Perhaps **אלהים** (*ʾelohîm*) has more backbone than **יהוה** (YHWH) and will actually kill him. The bluff that she calls is that Job can curse **אלהים** (*ʾelohîm*) and not die.[14] Our author takes his cue from Jud.13^{23}:

ותאמר לו אשתו
לו חפץ יהוה להמיתנו לא לקח מידנו עלה או מנחה
ולא הראנו את כל אלה
wtʾmr lw ʾštw
lw ḥpṣ yhwh lhmytnw lʾ lqḥ mydnw ʿlh ʾw mnḥh
wlʾ hrʾnw ʾt kl ʾlh
And his wife said to him, "Had YHWH wished to kill us,
He would not have accepted either offerings or sacrifice from us
Nor would he have shown us all these things."

This is the classic story of Manoaḥ and his wife, who were childless. They encountered a "messenger of **יהוה** (YHWH)" who foretold the birth of Samson. The encounter had left Manoaḥ in fear for their lives. Our author takes the innocent response of Manoaḥ's wife and puts it into the sarcastic mouth of Job's wife. Job's response is a mixture of pathos and the anger that seethes just below the surface:

---

[13] *Pace* Clines (1989, 51)

[14] Just as the serpent (**הנחש** *hannaḥaš*) suggested to (**האשה** *haʾišah*) in Gen.3^4 as a foil to **יהוה** (YHWH)'s pronouncement of Gen.2^{17} that eating form the tree would result in certain death.

2:10

ויאמר אליה כדבר אחת הנבלות תדברי
גם את הטוב נקבל מאת האלהים ואת הרע לא נקבל
בכל זאת לא חטא איוב בשפתיו

wyʾmr ʾlyh kdbr ʾḥt hnblwt tdbry
gm ʾt hṭwb nqbl mʾt hʾlhym wʾt hrʿ lʾ nqbl
bkl zʾt lʾ ḥṭʾ ʾywb bśptyw

And he said to her, "You speak like one of the loutish women,"
"Shall we accept only the good from the gods and not accept the evil?"
In all of this, Job did not sin with his lips.

Our author has crafted a brilliant response. When Job refers to his wife as **אחת הנבלות** (*ʾḥt hnblwt*) – "one of the loutish women," he refers us to $\psi 14^{1}$:

אמר נבל בלבבו אין אלהים
ʾmr nbl blbw ʾyn ʾlhym
A loutish man says in his heart, "there is no *ʾelohîm*."

The epithet **נבל** (*nbl*) explicitly describes one who denies **אלהים** (*ʾelohîm*) and Job defines his wife as such. After all, **אלהים** (*ʾelohîm*) is the institution of justice, the immutable principle that lights the path of Job's life.

Job must answer his wife but he cannot respond to her existential philosophy in terms of **אלהים** (*ʾelohîm*). However, he can understand her point of view in terms of **יהוה** (YHWH). Job can now easily understand **יהוה** (YHWH)'s capriciousness, whims and vacillation. He has cursed him and he is still alive.

Thus Job's answer comes in the form of a rhetorical question that apparently incorporates "good and evil" in the context of **אלהים** (*ʾelohîm*). Our author makes certain that we understand that Job himself is referring not to **אלהים** (*ʾelohîm*) but to **האלהים** (*hʾlhym*) "the gods." The careless reader might think that these are the same "gods" as are referenced in 1^{6} and 2^{1}; however, our author utilizes a clever *double entendre*. He is mindful of the famous passage in 1Kings 18^{39}, in which the Israelites declare the following equation:

יהוה הוא האלהים יהוה הוא האלהים
yhwh hwʾ hʾlhym yhwh hwʾ hʾlhym
"YHWH is *haʾelohîm*, YHWH is *haʾelohîm*."

Thus Job effectively reiterates his declaration of 1^{21} making **יהוה** (YHWH) the object of his invective and keeping intact his status as **ירא אלהים** (*yrʾ ʾlhym*) "revering *ʾelohîm*." He never explicitly even mentions **אלהים** (*ʾlhym*) by name.

Instead, by using the word האלהים (*h'lhym*), he lays his fate at the feet of יהוה (YHWH). Job neither "sinned with his lips" nor was he "offensive to *'elohîm*."[15]

There is one peculiarity about the phrase:

גם את הטוב נקבל מאת האלהים ואת הרע לא נקבל
gm 't hṭwb nqbl m't h'lhym w't hr' l' nqbl
"Shall we accept only the good from the gods and not accept the evil?"

Aside from in this passage, √קבל (*qbl*) occurs in the *pi'el* conjugation in *BH* in Prov.19[20], Esther 9[22,27], 1Chron.11 [22],12[18], and 2Chron.29[16,22], where it does not fit any relevant context. We have previously cited this as one of the instances of late usages that occur in the Book of Job.[16] The appearance of √קבל (*qbl*) in the Prologue argues against the chronological separation of the prose Prologue and 3rd Epilogue from the poetic section of the Book of Job.

בכל זאת לא חטא איוב בשפתיו (*bkl z't l' ḥṭ' 'ywb bśptyw*)—In all of this, Job did not sin with his lips. Our author, by his use of √חטא (*ḥṭ'*), demonstrates that he full well comprehends the "lack of intention" that it connotes. We remember that Noah is described in Gen.6[9] as צדיק תמים (*ṣdyq tmym*), the archetypal "absolutely whole" man. The statement of Ecc.7[20]:

כי אדם אין צדיק בארץ אשר יעשה טוב ולא יחטא
ky 'dm 'yn ṣdyq b'rṣ 'šr y'śh ṭwb wl' yḥṭ'
For there is no man who is a *ṣaddîq* in the world, who does good and does not sin.

does not apply to Noah. Even though Noah strays in Gen.9 [19-28], becoming drunk and sexually promiscuous with his son Ham, he is never charged with having "sinned." Similarly, Job's "absolute wholeness" is protected by the statement that חטא (*ḥṭ'*) "was never on his lips." Thus, when we return to the Talmudic citation attributed to Rava:

בשפתיו לא חטא בלבו חטא
bśptyw l' ḥṭ' blbw ḥṭ'
He did not sin with his lips, he sinned with his heart."[17]

---

[15] See above 1[21].

[16] Although Clines (1989, 54-55) maintains that √קבל (*qbl*) "is attested in Canaanite as early as the 14th century BCE."

[17] T. Bavli *B. Bathra* 16a; also *Midrash Rabbah, Bereshith* 19:12.

we see its superficiality. Rava understands intuitively that Job has indeed sinned; however, the *nuance* of √**חטא** (*ḥṭʾ*) and comprehension of **צדיק תמים** (*ṣdyq tmym*) has eluded him.

2:11

וישמעו שלשת רעי איוב את כל הרעה הזאת הבאה עליו
ויבאו איש ממקמו
אליפז התימני ובלדד השוחי וצופר הנעמתי
ויועדו יחדו לבוא לנוד לו ולנחמו

wyšmʿw šlšt rʿy ʾywb ʾt kl hrʿh hbʾh ʿlyw
wybʾw ʾyš mmqmw
ʾlypz htymny wbldd hšwḥy wṣwpr hnʿmty
wywʿdw yḥdw lbwʾ lnwd lw wlnḥmw

And the three friends of Job heard of all the evil that was befalling him
And each came from his place;
ʾEliphaz the Temanite, Bildad the Shuhite, and Zophar the Naʿamathite.
And they met together to come to console him and to comfort him.

Our author wishes to make several points in this verse. First, it is quite evident that Job was not a social being. If he was not a hermit, he certainly did not have a close circle of friends who might care about him.[18] Quite the opposite, it would appear that anyone living in Job's vicinity could do no better than to spread the gossip about his misfortunes. The three "friends" who have come to ostensibly comfort him have heard the news through the grapevine. They are not familiar with the details of his circumstances; as we will see, they are stunned by the sight that they encounter.

Pope[19] and Clines[20] each devote considerable effort in an attempt to make sense of the names of the friends, however with little success. The following is our analysis:

אליפז התימני (*ʾlypz htymny*) – Only the name of ʾEliphaz the Temanite has real relevance to the author's message. Consistent with his character portraits using the Book of Genesis as the source text, the author sets up ʾEliphaz (**אליפז**) as Job's prime antagonist. The name ʾEliphaz (**אליפז**) occurs in Gen.36 *passim* with a full genealogy that is revealing. ʾEliphaz (**אליפז**) is the son of ʿEsau (**עשו**) and his wife ʿAdah (**עדה**).[21] 'Edom (**אדום**) is another name for ʿEsau (**עשו**).

---

[18] With perhaps the exception of ʾEliphaz the Temanite who, while situated geographically closest to Job, hardly qualified as a "friend," as we shall see.
[19] Pope (1974, 23-24).
[20] Clines (1989, 57-58).
[21] See below in the genealogy of **צופר** (Zophar).

Teman (תימן) is the firstborn son of ʿEsau (עשו). We have already identified Job as an inhabitant of ʾEdom (אדום), which is synonymous with "the Land of ʿUz" (עוץ).[22] ʾEliphaz (אליפז) is the father of the Israelites' archenemy ʿAmalek (עמלק) by his concubine Timnaʿ (תמנע). This is indeed a wealth of information. First, there is the clear intimation that there is but a fine line between the "friendly territory of the east" and "the enemy territory of ʾEdom" (אדום). This same territory, also known as Teman (תימן), is at the same time the birthplace of יהוה (YHWH) the deity and ʿEsau (עשו) the enemy. The identification of יהוה (YHWH) with Jacob (יעקב) has already been demonstrated; the dysfunctional relationship of Jacob (יעקב) and ʿEsau (עשו) occupies a significant chunk of Genesis.[23] It is almost as if the author is describing a relationship synonymous with that of יהוה (YHWH) and השטן (*haśśaṭan*). This tension of opposites and apposites is almost palpable. As we shall see presently, the author follows up his premonition of disaster with the use of the term ויועדו יחדו (*wywʿdw yḥdw*) – "and they met together" later in this very verse.

It is possible that the name בלדד השוחי (*bldd hšwḥy*) – Bildad the Shuḥite may derive from the Akkadian *apla-adad*, (son of Hadad) a deity worshiped in the Middle Euphrates region. It occurs in the *Annal of Ninurta-Kudurrī-Uṣur*, who was "governor of the land of Suḫu." The names Temā and Šabaʾ also appear in this monumental inscription.[24] However, the name Shuaḥ (שוח) appears as one of the sons of Abraham by his wife Qeturah (קטורה).[25]

The name Zophar (צופר) is as yet unidentified although he is described as being הנעמתי (*hnʿmty*) – "the Naʿamathite" or ʿone of the family of Naʿamah. The name Naʿamah (נעמה) is mentioned in Gen.4[22] as the daughter of Ṣillah (צלה), one of the two wives of Lemek̲ (למך). It is important to know that the name of Lemek's (למך) other wife was ʿAdah (עדה).

The common thread that runs through these three names is that all or part of each name has a unique *BH* antecedent in the Book of Genesis.

את כל הרעה הזאת הבאה עליו (*ʾt kl hrʿh hbʾh ʿlyw*) "all the evil that was befalling him." On its face, this phrase appears simple enough; however, we are being directed to the one other place in *BH* where this phrase occurs, namely, 1Kings 9[8b-9]:

---

[22] See 1[1].
[23] See Gen 26[14]-27[46].and 32[4]-33[16].
[24] See *COS* 2.115B.
[25] See Gen.25[2].

ואמרו על מה עשה יהוה ככה לארץ הזאת ולבית הזה
ואמרו על אשר עזבו יהוה אלהיהם אשר הוציא את אבתם מארץ מצרים
ויחזקו באלהים אחרים וישתחו להם ויעבדם על כן הביא יהוה עליהם את כל הרעה הזאת
w'mrw ʿl mh ʿśh yhw hkkh l'rṣ hz't wlbyt hzh
w'mtw ʿl 'šr ʿzbw 't yhwh 'lhyhm 'šr hwṣy' 't 'btm m'rṣ mṣrym
wyḥzqw b'lhym 'ḥrym wyšthw lhm wyʿbdm ʿl kn hby' yhwh 'lyhm 't kl hrʿh hz't
And they will say, "Why has YHWH done such things to this land and to this house?"
And they will say (also), "It is because they have forsaken YHWH their god,
Who brought their fathers out of the land of Egypt,
And because they clung to other gods and worshipped and served them."
"That is why YHWH has brought all this evil upon them."

This passage is quite clear that the wrath of יהוה (YHWH) is perceived as a consequence of the worship of gods other than him.[26] Job has been right about his children's blasphemy and the possibility of their idolatry during their annual birthday feasts. So why is he being punished? Since it is explicitly declared in the 3rd commandment of the Decalogue in Exodus 20^{4} that יהוה (YHWH) is:

פקד עון אבת על בנים
pqd ʿwn 'bt ʿl bnym
(YHWH) visits the iniquity of the fathers on the sons…

and not *vice versa*,[27] it cannot be on account of his children's actions. Therefore it must be Job himself who has sinned and his sin is either his mere suspicion of his children's misdoings or it is the subliminal curse that יהוה (YHWH) has so well understood.[28] Therein lies the problem; יהוה (YHWH) has materially modified his position of the 3rd commandment of the Decalogue[29] first in Deut.24^{16}:

לא יומתו אבות על בנים ובנים לא יומתו על אבות
איש בחטאו יומת
l' ywmtw 'bwt ʿl bnym wbnym l' ywmtwʿl 'bwt
'yš bḥṭ'w ywmt

---

[26] The connection to our text is all the tighter for the reference to "this house." This passage may be compared to Deut.29^{23}, for which it may well have been the source.
[27] See Ezek.$18^{19,20}$.
[28] In 1^{21}: יהוה נתן ויהוה לקח יהי שם יהוה מברך (*yhwh ntn wyhwh lqḥ yhy šm yhwh mbrk*) "YHWH has given and YHWH has taken; cursed (blessed) be the name of YHWH." However, we shall discover in the 3rd Epilogue that Job's sin does not involve the "curse."
[29] Ex.20^{4} and Deut.5^{8}.

Fathers shall not be put to death on account of sons,
And sons shall not be put to death on account of fathers.
Each shall be put to death for his own sin.[30]

and then more fully in Ezek.18[20]:

הנפש החטאת היא תמות
בן לא ישא בעון האב ואב לא ישא בעון הבן
צדקת הצדיק עליו תהיה ורשעת רשע עליו תהיה
hnpš hḥṭ't hy' tmwt
bn l' yś' b'wn h'b w'b l' yś' b'wn hbn
ṣdqt hṣdyq 'lyw thyh wrš't hrš' 'lyw thyh
The person that sins shall die; Son shall not bear the iniquity of the father
And father shall not bear the iniquity of the son.

Wholeness shall accrue to the whole, And wickedness shall accrue to the wicked.

Of course, we the readers comprehend this underlying subtext; Job is dealing with his situation viscerally and does not know that all his efforts are in vain.

ויבאו איש ממקמו (*wyb'w 'yš mmqmw*) And each came from his place". Just as Job is unaware that he is a mere pawn in the mind-wrenching turmoil of YHWH/*haśśaṭan* and *haśśaṭan*/YHWH, the same applies to the three friends. Our author wishes us to read the prophecy to Gog from Ezek.38[15-16]:

ובאת ממקמך מירכתי צפון אתה ועמים רבים אתך...על עמי ישראל
wb't mmqwmk 'th w'mym rbym 'tk... 'l 'my yśr'l
"And you will come from you place from the far reaches of the north,
And many nations with you…against my people Israel."

As we have already mentioned, these three "friends" must have heard about Job indirectly; likewise, the prophecy is directed at an unwitting foe. The action of "coming from one's place" does not bode well either for Israel or for Job.

---

[30] See also Num.27[3], in which the daughters of Zelophehad complained to Moses that their father had died and left no male heir, only daughters. As such, the law made no provision for them to inherit their father's property. The phrase that *BH* used to describe the circumstances of his death was—**כי בחטאו מת ובנים לא היו לו** (*ky bhṭ'w mt wbnym l' hyw lw*)—"For he died on account of his own sin and had no sons." Our author's reference to this language is no accident; the story of the daughters of Zelophehad is the final twist in the Book of Job 42[14,15]. This language occurs *verbatim* in 2Kings 14[6], when King Amaziah killed the men who murdered his father but spares their sons, invoking Deut.24[16].

ויועדו יחדו (*wyw'dw yḥdw*) "And they met together" is another innocent expression with a not so innocent subtext. The term ויועדו...יחדו (*wyw'dw...yḥdw*) occurs only here and in the passage in Jos.11[5], in which the enemy kings "met together" to make war on Israel:

ויועדו כל המלכים האלה ויבאו ויחנו יחדו אל מי מרום להלחם עם ישראל
wyw'dw kl hmlkym h'lh wyb'w wyḥnw yḥdw 'l my mrwm lhlḥm 'm yśr'l
And all these kings met and they came and camped together at Mey Merom
To declare war with Israel

The author is letting us know that this visit is destined to fail to achieve its purpose. The three "friends" will neither comfort Job nor provide him with a rational explanation of this *lusus naturae*. They are merely a vehicle for connecting the Prologue with the body proper and the Epilogue. They are not present at the final *dénouement*.

לבוא לנוד לו ולנחמו (*lbw' lnwd lw wlnḥmw*) "to come to console him and to comfort him." The pairing of √נוד (*nwd*) and √נחם (*nḥm*) occurs in similar form in 42[11], Isa.51[19], Nah.3[7], and ψ69[21]. The latter is an unlikely choice for *BH* antecedent because it speaks in the first person. We read from Isaiah 51[19]:

שתים הנה קראתיך מי ינוד לך השד והשבר הרעב והחרב מי אנחמך
štym hnh qr'tyk my ynwd lk hšd whšbr hr'b whḥrb my 'nḥmk
These two things have befallen you; who will grieve with you?
Devastation and destruction, famine and sword; who will comfort you?

and Nahum 3[7]:

והיה כל ראיך ידוד ממך ואמר שדדה נינוה מי ינוד לה מאין אבקש מנחמים לך
whyh kl r'yk ydwd mmk w'mr šddh nynwh my ynwd lh m'yn 'bqš mnḥmym lk
And all who see you will flee from you and say,
"Nineveh is laid waste, no one will console her,
Where shall I look for comforters for you?"

All three occurrences of the pairing of √נוד (*nwd*) and √נחם (*nḥm*) indicate impending failure and are consistent with the sense of impending doom that we have identified in ויועדו...יחדו (*wyw'dw...yḥdw*).

The citation from Isaiah is the likely source since it speaks of four "disasters" which are similar to those described in Chapter 1 by number if not by actual description.

We might consider the quote from Nahum if we substitute the name "Job" for "Nineveh." Here we are again reminded of the futility of comfort and consolation for Job.

To what end is the author laying so much emphasis on this point? It is to tell us that Job does not want comfort and consolation. He is livid, seething with rage and frustration. For perhaps the first time, we understand the true meaning of name **איוב** (*ʾywb*) as "intense hater" as we explained above in 1^{1a}.

Newsom asserts that "although grief and consolation are universal human experiences, the particular forms they take are culturally specific." She then attempts to understand the *nuances* of √**נוד** (*nwd*) and √**נחם** (*nḥm*) in the context of Greco-Roman and Mesopotamian practices. Her admission that "the value of such a comparison is hermeneutical" serves only to highlight the inability of modern scholars to tackle the Book of Job without using exegesis.[31]

2:12

וישאו את עיניהם מרחוק ולא הכירהו וישאו קולם ויבכו
ויקרעו איש מעלו ויזרקו עפר על ראשהם השמימה
wyśʾw ʾt ʿynyhm mrḥwq wlʾ hkyrhw wyśʾw qwlm wybkw
wyqrʿw ʾyš mʿlw wyzrqw ʿpr ʿl rʾšyhm hšmymh
And they lifted their eyes from afar and did not recognize him
And they raised their voices and wept;
And each of them tore his coat
And sprinkled dust on their heads towards the heavens.

This verse is a perfect example of the patchwork quilt that is the material of which this story of Job is crafted.

וישאו את עיניהם מרחוק (*wyśʾw ʾt ʿynyhm mrḥwq*) appears only here and in Gen.22^4, where we read:

וישא אברהם את עיניו וירא את המקום מרחק
wyśʾ ʾbrhm ʾt ʿynyw wyrʾ ʾt hmqwm mrḥq
And Abraham lifted his eyes and saw the place from afar

We are back to the story of the "sacrifice" of Isaac. Abraham has set off on a journey without knowing his destination. Here, the three "friends" know their destination but are unaware of the scene that they are about to behold.

ולא הכירהו (*wlʾ hkyrhw*) is another expression of the unexpected, taken this time from Gen.42^8, where we read:

---

[31] Newsom (2003a, 347-358).

ויכר יוסף את אחיו והם לא הכרהו
wykr ywsp ʾt ʾḥyw whm lʾ hkrhw
And Joseph recognized his brothers and they did not recognize him.

The contrast is stark. Joseph's identity is concealed by the trappings of wealth and power; Job is unrecognizable in his abject physical state.

וישאו קלם ויבכו (*wyśʾw qwlm wybkw*) – This phrase is not uncommon on *BH*[32] but only Jud.21[2] fits our context:

ויבא העם בית אל וישבו שם עד הערב לפני האלהים
וישאו קלם ויבכו בכי גדול
wybʾ hʿm bytʾl wyšbw šm ʿd hʿrb lpny hʾlhym
wyśʾw qwlm wybkw bky gdwl
And the people came to Bethel and sat there before *haʾelohîm*[33] until the evening;
And the people raised their voice and wept greatly.

Here, the verse involves the unhappiness of the Israelites about the act that they are about to commit against the tribe of Benjamin despite the fact that the Benjaminites have committed a heinous crime. The application to our text is to suggest that the three "friends" are weeping at the way in which they are about to treat Job despite the fact that Job has committed the sin of blasphemy.

ויקרעו איש מעלו (*wyqrʿw ʾyš mʿlw*) – This phrase has already been demonstrated above to be an act of defiance.[34] The three "friends" were not present when Job tore his coat, so we can draw two inferences from their action in tearing their own coats. Either they saw what Job had done and acted innocently out of pure sympathy or they understood the real meaning of Job's action and committed their own act of defiance. We will see from the following phrase that their motive was innocent.

ויזרקו עפר על ראשיהם השמימה (*wyzrqw ʿpr ʿl rʾšyhm hšmymh*) is somewhat less obvious as to its *BH* antecedent. It would appear to have its origin in Ex.9[8,9]:

ויאמר יהוה אל משה ואל אהרן
קחו לכם מלא חפניכם פיח כבשן וזרקו משה השמימה לעיני פרעה
והיה לאבק על כל ארץ מצרים
והיה על האדם ועל הבהמה לשחין פרח אבעבעת בכל ארץ מצרים

---

32 See for example 2Sam.13[36].

33 Note the use of the term האלהים (*hʾlhym*) as a synonym for יהוה (YHWH), which occurs in the following verse.

34 See 1[20].

wyʾmr yhwh ʾl mšh wʾl ʾhrn
qḥw lkm mlʾ ḥpnykm pyḥ kbšn wzrqw mšh hšmymh lʿyny prʿh
whyh lʾbq ʿl kl ʾrṣ mṣrym
whyh ʿl hʾdm wʿl hbhmh lšḥyn prḥ ʾbʿbʿt bkl ʾrṣ mṣrym
And YHWH said to Moses and Aaron,
"Take handfuls of furnace soot
And let Moses throw it toward the heavens in the presence of Pharaoh.
And it shall become dust over all the land of Egypt,
And it will become sores sprouting blisters
On the people and cattle of all the land of Egypt."

Clearly then, the "friends" are acting out of sympathy for Job, trying to bring upon themselves the same affliction that has overtaken Job. However, their inability to put themselves in the same physical and emotional state as Job is symbolic of their subsequent failure to understand either Job or יהוה (YHWH).[35] Thus our author has set up the visit to fail and the "friends" are set up for יהוה (YHWH)'s petulant irritation in the Epilogue.[36]

2:13

וישבו אתו לארץ שבעת ימים ושבעת לילות
ואין דבר אליו דבר כי ראו כי גדל הכאב מאד
wyšbw ʾtw lʾrṣ šbʿt ymym wšbʿt lylwt
wʾyn dbr ʾlyw dbr ky rʾw ky gdl hkʾb mʾd
And they sat with him on the ground for seven days and seven nights
And no one said a word to him, for they saw that his pain was very great.

וישבו אתו לארץ (*wyšbw ʾtw lʾrṣ*) is a unique construction. The closest that occurs in *BH* is Gen.34^{15-16}, which takes us back to the story of Jacob's daughter Dinah and her brothers' murderous deception of Shechem the son of Hamor. We pick up the story at the point of the deceit:

אך בזאת נאות לכם אם תהיו כמנו להמל לכם כל זכר
ונתנו את בנתינו לכם ואת בנתיכם נקח לנו וישבנו אתכם והיינו לעם אחד
ʾk bzʾt nʾwt lkm ʾm thyw kmnw lhml lkm kl zkr
wntnw ʾtbntynw lkm wʾt bntykm nqḥ lnw wyšbnw ʾtkm whyynw lʿm ʾḥd

---

[35] In the body of the book, chapters 3^2 through 32^2. The Elihu speeches (32^3 through 40^2) and the dialogue of Job and יהוה (YHWH) in 40^3 through 42^6 will be treated separately.
[36] 42^7ff.

On this (condition) we will agree(?)[37] with you;
That is that you become like us and circumcise all your males.
Then we will give our daughters to you and we will take your daughters (as wives)
And we shall dwell[38] with you and we shall become as one people.

If this is indeed the source, then our phrase displays a hint of disingenuousness. Job's three "friends" appear to be trying to be sympathetic, yet we are not sure that they are convinced that Job has not somehow transgressed. Job is not inviting any conversation, indeed, he himself has uttered but two sentences in this entire episode. He has spoken once to himself (1^{21}) and once to his wife (2^{10}). Thus it is hardly surprising to read:

ואין דבר אליו דבר
w'yn dbr 'lyw dbr
And no one said a word to him

The *BH* antecedent for this phrase is Zech.1^{14}, where we read:

ויען יהוה את המלאך הדבר בי דברים טובים דברים נחמים
wy'n yhwh 't hml'k hdbr by dbrym ṭwbym dbrym nḥmym
And YHWH answered the messenger who was speaking with me
With good words, words of comfort.[39]

The silence of the "friends" lies in stark contrast with the "comfort" of **יהוה** (YHWH). Once again, the author injects a premonition of their ultimate failure to either "comfort" or reassure Job.[40] We have learned from **ויועדו יחדו** (*wyw'dw yḥdw*) in 2^{11} how an apparently innocent expression can have a sinister undertone.

The √**דבר** (*dbr*) is not frequently conjugated in the *Qal*; however, this form of √**דבר** (*dbr*) appears to carry a subtext consistent with Zech.1^{14}. For example we read in $\psi 15^{1\text{-}3}$:

---

[37] There is no agreement on the etymology of **נאות** (*n'wt*). The meaning is taken from the context.
[38] Lit. "sit."
[39] This denominative of √**נחם** (*nḥm*) is used here adjectivally. Neither *BDB*, p.637 nor *HALOT*, p.689 give a satisfactory explanation.
[40] In fact, Job will rebuke them in 16^2 and $21^{2,34}$.

יהוה מי יגור באהלך מי ישכן בהר קדשך
הולך תמים ופעל צדק ודבר אמת בלבבו
לא רגל על לשנו ולא עשה לרעהו רעה והרפה לא נשא על קרובו
yhwh my ygwr bʾhlk wmy yškn bhr qdšk
hwlk tmym wpʿl ṣdq wdbr ʾmt blbbw
lʾ rgl ʿl lšnw wlʾ ʿśh lrʿhw rʿh wḥrph lʾ nśʾ ʿl qrwbw
O YHWH! Who will sojourn in your tent, who will dwell on your holy mountain?
[It is] one who walks in purity, does whole deeds, and speaks the truth in his heart.
[It is] one who does not speak falsehood, nor does evil to his fellow man,
nor brings shame on a relative.

In selecting this *BH* antecedent, our author subtly defines the three visitors, not as "friends," but rather as quite the opposite, as people whose interest is neither in יהוה (YHWH) nor in the well-being of Job.[41] For the uninitiated, our author feels constrained to supply a plausible explanation for their silence:

כי ראו כי גדל הכאב מאד
ky rʾw ky gdl hkʾb mʾd
For they saw that his pain was very great

This is not simply pain; it is the agony resulting from יהוה (YHWH)'s wrath as articulated in Lam.1[12]:

לא אליכם כל עברי דרך הביטו וראו
אם יש מכאוב כמכאבי אשר עולל לי אשר הוגה יהוה ביום חרון אפו
lʾ ʾlykm[42] *kl ʿbry drk hbyṭw wrʾw*
ʾm yš mkʾwb kmkʾby ʾšr ʿwll ly ʾšr hwgh yhwh bywm ḥrwn ʾpw
You who pass by on the way, look around and see
If there is a pain like that which has burdened[43] me
That YHWH made (me) suffer on the day of his anger.

This passage contains some very difficult Hebrew; however, that is parenthetical to the message that it carries. Our author wants us to know that the pain comes from יהוה (YHWH) and that the "friends" realize this and will judge

---

[41] This contrasts also with Num.27[6], where the form occurs again in the story of the "daughters of Zelophehad," who spoke "correctly." See 42[14,15].
[42] Omitted in *LXX*.
[43] There is no agreed upon derivation for עולל (*ʿwll*). We are treating it as the *polel* of √עול "to burden," cf. Arabic عوّل *ʿawwala* (*AED*, 510).

Job using this assumption as a starting point. Job's pain is a direct divine retribution; he must have committed a sin.

THE PROLOGUE
PART 3

Chapter Three

These first two verses of this chapter provide the *segue* from the Prologue to Job's outpouring and at the same time inform the reader of the author's means of connecting the salient chapters of the book.

3:1-2

אחרי כן פתח איוב את פיהו ויקלל את יומו
ויען איוב ויאמר
ʾḥry kn ptḥ ʾywb ʾt pyhw wyqll ʾt ywmw
wyʿn ʾywb wyʾmr
After [all] that, Job opened his mouth and cursed the day of his birth.
And Job answered and said.

The idiom **פתח פי** (*ptḥ py*) meaning "to make speak" occurs on only three other occasions in *BH* and two of them literally mean "to open the mouth" as in enabling speech after a state of muteness.[1] The other occurrence is Num.22[28,30] where **יהוה** (YHWH) puts words into the mouth of Bilʿam's she-ass[2] and she speaks:

ויפתח יהוה את פי האתון ותאמר לבלעם מה עשיתי לך הכיתני זה שלש רגלים...
...הלא אנכי אתנך אשר רכבת עלי מעודך עד היום הזה ההסכן הסכנתי לעשות לך כה
wypt ḥyhwh ʾt py hʾtwn wtʾmr lblʿm mh ʿśyty lk ky hkytny zh šlš rglym...
...hlʾ ʾnky ʾtnk ʾšr rkbt ʿly mʿwdk ʿd hywm hzh hhskn hsknty lʿśwt lk kh
And YHWH opened the mouth of the she-ass and she said to Bilʿam:
"What have I done to you that you have struck me thus thrice?...
Am I not your she-ass whom you have ridden forever until this day?
Have I ever been in the habit of doing such a thing to you?"

There is both pathos and a hint of anger in the question and our author wishes to ascribe this to Job. On one level, the question that Bilʿam's she-ass asks conveys exactly the state of Job's mind and emotions. In addition, he is

---

[1] See Ezek.3[27]; 33[22].
[2] This theme is further explained in our chapter on Jewish Messianism.

informing us that Job now knows that it is his יהוה (YHWH) who is the source of his predicament. On a more profound level, the author is using the Bilʿam story to cast light on the Messianic movements of the day, as we shall show later.

The contrast between the foregoing citation and our text is the control over speech. In our text, Job has control (to the extent possible, given his emotional state). All of the anger, sorrow, and frustration that have been percolating in Job now surface in the explosion of volcanic magnitude that is Chapter $3^{3\text{-}26}$.

Chapter $3^{3\text{-}26}$

Chapter $3^{3\text{-}26}$ is an eloquent outpouring of Job's utter frustration and unfettered rage. It is not sufficient for him to have cursed יהוה (YHWH); he now strikes out at every aspect of his birth, including the accidental day on which it occurred. The assembled sections of $3^{3\text{-}26}$ constitute a work that is capable of standing on its own and further highlight the brilliance of our author. The chapter may be divided into five sections as follows: vs. 3-12,[3], vs.13-16, vs.17-19, vs.20-23, vs.24-26.

3:3-4

יאבד יום אולד בו והלילה אמר הרה גבר
היום ההוא יהי חשך אל ידרשהו אלוה ממעל ואל תופע עליו נהרה
yʾbd ywm ʾwld bw whlyh ʾmr hrh gbr
hywm hhwʾ yhy ḥšk ʾl ydršhw ʾlwh mmʿl wʾl twpʿ ʿlyw nhrh
May the day on which I was born perish;
And the night that said "a man is conceived."
Let that day be darkness,[4] let *ʾeloah* above not seek it out;
May no light shine upon it.

Clines' strong exegetical bent once again clouds his perspective. He writes:

> In this speech we are suddenly plunged out of the epic grandeur and deliberateness of the prologue into the dramatic turmoil of the poetry, from the external description of suffering to Job's inner experience.[5]

First, it is at best awkward to imagine being "plunged out" of a situation. Especially in light of our reading thus far, it is difficult, if not impossible, to discern any "epic grandeur" with respect to the person of Job. The forces well up from within Job to give external expression and not *vice versa*.

---

[3] To which Jer.$20^{14\text{-}18}$ bear great resemblance.
[4] Contrast Gen.1^{3} יהי אור (*yhy ʾwr*)—"let it be light."
[5] Clines (1989, 77)

3:10-11

כי לא סגר דלתי בטני ויסתר עמל מעיני
למה לא מרחם אמות מבטן יצאתי ואגוע
ky lʾ sgr dlty bṭny wystr ʿml mʿyny
lmh lʾ mrḥm ʾmwt mbṭn yṣʾty wʾgwʿ
For he did not close the doors of my womb and hid trouble from my sight.
Why could I not have died at the womb?;
[Why could] I [not have] exited the womb and expired?

As we have remarked above, there is a strong thematic similarity between $3^{3-4,10-11}$ and Jer.$20^{14, 17-18}$:

ארור היום אשר ילדתי בו יום אשר ילדתני אמי אל יהי ברוך
אשר לא מותתני מרחם ותהי לי אמי קברי ורחמה הרת עולם
למה זה מרחם יצאתי לראות עמל ויגון ויכלו בבשת ימי
ʾrwr hywm ʾšr yldty bw ywm ʾšry yldtny ʾmy ʾl yhy brwk
ʾšr lʾ mwttny mrḥm wthy ly ʾmy qbry wrḥmh hrt ʿwlm
lmh zh mrḥm yṣʾty lrʾwt ʿml wygwn wyklw bbšt ymy
Cursed be the day on which I was born!
Let the day on which my mother bore me be not blessed.
Why did he not kill me at the womb?
That my mother might be my grave, her womb eternally pregnant?
Why did I come out of the womb to see trouble and sorrow?
To finish out my days in shame?

While these passages express similar sentiments, there is nothing to indicate a *BH* antecedent relationship as our author's code requires. The only thing that can be said with certainty is that Jeremiah's curse bears the mark of the ritual curses of Deut. 27^{14-26} and 28^{16-19}. Job's sentiment is far more profound—he wills the day of his birth (and therefore all creation) into non-existence. Jeremiah bewails his predicament; Job denies his deity the act of creation.

Verse 10, one of four verses in the chapter that appears to be obviously out of place, appears to be a composite of Jer.20^{17-18}:

כי לא סגר דלתי בטני ויסתר עמל מעיני
ky lʾ sgr dlty bṭny wystr ʿml mʿyny
For he did not close the doors of my [mother's] womb
And [did not] hide trouble from my sight.[6]

---

[6] We should make note that the phrase ויסתר עמל מעיני (*wystr ʿml mʿyny*) occurs only here in *BH*. The phrase is found in the *DSS* $1QH^a$ col.xix l.19 as לא נסתר עמל מעיני (*lʾ nstr ʿml mʿyny*).

Pope, Habel, and Clines, have strikingly different translations:

"Since it closed not the womb's doors, To hide trouble from my eyes."[7]
"Because it did not shut the womb doors And so hide misery from my eyes."[8]
"Because it did not shut the doors of the womb, nor shield my eyes from trouble."[9]

None of these translations are accurate representations of the text. Pope and Clines each summarily dismiss the problem by stating that the subject womb belongs to Job's mother[10] and that the object of the complaint is either "day" or "night" depending on whose exegesis one is following. Habel remarks that:

> The grounds for Job's curses lie in the fact that the night, like some goddess of infertility, did not block the womb to prevent his conception.

How Habel adduces a "goddess of infertility" is at the very least puzzling. The only deity who might be perceived as causing infertility is יהוה (YHWH) himself.[11] However, it remains an inescapable fact that this is a complaint that can be uttered only by a woman and that our author knew exactly what he was doing. The thought that it expresses runs diametrically counter to the preceding thoughts. This is the direct criticism of the Deity misdirected by the author in order to preserve the appearance of theological correctness.

Verses 24-26 reflect the depth of Job's anger and frustration:

כי לפני לחמי אנחתי תבא ויתכו כמים שאגתי
כי פחד פחדתי ויאתיני ואשר יגרתי יבא לי
לא שלותי ולא שקטתי ולא נחתי ויבא רגז
ky lpny lḥmy ʾnḥty tbʾ wytkw kmym šʾgty
ky pḥd pḥdty wyʾtyny wʾšr ygrty ybʾ ly
lʾ šlwty wlʾ šqṭty wlʾ nḥty wybʾ rgz
For my groans come before my food,[12] my roars pour out like water.
For I feared *paḥad* and he came to me, and he whom I have dreaded comes to me.
I have no peace, I have no quiet, and I have no rest; and anger has come.

---

[7] Pope (1989, 26).
[8] Habel (1985, 99).
[9] Clines (1989, 68).
[10] Perhaps referring to Jer.20[18] in which Jeremiah specifically refers to his mother's womb being his grave.
[11] See Gen.18[18], 1Sam.1[5,6].
[12] Lit. "comes before my bread."

Once again we visit the renderings of Pope, Habel, and Clines.

Instead of my food come sighs, Groans are poured me as water
What I most feared has befallen me, What I dreaded has o'ertaken me.
I have no rest, no quiet, No repose, but continual agony.[13]

For my groaning arrives like daily bread, My roaring pours forth like water,
For the fear I feared has reached me, And what I dreaded has overtaken me.
I have no repose, no quiet, No peace—what comes is turmoil![14]

For my sighs are my daily bread, groans pour from me like water
For what I most feared has befallen me, all that I dreaded has come upon me.
I have no repose, no quiet, no rest. Turmoil has come.[15]

As was the case for verse 10, we find once again three materially differing translations, each of which inserts a less than subtle bias. None of the three renderings of כי לפני לחמי אנחתי תבא (*ky lpny lḥmy ʾnḥty tbʾ*) make any sense. The comparison of "bread" with "sighing" is absurd. The meaning of לפני (*lpny*) is "before"—literally, "in the face of" or "prior to" as in time—which is intended in this case." The term פחד (*paḥad*) which normally means "fear" performs in a brilliant *double entendre* as the deity mentioned in Gen.31[42,53], as the deity of Isaac.[16] Last, and perhaps most important, is the word רגז (*rgz*), translated as "trouble," "turmoil," and "agony." Nowhere does רגז (*rgz*) carry such a connotation; it simply means "anger" or "rage."

These three renditions are clearly exegetical. They are designed to promulgate the concept of "suffering" right at the outset since that is the premise that each translator has established in his reading of the Prologue. Clines reveals his exegetical problems of the story of Job at the conclusion of his "explanation" of Chapter 3.

> This [restlessness or turmoil] is not self-evidently the emotion people in Job's position would feel about their suffering: self-pity, *anger*, disgust, hopelessness, *yes*: but anxiety and *turmoil, hardly*. The reason can only be that it is the intellectual-existential implications of his suffering that "disturb Job; though he will not ventilate them here,

---

[13] Pope (1974, 27).
[14] Habel (1985, 99-100).
[15] Clines (1989, 68).
[16] Isaac's god was also known as האלהים (*hʾlhym*) whom we have shown is to be equated with יהוה (YHWH). See 2[10] above.

> *we are to understand*[17] that already he has been meditating on the religious significance of the disasters.[18]

Clines' entire thought process becomes unstuck around the meaning of the word רגז (*rgz*) and his preconception of Job's "suffering." We know that the Prologue nowhere speaks of "suffering" but rather describes Job the "Hater" as an increasingly unhappy, very angry man. Clines finds himself compelled to agree that a complaint about "trouble" or "turmoil" or "agony" does not fit the profile of a sad or depressed person. Silence and withdrawal are the outward symptoms of depression. Clines expects anger; however, when presented with it, he is forced to retreat into a wilderness of polysyllabic words that suitably obfuscate any real explanation.

Job is highly articulate about his feelings. He vents his spleen at whomever and whatever. It is of no concern to him at this stage whether the listener agrees, disagrees, sympathizes or not. We may paraphrase the "nodal"[19] verses 10 and 24-26:

[Job speaks in the name of his mother]:

> God could have spared me all this trouble
> had he only prevented my (mother's) womb from becoming pregnant.

[Job adds on his own behalf]:

> My guts are in such a knot that I cannot eat.
> I feared God [thinking it to be the right thing to do]
> And now my worst fears are reality.
> My rage gives me no pause for peace, quiet or rest.

---

[17] The italics are added.
[18] Clines (1989, 105).
[19] See below p.119.

THE DISCOURSE OF JOB AND HIS "FRIENDS"

The "Discourse" section of the Book of Job brings into sharp focus √צדק (*ṣdq*)) – "relative wholeness" as the "nodal" word that we mentioned earlier. In the Prologue our author asks the reader to induce √צדק (*ṣdq*) from the clues provided by the code; in this section, the subject of "wholeness" is tackled head on, although the uninitiated reader may still be unable to recognize it as "nodal."

Chapters 4[1]-26[14]

As we established in 2[11,12], the author has made it quite clear that the three "friends" have not come to "comfort" Job. There is a not so subtle subtext that strongly suggests that Job must have done something to incur divine wrath. Divine justice is not dispensed indiscriminately.

In the opening eight verses of this speech, ʾEliphaz begins almost cagily; however, he cannot restrain himself for long.

4:2-9

הנסה דבר אליך תלאה ועצר במלין מי יוכל
הנה יסרת רבים וידים רפות תחזק
כושל יקימון מליך וברכים כרעות תאמץ
כי עתה תבוא אליך ותלא תגע עדיך ותבהל
הלא יראתך כסלתך תקותך ותם דרכיך
זכר נא מי הוא נקי אבד ואיפה ישרים נכחדו
כאשר ראיתי חרשי און וזרעי עמל יקצרהו
מנשמת אלוה יאבדו ומרוח אפו יכלו

hnsh dbr ʾlyk tlʾh wʿṣr bmlyn my ywkl
hnh ysrt rbym wydym rpwt tʾmṣ
kwšl yqymn mlyk wbrkym krʿwt tḥzq
hlʾ yrʾtk ksltk tqwtk wtm drkyk
zkr nʾ my hwʾ nqy ʾbd wʾyph yšrym nkḥdw
kʾšr rʾyty ḥršy ʾwn wzrʿy ʿml yqṣrhw
mnšmt ʾlwh yʾbdw wmrwḥ ʾpw yklw

If one tries to talk to you will you be weary? Yet who can restrain words?
Indeed you chastise many, yet you [also] strengthen weak hands.
Your words enable the stumbler to rise and you fortify kneeling knees.
Yet now, when [your evil] comes, you are weary;
When it touches you, you are overwhelmed.
Are not your reverence, hope and integrity your [foolish] confidence?
Remember now, what innocent man has perished, and where are the upright cut down?
I have seen those who sow iniquity and how the sowers of trouble reap it.
They perish at a breath of *ʾeloah* and are annihilated by the wind of his anger.

The attempt to show concern does not go beyond the first phrase. ʾEliphaz cannot restrain himself. He concedes to Job that he has helped many people with his "good words" although he does not really believe it. The proof is that when the time comes to heed those very words, they are found to be empty. As long as Job prospered, he could dispense his counsel with magnanimity. Verse 5 can be understood in the context of Jer.2[19]:

תיסרך רעתך ומשבותיך תוכחך
ודעי וראי כי רע ומר עזבך את יהוה אלהיך
ולא פחדתי אליך נאם אדני יהוה צבאות
tysrk rʿtk wmšbwtyk twkḥk
wdʿy wrʾy ky rʿ wmr ʿzbk ʾt yhwh ʾlhyk
wlʾ pḥdty ʾlyk nʾm ʾdny yhwh ṣbʾwt
Your evil shall chastise you and your apostasies reprove you,
Know and see how evil and bitter is your abandonment of YHWH your God.
Fear of me is not upon you, says *ʾadonai YHWH ṣᵉbaʾot*

Jeremiah's indictment of Israel is mirrored in the words of ʾEliphaz. Job has abandoned יהוה (YHWH) his god and he must bear the consequences. Weariness will be no excuse for mercy.

זכר נא מי הוא נקי אבד (*zkr nʾ my hwʾ nqy ʾbd*)–" Remember now, what innocent man has perished?" ʾEliphaz mockingly exhorts Job to return to his basic beliefs, those that have enabled him to help so many. In an instant his tone becomes harsh. He taunts Job with the "facts"—no innocent (meaning "whole," as we are about to see), upstanding person has ever been penalized, in fact, the wicked are almost summarily snuffed out. The same question is posed in the *DSS Apostrophe to Zion* where we read:[1]

---

[1] *11QPs^a* XXII. l.9

מי זה אבד צדק
my zh ʾbd ṣdq
"Who is this that has perished whole?"

The construction **מי...אבד** (*my... ʾbd*) occurs only in these two places. Our author is clearly aware of this "apocryphal" text and Isa.57[1] which reads:

הצדיק אבד ואין איש שם על לב
hṣdyq ʾbd wʾyn ʾyš śm ʿl lb
Does a whole man perish and no man cares?

Both *DSS* and Deutero-Isaiah ask the question about a **צדיק** (*ṣdyq*) and one might wonder why the author has chosen to avoid this seemingly perfect antecedent. The answer lies in 4[17] where he needs √**צדק** (*ṣdq*) to pose the pivotal question of his investigation. We recall 1[5] where our author relies on a parallel usage to find the synonymous √קדש (*qdš*) for √ברך (*brk*). He now employs the same technique in substituting נקי (*nqy*) for **צדיק** (*ṣdyq*).[2]

The barely concealed implication is that Job cannot be one of the "whole" people. He now brutally shows his scorn for Job (the "nodal" verse):

4:17

האנוש מאלוה יצדק אם מעשהו יטהר גבר
hʾnwš mʾlwh yṣdq ʾm mʿśhw yṭhr gbr
Can man be more whole than *ʾeloah*?
Can man be purer than his Creator?

This verse constitutes the paradigmatic position statement of the "three friends." It is also set as a rhetorical question to which Job's answer would be undoubtedly positive. None of the "friends" recognizes the double meaning of **צדק** (*ṣdq*), with its dual meaning of both "godly" and "human" wholeness. Similarly, at this *crux*, our three major translators and commentators cannot agree on a single, unified translation. Our simple translation carries the full force of our author's question. Yet this notion is so unthinkable to our scholars that they find themselves compelled to assume reverential positions that force paraphrases that totally distort the meaning of the text. This is another case of

---

[2] See Ex.23[7]; ψ94[21].

exegesis begetting "meaning."[3] As a demonstration of what is typically to follow, let us analyze each translation:[4]

Pope: "Can a mortal be just before God? A man pure to his maker?" Pope explains his rendition as follows: "*KJ* renders 'more just than God, more pure than his Maker,' which is the meaning ordinarily conveyed by this construction, the normal device for expressing the comparative sense. It is obvious, however, that this is not the sense intended."[5] Pope clearly recognizes the construction and its proper meaning but needs to meddle in order to establish a context that he has set up by surrounding (both prior and subsequent) mistranslations. His justification using rare occurrences (where the meaning is not obvious) is tantamount to emendation. As far as יצדק (*yṣdq*) is concerned, he opts for "just" without any explanation.

Habel: "Can mortals be righteous before God? Humans pure before their Maker?" Habel's note is identical *verbatim* to Pope's;[6] however, he translates יצדק (*yṣdq*) as "be righteous," noting that this is a "pivotal topic statement" and that "the ambiguity of the original is probably deliberate."[7] He goes on to say that "the verbs *ṣdq* 'righteous,' and *ṭhr*, 'pure,' are apparently used here in the sense of sinless, without blame, free from moral imperfection...Job obviously appropriates the forensic sense of *ṣdq* in later passages." Habel actually builds his entire interpretation of the Book of Job around the "forensic sense" of the verb *ṣdq*. Why must the sense be different here? If the author wished to say "...pure before their (sic) Maker (or God)", he need have looked no further than Lev.16^{30}, where the text says לפני יהוה תטהרו (*lpny yhwh tṭhrw*)[8] in the context of "expiation from sin."

Clines: Can a man be righteous before God? Can a man be pure in the sight of his maker?

Of the three translators, Clines offers the most prolix if the least insightful comment. We will quote only the beginning of a theological exegesis that that is difficult to fathom:

---

[3] To add to the confusion, *NJPS* translates: Can mortals be acquitted by God? Can man be cleared by his Maker? This rendition is absolutely without ground.
[4] For this and all subsequent comparisons see Pope (1973), Habel (1985) and Clines (1989).
[5] Pope (1973, 37) Pope goes on to add that "the preposition "from" is used in this same way—in the sense of "before" —in Num.32^{22} and Jer.2^{5b}.
[6] Habel (1985, 116) makes no mention of Pope.
[7] Habel (1985, 129).
[8] "You shall be pure before Yahweh."

> Almost every reader of ʾEliphaz's speech is struck by the apparent banality of the utterance that forms the climax of the scene portrayed in vv. 12-16. Especially if the more straightforwardly grammatical translation is accepted (Can man be more righteous than God?"), the comment of Peake[9] is wholly appropriate: "So trivial a commonplace as that man is not more righteous than God needed no vision to declare it; and it is quite irrelevant in this connection," since it is only later that Job questions the justice of God, and in each of these places an exposition of Job's attitude has to be subtly modulated. There is never a question of humans being *more* righteous than God.[10]

What appears quite certain is that Clines is sticking with the word "righteous" and is forced into a convoluted explication that serves only to highlight the mire in which he has become stuck.

The *Targum of Job* does not recognize יצדק (*yṣdq*) at all in the sense of "righteous." It reads as follows:[11]

האיפשר דבר נש מאלוה יזכי ואין מן מאן דעבדיה ידכי גבר
hʾpšr dbr nš mʾlwh yzky wʾyn mn mʾn dʿbdyh ydky gbr
Is it possible that a man be purer than *ʾeloah*,
Or that a man be purer than his maker?

In an otherwise absolutely literal translation of the text, the *Targum* chooses √זכי (*zky*) and its variant √דכי (*dky*) meaning "be pure, clean"—which are the exact equivalent of Hebrew √זכה (*zkh*)—for both יצדק (*yṣdq*) and יטהר (*yṭhr*).[12] This is notwithstanding the fact that Aramaic has a √צדק (*ṣdq*), with a meaning identical to that of the Hebrew root. We shall see that the *Targum* is inconsistent in its subsequent renderings of √צדק (*ṣdq*).

This indecision on the part of the *Targum* reveals the challenges posed by multiple translations of √צדק (*ṣdq*).

All of the aforementioned may be rendered *de minimis* when we read the following in *DSS 1QH^a* xvii ll.14-17:

---

[9] No citation given. W.A. Irwin, (1962, 393) essentially mirrors the attribution to Peake when he says, "any ignorant person of the street might also have told that mortal man cannot be pure by divine standards…how absurd, for man is weak and transient."

[10] Clines (1989, 132).

[11] Stec (1994, 31)

[12] We shall discuss below the possible lexical connection of the bilateral stem *זכ (*zk*) with the Greek stem δίκαι- (*díkai-*) which is used by *LXX* to render √צדק (*ṣdq*).

...כי לא יצדק כול במשפטכה ולא יזכה בריבכה
אנוש מאנוש יצדק וגבר מרעהו ישכיל
ובשר מיצר [חמר] יכבר ורוח מרוח תגבר
ובגבורתכה אין בכוח ולכבודכה אין חקר לחכמתכה אין מדה...

...ky lw' yṣdq kwl bmšpṭkh wl' yzkh brybkh
'nwš m'nwš yṣdq wgbr mr'hw yśkyl
wbśr myṣr [ḥmr] ykbr wrwḥ mrwḥ tgbr
... wkgbwrtkh 'yn bkwḥ wlkbwdkh 'ynḥ ḥqr lḥkmtkh 'yn mdh...

...For no one is whole in your judgment,
No one is innocent at your trial.
A MAN MAY BE MORE WHOLE THAN ANOTHER MAN;[13]
A man more discerning than his fellow man;
Flesh may be more powerful than a creation [from clay];
One spirit mightier than another.
But compared to your might, no one is as strong;
There is no searching (the limit) to your glory;
And for your wisdom, there is no measure...

This is surely the premise against which the author pitches his entire argument. Using vocabulary that is consistent word-for-word with that of the author Book of Job, the writer of this Dead Sea Scrolls psalm articulates the case for "Divine superiority."

This is the foil for our author's penetrating interrogation. Our author does indeed question the meaning of Divine "wholeness," which includes both the "good" and the "evil" sides of the bicameral mind of the Divine. He asserts the existence of Divine "wholeness," recounting divine actions, whether for better or worse. This declaration implies the equivalence of Divine "wholeness" to human "wholeness." It is the consequence of the questioning of this statement of dogma that compels the author to seek the shelter of concealment behind his code. One can clearly comprehend our author's reluctance to face dogma head-on.

This is the exact corollary to the question of 'Eliphaz. It stands at face value and is consistent with the *crux* that we have identified. We can now be sure that the issue of "human" and "divine" wholeness was both current and immediate. Any suggestion of an early dating for the Book of Job can now be put to rest.

---

[13] The capitalization is mine for emphasis.

5:1

קרא נא היש עונך ואל מי מקדשים תפנה
qr' n' hyš 'wnk w'l my mqdšym tpnh
"Call out, is there anyone to answer you,
And to which of the *qᵉdošîm* will you turn?

The real barb lies not in the first colon but rather in the second, "and to which of the קדשים (*qᵉdošîm*)[14] will you turn?" If we refer back to our author's sources for the synonymy of אלוה (*'lwh*) and יהוה (YHWH), namely, Hab.3[3] and Deut.33[2], we note the presence of the word קדוש (*qdwš*) both in the singular and plural. קדוש (*qdwš*) is commonly translated as "holy"; however, in these two instances, the term is synonymous with the deity. Thus 5[1b] should be rendered "And to which of the deities will you turn?" as in Hos.12[1b]:

ויהודה עד רד עם אל ועם קדושים נאמן
wyhwdh 'd rd 'm 'l w'm qdšym n'mn
Yet Judah still walks freely with 'El,
And stands firm with *qᵉdôšîm*[15]

This citation gains credibility in terms of Job since it occurs in 15[15a] in the context of יצדק (*yṣdq*):[16]

הן בקדשו לא יאמין ושמים לא זכו בעיניו
hn bqdšw l' y'myn wšmym l' zkw b'ynyw
Lo! He has no faith in his *qᵉdôšîm*,
And the heavens have no merit in his eyes.

---

[14] Wilson (2001, 105ff.)

[15] Both *BDB* (923—"wander restlessly, roam") and *HALOT* (1195 "roam about freely") have trouble assigning a meaning to √רוד (*rwd*). The context demands a parallel to נאמן (*n'mn*). The closest root with an appropriate meaning would be √רדה (*rdh*)—"to rule." However, the participle parallel to נאמן (*n'mn*) would be רדה (*rdh*) vocalized *rodêh*. One might suggest that √רוד (*rwd*) and √רדה (*rdh*) (and probably √רדד (*rdd*)) share a common origin (compare √בוז (*bwz*), √בזה (*bzh*), and √בזז (*bzz*)), thus allowing for odd forms; however, that connection is speculative and we have tempered the "roaming freely" with a rendering of "walks freely."

[16] See also the parallel in 4[18]:

הן בעבדיו לא יאמין ובמלאכיו ישים תהלה
hn b'bdyw l' y'myn wbml'kyw yśym thlh
Lo! He has no faith in his servants (creations?),
And he makes fools of his messengers.

ʾEliphaz perhaps understands the plurality of the nature of the deity and turns Job's recent recognition of at least a duality in the nature of his god יהוה (YHWH) against him.

5:6

כי לא יצא מעפר און ומאדמה לא יצמח עמל
כי אדם לעמל יולד ובני רשף יגביהו עוף

ky lʾ yṣʾ mʿpr ʾwn wmʾdmh lʾ yṣmḥ ʿml
kyʾ dm lʿml ywld wbny ršp ygbyhw ʿwp

For nothingness comes not from the ground, nor does trouble sprout from the earth.
For man was born to [have] trouble, as disease takes wing aloft.

ʾEliphaz's tone becomes harsh and judgmental. He rejects Job's plea of $3^{10,11}$, in which he berates his fate of "having been born to see trouble." Trouble is not spontaneously generated, says ʾEliphaz; man (Job) must have something to do with it. The very fact of his birth ensures trouble, just as disease exists. This latter thought reflects Aristotle's axiomatic statement:

> It is altogether impossible that men should attain the highest good; they cannot share in the nature of the highest (μετασχεῖν τῆς τοῦ βελτίστου φυσέως). For the highest good for all men and women is not to be born (τὸ μὴ γενέσθαι). But, if they are born, the best—and *this* men can attain—is to die as quickly as possible.[17]

בני רשף (*bny ršp*) is often translated as "sparks"; however, it must in this instance refer to the deity *ršp* as the god of pestilence and the underworld. [18] "Disease" in an appropriate parallel for "trouble." We find the denominative רשף (*ršp*) as a parallel to דבר (*dbr*) "pestilence" in Hab. 3^5, just three verses after the identification of the source of אלוה (*ʾlwh*). In addition, דבר (*dbr*) "pestilence" is one of the four disasters enumerated in Ezekiel Chapter 14.

---

[17] From the *Eudemus* Jaeger (1967, 48), Rose (1886, 48-49 [frag. 44]).

[18] *ršp* appears in the Ugaritic pantheon as the equivalent of the Mesopotamian god *Nergal*, who was king of the netherworld and god of pestilence (Fulco 1976). See also Hab.3^5, Deut. 32^{29}.

5:8

אולם אני אדרש אל אל ואל אלהם אשם דברתי

ʾwlm ʾny ʾdrš ʾl ʾl wʾl ʾlhym ʾśym dbrty

But [I swear that] I would seek out *ʾel* and set my matter before *ʾelohîm*.[19]

Now ʾEliphaz thrusts at the heart of Job's disappointment. He does not know **יהוה** (YHWH) by name at all. He seems to know of the other deity, **אלהים** (*ʾelohîm*); however, he is not aware that Job's **אלהים** (*ʾelohîm*) does not speak or render judicial opinions. He is the immutable institution of justice. Is ʾEliphaz aware of the true nature of **אלהים** (*ʾelohîm*), or is he unintentionally intimidating Job out of ignorance?

5:17-18

הנה אשרי אנוש יוכחנו אלוה ומוסר שדי אל תמאס
כי הוא יכאיב ויחבש ימחץ וידו תרפינה

hnh ʾšry ʾnwš ywkḥnw ʾlwh wmwsr šdy ʾl tmʾs
ky hwʾ ykʾyb wyḥbš ymhṣ wydw trpynh

Behold! Happy is the man whom *ʾeloah* reproves;[20]
Do not reject the instruction of *šadday*.
For he inflicts pain and binds [the wound];
He shatters and his hands heal.[21]

ʾEliphaz opens a new vision wherein he conceives of the deity as a duality. He unknowingly describes the two diametrically polar natures of the divine that have been portrayed in the Prologue.

6:29

שבו נא אל תהי עולה ושבי עוד צדקי בה

šbw nʾ ʾl thy ʿwlh wšby ʿwd ṣdqy bh

Return, I pray you, let there not be injustice;
And my wholeness is yet in my return.[22]

Pope: No more, have done with injustice. Relent, for my cause is just. Pope's only comment is "the same word, *šûḇû*, "return you." The injustice is the unfair assumption that Job must be guilty." He also allows himself extensive

---

[19] Note the assonance and alliteration of **אל אל ואל אלהים** (*ʾl ʾl wʾl ʾlhym*).

[20] See ψ94[10,12], for analogies wherein the name **יהוה** (YHWH) has been substituted.

[21] See Deut.32[39] for the *BH* antecedent.

[22] Reading **ושבתי** (*wšbty*) vocalized *wᵉšuḇaṯî* "and my return" given the presence of a Masoretic *Qere* and *Kethib*.

license in his translation. There is nothing in the text that can support "Relent, for my cause is just."

Habel: Relent! Away with deceit! Relent! I am still in the right! Habel focuses on the words *ʿawlah* and *šûḇû*. The former, he says, "may mean 'injustice' in general. However, in Job it is associated with speech in such a way as to suggest the rendering 'deceit' or 'deception'…The twofold imperative 'relent' (*šûḇû*) is equivalent to a call of repentance, an ironic reversal of what the friends ultimately expect from Job."

Clines: Turn to me; there is no iniquity here! Turn to me; my integrity is still intact! Clines' primary interpretation is that "the 'turning,' lit. 'returning' (שוב) may involve physical movement….It is far more than that his lament is justified: it is that his integrity or innocence is still intact…and that he demands that they should recognize it."

Our three scholars find reasons to adjust the literal meaning of the text, each focusing on a *nuance* that they observe either explicitly or implicitly. Pope's rendering is probably the least tainted by a translator's *agenda*. Clines' "Turn to me" has absolutely no basis in the text. None of the three have anything to say either about the word צדקי (*ṣdqy*), which is the key to all of Job's arguments, or בה (*bh*), which must refer back to something in the verse.[23]

8:3

האל יעות משפט ואם שדי יעות צדק

h'l yʿwt mšpṭ w'm šdy yʿwt ṣdq

Does 'El twist justice? Does Šadday twist wholeness?

Pope: Does God pervert justice? Does Shaddai distort the right? While translating literally for the most part, Pope explains his use of two different English words in the translation of the same Hebrew word יעות (*yʿwt*), arguing that there is a corruption of one of the words יעות (*yʿwt*) that should be emended.[24]

Habel: Does 'El pervert justice? Does Shaddai pervert the right? Habel finds "no need to change the second occurrence of the colorful verb *ʿwt*." He ignores צדק (*ṣdq*) completely, turning his full attention to משפט (*mšpṭ*) – "justice" in support of his theory of the "legal metaphor" as the basis of the Book of Job.

---

[23] See n.17 above. The *Targum* (Stec, 1994, 49) renders צדקי (*ṣdqy*) with לדכאותי (*ldk'wty*), which is a variant spelling of √דכי (*dky*) meaning "be pure, clean" that has been described above.

[24] Pope (1973, 65) suggests this need for emendation perhaps to יעוה (*yʿwh*), on the grounds that *LXX*, Vulgate and *Targum* all use different verbs.

Clines: Can God pervert justice? Can the Almighty pervert what is right? By inserting the word "can," implying "ability," Clines puts himself in interpretive mode. The outcome of his discussion is that "Bildad has a static view of God as guarantor of the world order. Job's sense that it is God and not himself that has changed threatens that view of God."

The *Targum* uses the word צדקא (*ṣdqʾ*) as its rendering of צדק (*ṣdq*).[25] This verse finds Bildad asking the rhetorical question that Job refuses to accept. Our author is precisely on point when he puts the rhetorical question, with its expected negative answer, in the mouth of an antagonist.

Our author is playing with the word צדק (*ṣdq*). He defines צדק (*ṣdq*) as both "human wholeness" and "godly wholeness." Bildad presumably knows nothing of "human wholeness" and finds the notion of divine perverseness unimaginable. Our author also leaves us with the unspoken corollary, namely, that humanity can and does pervert "human wholeness."

8:6

אם זך וישר אתה כי עתה יעיר עליך ושלם נות צדקך
ʾm zk wyšr ʾth ky ʿth yʿyr ʿlyk wšlm nwt ṣdqk
Indeed, you are not pure and upright;[26]
For he will now awaken against you
And YHWH will have vengeance upon you.

Pope: If you are pure and upright, he will bestir himself for you and restore your righteous estate.

Habel: If you are pure and upright, then he will rouse himself for you and restore your righteous estate.

Clines: If you are pure and upright, he will surely now rouse himself for you, and restore your righteous abode.

What we have here is a demonstration of the use of the particle אם (*ʾm*) as an asseverative.[27] The statement is clearly rhetorical, expecting a negative response.

The *Targum* uses the Aramaic צדקך (*ṣdqk*) as its rendering of the Hebrew צדקך (*ṣdqk*) and both our translators and the *Targum* seem to agree on their understanding of צדק (*ṣdq*).[28]

---

[25] Stec (1994, 57).
[26] For the use of the preposition אם (*ʾm*) as the introduction to a negative statement, see *GKC* §149*e* for a discussion of simple particles of asseveration.
[27] For elaboration, see our treatment of $9^{19,20}$.

However, for all of their accord, our scholars miss the real meaning of this crucial statement. The phrase **נוה צדק** (*nwh ṣdq*) is a synonym for **יהוה** (YHWH), as evidenced by its occurrences in Jer.31[22] and 50[6,7,9]. While both citations clearly express this synonymy, our author, meticulously consistent with his methodology of unique *BH* antecedents, clearly wishes to utilize only the latter citation since it occurs in close proximity with √**עור** (*ʿwr*) as follows:

צאן אבדות היה עמי רעיהם התעום הרים שובבום מהר אל גבעה הלכו שכחו רבצם
כל מוצאיהם אכלום וצריהם אמרו לא נאשם
תחת אשר חטאו ליהוה נוה צדק ומקוה אבותיהם יהוה...
כי הנה אנכי מעיר ומעלה על בבל קהל גוים גדלים מארץ צפון...
ṣʾn ʾbdwt hyh ʿmy rʿyhm htʿwm hrym šwbbwm mhr ʾl gbʿh hlkw škḥw rbṣm
kl mwṣʾyhm ʾklwm wṣryhm ʾmrw lʾ nʾšm
tḥt ʾšr ḥṭʾw lyhwh nwh ṣdq wmqwh ʾbwtyhm yhwh...
ky hnh ʾnky mʿyr wmʿlh ʿl bbl qhl gwym gdlym mʾrṣ ṣpwn
My people are lost sheep, whose shepherds have led them astray;
The mountains have turned them away, they go from mountain to hill;
They have forgotten their fold.
All who find them devour them, their enemies say, "We are not to blame.
For they have sinned against YHWH, the abode of wholeness,
YHWH, the hope of their ancestors."...
For lo! I am going to stir up and lead against Babylon
A congregation of great nations from the land of the north...

While Bildad appears to be politely ambiguous, his words conceal a brutal accusation. He is implicitly stating that Job is "unwhole" and impure. Our translation, which is based on Jer. 50[6,7,9], provides the only sensible meaning of the verse.

This in turn leads us to the question of the meaning of **ושלם** (*wšlm*).[29] Normally rendered "to be whole" or "be peaceful," √**שלם** (*šlm*) in the *piʿel* form carries the meaning of "make whole" in the sense of "to requite," "to recompense," or "take vengeance," as Yahweh asserts in Deut.32[35]:[30]

---

[28] The *Targum* is significantly unaware of the author's agenda with its simple literal translation.

[29] The form *wᵉšillam* is almost certainly an Aramaism.

[30] *HALOT*, 1535 "to restore, replace" is based on Fohrer's interpretation of the phrase (*Hiob* 183, 190). Similarly *BDB*, 1022, "with accusative."

לי נקם ושלם...
ly nqm wšlm...
Mine are revenge and vengeance...

Our verse is further clarified by the parallel presence in Jer.50[9] of מעיר על (*mʿyr ʿl*)—"stir up against"—where the intended object is Babylon. Thus the intent is clearly adversarial and hostile.

This verse is probably the signal example for our contention that our sample translators were guided by preconceived notions. Even given their own *agenda*, they become completely unstuck. The true sense of the verse emerges only by application of the code that we have described.

9:2

אמנם ידעתי כי כן ומה יצדק אנוש עם אל
ʾmnm ydʿty ky kn wmh yṣdq ʾnwš ʿm ʾl
Certainly I know it to be true;
That man shares some[31] godly wholeness with ʾEl?

Pope: Indeed, I know it is so. But how can man be acquitted before God? Pope translates ומה (*wmh*) as "but how" without grounds, citing 4[17] as a comparison. The structure of the latter citation is completely different; one can therefore only assume that Pope derives his meaning from the context.

Habel: Of course, I know that this is so: A mortal cannot win a suit against El. Habel is now in forensic mode although the text simply cannot support his rendering. Both Habel and Newsom emphasize the legal aspects of √צדק (*ṣdq*) to varying degrees. Habel states that the court-like setting is "integral to the coherence of the Book of Job."[32] All of the subtitles of his rendering of Chap. 9 make this abundantly clear. [33] Newsom argues against Habel's generalization and attempts to recognize *nuances* in the author's use of √צדק (*ṣdq*).[34] However, she needs to resort to convoluted linguistic techniques to make her point.[35] We hold that, while our author utilized a sophisticated code, he did not deviate from its application.

---

[31] See *GKC* §137*c* for the use of מה (*mh*) as the indefinite pronoun.
[32] Habel (1985, 54)
[33] Habel (1985, 178-181)
[34] Newsom (2003, 152-160)
[35] Newsom (2003, 154-155) is a discussion of "localized metaphor" vs. "cognitive metaphor" with the latter identifying what might be termed *cruces* in the text.

Clines: I know that this is so; but how can man be justified by God? Clines, as ever entwined in preconceived theology, is compelled to invent an even less plausible rendering than the other two.

Job is the speaker and he is unswerving in his conviction that man must be capable of at least some "godly wholeness." We note the presence of the word **אמנם** (*ʾmnm*), commonly translated "indeed." Our author perhaps wishes us to understand the significance of √**אמן** (*ʾmn*) with its profound sense of "trustworthiness" in close proximity with √**צדק** (*ṣdq*).[36]

9:14-15

אף כי אנכי אעננו אבחרה דברי עמו
אשר אם צדקתי לא אענה למשפטי אתחנן
ʾp ky ʾnky ʾʿnnw ʾbḥrh dbry ʿmw
ʾšr ʾm ṣdqty lʾ ʾʿnh lmšpṭy ʾtḥnn
Even if I were to answer him,
I would choose my words with him
If I am not whole, I would not be answered;[37]
I would seek grace from my judge.

Pope: How then could I answer him, Or match my words with him? Though in the right, I could not answer; I would have to entreat my opponent.

Habel: How then can I answer him, Or select my charges against him? Even though I am in the right, I cannot answer; I must plead for mercy to my adversary at law.

Clines: How then could I respond to him, how choose words with which to answer him? Even if I were in the right, I could not defend myself; I could only appeal for mercy to my adversary.

None of the three translations is at all comprehensible, either grammatically or contextually. First, v.14 is not presented as a question, as the *Targum* accurately reflects. Second, if our author had truly set this up as a court case, it is unlikely that he would have made the deity both judge and adversary.[38] The notion of pleading for mercy from an adversary is more martial than legal. Third, this *poʿel* form of √**שפט** (*špṭ*) is *hapax legomenon* and thus its meaning is

---

[36] Both *HALOT*, 65 and *BDB*, 53 assert this relationship.

[37] Vocalizing **אֵעָנֶה** (*ʾʿnh*) as the passive *nip̱ʿal ʾêʿâneh* brings meaning to an otherwise obscure construction.

[38] As Pope (1973, 72) asserts.

not easily adduced.[39] The *Targum* renders **למשפטי** (*lmšpṭy*) with **למאן דדאין יתי** (*lm'n dd'yn yty*) "to the one who judges me." As to context, Job is affirming his "wholeness" and effectively chastising the deity for neither listening nor answering. Job's skepticism goes so far as to be unbelieving should an answer emanate from the deity.

9:19-20

אם לכח אמיץ הנה ואם למשפט מי יועידני
אם אצדק פי ירשיעני תם אני ויעקשני
'm lkḥ 'myṣ hnh w'm lmšpṭ my yw'ydny
'm 'ṣdq py yršy'ny tm 'ny wy'qšny
If this is a case of strength, Behold he is the mighty one;
If it is a matter of justice, who will arraign me?
If I am not whole, my mouth will convict me;
If I am [not] pure, it will make me perverse.

Pope: Be it power, he is strongest; Or litigation, who could arraign him? Though I be righteous, my mouth would condemn me; Though guiltless, he would declare me perverse.

Habel: If it be a trial of strength—he is the mighty one! If it be a trial at court—who will arraign him for me? Though I am innocent, my mouth would condemn me; Though I am blameless, he would declare me perverse.

Clines: If it is a matter of strength, behold he is the mighty one; if a matter of justice, who can arraign him? Though I am innocent, my own mouth would condemn me; though I am blameless, it would prove me guilty.

All three translators require similar extensive emendations to derive their versions. It is not constructive to go into the details since they add nothing constructive. In the final analysis, their wrestling with the text is driven by a "theological "rectitude" that is quite unnecessary.

What we have here is a brilliant demonstration of the contrasting uses of the particle **אם** (*'m*), both as a conditional and as an asseverative particle. Job stands defiant—while conceding the superior physical power of the deity, he accuses him as prejudiced and monomaniacal—the divine is not fit to swear him in, let alone pass "justice." In creating this unique syntactic device, our author is true to form. The superficial plot disguises his true agenda, namely, the diminution of the deity and the elevation of humanity.

---

[39] Pope, (*ibid.*) compares this form to the Arabic 3rd conjugation form قاطل (*qâṭala*), which he states "connotes conation and reciprocity," in order to extract his interpretation, which is unquestioningly followed by the others.

10:14-15

אם חטאתי ושמרתני ומעוני לא תנקני
אם רשעתי אללי לי וצדקתי לא אשא ראשי שבע קלון וראה עניי
ʾm ḥṭʾty wšmrtny wmʿwny lʾ tnqny
ʾm ršʿty ʾlly ly wṣdqty lʾ ʾśʾ rʾšy śbʿ qlwn wrʾh ʿnyy
Since I have not sinned, you have guarded me,
You would not find me innocent of my iniquity.
If I am guilty, woe is me;
Were I not whole I would not raise my head;
Be sated with humiliation! And see my affliction!

Pope: If I should sin, you are watching me, and would not acquit me of my guilt. If I am guilty, woe is me! Or innocent, I may not lift my head. Sated with shame, Drenched in misery.

Habel: To watch whether I would sin And not clear me from my guilt. If I am guilty—woe is me. But if I am innocent—I cannot lift my head, I am so sated with shame And so saturated with misery.

Clines: that, if I sinned, you would be watching me and would not acquit me of my guilt! If I am guilty, woe to me! And if I am innocent, I dare not lift my head, I am filled with shame and sated with affliction.

Once again we observe the contrasting uses of the particle **אם** (*ʾm*) and the meaning of the two verses immediately becomes apparent and sensible. Our three translators are once again forced to stretch the limits of the text. Even then, their renditions are not plausible.

The word **ושמרתני** (*wšmrtny*) does not connote simple "watching." The √**שמר** (*šmr*) always has the sense of "watch over," "guard" or "preserve."

שבע קלון (*śbʿ qlwn*) occurs as a phrase only once in *BH* in Hab.2[16], as follows:

שבעת קלון מכבוד...
śbʿt qlwn mkbwd
You are sated with humiliation rather than glory…

The context is a scathing rebuke by **יהוה** (YHWH) of the contemporary Israelite social practices, which will be punished by the invasion of the Babylonians. Now Job turns **יהוה** (YHWH)'s own words against **יהוה** (YHWH) himself.[40] Not coincidentally, Hab.2[4] ends with the phrase:

---

[40] This phrase occurs in the middle of a passage replete with lexical difficulties; however, even the Qumran *Pesher Habakkuk* (*1QpHab* Col.xi, l.8-9) is unequivocally in agreement with *BH*.

וצדיק באמונתו יחיה
wṣdyq b'mwntw yḥyh
And the whole man shall live by dint of his steadfastness

Similarly the phrase וראה עניי (*wr'h 'nyy*) – "and see my affliction," occurs only once in *BH*. Our author takes us back to ψ25[18,19], where we read:

ראה עניי ועמלי ושא לכל חטאותי
ראה איבי כי רבו ושנאת חמס שנאוני
r'h 'nyy w'mly ws''lkl ḥṭ'wty
r'h 'wyby ky rbw wśn't ḥms śn'wny

See my affliction and my toil and forgive all my sins.
See how many are my enemies and their violent hate for me.

This passage is not new to our author—he used it in the first verse of the first chapter of the Book of Job.

What we have then in this verse is a coherent statement rather than the disjointed series of phrases that so troubles scholars. Only Pope is non-committal in his translation; He leaves the final colon hanging out neutrally. The other two immediately assume that Job is referring to himself in his misery.

Each colon carries its own weight. Right or wrong, יהוה (YHWH) will not let Job prevail. "Shame on you, Yahweh, see your own injustice and give me relief. You yourself have said that a whole man shall live by dint of his faith and trust in you"

11:2

הרב דברים לא יענה ואם איש שפתים יצדק
hrb dbrym l' y'nh w'm 'yš śptym yṣdq
One who strives with words shall not be answered;
Nor shall a man of lips be whole.

Pope: Shall this spate of words go unanswered? Shall the glib one be innocent? Pope has no useful comment.

Habel: Should a spate of words go unanswered? Must a loquacious person be in the right? Habel, similarly, lets this pass without comment.

Clines: Should a multitude of words go unanswered? Should a man win vindication by mere talk? In his notes, Clines modifies his translation with "perhaps איש שפתים (*'yš śptym*) means "a glib talker by contrast with איש דברים (*'yš dbrym*), "a fluent speaker" (Ex.4[10]). He then remarks that "since there is no interrogative particle in v.3, it must be continued from the previous verse." If our author wanted to say איש דברים (*ʾyš dbrym*), there would have been no reason for him not to do so.

All three see this verse as a pair of rhetorical questions when it is in fact a direct statement. Zophar's opening is a brusque accusation, a frontal attack on Job. There is no rhetorical question demanded by context; this is a stark refutation.

The sense of fighting is obtained by simply adjusting the vocalization of הרב דברים (*hrb dbrym*) from *harôb dᵉbarîm* to *harâb dᵉbarîm*. The prefixed letter *he* is an Aramaized definite article rather than an interrogative, as is reflected in the *Targum*'s rendering of הרב דברים (*hrb dbrym*) with הא דמסגי מליא *(hʾ dmsgy mlyʾ)* – "The man of many words," which is dispositive and not interrogative.

איש שפתים (*ʾyš śptym*) does not occur as such anywhere else in *BH*. However, our author does not intend to convey a sense of "glibness." He is directing the reader to Isa.6[5] where the prophet refers to himself as איש טמא שפתים (*ʾyš ṭmʾ śptym*) – "a man of impure lips," which conveys a sense of "being inarticulate"—quite the opposite of "glib." The *Targum* clearly fails to understand the reference to Isaiah, reading בר נש מרי ספוון (*br nš mry spwwn*) – "a man, a master of lips."[41]

In referring to Isaiah, our author reveals his subtext, namely, that since Isaiah, a self-described "man of impure lips," was answered by the deity, the same applies to Job.

12:2-4,9

אמנם כי אתם עם ועמכם תמות חכמה
גם לי לבב כמוכם לא נפל אנכי מכם ואת מי אין כמו אלה
שחק לרעהו אהיה קרא לאלוה ויענהו שחוק צדיק תמים...
ומי לא ידע בכל אלה כי יד יהוה עשתה כל זאת

ʾmnm ky ʾtm ʿm wʿmkm tmwt ḥkmh
gm ly lbb kmwkm lʾ npl ʾnky mkm wʾt my ʾyn kmw ʾlh
śḥq lrʿhw ʾhyh qwrʾ lʾlwh wyʿnhw śḥwq ṣdyq tmym...
wmy lʾ ydʿ bkl ʾlh ky yd yhwh ʿśth kl zʾt

---

[41] Stec (1994, 74)

Indeed I know that you are [foolish] people,
And that wisdom shall die with you.
I, like you, also have a mind; I am not inferior to you.
Who does not know these things?
I am the one who jokes at his friend;
One who calls upon ʾEloah and afflicts him;
A whole, perfect joker…
Who among all these does not know that the hand of Yahweh has done this?

Pope: No doubt you are gentry, And with you wisdom will die. But I have a mind as well as you; I am not inferior to you. Who does not know such things? A derision to his neighbor I am become, One whom God answered when he called, The just and perfect a derision…Who does not know all these things, That God's hand has done this? Pope's rendering of עם (*ʿm*) as "gentry" harkens back to the usage of עם הארץ (*ʿm hʾrṣ*) in 2Kings and Jeremiah.[42] As we shall show, the meaning of is עם הארץ (*ʿm hʾrṣ*) is intended in its 2nd Temple period context.

Habel: Truly you are the people With whom wisdom will die. But I, like you, have a mind; I am not inferior to you. Who does not know such things? I am the one mocked by his friends As "The one who summons God for an answer," Yes, mocked as "The guiltless whole one"…Who among all these does not know That the hand of ʾEloah has done this? Habel's needless rendering of יהוה (YHWH) with "ʾEloah" is left unexplained.

Clines: Truly you are the last of the wise! With you wisdom will die! But I have intelligence as much as you; I am not inferior to you, Who does not know such things? For I have become a laughingstock to my friends, I, a man who would call upon God and be answered, I, an innocent man, a blameless man—a laughingstock…Which among all these does not know that Yahweh's hand has done this? Clines needlessly renders עם (*ʿm*) as "the last of the wise."

This citation is lengthy because our scholars demonstrate differences in translation and comprehension ranging from subtle to gross. First is the misconstruction of עם (*ʿm*) in v.2. Far from complimenting the "friends," for which he would have no reason, Job ridicules them as "fools." We are to understand עם (*ʿm*) as עם הארץ (*ʿm hʾrṣ*) – "ignorant people" (the term is used in its late pre-Mishnaic sense). Job has no reason to declare that wisdom will die

---

[42] In such contexts the term has been interpreted variously as an ancient Hebrew "parliament," the landed nobility, the free, male, property-owning citizenry, and the like. Some representative body of the population is evidently intended, though as a general, rather than a specific term (cf. the vague "all the people of Judah" who enthroned King Azariah, 2Kings 14:21).(M. Greenberg, *EJ AM HA-AREẒ*)

with these "three last wise men." Job's proclamation of their ignorance is affirmed by his question in v.9 "who does not know that the hand of Yahweh has done all of this?"[43]

Second, the triplet in v.4 is troublesome to both our scholars and the *Targum*, all of whom translate similarly and are unable to make any sense. The issue is that √שחק (*śḥq*) in the *qal* is active, that is to say that it means "to laugh (at)" and not "to be laughed at." Our scholars, needing to follow a preconception of Job's self deprecation, somehow, without any justification, turn √שחק (*śḥq*) into a stative "to be the object of laughter or derision."[44]

The third issue is the meaning of שחוק צדיק תמים (*śḥwq ṣdyq tmym*). Job has treated the "friends" with sarcastic disdain. In a rare moment of foresight, Job understands the paradox of the "whole, perfect joker" and recognizes the dual aspects that are the basis of יהוה (YHWH)'s personality. Our author harks back to the opening verse of the Book of Job and the subtext description of Job in terms attributed to Noah, who was the archetype for איש צדיק תמים (*ʾyš ṣdyq tmym*). Job comprehends now that the "friends" know nothing. They have never seen the deity, let alone communed with it. Job taunts them as "ignorant." Unlike Job, (see v.9) they are unaware of the power of יהוה (YHWH), a knowledge that every common beast possesses.

Last but not least is קורא לאלוה ויענהו (*qwrʾ lʾlwh wyʿnhw*), which has perplexed both our scholars and the *Targum*. Our author utilizes two meanings of √ענה (*ʿnh*), namely, "to answer" and "to afflict."[45] Job is clearly on the offensive, rejecting the slurs of ʾEliphaz, Bildad, and Zophar. Thus they may understand Job believes that the deity does indeed answer him, although they have no evidence to confirm this. Job, for his part, has no interest in a baseless

---

[43] The term עם הארץ (*ʿm hʾrṣ*) was a pejorative term that had a decidedly negative bias. It was used in Tannaitic times to describe those Jews who were not exiled to Babylon. They were considered "impure" in contrast to the returned exiles who, having been "purified" by the exile, were faithful to God. At the beginning of the period of the Second Temple the term עם הארץ (*ʿm hʾrṣ*) described a social distinction between people whose lives were governed by religious faith and observance and those whose conduct was not necessarily consistent with the prevailing orthodoxy. In middle and late Second Temple times, עם הארץ (*ʿm hʾrṣ*) became an idiom for ignorance, often of those who were unschooled in Torah and/or the laws connected with agriculture and ritual purity.

[44] Neither *BDB*, 966 nor *HALOT*, 1315 cites this verse as a definitive example of √שחק (*śḥq*). This would be the only example of √שחק (*śḥq*) in the sense of "object of derision," derived from the traditional translations.

[45] See *HALOT*, 851f. and *BDB*, 772ff.

claim; however he does assert that he has afflicted the deity both by his curse in 1[21] and his plea for the nullification of "Creation" in Chapter 3.

13:18

הנה נא ערכתי משפט ידעתי כי אני אצדק
hnh nʾ ʿrkty mšpṭ ydʿty ky ʾny ʾṣdq
Lo, I have prepared justice;
I know that I am whole.

Pope: See, now, I set forth my case. I know I will be acquitted.

Habel: Now then, I have prepared my lawsuit. I know I should be acquitted.

Clines: You will see that I have drawn up my case. I know that I am in the right!

Job, having scorned the cowardice of the "friends," once again asserts his ability to achieve or even surpass the level of divine "wholeness" **צדק** (*ṣdq*), **צדיק** (*ṣdyq*) and **צדקה** (*ṣdqh*). The *Targum*, anticipating Job's retreat in Chapter 14, reads **ידעית ארום לא אדכי** (*ydʿyt ʾrwm lʾ ʾdky*) – "I now know that I will ***not*** be found innocent."[46]

The phrase **ערך משפט** (*ʿrk mšpṭ*) is unique to the Book of Job, occurring only here and in 23[4].

15:14-15

מה אנוש כי יזכה וכי יצדק ילוד אשה
הן בקדשו לא יאמין ושמים לא זכו בעיניו
mh ʾnwš ky yzkh wky yṣdq ylwd ʾšh
hn bqdšw lʾ yʾmyn wšmym lʾ zkw bʿynyw
What is man that that he deserve merit?
Or how can one born of a woman be whole?
Lo! He has no faith in his *qᵉdôšîm*,
And the heavens have no merit in his eyes.

Pope: How can man be innocent, One born of woman righteous? Even his angels he distrusts, The heavens are not pure in his sight.

Habel: What are mortals that they should be pure, Those born of women that they should be in the right? If he does not trust his holy ones And the heavens are not pure in his eyes…

Clines: What is humankind, that it could be blameless, one born of woman, that such a one could be innocent? If God puts no trust in his holy ones, and the heavens are not clean in his eyes…

---

[46] Stec (1994, 90)

15^{14} is almost identical to 25^{4}, with the exception that the latter is explicit in its expression of comparison with the deity.[47]

Pope has translated בקדשו (*bqdšw*) as "angels" without a plausible reason[48]. Both Habel and Clines simply invoke other translators and commentators in order to justify הן (*hn*) as a conditional. This is simply a vicious circle of scholastic ignorance.[49]

17:9

ויאחז צדיק דרכו וטהר ידים יסיף אמץ

wy'ḥz ṣdyq drkw wṭhr ydym ysyp 'mṣ

And he who is whole holds on to his way;

And he whose hands are clean grows in strength.

Pope: But the righteous retains his force, The clean-handed grows in strength.

Habel: The righteous would hold to their way And the pure of hands grow stronger.

Clines: The righteous maintain their way; those whose hands are clean grow stronger still.

The idioms of each of the two cola of the verse are unique. This is a rejoinder to the rhetorical question that ʾEliphaz posed in his opening remarks of 4^{17}.[50]

None of the translators comprehends the complexity of the concept of **צדיק** (*ṣdyq*) or Job's insinuation that the deity has human physical attributes such as hands. Using ʾEliphaz's own words, Job strongly reaffirms that humanity can aspire to, and indeed achieve, "godly wholeness." "Human wholeness" can hold its own in the face of **יהוה** (YHWH). The "godly wholeness" that is unique to **יהוה** (YHWH) is but an illusion. Job still lives in reverence of **אלהים** (*ʾelohîm*) whose "justice" is immutable and carved in stone. If "wholeness" were to be defined in terms of **אלהים** (*ʾelohîm*), then it would not be relative but absolute—it would apply equally to all.

---

[47] See 25^{4} below

[48] Pope (1973, 116)

[49] For discussion of 15^{15}, see 5^{1} above.

[50] **האנוש מאלוה יצדק אם מעשהו יטהר גבר** (*h'nwš m'lwh yṣdq 'm m'śhw yṭhr gbr*) – Can man be more righteous than *ʾeloah*? Can man be purer than his Creator?

19:25-27

ואני ידעתי גאלי חי ואחרון על עפר יקום
ואחר עורי נקפו זאת ומבשרי אחזה אלוה
אשר אני אחזה לי ועיני ראו ולא זר כלו כליתי בחקי

w'ny yd'ty g'ly ḥy
w'ḥrwn 'l 'pr yqwm
w'ḥr 'wry nqpw z't wmbśry 'ḥzh 'lwh
'šr 'ny 'ḥzh ly
w'yny r'w wl' zr
klw klyty bḥqy

But I know that my Avenger is alive,
And that, as the last one, he will arise upon the dust.
And after they have blinded me, hit me, I will see 'Eloah from my flesh.
It is I who will see for myself;
It is my eyes that will see and not those of a stranger;
My kidneys fail within me.

Pope: I know my vindicator lives, A guarantor upon the dust will stand; Even after my skin is flayed, Without my flesh I shall see God. I will see him on my side, My own eyes will see him no stranger. My heart faints within me.

Habel: I, I know my redeemer lives And afterward he will rise on the dust—After, that is, my skin is peeled off! But from my flesh would I behold 'Eloah; I, I would behold him, not another's—My heart heaves in my breast.

From a Christian theological standpoint, these verses are the highlight of the Book of Job. They have been turned into the promise of unconditional everlasting salvation. Habel comfortingly cites the "voluminous literature" that is to be found. In fact, pursuit of the traditional lines of explanation is not fruitful.

The author's reasons for putting these words into Job's mouth are twofold. First, he recognizes the precariousness of his own stance in pursuing the congruence, if not the similarity of divine and human "wholeness," – **צדק** (*ṣdq*), **צדיק** (*ṣdyq*) and **צדקה** (*ṣdqh*). It is almost as though the arguments of the three "friends" have finally taken their toll. By sheer dint of the mass that opposes him, Job appears ready to crumble and surrender; however, his belief in the validity of his argument wins out. He may not see himself vindicated while in mortal form but he knows that time will prove him right.

Second, and more important, our author adds the eschatological element to his *cache* of weaponry. We may recall from our discussion of the uniqueness of the naming of Job and Ṣemaḥ in Job 1^1,42^7 and Zech.6^{12},3^8 respectively that there was an eschatological or Messianic component to the name of Job.[51] Thus there has existed the possibility of a failure to achieve resolution during the author's own lifetime.

As theologically crucial as these verses have been rendered, this neither surprises us nor constitutes any grand innovative thinking. This possibility has been in the mind of the author on his intellectual pursuit from the very outset.

Once again, the lexical challenges posed by $19^{25,26}$ seem to have provided scholars with the grand theological possibility. Let us examine these verses in detail in order to validate our translation.

גאלי (*g'ly*) – This term, which has been translated variously to suit a particular *agendum*, has specific *BH* antecedent meanings.[52] The Dead Sea Scrolls rarely mention √**גאל** (*g'l*) although they contain a plethora of would-be synonymous terms.[53] The *Targum* uses the √**פרק** (*prq*) "to redeem (through salvation?) for both **גאלי** (*g'ly*) and **אחרון** (*'ḥrwn*).[54] Our use of the tem "avenge" is clearly inadequate since it assumes a crime to which Job does not admit.

It seems that the focus of the problem is the identity of the **גאל** (*g'l*). It would appear on the surface that Job is appealing to the deity; however, it is from that very deity from whom he is seeking "ultimate release." One may well ask whether the author is positing another entity, divine or not, that can stand up to and indeed break the will of the deity that is Job's scourge.

If as we have suggested, our author is *au fait* with Aristotelian thought, then **גאל** (*g'l*) might well be inanimate. It would be the force of logic that prevails over time.

אחרון (*'ḥrwn*) – Pope would like to see this as a parallel to **גאל** (*g'l*), citing Isa.44^6 where the two words appear in parallel cola of the same verse. He states, if somewhat feebly, "If **אחרון** (*'ḥrwn*) is parallel to **גאל** (*g'l*) one may appeal to the Mishnaic and Talmudic term **אחראי** (*'ḥr'y*)[55] in the sense of 'guarantor'."[56]

---

[51] We show again the schematic laid out in our comments on Job 1^1 **איש...איוב שמו** – *'yš... 'ywb šmw* – "A man…Job was his name" and in 42^7 as **עבדי איוב** – *'bdy 'ywb* -" my servant Job." Ṣemaḥ is referred to in Zech.6^{12} as **איש צמח שמו** – *'yš ṣmḥ šmw* – "A man, Ṣemaḥ is his name" and in Zech.3^8 as **עבדי צמח** *'bdy ṣmh* – My servant Ṣemaḥ.

[52] *HALOT*, 169 gives four separate meanings and regards this particular citation as questionable.

[53] That is in an extra-Biblical setting. cf. *4QTanh* (*4Q176*) Frags. 8-11, line 7, which is still a quotation from Isa.54^5.

[54] Stec (1994, 132).

[55] *JAS*, 41.

Habel's arguments are similarly artificial, although he allows in the end that אחרון (*ʾḥrwn*) points "to a time "after" death when Job's vindication happens."[57]

עורי (*ʿwry*) is difficult to translate as either "my skin" or "my awakening." We revocalize עורי (*ʿowrî*) as *ʿawwrî*, the *piʿel* infinitive of √עור (*ʿwr*) – "to make blind" and render it "After my blinding." We thus juxtapose the blinding and the following phrase נקפו זאת (*nqpw zʾt*) "they have hit this [me]."[58]

ומבשרי (*wmbśry*) – "And from my flesh." There is an argument among translators and exegetes as to whether this means "from within my flesh" or "from without my flesh." Of course, all hinges upon the theological *agenda*. From our author's standpoint, the view is very clear. This is an "out-of-body" experience. Job's "ultimate release" will emanate from the force of his own argument, which will overcome all the physical tribulations that he may undergo.

אחזה (*ʾḥzh*) – Our author had any number of words at his disposal to convey the meaning of "seeing" or "beholding." His choice of the √חזה (*ḥzh*) is intended to convey the supernaturalism of the experience that he is describing. √חזה (*ḥzh*) is the verb of choice for prophetic visions and encounters with the deity.[59]

The literal translation of these two verses is entirely consistent with our author's search. If it takes him to his dying day, he will not concede omnipotence and omniscience to the deity. One might go so far as to speculate that our author ponders the role of השטן (*hašśaṭan*) in his role as *hašśaṭan*/YHWH from the Prologue. After all, we have established the character of *hašśaṭan*/YHWH as that of the hard pragmatist.

20:29

זה חלק אדם רשע מאלהים ונחלת אמרו מאל

zh ḥlq ʾdm ršʿ mʾlhym wnḥlt ʾmrw mʾl

This is the portion of a wicked man from *ʾelohîm*

His inheritance by the utterance of ʾEl.

---

[56] Pope (1974, 146) We have mentioned Pope's unexplained statement about the similarity of the Books of Job and Ruth (1974, lxxi). The Book of Ruth is in large part devoted to the concept of √גאל (*gʾl*) as "material redemption" or "reclamation."

[57] Habel (1985, 293).

[58] נקפו (*nqpw*) – derived from the Arabic cognate نقف (*naqafa*) – "to break open the skull." *AED*, 794. This usage is then the *piʿel* of √נקף (*nqp*). cf. Isa.10[34].

[59] See Gen.15[2]; Num.24[4]; Isa.1[1], and *passim* through the Prophets. Also Job 4[13], 7[15], 20[8], 33[16].

Pope: This is the fate of a wicked man. The heritage appointed to him by God.

Habel: This is God's portion for the wicked human, The inheritance ordained for him by ʾEl.

Pope simply omits מאלהים (*mʾlhym*) – "from *ʾelohîm*" citing comparable statements from 8[13] and 27[13] as his only explanation.[60] His discussion of אמרו (*ʾmrw*) is circular and unnecessary. Habel's rendition is literal and he offers no explanation other than that Zophar has sought to condemn Job with his own words.[61]

These words follow the immediately preceding declaration of Job in 19[25-29]. Of course, the crucial word in this verse is מאלהים (*mʾlhym*) – "from *ʾelohîm*." Its invocation by Zophar is the ultimate rebuttal of Job's declaration of relief and salvation. It suddenly places Zophar in a position that merits respect. Our author's placement of the understanding of the significance of אלהים (*ʾlhym*) into the words of Zophar should elevate him *vis-à-vis* Job. Zophar is flatly stating that אלהים (*ʾlhym*) will not rise to the occasion on Job's behalf. Of course, unlike Job, Zophar does not comprehend the immutability of אלהים (*ʾlhym*) and the world order that he represents.[62]

22:3

החפץ לשדי כי תצדק ואם בצע כי תתם דרכיך
hḥpṣ lšdy ky tṣdq wʾm bṣʿ ky ttm drkyk
Does Šadday take pleasure that you are whole?
Of is it of benefit [to him] that you perfect your integrity?

Pope: What good to Shaddai if you are just? What gain if your conduct be perfect?

Habel: Is it a favor to Shaddai if you are righteous? Or his gain if you perfect your ways?[63]

We find the phrase החפץ ליהוה (*hḥpṣ lyhwh*) – "Does YHWH take pleasure" only in 1Sam.15[22]. We read:

---

[60] Pope (1974, 154).
[61] Habel (1985, 315).
[62] That has already been established in 1[1].
[63] Clines' contribution ends at Chapter 20.

החפץ ליהוה בעלות וזבחים כשמע בקול יהוה
הנה שמע מזבח טוב להקשיב מחלב אילים
hḥpṣ lyhwh bʿlwt wzbḥym kšmʿ bqwl yhwh
hnh šmʿ mzbḥ ṭwb lhqšyb mḥlb ʾylym
Does YHWH take [as much] pleasure in burnt offerings and sacrifices,
As in listening to the voice of YHWH?
Behold, listening is better than sacrifice,
Giving ear [better] than the fat of rams.

There can be little doubt that the sentiment of 1Sam.15[22] is being put into the words of ʾEliphaz. In what is the first hint that ʾEliphaz comprehends that Job's *agenda* is the nature of √צדק (*ṣdq*), comes the stinging criticism that Job's ritual piety is of no worth. Of course, our author has made this very suggestion, albeit subliminally, in 1[4,5].

The same principle applies to the phrase ואם בצע (*wʾm bṣʿ*). While the actual wording of the phrase is *hapax legomenon*, the variant מה בצע (*mh bṣʿ*) occurs significantly in two other places in *BH*. We find the question asked by Judah in Gen.37[26] concerning the benefit of killing Joseph and, more to the point in Mal.3[14], where we read:

אמרתם שוא עבד אלהים ומה בצע כי שמרנו משמרתו
ʾmrtm šwʾ ʿbd ʾlhym wmh bṣʿ ky šmrnw mšmrtw
You have said: "The worship of *elohîm* is worthless;
And there no benefit in observing his commandment."

ʾEliphaz drives home his indictment of Job's entire belief structure with a devastating attack on the institution of אלהים (*ʾelohîm*). In a moment of brilliant clarity, our author articulates the core of his quest. It is the suggestion that neither יהוה (YHWH) nor אלהים (*ʾelohîm*) is interested in human destiny, regardless of the degree of perfection of "wholeness" – צדק (*ṣdq*), צדיק (*ṣdyq*) and צדקה (*ṣdqh*).

כי תתם דרכיך (*ky ttm drkyk*)—"that you perfect your integrity" certainly harks back to 4[6], where ʾEliphaz first suggested the futility of תם דרכיך (*tm drkyk*)—"your (Job's) integrity" as a means of influencing the behavior of the deity. It would seem, however, that our author now wishes to probe further. ʾEliphaz is not simply taunting Job's ritual piety; he is asserting the perfection of the way(s) of the deity. He is recalling 2Sam.22[31]:[64]

---

[64] See also the parallel occurrence in ψ18[31].

האל תמים דרכו אמרת יהוה צרופה מגן הוא לכל החסים בו
h'l tmym drkw 'mrt yhwh ṣrwph mgn hw' lkl hḥsym bw
The way of 'El is perfect; The *dictum* of YHWH is pure;
He is a shield for all who take refuge with him.

Perfection, like uniqueness, is absolute and not relative. If the deity already possesses perfection, then perfection is not attainable by anyone else. Our author provides us with a glimpse into the "mindset" of יהוה (YHWH) when he observed to השטן (*haśśaṭan*) in 2^3:

ועדנו מחזיק בתמתו
w'dnw mḥzyq btmtw
Yet he still holds on to his integrity

and an affirmation of the perceptiveness of Job's wife, when she savaged Job in 2^9 with:

עדך מחזיק בתמתך
'dk mḥzyq btmtk
"Do you still hold on to your integrity?"

Both understand clearly that Job's aspiration to perfection is an impossibility. Our author is asking the question, "If man and deity are in the same image, how can a condition of uniqueness apply to either of them?

The superficial meaning of the sentence would appear to affirm that Job must have committed some wrong that incurred the divine wrath. Our application of the author's encrypted system of unique *BH* antecedents reveals his philosophical paradox.

22:19

יראו צדיקים וישמחו ונקי ילעג למו
yr'w ṣdyqym wyśmḥw wnqy yl'g lmw
They see the whole and rejoice;
And scorn the innocent.

Pope: The righteous see and rejoice, The innocent deride them.

Habel: The righteous see and they celebrate; The innocent laugh them to scorn.

Our translators' renditions of this verse are somewhat enigmatic. Contextually, the preceding verses are 'Eliphaz's harangue that demonstrates the futility of wholeness and affirms the success of the wicked despite their sins.

The following verses are an exhortation to put one's trust in the deity. Neither of these scenarios presents an occasion for the whole to rejoice and be scornful. Even as a stand-alone statement, it is internally inconsistent. The only actors in this speech are the "impious wicked"; consequently, they must be the subject and the "whole innocent." the object.

That our rendition is correct is clearly demonstrated if we revisit ψ2⁴:[65]

יושב בשמים ישחק אדני ילעג למו
ywšb bšmym yśḥq ʾdny ylʿg lmw
He that dwells in the heavens shall laugh; *ʾadonay* will scorn them.

The parallel of **יושב בשמים** (*ywšb bšmym*) with **צדיקים** (*ṣdyqym*) and **אדני** (*ʾdny*) with **נקי** (*nqy*) underscores both the sarcasm of ʾEliphaz and the *agenda* of the author. It is consistent with 22³ and is also consistent with the ascription of √**צדק** (*ṣdq*) to both deity and humanity.

25:4

ומה יצדק אנוש עם אל ומה יזכה ילוד אשה
wmh yṣdq ʾnwš ʿm ʾl wmh yzkh ylwd ʾšh
And can man be more whole than ʾEl
And how can one born of a woman be of [more] merit?

Pope: How can a man be just before God, one born of a woman be clean?
Habel: What mortal can be in the right before El? How can one born of woman be cleared of guilt?

This verse is an analog of 15¹⁴ this time out of the mouth of Bildad. Its tone is somber, dark, and pessimistic. No mortal can achieve √**צדק** (*ṣdq*) under any circumstances. Any relational connection between divine √**צדק** (*ṣdq*) and its human counterpart is off the table. The three "friends" have nothing further to say on the subject of **צדק** (*ṣdq*), **צדיק** (*ṣdyq*) and **צדקה** (*ṣdqh*).

A Note on Chapter 26
26:2-4

While chapter 26 contains no reference to √**צדק** (*ṣdq*), it is important to point out that it contains Job's concluding remarks regarding the usefulness of the comments of his "friends." The English idiomatic equivalent of his remarks in

---

[65] We have referenced ψ2 in our discussion of 1⁶ as a *BH* antecedent.

verses 2-4 would be that of the “sunshine soldier,” who is never there when one is in need and armed only with platitudes when he arrives.

26:5-13

In verses 5-13, Job asserts the physical power of a deity whose name is unknown. Also included in this very short chapter (vs. 12-13) is the victory of the deity over his cosmic rivals רהב (*rhb*) and נחש ברח (*nḥš brḥ*). The mention of the cosmic foes also harks back to 7^{12}, where Job bristles at any comparison with them saying:

הים אני אם תנין כי תשים עלי משמר
hym ʾny ʾm tnyn ky tśym ʿly mšmr
Am I Yam or Tannin that you set a watch over me?

26:14

הן אלה קצות דרכו ומה שמץ דבר נשמע בו ורעם גבורתו מי יתבונן
hn ʾlh qṣwt drkw wmh šmṣ dbr nšmʿ bw wrʿm gbwrtw my ytbwnn
Lo! These are the ends of his way,
And nary a whisper is heard on it.
Who comprehends the thunder of his power?[66]

This verse concludes the chapter with the open challenge questioning the meaning of the ways of the deity.

The significance of Chapter 26 lies both in its concise summation of the entire content of Chapters 4-25 and its anticipation of the final dialog between יהוה (YHWH) and Job in 38^{1}-42^{6}.

---

[66] MT corrects with a plural *Qere* דרכיו (*drkyw*)and גבורתיו (*gbwrtyw*) which does not materially alter the sense of the text.

Continuity and Messianism: The Blessing and the Curse The Story of Bilᶜam and the Book of Job

Continuity in the Book of Job

Before continuing further in our investigation, we need to understand how the author is transporting us through this work. As is the case with his method of encryption for the salient portions of the book on which he wishes us to concentrate, he utilizes the story of Bilᶜam (Num.22-24) both as the vehicle of continuity throughout the book and as a contrasting paradigm for Messianism in the Prologue.

Before proceeding to the anatomical analysis of this passage, we must demonstrate the way in which our author used language of the Bilᶜam story as the connective tissue between the various parts of the book. We begin with 3^1:

אחרי כן פתח איוב את פיהו ויקלל את יומו

ʾḥry kn ptḥ ʾywb ʾt pyhw wyqll ʾt ywmw

After that, Job opened his mouth and cursed the day of his birth.

This verse is the analog of the speech of Bilᶜam's ass beginning at Num.22^{28}:

ויפתח יהוה את פי האתון...

wyptḥ yhwh ʾt py h ʾtwn...

And YHWH opened the she-ass' mouth…

3^1 is followed immediately by the formulaic rubric that begins with the words ויען...ויאמר (*wyʾn... wyʾmr*), which literally mean, "and he answered…and said." These are the verbs used in the *BH* to describe Bilᶜam's communication with Balak in Num.22^{18}, 23^{12}, and 23^{26} and it provides a connective tissue throughout the book.

This "Bilᶜam connection" is confirmed at 27^1, and again in 29^1, where we read:

ויסף איוב שאת משלו ויאמר
wysp ʾywb śʾt mšlw wyʾmr
And Job continued to raise his *mašal* and he said:

Consistent with the author's method, the idiom, worded exactly this way, is unique to Job and the *BH* antecedent in Num. 23 and 24:[1]

וישא משלו ויאמר
wyśʾ mšlw wyʾmr
And he raised his *mašal* and he said:

that Bilʿam utters seven times.

Excursus on the Meaning of *BH* משל (*mšl*)

The *BH* **משל** (*mšl*) is not satisfactorily explained by the lexicons.[2] They assign its meaning to a number of possible categories such as "saying," "prophetic, figurative discourse," "wisdom saying," or "song of jest, mocking." However, we may be able to narrow the meaning considerably if we examine the three other occurrences of **נשא משל** (*nśʾ mšl*) and the synonyms that occur as parallels to **משל** (*mšl*).

In addition to its appearance in Job and Numbers as described above, we find **נשא משל** (*nśʾ mšl*) on three other occasions as follows:

Isa.14:3,4

והיה ביום הניח יהוה לך מעצבך ומרגזך
ומן העבודה הקשה אשר עבד בך
ונשאת את המשל הזה מלך בבל ואמרת
איך שבת נגש איך שבתה מדהבה
whyh bywm hnyḥ yhwh lk mʿṣbk wmrgzk
wmn hʿbwdh hqšh ʾšr ʿbd bk
wnśʾtt hmšl hzh ʿl mlk bbl wʾmrt
ʾyk šbt ngś ʾyk šbth mdhbh
When the LORD has given you rest from your pain and turmoil
and the hard service with which you were made to serve,
You will take up this *mašal* against the king of Babylon:
How the oppressor has ceased! How his insolence has ceased!

---

[1] Job 27[1] and 29[1] and Num.23[7,18] and 24[3,15,20,21,23]..
[2] See *BDB* 605 and *HALOT* 648.

LXX reads:

καὶ λήμψῃ τὸν θρῆνον τοῦτον ἐπὶ τὸν βασιλέα Βαβυλῶνος
And you shall take up this lamentation against the king of Babylon

rendering **משל** (*mšl*) as θρῆνος – "dirge" or "lament."

Micah 2:3,4

לכן כה אמר יהוה הנני חשב על המשפחה הזאת רעה
אשר לא תמישו משם צוארתיכם
ולא תלכו רומה כי עת רעה היא
ביום ההוא ישא עליכם משל ונהה נהי נהיה
אמר שדוד נשדנו חלק עמי ימיר
איך ימיש לי לשובב שדינו יחלק

lkn kh ʾmr yhwh hnny ḥšb ʿl hmšpḥh hzʾt rʿh
ʾšr lʾ tmyšw mšm ṣwʾrtykm
wlʾ tlkw rwmh ky ʿt rʿh hyʾ
bywm hhwʾ yśʾ ʿlykm mšl wnhh nhy nyhh
ʾmr šdwd nšdnw ḥlq ʿmy ymyr
ʾyk ymyš ly lšwbb sdynw yḥlq

Therefore thus says the LORD:
I am devising against this family an evil from which you cannot remove your necks;
And you shall not walk haughtily, for it will be an evil time.
On that day they shall take up a *mašal* against you,
And wail with bitter lamentation, and say,
"We are utterly ruined; the LORD alters the inheritance of my people;
How he removes it from me! Among our captors he parcels out our fields."

LXX reads:

ἐν τῇ ἡμέρᾳ ἐκείνῃ λημφθήσεται ἐφ᾽ ὑμᾶς παραβολή
In that day shall a parable be taken up against you,

rendering **משל** (*mšl*) as παραβολή – "parable."

Hab.2:6

הלא אלה כלם עליו משל ישאו ומליצה חידות לו
ויאמר הוי המרבה לא לו עד מתי ומכביד עליו עבטיט

hlʾ ʾlh klm mšl yśʾw wmlyṣh ḥydwt lw
wyʾmr hwy hmrbh lʾ lw ʿd mty wmkbyd ʿlyw ʿbṭyṭ

Shall not everyone raise a *mašal* against him and, with mocking riddles,
Say about him, "Alas for you who heap up what is not your own!"
How long will you load yourselves with goods taken in pledge?

LXX reads:

οὐχὶ ταῦτα πάντα παραβολὴν κατ' αὐτοῦ λήμψονταί
Shall not all these take up a parable against him?

rendering משל (*mšl*) as παραβολη – "parable."

In the Bilʿam story and the three instances cited above, *LXX* is consistent in translating √נשא with λαμβάνειν – "to take."[3] *NRSV* recognizes a problem when it renders משל (*mšl*) both as "taunt" and "taunt song."

In the Bilʿam story. *LXX*[4] translates וישא משלו ויאמר - (*wyśʾ mšlw wyʾmr*) with:

καὶ ἀναλαβὼν τὴν παραβολὴν αὐτοῦ εἶπε
"Taking up his parable, he said"

However, in the Book of Job, *LXX* inexplicably renders שאת משלו ויאמר (*śʾt mšlw wyʾmr*) with:

εἶπεν τῷ προοιμίῳ
[He]said in [his] parable.

The word שאת (*śʾt*) is left untranslated. The translator of the Book of Job seems not only unaware of the idiom but was also unaware of the efforts of his would-be co-translators.

The occurrences of *BH* משל (*mšl*) and its parallel synonyms (other than in Job and Numbers) are as follows:

- שנינה (*šnynh*) – Deut.28[37], 1Kings 9[7], Jer.24[9], 2Chron.7[20].
- מליצה (*mlyṣh*) – Hab.2[6], Prov.1[6].
- חידה (*ḥydh*) – Hab.2[6], ψ49[5], ψ78[2], Prov.1[6].
- קללה (*qllh*) – Jer.24[9].

---

[3] In *BH* Numbers, *LXX* reads – ἀναλαβὼν τὴν παραβολὴν – "taking up his parable." In Job it reads – ἔτι δὲ προσθεὶς Ιωβ εἶπεν τῷ προοιμίῳ – ""

[4] *LXX* evidence may be important since it probably postdates Job by only a short time. Tradition traces the composition of the Septuagint to Alexandria in Egypt in the late 3rd century BCE. However, the *LXX* of Job resembles more a paraphrastic commentary than a strict translation and its wording should be treated with appropriate circumspection. Nonetheless, its Pentateuchal renderings may well reflect current Messianic thinking of the time.

These citations are shown below *in situ* along with the *LXX* rendering:

Deut.28[37]	αἰνίγματι (משל) καὶ παραβολῇ (שנינה)
1Kings 9[7]	εἰς ἀφανισμὸν ((משל)) καὶ εἰς λάλημα (שנינה)
Jer.24[9]	εἰς παραβολὴν (משל) καὶ εἰς μῖσος (שנינה) καὶ εἰς κατάραν (קללה)
Hab.2[6]	παραβολὴν (משל)...καὶ πρόβλημα (מליצה)...καὶ ἐροῦσιν (חידה)
ψ49[5]	εἰς παραβολὴν (משל)...τὸ πρόβλημα (חידה) μου
ψ78[2]	ἐν παραβολαῖς (משל)...προβλήματα (חידה)
Prov.1[6]	παραβολὴν (משל) καὶ σκοτεινὸν (מליצה)...καὶ αἰνίγματα(חידה)
2Chron.7[20]	εἰς παραβολὴν (משל) καὶ εἰς διήγημα (שנינה)

The sheer variety of synonyms offered by *LXX* and the inconsistent application of the Greek to *BH* adequately demonstrate the uncertainty of the understanding of both משל (*mšl*) and its synonyms. What is certain is that In none of these cases does the word משל (*mšl*) or any of its synonyms carry a positive connotation. In fact, in all of the instances cited, there is the air of adversity and uncertainty. This is clearly reflected in the words used in *LXX*. Jer.24[9] specifically equates משל (*mšl*) with קללה (*qllh*) "curse." The idiom משל נשא (*nśʾ mšl*) therefore means "to curse," which is after all precisely what we are talking about. Job's final monologue is an indictment of יהוה (YHWH); משל נשא (*nśʾ mšl*) means "to curse" without actually saying the words—just as described in 1[22] and 2[10].

Thus, if we understand the idiom as just explained, we can surmise that the action intended results in failure or adversity. Bilʿam similarly intends to "curse" Israel but fails. When he opens his mouth he thinks curses but articulates a blessing.

The other side of the connection occurs at 42[8] in the 3rd Epilogue with יהוה (YHWH)'s excoriation of the three "friends" and the description of the sacrifices prescribed by יהוה (YHWH) for their atonement which is an exact reflection of Num.23[1,29].

So much for the Bilʿam[5] story as the major vehicle of continuity in the Book of Job; however, we will now concentrate on the author's "hidden" *agenda* in utilizing the same narrative.[6]

---

[5] The rabbis considered Bilʿam as a major factor in the context of Moses. They thought that Bilʿam was a "wiser, more divinely informed" prophet. See *Sifré* on Deut.34[10].

[6] The Bilʿam story certainly reaches back into antiquity. He is mentioned by his full name as a seer in the Deir ʿAlla inscription, which probably dates to the 7th century BCE. See Hackett (1984).

Bil'am and the Messianic Agenda in the Book of Job

Num.22$^{20\text{-}35}$ may be said to represent the Messianic paradigm for both the Prologue and 3rd Epilogue.[7] We shall deal with it by relevant segment:

Num. 22:20-22

ויבא אלהים אל בלעם לילה ויאמר לו אם לקרא לך באו האנשים קום לך אתם ואך את הדבר אשר אדבר אליך אתו תעשה. ויקם בלעם בבקר ויחבש את אתנו וילך אם שרי מואב.
ויחר אף אלהים כי הולך הוא ויתיצב מלאך יהוה בדרך לשטן לו והוא רכב אתנו ושני נעריו עמו.

wyb' 'lhym 'l bl'm lylh wy'mr lw 'm lqr' lk b'w h'nšym qwm lk 'tm w'k 't hdbr 'šr 'dbr 'lyk 'tw t'śh. wyqm bl'm bbqr wyḥbš 't 'tnw wylk 'm śry mw'b. wyḥr 'p 'lhym ky hwlk hw' wytyṣb ml'k yhwh bdrk lśṭn lw whw' rkb 'l 'tnw wšny n'ryw 'mw.

That night *'elohîm* came to Bil'am and said to him, "If the men have come to summon you, get up and go with them; but do only what I tell you to do." So Bil'am got up in the morning, saddled his she-ass, and went with the officials of Moab. However, *'elohîm*'s anger was kindled because he was going. and YHWH's messenger took his stand in the road as his adversary. Now he was riding on the she-ass, and his two servants were with him.

ויבא אלהים...(ה)לילה (*wyb' 'lhym...(h)lylh*)—"and *'elohîm* came…at night" occurs four times in *BH*, twice in the Bil'am story,[8] once in the case of Abimelech and once in the case of Laban.[9] Both Abimelech and Laban[10] were "evil" characters and we should therefore already expect an unfortunate outcome of the visitation. We might have expected to read **יהוה** (YHWH) for **אלהים** (*'lhym*) in verses 20 and 22. We have shown that Job's **אלהים** (*'lhym*) neither speaks nor "changes his mind," whereas **יהוה** (YHWH) displays both of these attributes.[11] However, we shall see that this narrative places its characters in diametric contrast to those of the Prologue and 3rd Epilogue both thematically and literarily. Thus **אלהים** (*'lhym*) and **יהוה** (YHWH) display the identical polar mood swing that we attribute to **יהוה** (YHWH) alone in the Prologue. **אלהים** (*'lhym*) at first tells Bil'am not to go along with the emissaries of Balak and

---

[7] Num.22$^{20\text{-}35}$ is presented in full in Appendix 1.
[8] See Num.22^{9,20}.
[9] See Gen.20^{3} and 31^{24} respectively.
[10] While the Bil'am story is the most significant, the author avails himself of other literary *BH* devices that have common themes. He uses the stories of Abimelech, in both the Books of Genesis (chapters 20, 21 and 26) and in Judges (chapter 9), as contrasts in evil and the way in which humanity and the deity deal with it.
[11] Adherents of the *Documentary Hypothesis* will identify Num.22$^{20\text{-}22}$ as an E story and Num.20$^{22\text{-}35}$ as a J story—two separate stories of the circumstances under which Bil'am went to see Balak. Our author is looking at the two stories as a single whole (perhaps JE).

Bilʿam complies, then he changes his mind and allows him to go; however, no sooner had Bilʿam saddled up than אלהים (*ʾlhym*) changes his mind in a fit of anger—ויחר אף אלהים (*wyḥr ʾp ʾlhym*)—the same expression used by the author to describe יהוה (YHWH) in 42⁷.[12] The same phrase is then used later in Num.22²⁷ with reference to Bilʿam himself. The ironic humor of the author should not go unnoticed since it is a key part of his reflection on contemporary Messianism.

ויקם בלעם בבקר ויחבש את אתנו...ושני נעריו עמו (*wyqm blʿm bbqr wyḥbš ʾt ʾtnw... wšny nʿryw ʿmw*)—"and Bilʿam arose in the morning and saddled his she-ass... and his two servants were with him." In Gen.22³, we read the following regarding Abraham on his way to sacrifice Isaac:

וישכם אברהם בבקר ויחבש את חמרו...שני נעריו עמו
(*wyšqm ʾbrhm bbqr wyḥbš ʾt ḥmrw... šny nʿryw ʿmw*
So Abraham got up early in the morning,
saddled his ass...and his two servants were with him.

The two phrases are identical in structure; they differ only as to the following vocabulary: ויקם (*wyqm*) for וישכם (*wyšqm*) and אתנו (*ʾtnw*) for חמרו(*ḥmrw*). The differences are subtle but telling. וישכם (*wyšqm*)has a cultic connotation, as in "getting up early to perform a ritual" (והשכים (*whšqym*) as we read in the case of Job in 1⁵), whereas ויקם (*wyqm*) has the simple meaning of "getting up in the morning." אתנו (*ʾtnw*) and חמרו (*ḥmrw*) are the she-ass and the male ass respectively. While the male ass is simply a beast of burden in Gen.20³, the she-ass plays an active role in the Bilʿam story.

ויתיצב מלאך יהוה בדרך לשטן לו (*wytyṣb mlʾk yhwh bdrk lśṭn lw*)—"and YHWH's messenger took his stand in the road in order to be his adversary." Here we have a phrase with compound relevant associations. ויתיצב (*wytyṣb*) is the verb used in 1⁶ of the בני האלהים (*bny hʾlhym*)—"the sons of the gods." While we have identified the *BH* antecedent of this phrase as ψ2², there can be no doubting that this occurrence is congruent, especially since we have the explanation that follows, namely, לשטן לו (*lśṭn lw*)—"in order to be his

---

[12] There is a case to be made for reading האלהים (*hʾlhym*) for אלהים (*ʾlhym*) in Num.22^{9,12,20} since האלהים (*hʾlhym*) appears in Num.22¹⁰ and 23²⁷. We have already established the equivalence of האלהים (*hʾlhym*) and יהוה (YHWH); thus we would eliminate the need to assign אלהים (*ʾlhym*) and יהוה (YHWH) the same character attributes.

adversary." We are informed quite clearly that the purpose of מלאך יהוה (*ml'k yhwh*)—"YHWH's messenger" is to prevent Bilʿam from fulfilling the mission on which he had been divinely sent. This notion is reinforced by the scene set in Zech.3^{1}, in which we read:[13]

ויראני את יהושע הכהן הגדול עמד לפני מלאך יהוה והשטן עמד על ימינו לשטנו
wyr'ny 't yhwšʿ hkhn hgdwl ʿmd lpny ml'k yhwh whśṭn ʿmd ʿl ymynw lśṭnw
And he (Yahweh) showed me Joshua the High Priest
Standing before YHWH's messenger;
And *haśśaṭan* was standing to his (Joshua's) right side to be his adversary.

We shall return to Zech. 3^{1} later in our discussion of Messianism.

Num. 22:23

ותרא האתון את מלאך יהוה נצב בדרך וחרבו שלופה בידו
ויך בלעם את האתון להטתה הדרך

wtr' h'twn 't ml'k yhwh nṣb bdrk wḥrbw šlwph bydw
ʿmw. wtr' h'twn 't ml'k yhwh nṣb bdrk wḥrbw šlwph bydw
wtṭ h'twn wtlk bśdh yk blʿm 't h'twn lhṭth hdrk.
And the she-ass saw YHWH's messenger standing in the road,
With a drawn sword in his hand;
So the she-ass turned off the road, and went into the field;
And Bilʿam struck the she-ass, to turn it back onto the road.

ותרא האתון את מלאך יהוה נצב בדרך וחרבו שלופה בידו (*wtr' h'twn 't ml'k yhwh nṣb bdrk wḥrbw šlwph bydw*)—" The she-ass saw YHWH's messenger standing in the road, with a drawn sword in his hand." In keeping with the author's methodology, we find that this phrase occurs in *BH* only here and in 1Chron.21^{16} where we read of David:

(וישא דויד את עיניו) וירא את מלאך יהוה
(עמד בין הארץ ובין השמים) וחרבו שלופה בידו
(*wyś' dwyd 't ʿynyw*) *wyr' 't ml'k yhwh*
(*ʿmd byn h'rṣ wbyn hšmym*) *wḥrbw šlwph bydw*

---

[13] In the same way, we find מלאך יהוה (*ml'k yhwh*)—"YHWH's messenger" in Gen.22^{11} where he prevents Abraham from sacrificing his son Isaac.

(And David looked up) and he saw YHWH's messenger
(Standing between the earth and the heavens,) with a drawn sword in his hand.[14]

While this observation may appear to be tangential, we must include it since it links yet another passage to the Job and Bilʿam stories and the Messianic discussion. 1Chron.21[1] reads as follows.

ויעמד שטן על ישראל ויסת את דויד למנות את ישראל
yʿmd śṭn ʿl yśrʾl wyst ʾ tdwyd lmnwt ʾt yśrʾl
And Satan stood against Israel
And incited David to count (the people of) Israel.

We compare this verse to its parallel in 2Sam.24[1]:

ויסף אף יהוה לחרות בישראל ויסת את דוד בהם לאמר
לך מנה את ישראל ואת יהודה
wysp ʾp yhwh lḥrwt byśrʾl wyst ʾt dwd bhm lʾmr
lk mnh ʾt yśrʾl wʾt yhwdh
And YHWH was again angry with Israel and he incited David against them, saying;
Go count (the people of) Israel and Judah.

We have here a crystal clear example of the dichotomous, polarized relationship between **יהוה** (YHWH) and **(ה)שטן** ([*haś*]*śaṭan*) that we have described in our treatment of the Prologue. There was a clear prohibition[15] against the taking of a military census. While the author(s) of 1Chronicles and 2Samuel split the identity of the protagonist, they both agree that David was (deceitfully) "incited" to take such a census. The word they both use to describe "incite" is √**סות** (*swt*) which is the term used in the Prologue by **יהוה** (YHWH) in his accusation of **השטן** (*haśśaṭan*).[16]

Num.22: 26-31

ויפתח יהוה את פי האתון ותאמר לבלעם מה עשיתי לך כי הכיתני זה שלש רגלים.
ויאמר בלעם לאתון כי התעללת בי לו יש חרב בידי כי עתה הרגתיך. ותאמר האתון אל בלעם
כי אנכי אתנך אשר רכבת עלי מעודך עד היום הזה ההסכן הסכנתי לעשת לך כה . ויגל יהוה
את עיני בלעם וירא את מלאך יהוה נצב בדרך וחרבו שלפה בידו ויקד וישתחו לאפיו.

---

[14] The only other occurrence of **וחרבו שלופה בידו** (*wḥrbw šlwph bydw*) is in Jos.5[13] where the holder of the sword is described as **שר צבא יהוה** (*śr ṣbʾ yhwh*) "commander of the army of the Yahweh."

[15] See 1Chron.21[7] and 2Sam.24[1].

[16] See 2[3].

wyptḥ yhwh ʾt py hʾtwn wtʾmr lblʿm mh ʿśyty lk ky hkytny zh šlš rglym. wyʾmr blʿm lʾtwn ky htʿllt by lw yš ḥrb bydy ky ʿth hrgtyk. wtʾmr hʾtwn ʾlblʿm ky ʾnky ʾtnk ʾšr rkbt ʿly mʿwdk ʿd hywm hzh hhskn hsknty lʿśt lk kh. wygl yhwh ʾt ʿyny blʿm wyrʾ ʾt mlʾk yhwh nṣb bdrk wḥrbw šlwph bydw wyqd wyštḥw lʾpyw.

Then YHWH opened the mouth of the she-ass, and it said to Bilʿam, "What have I done to you, that you have struck me these three times?" Bilʿam said to the she-ass, "Because you have made a fool of me! I wish I had a sword in my hand! I would kill you right now!" But the she-ass said to Bilʿam, "Am I not your she-ass, which you have ridden all your life to this day? Do I take care of you in such a way?" And he said, "No." Then YHWH opened Bilʿam's eyes, and he saw YHWH's messenger standing in the road, with his drawn sword in his hand; and fell prostrate on his face.

We can compare, albeit more loosely, the pragmatic questions posed by the she-ass to Bilʿam and his answers in the passage cited above with the fantastical interchange between Isaac and Abraham in Gen.22 [7-8,10]:

ויאמר יצחק אל אברהם אביו ויאמר אבי ויאמר הנני בני
ויאמר הנה האש והעצים ואיה השה לעלה.
ויאמר אברהם אלהים יראה לו לעלה בני וילכו שניהם יחדו...
וישלח אברהם את ידו ויקח את המאכלת לשחט את בנו.

wyʾmr yṣḥq ʾl ʾbrhm ʾbyw wyʾmr ʾby wyʾmr hnny bny
wyʾmr hnh hʾš whʿṣym wʾyh hśh lʿlh
wyʾmr ʾbrhm ʾlhym yrʾh lw hśh lʿlh bny wylkw šnyhm yḥdw...
wyšlḥ ʾbrhm ʾt ydw wyqḥ ʾt hmʾklt lšḥṭ ʾt bnw

And Isaac said to his father Abraham "My father."
And Abraham answered, "I am here, my son."
And (Isaac) said, "Here are the fire and the timbers,
But where is the lamb for the burnt offering?"
And Abraham said, " *ʾelohîm* will provide the lamb for the burnt offering."
And the two of them went off together…
And Abraham stretched forth his hand and took the sacrificial knife to slaughter his son.

Bilʿam's she-ass asks the practical question after the fact. Bilʿam answers weakly about looking foolish and volunteers an action that he might undertake were the circumstances right. The she-ass cannot accept Bilʿam's answer and takes him to task with a further question in Num.22[30]:

ההסכן הסכנתי לעשות לך כה
hskn hskty lʿśwt lk kh
…do I take care of you in such a way?...

to which Bilʿam can only answer with a dumbstruck "no."

√סכן (*skn*) occurs in *BH* only in the Books of Numbers and Job.[17] This is no coincidence. The speakers are ʾEliphaz and ʾElihu, who are at complete odds on the subject of access to and care of the deity. ʾEliphaz maintains that interaction between humanity and the deity may be direct while ʾElihu advocates the need for an intermediary, for which position he fancies himself a candidate. It would seem quite clear that by putting the words of Bilʿam's she-ass in their respective mouths, our author drives the Messianic theme with a markedly pejorative and ironic slant.[18]

Isaac asks a matter-of-fact question of Abraham about an event that is to take place in the future. Abraham gives a fantastical answer about divine assistance (which Isaac unquestioningly accepts) and proceeds to go about his business. Neither the she-ass nor Isaac is in any position to affect the outcome of their predicament.

By way of contrast, it is not Job who questions or is questioned. It is יהוה (YHWH) himself who asks the question of השטן *haśśaṭan*, who in turn gives him the unsparing answer. The divine is intervening in human affairs without invitation. Job is himself aware only of his immediate circumstances; when he realizes what is happening, he understands that he is not in control of his predicament—he "fails" because he is not divine.

The pervasiveness of Bilʿam-linked vocabulary through both the prose and poetic portions argues strongly for the single authorship of the entire Book of Job. We shall see this further supported when we deal with Num.23^{20}.

The "Blessing" and the "Curse": √ברך(*brk*) in the Bilʿam Story

We have treated √ברך(*brk*) on several occasions in our discussion of the Prologue. These occasions are somewhat widespread since they are based on the

---

[17] Num.22^{30} and Job 15^{3}, 22^{2}, 22^{21}, 34^{9},35^{3}. There are several forms of √סכן (*skn*)—we refer to I √סכן (*skn*) which has an underlying meaning of "to care for." See *BDB*, 698; *HALOT*, 755. The word occurs in the El Amarna tablets as *sú-ki-na* (sing. abs. 362^{69}) and *sú-ki-ni* (sing. cons. 256^{9}) see *DNWSI*, 755; *AHw*. 1011a.

[18] It is interesting to note that the entire *dramatis personae* of the Book of Job is linked together at once in a *midrash* of *Tanna d'Bei Eliahu Rabbah* 26,5:

אליפז התימני וצופר הנעמתי ובלדד השוחי ואליהוא בן ברכאל הבוזי
ואיוב מארץ עוץ בלעם בן בעור האחרון שבכולם

This is an interesting aside in that the story concerns the fact that God had to reveal everything that he was planning for the world to Bilʿam so that when the Israelites accepted of the Torah, the nations of the world could not plead ignorance for not having accepted it first. This grouping of the cast of the Book of Job does not portray any of them favorably.

individual occurrences of the verb. The story of Bilʿam is the showcase *par excellence* not only for the verb and its semantic range but also for its antonym, "to curse."[19]

√ברך(*brk*) occurs in the Bilʿam story on seven separate occasions.[20] On each of these occasions it carries the explicit meaning of "to bless." It is also the only word used to express "blessing."

On the other hand, we find several expressions of "cursing." They are √קבב(*qbb*),[21] √ארר(*ʾrr*),[22] and √זעם(*zʿm*)[23], Each of these carries a subtle *nuance*; however, the overall intent is clear.

The one other instance of "blessing" and "cursing" is Num.23^{20}, which reads as follows:

הנה ברך לקחתי וברך ולא אשיבנה
hnh brk lqḥty wbrk wlʾ ʾšybnh

The verse seems to pose a problem for all translators. *NRSV*, along with other translations, renders this verse:

> See, I received a command to bless; he has blessed, and I cannot revoke it.

LXX recognizes a problem and reads:

> ἰδοὺ εὐλογεῖν παρείλημμαι εὐλογήσω καὶ οὐ μὴ ἀποστρέψω
> Behold, I have received (an order) to bless: I will bless, and not turn back.

Perhaps LXX is reading ואברך (*wʾbrk*). The 3rd person perfect of the Hebrew (albeit with an irregular vocalization) is rendered in the 1st person future but the verb is still translated as meaning "blessing."

We render the verse as follows:

---

[19] We use the English translation since *BH* uses a variety of verbs as we shall demonstrate. It is one of the rare occasions when the translation may be more succinct than the original text.
[20] Num.$22^{6,12}$, $23^{11,20}$, 23^{25}, $24^{1,9,10}$ not including emphatic reduplications in Num.22^{6}, $23^{11,25}$, and 24^{10}.
[21] See Num.$22^{11,17}$,$23^{8,11,13,25,27}$, 24^{10}. See also Job 3^{8}, 5^{3}.
[22] See Num.$22^{6,12}$, 23^{7}, 24^{9}. See also Job 3^{8}.
[23] See Num. $23^{7,8}$,

הנה ברך לקחתי וברך ולא אשיבנה
hnh brk lqḥty wbrk wlʾ ʾšybnh
Behold, I took a curse (with me);
But he (Yahweh) has blessed and I will not answer (it).

Only on this occasion do we find √ברך (*brk*) meaning both "to bless" and "to curse" in the same verse. This is usage of √ברך (*brk*) is entirely consistent with our author's application in the Prologue.[24] It is in fact the *locus classicus* for the contrasting uses of√ברך (*brk*).

If we analyze the syntax, we find that it is really the only reasonable sense of the verse. ברך (*brk*) is the infinitive absolute in the first colon; וברך (*wbrk*) is the 3rd person singular perfect. The word play is exquisite.

Even more remarkable is the way the turn of phrase is exactly reflected in Job's rejection of יהוה (YHWH) in 40^4:[25]

הן קלתי מה אשיבך
hn qlty mh ʾšybk
Behold, I have cursed [you], what shall I answer you?

The form is uncannily true. If we juxtapose the two passages (citing Numbers first and Job second) we find that for הנה (*hnh*) we have the Aramaized הן (*hn*)[26]. וברך (*wbrk*) is paralleled by קלתי (*qlty*). ולא (*wlʾ*) has its equivalent in מה (*mh*)—which can carry a negative connotation.[27] Finally, אשיבנה (*ʾšybnh*) and אשיבך (*ʾšybk*) are from the same root and require no further comment..

Jewish Messianism in the Book of Job

We have already made comment regarding the political and religious unrest of the Second Temple period and how it spawned a variety of Messianic movements.

Before dealing with programmatic Messianism, we need to deal with its terminology, specifically as it relates to the Book of Job. It is axiomatic that our author expresses his views in a code that we have described in detail in the Introduction. It is therefore not surprising that there is no explicit mention of any Messianic nomenclature in the Book of Job. We must then turn to the underlying texts that form the basis of the code.

---

[24] See discussion of 1^5 above.
[25] See discussion of $40^{1\text{-}5}$ below.
[26] This form occurs (27) times in Pentateuch and more frequently in the remainder of *BH*.
[27] See *GKC* §137 *b*.

The eschatological term באחרית הימים (*b'ḥryt hymym*) appears in the Pentateuch in Gen.49[1], Num.24[14], and Deut.4[30], 31[29]. The first is the "prognostication" of Jacob to each of his sons individually by name; the second is the final "oracle" of Bilʿam regarding Israel and its neighbors; the last two are from "testamentary" speeches of Moses (the first regarding a return of Israel to Yahweh after a time of trouble and the second predicting the departure of Israel from Yahweh after Moses' death). In the rest of *BH*, Hosea 3[5] is a lone specific reference to David.[28]

We have already described the *nexus* between Job, Genesis, and Numbers; we can therefore conclude that it is to either or both Gen.49[1] and Num.24[14] that the author intends us to refer.

The Messianic reference in the speech of Jacob to his sons appears in his prediction for Judah in Gen.49 [8-12], specifically verse 10:

לא יסור שבט מיהודה ומחקק מבין רגליו...
l' yswr šbṭ myhwdh wmḥqq mbyn rglyw...
The scepter shall not depart from Judah, or the ruler's staff from between his feet...

which *LXX* translates somewhat obliquely:

οὐκ ἐκλείψει ἄρχων ἐξ Ιουδα καὶ ἡγούμενος ἐκ τῶν μηρῶν αὐτοῦ...
A ruler shall not fail from Judah, nor a prince from his thighs...

The equivalent reference in the final "oracle" of Bilʿam[29] is Num.24[17], which reads in part as follows:

...דרך כוכב מיעקב וקם שבט מישראל...
... *drk kwkb myʿqb wqm šbṭ myśr'l*...
...a star shall come out of Jacob, and a scepter shall rise out of Israel...

LXX renders the verse:

ἀνατελεῖ ἄστρον ἐξ Ιακωβ καὶ ἀναστήσεται ἄνθρωπος ἐξ Ισραηλ[30]
...a star shall arise out of Jacob and a man stand up out of Israel...

---

[28] Other *BH* occurrences are Isa.2[2] (the eschatological supremacy of Zion echoed in Mic.4[1]); Jer.23[20] (a very bizarre promise echoed in 30[24]); Jer.48[47], 49[39] (prophecies against Moab and Elam respectively); Ezek.38[16] (the coming reign of Gog). See also *4Q504* 1-2 iii,13; *11Q12* ii, 4.

[29] See Num.24[14-24].

[30] *LXX* renders דרך (*drk*) as ἀνατελει – "will rise." Similarly, *LXX* renders צמח (*ṣmḥ*) – literally "branch" and ἀνατολή – "the rising."

We can immediately notice the discrepancy between the *LXX* renditions of the two occurrences of the word **שבט** (*šbṭ*). It is confusing enough knowing that the Hebrew **שבט** (*šbṭ*) can normally signify both "scepter" and "tribe" (although the meaning of "scepter" is quite clearly intended in this case). *LXX* renders **שבט** (*šbṭ*) as ἄρχων – "ruler" in Gen.49[10], and ἄνθρωπος – "man" in Num.24[17]. *LXX* sheds no light on the problem other than to expose the fact that there exists the possibility either of alternate readings or a difference in politico-religious leaning.

The other key difference between the two verses lies in the names mentioned therein. Gen.49[10] speaks of "Judah" while Num.24[17] addresses "Israel." This is significant in that it potentially identifies the "messiah" as either being from Judah in the south or from Israel in the north. The two regions seem to have differed on whether the "messiah" would be "royal/military" (i.e. of Davidic lineage) or "priestly" (i.e. Aaronide or Zadokite) or perhaps even a combination of the two.

The Dead Sea Scrolls, while quite explicit on the subject of Messianism, are ambiguous as to the attributes of the "messiah." All three possibilities just mentioned are contained within them.

The Davidic "messiah" is clearly articulated in *4Q252 Commentary on Genesis A* v ll.1-4:

...]לו[א יסור שליט משבט יהודה בהיות ישראל ממשל
[לוא י]כרת יושב כסא לדויד כי המחקק היא ברית המלכות [ואל]פי ישראל המה הדגלים
עד בוא משיח הצדק צמח דויד כי לו ולזרעו נתנה ברית מלכות עמו עד דורות עולם

lw᾿ yswr šlyṭ mšbṭ yhwdh bhywt yśr᾿l mmšl
lw᾿ ykrt ywšb ks᾿ dwyd ky hmḥqq hy᾿ bryt hmlkwt w᾿lpy yśr᾿l hmh hdglym
ʿd bw᾿ mšyḥ hṣdq ṣmḥ dwyd ky lw wlzrʿw ntnh bryt mlkwt ʿmw ʿd dwrwt ʿwlm

The scepter shall [no]t depart from the tribe of Judah.
While Israel has dominion, there [shall not] be cut off
One who sits on the throne of David.
For the "staff" is the covenant of kingship,
[And the thou]sands of Israel are the "standards."
Until the Messiah of Righteousness comes, the branch of David.
For to him and to his descendants has been given
The covenant of the kingship of his people for generations everlasting.

There are several points of interest in the *DSS* citation. First, we find the use of the word **שליט** (*šlyṭ*) for "scepter" and the word **שבט** (*šbṭ*) used to mean "tribe." Second, the "messiah" is described as **משיח הצדק צמח דויד** (*mšyḥ hṣdq ṣmḥ dwyd*) – "Messiah of Righteousness, the branch of David." This latter description contains the two key words צמח (*ṣmḥ*) – "branch" and צדק (*ṣdq*) – "wholeness" that we have identified as the object of the author's investigation.

In our discussion of 1[1] above, we identified Job with the "messiah" named *Ṣemaḥ* (צמח) as described in Zech.3[1], 6[12]. This *Ṣemaḥ* (צמח), as articulated by Zechariah, finds its origins both in the Pentateuch and in the words of Isaiah[31] and especially Jeremiah[32] who operated during late First Temple times.

Zechariah's Visions (Zech. 3-6)

יהושע (Joshua) the son of Jehozadak the High Priest is pictured in a scene standing before the "messenger of YHWH,"[33] with the Satan—השטן (*haśśaṭan*)—standing to his right as adversary[34]. The Satan—השטן (*haśśaṭan*) is rebuked by the Lord, and יהושע (Joshua) is called "a brand plucked from the fire" and is commanded to remove his filthy clothing and to put on apparel prepared for him by Yahweh.

After the "messenger of YHWH" challenges יהושע (Joshua) to "walk in the way of YHWH," as a condition for fulfilling the role of judge and leader in the reconstructed Jerusalem, the following promise is given: "Hear now, O יהושע (Joshua) the high priest...for behold, I will bring forth my servant the "Branch."[35]

In the following context, the "Branch" seems to refer to Zerubbabel (who was the "royal Davidic pretender" among the returnees from the Babylonian Exile), and in 4[14], the prophet Zechariah receives a vision of "two olive branches" which symbolize "the two anointed ones that stand by the Lord of the whole earth"—apparently יהושע (Joshua) and Zerubbabel (זרבבל). A little later, Zechariah is told to make a crown and set it on the head of יהושע (Joshua) the high priest, and to say to him "Behold a man whose name is "Branch" (צמח—*ṣmḥ*—ἀνατολή) —he shall rise out of his place and he shall build the temple of YHWH... and shall sit and rule on his throne, and the council of peace shall be between them both...."

---

[31] See Isaiah 4[2], although this reference is not clearly proto-Messianic.

[32] See Jer.23[5] in particular and also 33[14].

[33] מלאך יהוה (*ml'k yhwh*).

[34] This is the same השטן (*haśśaṭan*) that we encountered in the first two chapters of the Book of Job.

[35] *LXX* 'Ανατολη "rising/sprouting." See above.

Those scholars who would identify *Ṣemaḥ* (צמח) with Zerubbabel (זרבבל) do so on the basis of Zech.4^{9}:[36]

ידי זרבבל יסדו את הבית הזה וידיו תבצענה
ydy zrbbl ysdw ʾt hbyt hzh wydyw tbṣʿnh
The hands of Zerubbabel shall found this house
And his hands shall complete it.[37]

יהושע (Joshua) the son of Jehozadak

Apart from the verse just cited, Zechariah's vision of *Ṣemaḥ* (צמח) leans more toward the portrayal of a "priestly Messiah." This would be the High Priest יהושע (Joshua) the son of Jehozadak, the high priestly associate of Zerubbabel and Nehemiah during the return of the Jews from Babylon and the rebuilding of the Temple.[38] As is perhaps to be expected for both lexical and historical reasons, the name יהושע (Joshua) figures prominently in the propagation of Messianic movements.

It may well be that this יהושע (Joshua) was a member of the rather extensive division of the priesthood which was also known as "the house of יהושע (Joshua)."[39]

Another possible source for an early יהושע (Joshua) Messianology, is the third chapter of Habakkuk, which at one time circulated both separately from, and, as we now have it, appended to the Book of Habakkuk.[40] For the most part, chapter 3, sometimes known as the *Psalm of Habakkuk*, recounts the glory of Yahweh in his mastery over nature, and his mighty deeds on behalf of his people. However, Hab.3^{13a} reads:

---

[36] See Rose (2000,17ff.). Rose's entire work is devoted to this subject. He ultimately throws doubt upon any theory, be it either of a "priestly" or "monarchic" Messiah. He is not aware of the evidentiary material adduced by the author of the Book of Job, which, although encrypted, nevertheless forces some kind of Messianic identification for the mid-2nd Temple period.

[37] The etymology of תבצענה (*tbṣʿnh*) is uncertain. The translation is based on the *LXX* rendering ἐπιτελέσουσιν – "will successfully complete," for which there is no lexical or cognate basis. √בצע (*bṣʿ*) means "to cut, sever" and in Mishnaic Hebrew "to settle, compromise."

[38] See Collins (1995, 29ff.).

[39] See 1Chron.24^{11}; Ezra 2^{36,40}; Neh.7^{39}.

[40] The third chapter of Habakkuk is not addressed in the Dead Sea Scrolls *pesher* on Habakkuk (*1QpHab*).

יצאת לישע עמך לישע את משיחך
yṣʾt lyšʿ ʿmk lyšʿ ʾt mšyyḥk
You came forth to save your people, to save your anointed.

One might well imagine the potential that the words ישע (*yšʿ*) and משיח (*mšyḥ*) would offer to an *eschaton*-oriented communities. The Qumran *pesher* on Habakkuk does not include an interpretation of chapter 3.

Given the expectation of a "priestly" as well as a "military" or "royal" Messiah, *LXX* interpretation could also integrate the high priestly יהושע (Joshua) figure into this "Joshua" - based Messianology by means of the *LXX* ἀνατολὴ-ἀνατελεῖ similarities between Zech.3[8], 6[12] and Num.24[17], as mentioned above.

יהושע (Joshua son of Nun) or Ἰησοῦς ὁ τοῦ Ναυη

The name יהושע (Joshua) in *BH* includes an otherwise unknown "city governor,"[41] and the land-owner of Beth Shemesh into whose field the cows draw the cart that carried the Ark of the Covenant when it was recovered from the Philistines.[42] Most familiar, however, is יהושע (Joshua son of Nun), or, as the *LXX* idiomatically calls him, Ἰησοῦς ὁ τοῦ Ναυη.[43] This ancient יהושע (Joshua son of Nun) is mentioned in several Pentateuchal episodes before he finally becomes Moses' successor and leads Israel into the "promised land." We first see him leading the Israelite army against ʿAmalek and the ʿAmalekites.[44] Moses, Aaron, and Ḥur watch the battle from a nearby hill, and whenever Moses' arms are raised, the battle favors Israel, but when they are lowered, ʿAmalek gains the advantage. יהושע (Joshua son of Nun) and his forces defeat ʿAmalek. Moses conveys to יהושע (Joshua son of Nun) YHWH's promise that the name and memory of ʿAmalek will ultimately be blotted out forever.

Later in Exodus, we find יהושע (Joshua son of Nun) on Mt. Sinai with Moses[45] and ministering in the "Tent of Meeting" after YHWH speaks to Moses.[46] In Numbers-Deuteronomy, the story is told how Moses had changed יהושע (Joshua son of Nun)'s name from הושע (*hosheʿa*) to יהושע (*yehoshuʿa*),[47] how of the twenty spies he and Caleb alone encouraged the conquest of

---

[41] See 2 Kings 23[8].
[42] See 1 Sam.6[14]ff.
[43] *LXX* also refers to him as Ιησοῦς υἱὸς Ναυη, the literal rendition of יהושע בן נון.
[44] See Ex.17[8].
[45] See Ex.24[13], 32[17].
[46] See Ex.33[11].
[47] See Num.13[16] ff.

Canaan,[48] and how he was divinely chosen and dedicated for the task of leading Israel into the land and distributing the land to the tribes.[49] For this latter role, he received the "spirit of wisdom," like Moses,[50] and the commission of YHWH.[51]

We also find clues to the existence of a "יהושע (Joshua son of Nun)" Messianology in certain *DSS* passages. *4Q175 Testimonia* in particular juxtaposes the Mosaic "prophet" passage from Deut.18^{15},[52] the "star and scepter" oracle from Num.24^{15}, a portion from the "blessing" on Levi in Deut.33^{8}, and a passage from *4Q379 Psalms of Joshua* dealing with Joshua's curse on the city of Jericho.[53] Similarly, the "star and scepter" testimony appears in the *War Scroll* in the context of the final battle between the forces of God and the evil world dominion.[54] It is unlikely that these similarities are purely coincidental.

Perhaps the most important Jewish יהושע (Joshua) Messianology comes from the Samaritan book of the *Secrets of Moses* or *ʾAsatir*.[55] According to Gaster, the *ʾAsatir* was compiled around the end of the 3rd century BCE[56] and has close affinities with the Palestinian *Targum* to the Pentateuch, the *Sibylline Oracles* and with some of Josephus' extra-canonical traditions. In its comments on the "oracles" of Bilʿam, we find the following passage:[57]

ומה דאמר מלאכה לבלעם
דרך כוכב מיעקב והו פינחס
וקם שבט מישראל זה יהושע

wmh dʾmr mlʾkh lblʿm
drk kwkb myʿqb whw pynḥs
wqm šbṭ myśrʾl whw yhwšʿ

and what did the "Messenger" say to Bilʿam?
"A star shall arise from Jacob"—that is Phinehas,
"and a scepter shall come from Israel"—that is Joshua.

---

[48] See Num.14^{6} ff. Levin (1978, 4ff.) makes a persuasive argument for בן נון (*bn nwn*) as a theophoric patronym. If Levin is right, then the Moses/Joshua association described below is all the more reinforced.

[49] Num.27^{18} ff; 34^{17}

[50] See Deut.34^{9}.

[51] See Note 20 above.

[52] See also Samaritan Pentateuch Ex.20^{21},

[53] See also Jos.6^{26}.

[54] See *1QM* 11.6ff.

[55] Gaster (1927)

[56] Although the earliest MSS are dated much later.

[57] *ʾAsatir* 10.45 to Num.24^{17}.

פינחס (Pinḥas) was the young priest hero, the grandson of Aaron, who had applied preventive measures against the plague sent upon Israel for immoral conduct by impaling on his spear a young Israelite and his Midianite sexual partner. In Rabbinic thought, one meets with the idea that פינחס (Pinḥas) will return in the form of Elijah.[58] Upon his death, יהושע (Joshua son of Nun) is referred to as "servant of YHWH."[59] In the Samaritan *Asatir*, it seems that פינחס (Pinḥas) and יהושע (Joshua son of Nun) are pictured respectively as the priestly and royal successors to Aaron and Moses—the priestly and kingly "messiahs."

Perhaps the most significant attribute of יהושע (Joshua son of Nun) is that he was of the tribe of Ephraim. The implication is that he was from Israel in the north in contrast to David who represented the Messianic hopes of Judah in the south. The appearance of his name in a Samaritan Messianology is not out of place.

Thus יהושע (Joshua son of Nun) and פינחס (Pinḥas in the Samaritan tradition) replace Moses and Aaron as the civil and priestly leaders of Israel.[60] Nodet makes a strong case for the existence of Moses and Joshua as legislators each in their own right. Joshua's support base was non-Levitical in Shechem, while Moses and Aaron were connected to a patriarchal, pre-Sinaitic Bethel.[61] While Nodet regards the argument as hypothetical, it certainly explains the promotion of יהושע (Joshua son of Nun) in the Samaritan *Asatir* citation above.

The usual application of the "star and scepter" passage in later Samaritan literature, however, is not to פינחס (Pinḥas) and יהושע (Joshua son of Nun) but to the expected "Restorer," the *Taheb* (תהב *thb*), who fulfills the role of the "prophet like Moses" promised in Deut. 34^{10}. The *Taheb* (תהב *thb*) is indeed a second Moses. He will rebuild the Temple at Gerizim and give his Law to the world; he will be of the house of Levi or will be accompanied by a high priest from the order of פינחס (Pinḥas) and will restore the favor of God to his people.

The Samaritan "Messianic doctrine" is relatively clearly articulated. The term used is התהב (*hthb*) or תהבה (*thbh*), which has been variously explained as "the restorer" or "he who returns." During all the time that has elapsed since the schism of Eli (1 Sam.1 *passim* for the story of the establishment of a priestly worship center at Shiloh) and the disappearance of the Tabernacle (see Amos 9^{11} סכת דויד הנפלת – *śkt dwd hnplt*), Israel has been suffering by reason of divine

---

[58] See *Pirke d'Rabbi Eliezer*, 46.
[59] See Jos.24^{29}.
[60] Nodet (1997, 169 ff.).
[61] Nodet (1997, 191 ff.) sees the first appearance of the Pentateuch as a very late redaction, perhaps 250-200 BCE originating from Samaria.

displeasure פנותה (*fanuṯah*). It will be terminated by the coming of the *Taheb* (תהב *thb*), who will restore the period of favor רעותה (*re'uṯah*),[62] establish the true religion, and destroy the followers of Ezra. He will live 110 years on earth, and then die. The resurrection, which will take place after the death of the *Taheb* (תהב *thb*), and will be accompanied by the final judgment יום נקם יום גדול (*yom naqam yom gadol*—"A Day of Vengeance, a Great Day"), when the righteous will go into the Garden of Eden, and the wicked shall be burned with fire.

The stages in the development of this *Taheb* (תהב *thb*) concept are not clear, but it is quite possible that earlier, more historically based interpretations of eschatological texts came to be projected and harmonized into a fairly consistent picture of one future *Taheb* (תהב *thb*) figure, on the model of Moses. The place of פינחס (Pinḥas) in the *'Asatir* is one clue to such a development; similarly, the early identification of יהושע (Joshua son of Nun) with the promised "scepter" may be a further clue. That is to say, perhaps the earlier stages of speculation about the eschatological restoration looked to figures like פינחס (Pinḥas) and יהושע (Joshua son of Nun) as typical of what was to come. However, as the future hopes became more streamlined and idealized, the more general comprehensive concept of the *Taheb* (תהב *thb*) emerged and replaced the earlier figures. Thus פינחס (Pinḥas) and יהושע (Joshua son of Nun) fulfill the "star-scepter" image, but soon it is applied in general to the Moses-reflecting *Taheb* (תהב *thb*).

The interpretation of the "star and scepter" passage in the *Damascus Document* fragment CD*B*) bears further possible witness to the kind of background from which the Samaritan *Taheb* (תהב *thb*) Messianology was forged, for in CD*B* the "star" is the priestly interpreter of the Law while the "scepter" is the prince of the congregation (who exercises military power)—a striking parallel. Interestingly enough, by the time of the second revolt c.132 CE, the distinction of "star"—priestly "messiah"—and "scepter"—military/royal "messiah"—either had broken down or had been reversed, for Bar-Kochba received the Messianic title "star" from R. Aqiba[63].

As to the origins of a "יהושע (Joshua son of Nun)" Messianology, if indeed it had any *one* place of origin, the Northern Kingdom and particularly Samaria is a likely candidate given its antipathy to any suggestions of a Davidic "messiah." From Samaria, and perhaps by means of diaspora Samaritan communities such

---

[62] The first רעותה (*re'uṯah*) is said to have been the period of the Judges prior to the time of Eli at Shiloh. Hebrew עת רצון (*'t rṣwn*), see ψ69[14].
[63] See *1QM* xi:4-6.

as Alexandria, the rudimentary "Joshua" Messianology came to influence Hellenist as well as traditional Judaism.

Job and the Messiah Redux

In summary, we have attempted to describe some of the propaganda that underlie the various Messianic movements of the early Second Temple period. It is clear that the "messiah" was envisioned either as someone either of royal Davidic lineage, Aaronide/Zadokite High Priestly stock, or even possibly a combination of the two. The relevant question for us is what the author envisioned as the Joban "messiah."

On the one hand, the encrypted language linking Job with Ṣemaḥ (צמח) and Zerubbabel (זרבבל) would seem to point us in the direction of a "royal messiah." On the other hand, the language of the Prologue and 3rd Epilogue indicate a leaning toward a "priestly" messiah." Job is seen as performing priestly functions and wearing priestly garb and the central character in the prophet Zechariah's vision was יהושע (Joshua) the son of Jehozadak.

The Samaritan interpretation of Num.24[17] provides a combination of the "royal" and the "priestly" in the characters of פינחס (Pinḥas) and יהושע (Joshua). פינחס (Pinḥas) was Aaron's grandson and there is no questioning his lineage. יהושע (Joshua) is neither the priest of Zechariah's vision nor the military monarch of Davidic lineage (since he predates David by at least one or two centuries). He is יהושע (Joshua son of Nun) who was (according to *BH*) Moses' *aide de camp* and appointed successor. He fills the character of the royal/military "messiah" that we have mentioned.

Perhaps the most persuasive case for Job as the combined "priestly" and "royal" messiah" is its Samaritan provenance. The Samaritans followed, if they did not originate, the Israelite Judaism that was based solely on the Pentateuch; hence their Messianic aspirations could not be defined in terms of extra-Pentateuchal characters. The similarity of the Samaritan and Sadducee reliance on the Pentateuch alone cannot be ignored. The two groups diverge over their respective centers of worship, the Samaritans on Mt. Gerizim and the Sadducees in Jerusalem. The Samaritans' disapproval of the Zadokite High Priesthood (בני צדוק – *bny ṣdwq*) and the Temple in Jerusalem was well known as was their aversion to any Judaean Davidic tradition.

While the Samaritans may have later disavowed any association with the Jerusalem Zadokite Priesthood (בני צדוק – *bny ṣdwq*), they themselves were referred to, albeit anachronistically, in Rabbinic times as Sadduceans (צדוקים –

ṣdwqym).[64] This attribution probably had early antecedents reaching back to pre-Hasmonaean times in the middle of the 2nd century BCE. We see here the play on words involving√צדק (*ṣdq*). Our author would certainly have been familiar with this subtlety.

It is in this context that we will later consider √צדק (*ṣdq*) both as a verb and as a source of different onomastica that seem to have been prevalent in the mid-to-late 2nd Temple period.

[64] See Driver (1965, 259 ff.). Although Driver is dealing with the dating of the Dead Sea Scrolls, his subject material is nevertheless on point.

JOB'S LAST WORD
ANATOMY OF A CURSE

Now that we have demonstrated that נשא משל (*nś᾽ mšl*) is a euphemism for "cursing," we can examine Job's final monologue in its true light. Through Job's words, the author serves up an open frustration with the orthodox "order of things." The "friends" have not contributed anything useful by way of logical reasoning.

27:5,6

חלילה לי אם אצדיק אתכם עד אגוע לא אסיר תמתי ממני
בצדקתי החזקתי ולא ארפה ולא יחרף לבבי מימי
ḥlylh ly ᾽m ᾽ṣdyq ᾽tkm ʿd ᾽gwʿ l᾽ ᾽syr tmty mmny
bṣdqty hḥzqty wl᾽ ᾽rph wl᾽ yḥrp lbby mymy
Far be it from me that I declare you to be whole;
Even until I perish will I not turn aside my purity from me.
I have held strong to my wholeness and I will not weaken it,
And my heart will not be scornful as long as I live.

Pope: Far be it from me to declare you right; Till I die I will not renounce my integrity. My innocence I maintain, I will not relinquish it; My conscience gives no reproach my life long.

Habel: Far be it from me to declare you in the right! Until I die I will not be deprived of my integrity. I hold fast to my righteousness and will not let go. My heart has not blasphemed all my days.

Our translators each give a subtly different expression to the Hebrew text. Pope's "I will not renounce my integrity" is Habel's "I will not be deprived of my integrity." Similarly, Pope's "My conscience gives no reproach my life long" is Habel's "My heart has not blasphemed all my days." "Renunciation is active"; "being deprived" is passive. The text clearly describes an active Job and, in a work where every *nuance* is critical, Habel's translation is at the very least misleading.

There is a finality to Job's statement that he would never declare his three "friends" to be "whole." (אם אצדיק אתכם עד אגוע – *᾽m ᾽ṣdyq ᾽tkm ʿd ᾽gwʿ*) He has irrevocably rejected not only their arguments but also the essence of their entire being. This rejection will be affirmed by יהוה (YHWH) in 42^7, when he says to ʾEliphaz:

חרה אפי בך ובשני רעיך כי לא דברתם אלי נכונה כעבדי איוב
ḥrh ʾpy bk wbšny rʿyk ky lʾ dbrtm ʾly nkwnh kʿbdy ʾywb
"I am very angry with you and your two friends,
For you have not spoken the truth to me as has my servant Job."

Then follows the crucial phrase בצדקתי החזקתי (*bṣdqty hḥzqty*) – "I have held strong to my wholeness." The צדקה (*ṣdqh*) to which Job refers is that of Ezek.14^{14}, the root quality that guarantees his survival.

Our author, through the mouth of Job, now affirms the relative status of צדקה (*ṣdqh*). He is quite certain of his own survival but not quite so sure that the deity יהוה (YHWH) will survive with him.

27:16-17

אם יצבר כעפר כסף וכחמר יכין מלבוש
יכין וצדיק ילבש וכסף נקי יחלק
ʾm yṣbr kʿpr ksp wkḥmr ykyn mlbwš
ykyn wṣdyq ylbš wksp nqy yḥlq
Though he store up silver like dust,
And prepares his clothing like clay;
What he prepares, the whole will wear;
And the innocent will share the silver.

Pope: Though he heap silver like dust, And lay up stacks of raiment, What he stored the righteous will wear, The innocent will divide the silver.

Habel: Though they pile up silver like dust And store up clothing like clay, Yes, though they store it up, the righteous will wear it and the innocent will share in the silver.

The *BH* antecedent for אם יצבר כעפר כסף (*ʾm yṣbr kʿpr ksp*) is Zech.9^3, where we read:

ותבן צר מצור לה ותצבר כסף כעפר וחרוץ כטיט חוצות
הנה אדני יורשנה והכה בים חילה והיא באש תאכל
wtbn ṣr mṣwr lh wtṣbr ksp kʿpr wḥrwṣ kṭyṭ ḥwṣwt
hnh ʾdny ywršnh whkh bym ḥylh whyʾ bʾš tʾkl
And Tyre built a fortress for herself;
She has gathered in silver like dust, and gold like the clay of the streets.
Behold *ʾadonay* will dispossess her;
He will smite her wealth into the sea, and she shall be consumed by fire.

וכחמר יכין מלבוש (*wkḥmr ykyn mlbwš*) is the second part of the author's construct of a complex word-play consisting of Zech.9[3],Zeph.1[7,8], and Isa.41[25,26].

Zeph.1:7,8

הס מפני יהוה אדני כי קרוב יום יהוה
כי הכין יהוה זבח הקדיש קראיו
והיה ביום זבח יהוה ופקדתי על השרים ועל בני המלך
וכל הלבשים מלבוש נכרי
hs mpny yhwh ʾdn yk yqrwb ywm yhwh
ky hkyn yhwh zbḥ hqdyš qrwʾyw
whyh bywm zbḥ yhwh wpqdty ʿl hśrym wʿl bny hmlk
wkl hlbšym mlbwš nkry
Be silent before YHWH God! For the day of YHWH is at hand;
YHWH has prepared a sacrifice, he has consecrated his guests.
And on the day of YHWH's sacrifice I will punish the officials and the king's sons
And all who dress themselves in foreign attire.

Isa.41:25,26

העירותי מצפון ויאת ממזרח השמש יקרא בשמי
ויבא סגנים כמו חמר וכמו יוצר ירמס טיט
מי הגיד מראש ונדעה ומלפנים ונאמר צדיק
אף אין מגיד אף אין משמיע אף אין שמע אמריכם
hʿyrwty mṣpwn wyʾt mmzrḥ hšmš yqrʾ bšmy
wybʾ sgnym kmw ḥmr wkmw ywṣr yrms ṭyṭ
my hgyd mrʾš wndʿh wmlpnym wnʾmr ṣdyq
ʾp ʾyn mgyd ʾp ʾyn mšmyʿ ʾp ʾyn šmʿ ʾmrykm
I stirred up one from the north,[1] and he has come,
From the rising of the sun he calls my name.
He shall bring[2] rulers as mortar, as the potter treads clay.
Who declared it from the beginning, so that we might know,
And beforehand, so that we might say, "He is whole"?
There was no one who declared it, none who proclaimed,
None who heard your words.

The combination of these three separate sources for 27[16-17] is truly elegant. Not only does it flesh out Job's excoriation of his "friends" whom he has characterized throughout as "wicked," it provides an insight to 42[7] to which we have referred above. We have identified the author's use of the *BH* story of Bilʿam as the vehicle for continuity throughout the book and this instance

---

[1] Compare Jer.50[9], which is cited in connection with Job 8[6].

[2] Vocalizing ויבא (*wybʾ*) as *wᵉyabêʾ*.

provides the powerful example of an attempt to say one thing by articulating its opposite. While וכחמר יכין מלבוש (*wkḥmr ykyn mlbwš*) might convey the image of "one preparing clothing [carefully] as [the potter shapes] clay," the author intends something quite different. חמר (*ḥmr*)[3] represents the evil rulers[4] upon whom יהוה (YHWH) will trample. יכין (*ykyn*) is יהוה (YHWH)preparing the sacrifice of these evil rulers.[5] מלבוש (*mlbwš*) is the inappropriate clothing of the evil foreigner.[6] Thus we now look at a picture of material greed and cultic negligence. Now 27^{17} makes sense; the spoils of the "wicked" shall be the reward of the "whole" צדיק (*ṣdyq*).

The context of this verse is the terrifying fate of idolatrous Tyre and Job predicts likewise for his "friends." It is interesting that our author makes a direct parallel between the divine אדני (*ʾdny*)[7] and the human צדיק (*ṣdyq*). It seems that he may no longer be asserting the ability of, or necessity for, humanity to surpass the level of divine צדק (*ṣdq*), צדיק (*ṣdyq*) and צדקה (*ṣdqh*)[8] and is recognizing a level of equality or equivalence.

A Note on Chapter 28

There has been much scholarly discussion about the placement of Chapter 28, its relevance to the discourse, and the possibility that it is a late addition or interpolation. As we are about to demonstrate, these scholarly opinions are fundamentally incorrect—chapter 28 goes to the very root of the author's quest and argument.

Chapter 28 does not deal specifically with צדק (*ṣdq*), צדיק (*ṣdyq*) and צדקה (*ṣdqh*). Our author picks up on the imagery of "silver and dust" used in 27^{16} and elaborates on their terrestrial subterranean provenance. The deity, who is not named in $28^{1\text{-}11}$, sees through the nether darkness and creates the physical world using the natural resources of the underworld. He produces light out of its darkness.[9]

$28^{12\text{-}22}$ contrasts the possible provenances of "wisdom" while implicitly comparing "wisdom" to "silver and dust." "Wisdom" is not to be found either on earth or in the underworld. Only אלהים (*ʾelohîm*) knows its source (28^{23}) and we

---

[3] Isa.41^{25}.
[4] Literally, "from the north."
[5] Zeph.1^{7}.
[6] Zeph.1^{8}.
[7] Whom we shall identify below as אלהים (*ʾelohîm*).
[8] As he seems to have been doing in 13^{18}.
[9] Although the antecedent of the possessive suffix of תעלמה (*tʾlmh*) is not clear.

know from 1[1] that Job is **ירא אלהים** (*yr' 'lhym*)—"revering *'elohîm*." The chapter ends with verse 28:

ויאמר לאדם הן יראת אדני היא חכמה וסר מרע בינה
wy'mr l'dm hn yr't 'dny hy' ḥkmh wswr mr' bynh
And He said to the man,
"Reverence for God is wisdom, and shunning evil is understanding."

This verse ties in so closely with 1[1]:

והיה האיש ההוא תם וישר וירא אלהים וסר מרע
whyh h'yš hhw' tm wyšr wyr' 'lhym wsr mr'
And that man was honest and upright, revering *'elohîm* and shunning evil.

that it is impossible to ignore the author's intent to promote the institution of **אלהים** (*'elohîm*). As we have seen in Zeph.1[7] above, the term **אדני** (*'dny*) refers to **אלהים** (*'elohîm*) as it does in 28[28].[10]

29:14

צדק לבשתי וילבשני כמעיל וצניף משפטי
ṣdq lbšty wylbšny km'yl wṣnyp mšpṭy
I put on clothes of wholeness and it clothed me;
My justice was like a cloak and turban.

Pope: I was clothed in righteousness and it with me; Like robe and turban was my justice.

Habel: Righteousness was my robe And it robed me like a cloak, Like a turban was my justice.

This is a deceptively simple verse that reveals a small part of its complex structure in the two translations of Pope and Habel. Pope treats the verse as a couplet, while Habel sees a triplet. The verse is a couplet; Habel's rendition requires emendation and adds nothing to the meaning of the verse. Pope's rendition of the first colon is absolutely correct, although he does not pause to understand what he has said.

Contextually, this verse stands out from the others in the chapter; it departs from the theme of Job recounting his good deeds. However, our author has his

---

[10] See also Gen.15[2,8] in particular (and *passim* throughout *BH*) for the more conventional **אדני יהוה**, which is vocalized *'dny 'elohîm.*

agenda and this verse fits in neatly. There are three elements to the verse, all of which describe "priestly" attributes,[11] namely:

צדק לבשתי – (*ṣdq lbšty*) "I put on clothes of wholeness" is a pairing that occurs only once in *BH*, namely in ψ132⁹:[12]

כהניך ילבשו צדק וחסידיך ירננו
khnyk ylbšw ṣdq wḥsydyk yrnnw
Your priests shall be clothed in wholeness,
And those loyal to you shall break out in song.

כמעיל (*km'yl*) – "like a cloak." We have already put forward the idea of Job as priest and discussed the "priestly" significance of the **מעיל** (*m'yl*) in our treatment of 1²⁰. Isa.61¹⁰ reads **מעיל צדקה** (*m'yl ṣdqh*); however, there is no explicit "priestly" connotation there.

וצניף (*wṣnyp*) – "and turban." The word **צניף** (*ṣnyp*) is of relatively recent vintage, occurring only here and in Zech.3⁴.[13] Here we have the classic dream of the prophet Zechariah in which the High Priest Joshua appears wearing soiled clothes. The other characters in the dream are **השטן** (*haśśaṭan*) and **מלאך יהוה** (*ml'k yhwh*)[14] who meld together into one character—**מלאך יהוה** (*ml'k yhwh*)—after Zech.3².

The author has picked his words very carefully, since he could have covered **כמעיל וצניף** (*km'yl wṣnyp*) in a single stroke by using the word **מצנפת** (*mṣnpt*) for **צניף** (*ṣnyp*). Then he would have had available to him the combination from Ex.28⁴:

ואלה הבגדים אשר יעשו חשן ואפוד ומעיל וכתנת תשבץ מצנפת ואבנט
w'lh hbgdym 'šr y'św ḥšn w'pwd wm'yl ktnt tšbṣ mṣnpt w'bnṭ
These are the vestments that they shall make:
A breast piece, an ephod, a cloak, a checkered tunic, a turban, and a sash.

---

[11] Which Job had assumed for himself in 1⁵, wherein he offers sacrifices for his children.

[12] Both Pope and Habel cite Isa.59¹⁷ as a comparison; however the text there reads **צדקה** (*ṣdqh*) rather than **צדק** (*ṣdq*) and is not in the direct context of priesthood.

[13] There is an occurrence of **צניף** (*ṣnyp*) in Isa.62³, where it is written **צנוף** (*ṣnwp*) and corrected by *BH*. However, this is a reference to the "turban of kingship" and not "priesthood." Its appearance in the latest section of Isaiah attests to its recent provenance.

[14] We have dealt extensively with **השטן** (*haśśaṭan*) in our treatment of 1⁶. We have shown that **מלאך יהוה** (*ml'k yhwh*) is synonymous with **השטן** (*haśśaṭan*).

Thus our author is making two quite distinctly different points in this one small verse. First, he is investigating human "wholeness" to see if there are subsets such as "priestly wholeness." Second, he is once again allowing the reader to recognize the contemporaneousness of his investigation.

31:6

ישקלני במאזני צדק וידע אלוה תמתי
yšqlny bmʾzny ṣdq wydʿ ʾlwh tmty
Let him weigh me in scales of wholeness;
And let ʾEloah know my integrity

Pope: Let him weigh me in just scales, And let God know my innocence.

Habel: Let him weigh me on the scales of righteousness And let Eloah know my integrity.

Pope muses about Biblical condemnation of "false scales and weights." Habel digresses into Egyptian mythical rituals of justice and cites Pope on "false balances" without giving any credit. The last portion of his insight is worth quoting:

> However, the term "just" (*ṣedeq*) also means "righteousness," while "full weight" (*tumma*) is a key thematic word designating Job's personal "integrity." "Just scales" would be those on which Job wants his "righteousness" and "integrity" to be weighed so that God will "know" his full weight and be forced to acknowledge it (cf. 10:7). Thus Job's oath of purity is framed by a challenge that God would test Job's claim in public by the ultimate standard of truth.[15]

There are only two references in *BH* to **מאזני צדק** (*mʾzny ṣdq*), namely, Lev.19[36] and Ezek.45[10]. Either would be a suitable antecedent; both come from "priestly" sources. The latter, however, is embedded in the technicalities of Temple weights and measures while the former is divine commandment. Thus we read in Lev.19 [35,36]:

לא תעשו עול במשפט במדה במשקל ובמשורה
מאזני צדק אבני צדק איפת צדק והין צדק יהיה לכם...
lʾ tʿśw ʿwl bmšpṭ bmdh bmšql wbmśwrh
mʾzny ṣdq ʾbny ṣdq ʾypt ṣdq whyn ṣdq yhyh lkm
You shall not deal perversely in justice, measure, weight or quantity.
You shall have "whole" scales, "whole" weights, a 'whole" ephah, and a "whole" hin...

---

[15] Habel (1985, 433).

The objective here is not to contrast "honest" and "dishonest" scales.[16] It is to emphasize that it is by the standards of divine צדק (*ṣdq*) – "wholeness" that Job demands to be judged.

Our author has shifted his position slightly. As we have seen earlier, he has asserted the possibility that human "wholeness" might exceed divine "wholeness" based on the statement that, since God created humanity in his own image, humanity must possess all the divine attributes. Since we know that humanity is not perfect, the same must apply to the divine. We have remarked that this position has been modified to admit that human and divine "wholeness" may be on a par.

We see in this verse a dying search for the source of "wholeness" within the divine, outside of humanity. It is a challenge that the author knows will not be answered. The only possibility that remains is that divine "wholeness" and human "wholeness" are essentially and fundamentally incompatible and mutually exclusive.

---

[16] The opposite of מאזני צדק (*m'zny ṣdq*) is מאזני מרמה (*m'zny mrmh*) – "scales of guile," as occurs in Hos.12[8], Amos 8[6], and Prov.11[1]; 20[23]. The term מאזני רשע (*m'zny rš'*) – "scales of evil," occurs only in Mic.6[11], where it parallel to מרמה (*mrmh*).

DEUS OMNIPOTENS:
THE ʾELIHU EPILOGUE

Chapters 32^1 37^{24}

The Name of ʾElihu

Our author names the speaker in such a way as to leave little doubt as to his intended identity. The given name is:

אליהוא בן ברכאל הבוזי ממשפחת רם

ʾlyhwʾ bn brkʾl mmšpḥt hbwzy

ʾElihu ʻthe son of Berachʾel the Buzite of a noble family

The literal meaning of **אליהוא** (*ʾlyhwʾ*) is "He is my ʾEl (god)." The connection with **אליהו** (*ʾlyhw*) – ʾElijah is fairly unmistakable. The notion of a "messiah" as intercessor is intrinsic to the content of the ʾElihu Epilogue. .

Similarly, the literal rendering of **ברכאל** (*brkʾl*) is "the one who blessed ʾEl (god)."[1] Our author was clearly familiar with the prophet Zechariah, whose *floruit* was from 520-518 BCE. This is important, not just from the standpoint of the dating of the Book of Job, but it also reinforces the concept of Messianism and the *eschaton* within the *persona* of Job himself. Zechariah is himself named in Zech.1^1 as:

זכריה בן ברכיה

zkryh bn brkyh

Zechariah, the son of Berekiah

The patronym **ברכיה** (*brkyh*) – Berechiah is immediately reminiscent of **ברכאל** (*brkʾl*) – Berachʾel, which was the patronym of ʾElihu whom we meet later in 32^2. The only difference in between the patronyms is the name of the suffixed deity.

Third, and equally important, we read **הבוזי ממשפחת רם** (*hbwzy mmšpḥt rm*), "of a noble family of Buz." **בוזי** (*bwzy*) is the patronym of the prophet

---

[1] Possibly also "the one whom ʾEl blessed."

Ezekiel, whose relevance to the Book of Job has already been demonstrated.[2] Finally, though not least, בוזי (*bwzy*) contrasts directly with בארץ עוץ "in the land of ʿUz" (*bʾrṣ ʿwṣ*), which we know[3] was Job's homeland.

Thus we may postulate that ʾElihu is an invention by the author of a self-proclaimed intercessor.

32:1,2

וישבתו שלשת האנשים האלה מענות את איוב כי הוא צדיק בעיניו
ויחר אף אליהוא בן ברכאל הבוזי ממשפחת רם באיוב חרה אפו על צדקו נפשו מאלהים
wyšbtw šlšt hʾnšym hʾlh mʿnwt ʾt ʾywb ky ṣdyq hwʾ bʿynyw
wyḥr ʾp ʾlyhwʾ bn brkʾl hbwzy mmšpḥt rm bʾywb ḥrh ʾpw ʿl ṣdqw npšw mʾlhym
And these three men ceased replying to Job, For he considered himself to be whole.
And ʾElihu the son of Berachʾel the Buzite, of the family of Ram became angry.
He was angry with Job because he had made himself more whole than *ʾelohîm*..

Pope: Then these three men ceased answering Job because in his own opinion he was righteous. But the anger of ʾElihu, son of Berachel the Buzite from the clan of Ram, flared up against Job, because he held himself to be righteous rather than God.

Habel: So these three men ceased answering to Job because he was righteous in his own eyes. Then the anger of ʾElihu, son of Berachel the Buzite from the clan of Ram, flared up against Job because he thought himself more righteous than God.

צדק...נפש (*ṣdq... npš*) occurs as a phrase only here and Jer.3[11]:

ויאמר יהוה אלי צדקה נפשה משבה ישראל מבגדה יהודה
wyʾmr yhwh ʾly ṣdqh npšh mšbh yśrʾl mbgdh yhdh
And YHWH said to me:
"Apostate Israel has made herself more whole than treacherous Judah."

This occurrence confirms the comparative sense of √צדק (*ṣdq*) in the *piʿel* form. Pope does not recognize this *nuance* and *NRSV* paraphrases with "shown herself less guilty."

This introductory statement seemingly comes straight to the point in a seemingly innocuous (*sic*) manner. The "friends" have conceded and the focus is clearly on the statement that Job considers himself to be צדיק (*ṣdyq*) – "whole." The entrance of ʾElihu is ostensibly prompted by his own perception that Job

---

[2] See Ezek.1[3], יחזקאל בן בוזי הכהן (*yḥzqʾl bn bwzy hkhn*)—"Ezekiel the son of Buzi the priest."
[3] From 1[1].

considers himself to be more "whole" than אלהים (*elohîm*). This is the same אלהים (*elohîm*) whom Job has always regarded as the ultimate object of reverence.[4] This mention of אלהים (*elohîm*) is a clear signal that Job's entire belief system is now under attack.[5]

From the context of Jer.3[11], our author reconfirms יהוה (YHWH) as the antagonist He uses אלהים (*elohîm*) because Job has already indicted and cursed יהוה (YHWH). By introducing אלהים (*elohîm*) at this point, he uses ʾElihu to raise the stakes. We remember from 1[1] that our author has made it clear that Job is fully aware of his relationship with אלהים (*elohîm*)—his awareness of יהוה (YHWH) is not at all clear.

33:12-13

הן זאת לא צדקת אענך כי ירבה אלוה מאנוש
מדוע אליו ריבות כי כל דבריו לא יענה
hn zʾt lʾ ṣdqt ʾʿnk ky yrbh ʾlwh mʾnwš
mdwʿ ʾlyw rybwt ky kl dbryw lʾ yʿnh
Since in this case you are not whole, I shall afflict you.
For ʾEloah is more [whole] than man.
Why do you fight with him?
He will not answer for all of his actions.

Pope: You are not right in this, I tell you, For God is greater than man. Why do you charge him That he answers none of your words?

Habel: Well, in this you are not in the right. I will answer you. If "Eloah is greater than humans," Then why do you bring a suit against him, Since (as you claim) "He answers none of my charges."

It is plain that our exemplar translators are floundering in a morass of confusion. Their need to emend דבריו (*dbryw*) to reflect two diametrically opposite meanings speaks volumes.

In fact, our author has transformed ʾElihu into a *vox dei* so that he can turn Job and the "friends" into silent antagonists. He has positioned ʾElihu so that he can rail at will against both Job and the "friends." The elegant play on √רבה (*rbh*) – "to be great," √ריב (*ryb*) – "to strive, quarrel," and the two roots √ענה (*ʿnh*) – "to answer" and "to afflict" sets up the knowing reader for the inevitable posture and language of Job in the Second Epilogue.

---

[4] See 1[1].

[5] ʾElihu's reference to אלהים (*elohîm*) is reminiscent of the challenge of Job's wife to "curse אלהים (*elohîm*) and die" in 2[9].

33:26

יעתר אל אלוה וירצהו וירא פניו בתרועה וישב לאנוש צדקתו
yʿtr ʾl ʾlwh wyrṣhw wyrʾ pnyw btrwʿh wyšb lʾnwš ṣdqtw
He pleads with ʾEloah and he [ʾEloah] desires him;
He [ʾEloah] reveals his face with a fanfare;
And he returns wholeness to man.

Pope: He prays to God and he accepts him, he sees his face with joy. He announces to men his salvation…

Habel: He prays to Eloah, and he accepts him; Reveals his face amid festal shouting, And restores righteousness to the person.

Our translators continue to have serious difficulties with √צדק (*ṣdq*). The problem here is clear. "Righteousness" may not be an appropriate translation; the question is whose "wholeness is restored? Is it human "wholeness" that humanity has somehow forfeited? Or is it divine "wholeness" that is being freshly bestowed?

וירצהו (*wyrṣhw*) would thus appear to be the *crux* of a verse whose subject and object may be variously construed. Assuming that the Divine is the subject, then "acceptance" is an appropriate rendering. If humanity is the subject, then we might well ask why humanity would entreat with the divine and then "accept" him. Surely "and he (humanity) pleases him (the Divine) would be more appropriate. Alternatively, and perhaps most preferably, "desires" comes closest to the real intent of the author who is not above leaving a *double entendre* regarding subject and object.

ʾElihu certainly is the staunch proponent of the concept of divine "wholeness" that is bestowed upon humanity solely at the will of the deity. It is this portrayal of his theocentricity that is at once his hallmark and the evidence of his apparent *naïveté*. We shall see from the immediately following citation that this "apparent *naïveté*" is completely disingenuous.

33:32

אם יש מלין השיבני דבר כי חפצתי צדקך
ʾm yš mlyn hšybny dbr ky ḥpṣty ṣdqk
If there are words, answer me;
For it would please me to find you whole.

Pope: If you have something to say, answer me; Speak, I want you to show your righteousness.

Habel: If you have arguments, refute me! Testify, for I am eager to find you in the right.

Our translators find nothing remarkable in this verse; however, an examination of the *BH* antecedent is revealing. The phrase השיבני דבר (*hšybny dbr*) occurs only once, in Gen.37[14], where Jacob says to Joseph:

לך נא ראה את שלום אחיך ואת שלום הצאן והשבני דבר
lk nʾ rʾh ʾt šlwm ʾḥyk wʾt šlwm hṣʾn whšbny dbr
Go now, see about the welfare of your brothers and the flocks,
And come back to me with a report.

We recall from the Prologue that we have argued that our author assigned the character of Jacob to יהוה (YHWH). We know that Jacob sent Joseph on a mission from which he never returned. Our author is imputing the outcome of that story to this verse. By the use of the asseverative particle אם (ʾ*m*),[6] our author makes it clear that יהוה (YHWH) has no intention of ascribing anything to humanity, let alone "wholeness" – √צדק (*ṣdq*). The verse should probably be rendered:

> If there are (and I know that there are not) words, answer me (and it will not serve you well because I know that this turns out badly for you); for it would please me (and I have already told you that there are no words that will please me)[7] to find you whole.

34:5

כי אמר איוב צדקתי ואל הסיר משפטי
ky ʾmr ʾywb ṣdqty wʾl hsyr mšpṭy
For Job has said, "I am whole,
And ʾEl has set aside judgment against me.

Pope: Now Job has said, 'I am righteous, And God has robbed me of my right.'

Habel: For Job said, "I am in the right, But El denied me litigation."

Pope sloughs off this verse with the comment that this is simply ʾElihu quoting Job's opening statement in 27[2]. Habel comments similarly but finds a need to pursue the notion of "justice denied" and the reinterpretation of משפט (*mšpṭ*) as "litigation or lawsuit, rather than justice in general."

In order to understand the meaning of this verse, we must look to the *BH* antecedent of ואל הסיר משפטי (*wʾl hsyr mšpṭy*), which we find in Zeph.3[15]:

---

[6] Words in parentheses are my own explicative additions. See above in 9[19,20].

[7] See above in 22[3].

הסיר יהוה משפטיך פנה איבך

hsyr yhwh mšpṭyk pnh ʾybk

YHWH has set aside (his) judgments against you,

He has turned away your enemy.

Our first observation, while perhaps parenthetical, is that the *BH* antecedent has יהוה (YHWH) as the protagonist. Second, and far more important, the word משפטיך (*mšpṭyk*) carries the clear meaning of "judgments rendered against you." Our author wishes us to understand this meaning in this instance also—hence our rendering "has set aside judgment against me." As for the quotation from 27², it is fraught with problems of its own.

חי אל הסיר משפטי ושדי המר נפשי

ḥy ʾl hsyr mšpṭy wšdy hmr npšy

Would that! ʾEl had set aside judgment against me

And Shaddai had altered my soul.

The verse is Job's opening salvo as he prepares to wind up his rejection of the "friends" and their unwavering posture.

The term חי אל (*ḥy ʾl*) is *hapax legomenon* and all efforts to translate it somehow seem to contort its meaning. The idiom in *BH* is generally חי...אם (*ḥy... ʾm*) for a negative oath חי...כי (*ḥy...ky*) for a positive oath. The divine name normally follows the word חי (*ḥy*) immediately. That is not the case here and one might well wonder whether an oath is intended here at all. These two citations of אל הסיר משפטי (*ʾl hsyr mšpṭy*) are indeed equivalent and the word חי (*ḥy*) of 27² is left hanging by itself. We should probably look for an optative sense of "would that" for the word חי (*ḥy*).

Pope sees a similarity in the styles of the Prologue to Job and the Book of Ruth.[8] He does not elaborate on this statement; however, the one true similarity is the occurrence of the word המר (*hmr*) – "has embittered."[9] Since the two occurrences indicate different uses of the verb, we would suggest that המר (*hmr*) is not from √מרר (*mrr*) – "to be bitter" but rather from √מור (*mwr*) "to change," which in the *hiphʿil* takes on the transitive meaning "to alter."[10] This suggestion gains support from the alliterative character of the verse and the restoration of parallelism.

---

[8] Pope (1974, lxxi)

[9] In Ruth 1²⁰, המר (*hmr*) takes the indirect object particle לי (*ly*), whereas in our verse המר (*hmr*) takes the direct object. Thus the comparison may not be valid.

[10] We would thus vocalize המר (*hmr*) as *hêmir* spelled defectively.

Hence we arrive at our rendition of the verse above.

34:9

כי אמר לא יסכן גבר ברצתו עם אלהים

ky ʾmr lʾ yskn gbr brṣtw ʿm ʾlhym

For he has said, "Man does not offer care[11]

In exchange for being acceptable to *elohîm*."

This is the second time that ʾElihu has quoted Job incorrectly and out of context, the other occasion being 34^5:

There are two aspects of this verse that our author wishes the reader to recognize. First is the mention of **אלהים** (*elohîm*). If we recall 32^2, we see that the object of ʾElihu's criticism was Job's assertion that he was "more whole than *elohîm*."

The original citation to which ʾElihu refers is 33^{26}, with which we have dealt above.

יעתר אל אלוה וירצהו...וישב לאנוש צדקתו

yʿtr ʾl ʾlwh wyrṣhw... wyšb lʾnwš ṣdqtw

He pleads with ʾEloah and he [ʾEloah] accepts him...

And he returns wholeness to man.

As we remarked earlier, ʾElihu is the proponent of the concept of divine "wholeness" that is bestowed upon humanity solely at the will of the deity. We suspected him of being disingenuous and he shows it here when he clearly accuses Job of dissatisfaction with "divine wholeness."

However, the accusation against Job is not entirely specious. After all, having recognized that there may be a qualitative difference between divine and human wholeness, our author is intent on pursuing the matter further. The "ʾElihu Solution" cannot satisfy his quest; the best that he can get from a fundamentalist thinker is a suggestion that he is searching for the opposite of ʾElihu's position.

34:17

האף שונא משפט יחבוש ואם צדיק כביר תרשיע

hʾp śwnʾ mšpṭ yḥbwš wʾm ṣdyq kbyr tršyʿ

Will one who hates judgment imprison?

Or will you convict one who is whole and great?

---

[11] See discussion of Num.22^{30} in the story of Bilʿam above.

Pope: Can one who hates justice govern? Will you condemn the Just and Mighty One?

Habel: Would one who hates justice govern? Would you prove the Just and Mighty One wrong?

Without even considering the meaning of the entire verse, it is difficult to assign a rendering of "govern" to √חבש (*ḥbš*), which clearly has a meaning of "binding up," "harnessing," or "imprison."[12] The sense of imprisonment is inherent in the Arabic cognate.[13] ʾElihu is intensifying his rhetoric concerning divine even-handedness almost *ad absurdum*.

35:2

הזאת חשבת למשפט אמרת צדקי מאל
hzʾt ḥšbt lmšpṭ ʾmrt ṣdqy mʾl
Do you think that this is judgment,
That you say, "I am more whole than ʾEl?

Pope: Do you think this according to justice? You say, 'It is my right from God.'

Habel: Do you consider it just to claim, "I am right against El."

This is a throwback to 32^2, ʿElihu's purported original reason for chastising Job. Of course the question is rhetorical from ʿElihu's standpoint and he discards it as "ignorant" and "vain" in 35^{16}; however, Job's statement has penetrated ʿElihu's offensive shield and ʿElihu is not able to refute it.

35:7,8

אם צדקת מה תתן לו או מה מידך יקח
לאיש כמוך רשעך ולבן אדם צדקתך
ʾm ṣdqt mh ttn lw ʾw mh mydk yqḥ
lʾyš kmwk ršʿk wlbn ʾdm ṣdqtk
If you are whole, what will you give him?
Or what will he take from your hand?
Your wickedness [inheres] to one like you;
As does your wholeness to humankind.

---

[12] *BDB*, 290 cites this single instance as "fig. = restrain, control. *HALOT*, 289 recognizes the same meaning as *BDB*; however, it assigns a new meaning of "govern(?)" for just this one case. It is of note that this same word occurs in both the *ʿaqedâh* (Gen.22^3) and the story of Bilʿam (Num.22^{21}).

[13] *AED*, 109 حبس (*ḥabasa*) – "to confine, hold in custody."

Pope: If you are righteous, what do you give him? Or what does he get from your hand? Your wickedness concerns man like yourself; Your righteousness, only human beings.

Habel: If you are righteous, what do you render him? Or what does he receive from your hand? Your wickedness affects mortals like yourself; Your righteousness, fellow human beings.

This is a doctrinal statement that clearly separates the divine and human attributes of צדק (*ṣdq*), צדיק (*ṣdyq*) and צדקה (*ṣdqh*). The fundamentalist ʾElihu is cutting off all possibility of contact between humankind and the deity. There is a biting sarcasm to the suggestion that humanity has nothing to offer to the deity anything but itself. Job rejects this notion in 42[6].

36:3

אשא דעי למרחוק ולפעלי אתן צדק

ʾśʾ dʿy lmrḥwq wlpʿly ʾtn ṣdq

I will make my opinion known far and wide,

And I shall recount the wholeness of my maker.

Pope: I will fetch my speech from afar, I will ascribe righteousness to my Maker

Habel: I will glean my knowledge from far afield; I will prove my Creator in the right.

ʾElihu continues his defense of the deity in his bombastic style. Both Pope and Habel offer nuanced translations that offer little of substantive value.

The verse actually is comprised of six words, each of which can bear extensive discussion. Our interest is focused on the words אתן צדק (*ʾtn ṣdq*) which our translators render variously as "I will ascribe righteousness" (Pope) and "I will prove…in the right." (Habel). If the root of אתן (*ʾtn*) is √נתן (*ntn*), then we should simply translate אתן (*ʾtn*) as "I shall give, award, donate" or some other synonym of "to give." We do have a unique *BH* antecedent that curiously resembles this idiom in Jud.5[11]:

מקול מחצצים בין משאבים שם יתנו צדקות יהוה צדקת פרזנו בישראל

mqwl mḥṣṣym byn mšʾbym šm ytnw ṣdqwt yhwh ṣdqt prznw byśrʾl

From the voices of archers between the toughs,

There do they recount the whole deeds of YHWH,

His whole deeds of deliverance for Israel.

While the lexicons differ as to their degree of uncertainty of the original meaning of √תנה (*tnh*) ,the root of יתנו (*ytnw*),[14] we can plausibly suggest that the derivation of אתן (*ʾtn*) is indeed the same √תנה (*tnh*) especially since it occurs in an idiom יתנו צדקות יהוה (*ytnw ṣdqwt yhwh*), giving us both the contextual meaning of "narration" or "recounting" with reference to יהוה (YHWH).

36:7

לא יגרע מצדיק עיניו ואת מלכים לכסא וישיבם לנצח ויגבהו
lʾ ygrʿ mṣdyq ʿynyw wʾt mlkym lksʾ wyšybm lnṣḥ wygbhw
He does not withdraw his eyes from the whole,
And as regards messengers, he seats them on thrones forever and they are exalted

Pope: He does not withdraw his eyes from the righteous. With kings on the throne he seats them. Forever they are exalted.

Habel: He does not turn his eyes from the righteous, But with kings on thrones He seats them and exalts them forever.

Most scholars concede that this verse is singularly difficult. Our two translators tackle the verse as a *quasi* tricolon. The phrase לא יגרע מצדיק עיניו (*lʾ ygrʿ mṣdyq ʿynyw*) is generally agreed upon as to its meaning; the other two cola leave much room for disagreement.

There is a *BH* antecedent for the first colon in Ezek.5[11]:

...אם לא יען את מקדשי טמאת בכל שקוציך ובכל תועבתיך
וגם אני אגרע ולא תחוס עיני וגם אני לא אחמל
... *ʾm lʾ yʿn ʾt mqdšy ṭmʾt bkl šqwṣyk wbkl twʿbtyk*
wgm ʾny ʾgrʿ wlʾ tḥws ʿyny wgm ʾny lʾ ʾḥmwl
...because you have defiled my sanctuary
With all of your detestable things and all of your abominations,
I also will withdraw and my eye shall not be sparing,
And I shall have no pity.

Of course this is not the exact idiom of our verse, in fact, the √גרע (*grʿ*) is used transitively in Job and intransitively in Ezekiel. However, we must take note of the juxtaposition of the elements in both instances since it is the only occurrence in *BH*. It is also important to remember that Ezekiel is the prophet who gives us the definition of the צדיק (*ṣdyq*).[15]

---

[14] *HALOT*, 1759; *BDB*, 1072.
[15] See Ezek. Chapter 18.

The phrase from Ezekiel refers to the dire consequences of divine withdrawal from idolators, i.e. those who do not act in a "whole" manner. The phrase in Job describes the opposite, i.e. that the deity will not abandon those who act in a "whole" manner.

The remainder of the verse can only make sense with one small adjustment to the reading; namely, reading **מלאכים** (*mlʾkym*) "messengers"[16] for **מלכים** (*mlkym*) "kings." We know from the Dead Sea Scrolls that the idea of "messengers on the throne" was a probably a proto-Messianic idea that was in contemporary circulation.[17]

37:23

שדי לא מצאנהו שגיא כח ומשפט ורב צדקה לא יענה

šdy lʾmṣʾnhw śgyʾ kḥ wmšpṭ wrb ṣdqh lʾ yʿnh

Šadday, we do not find him

[though he be] great in power and justice

He does not answer the whole litigant.

Pope: Shaddai we cannot reach; Pre-eminent in power and judgment, Great in justice, he does not oppress.

Habel: Shaddai—we cannot reach him! Great in his might and justice, Mighty in his righteousness—He does not answer!

This is ʾElihu's parting harangue to Job. What has to be a clearly understood statement is curiously worded as to admit two opposite renditions.

Our two translators differ as to which form of √**ענה** (*ʿnh*) should prevail in this verse. Is it to be √**ענה** (*ʿnh*) – "to answer" or √**ענה** (*ʿnh*) – "to afflict?"[18] Is **רב צדקה** (*rb ṣdqh*) "abundant in righteousness" or is "the whole litigant" the object of **לא יענה** (*lʾ yʿnh*)?

---

16 Or "angels."

17 See *4Q405 Songs of the Sabbath Sacrifice* Frags.19-20; *4Q491c Self Glorification Hymn*;

18 As we have mentioned above in our treatment of $33^{12,13}$.

“FROM THE WHIRLWIND”
THE SECOND EPILOGUE

The Dialogue of YHWH and Job

Chapter 38^1-42^6

As we have already seen, the Book of Job is a work whose literary structure has been debated without resolution for centuries. We have posited a unified literary composition whose author conceals a “theologically incorrect” *agenda* beneath a superficially “correct” theme. We have uncovered the code method of the Prologue (1^1-3^2). The poetic chapters, although apparently enigmatic, contain a continuation of the basic code, along with the use of key vocabulary. This segment comprises the second of the three separate epilogues, each of which provides a plausible conclusion to the book.

In 38^1-41^{26}, יהוה (YHWH) speaks and rationalizes his existence in terms that resonate with Plato’s “Demiurge” and Aristotle’s “Prime Mover.”

We read in Plato, *Timaios* 40c:

> φύλακα καὶ δημιουργὸν νυκτός τε καὶ ἡμέρας ἐμηχανήσατο
> He was framed to be the guard and fashioner of night and day

and in Aristotle *Metaphysics* 1074a:

> ὅτι δὲ εἷς οὐρανός, φανερόν. εἰ γὰρ πλείους οὐρανοὶ ὥσπερ ἄνθρωποι, ἔσται εἴδει μία ἡ περὶ ἕκαστον ἀρχή, ἀριθμῷ δέ γε πολλαί. ἀλλ’ ὅσα ἀριθμῷ πολλά, ὕλην ἔχει (εἷς γὰρ λόγος καὶ ὁ αὐτὸς πολλῶν, οἷον ἀνθρώπου, Σωκράτης δὲ εἷς): τὸ δὲ τί ἦν εἶναι οὐκ ἔχει ὕλην τὸ πρῶτον: ἐντελέχεια γάρ. ἓν ἄρα καὶ λόγῳ καὶ ἀριθμῷ τὸ πρῶτον κινοῦν ἀκίνητον ὄν: καὶ τὸ κινούμενον ἄρα ἀεὶ καὶ συνεχῶς: εἷς ἄρα οὐρανὸς μόνος.
> It is evident that there is only one heaven. For if there is to be a plurality of heavens (as there is of men), the principle of each must be one in kind but many in number. But all things that are many in number have matter (for one and the same definition applies to many individuals, e.g. that of “man”; but Socrates is one), but the primary essence has no matter, because it is complete reality. Therefore the

> **prime mover**, which is immovable, is one both in formula and in number; and therefore so also is that which is eternally and continuously in motion.[1] Therefore there is only one heaven.

While these citations refer more to the metaphysical world, there is a clear articulation of divine singularity and creative power.

While the tone of יהוה (YHWH)'s speech is apparently aggressive, berating the arrogance of a human being who is not unquestioningly accepting, there is an air of pathos that is brought into sharp focus in a short but crucial interchange with Job at 40[1-5], in which the author reveals the true identity of יהוה (YHWH). There we read:

ויען יהוה את איוב ויאמר
הרב עם שדי יסור מוכיח אלוה יעננה
ויען איוב את יהוה ויאמר
הן קלתי מה אשיבך ידי שמתי למו פי
אחת דברתי ולא אענה ושתים ולא אוסיף
wyʿn yhwh ʾt ʾywb wyʾmr
hrb ʿm šdy yswr mwkyḥ ʾlwh yʿnnh
wyʿn ʾywb ʾt yhwh wyʾmr
hn qlty mh ʾšybk ydy śmty lmw py
ʾḥt dbrty wlʾ ʾʿnh wštym wlʾ ʾwsyp
And YHWH answered Job and said:
Will he who quarrels with Shaddai chastise [him]?
Will he who reproves ʾEloah afflict [him]?
And Job answered YHWH and said:
Behold, I have cursed [you], I have said my piece,[2] what shall I answer you?
I have spoken once and I shall not answer, twice and I shall not add

This exchange is a *crux*; יהוה (YHWH) identifies himself not as אלוה (*ʾlwh*) but rather as שדי אלוה (*šdy ʾlwh*). There are only three verses in the entire Book of Job in which the deity is addressed both as שדי (*šdy*) and אלוה (*ʾlwh*) (in that order) in the two parallel cola of each verse.[3] They are as follows:

---

[1] The definition of form is one and universal; it is the combination of form with matter that constitutes an individual. Thus a plurality of individuals is caused by the combination of the same form with different matter.

[2] ידי שמתי למו פי (*ydy śmty lmw py*)—literally, "I have put my hand to my mouth." Compare Jud.18[19].

[3] In 6[4] and 27[10], the speaker is Job; in 40[2], יהוה (YHWH) speaks.

6:4

כי חצי שדי עמדי אשר חמתם שתה רוחי בעותי אלוה יערכוני
ky ḥṣy šdy ʿmdy ʾšr ḥmtm šth rwḥy bʿwty ʾlwh yʿrkwny
For the arrows of Shaddai are in me,
Whose poison my spirit drinks;
The terrors of ʾEloah are set against me

The speaker is Job himself, reflecting upon his circumstances and **יהוה** (YHWH)'s direct responsibility for his misfortune.

27:10

אם על שדי יתענג יקרא אלוה בכל עת
ʾm ʿl šdy ytʿng yqrʾ ʾlwh bkl ʿt
He takes no pleasure in Shaddai, he calls not [upon] ʾEloah at all times.[4]

The context of this statement is Job's assertion that, despite the fact that his entire life has been wrecked, he will maintain his integrity and wholeness. He compares his enemy to the wicked, who know no rest and whose pleas for divine help go unanswered.

40:2

הרב עם שדי יסור מוכיח אלוה יעננה
hrb ʿm šdy yswr mwkyḥ ʾlwh yʿnnh
Shall he that has a quarrel with Shaddai chastise [him]?
Shall he that reproves ʾEloah afflict [him]?

יהוה (YHWH) reveals his true identity and, having raged at Job, asks almost plaintively that Job no longer attack him. Job's response is starkly unemotional:

הן קלתי מה אשיבך ידי שמתי למו פי
אחת דברתי ולא אענה ושתים ולא אוסיף
hn qlty mh ʾšybk ydy śmty lmw py
ʾḥt dbrty wlʾ ʾʿnh wštym wlʾ ʾwsyp
Behold, I have cursed [you], what shall I answer you? I have said my piece.[5]
I have spoken once and I shall not answer, twice and I shall not add.

---

[4] The sense of the Hebrew **אם** (*ʾm*) is clearly that of a negative oath in $27^{1\text{-}15}$. See GK §149*a*. The positive oath is expressed by **אם לא** (*ʾm lʾ*).

[5] **ידי שמתי למו פי** (*ydy śmty lmw py*)—literally, "I have put my hand to my mouth." Compare Jud.18^{19}.

Job reasserts his having cursed יהוה (YHWH) and states with some finality that he has spoken his piece. The reader is left with the overall impression of a stand-off between Job and יהוה (YHWH).

The pivotal word in Job's answer is קלתי (*qallôtî*), which we translate as "I have cursed" from √קלל 1st person singular perfect *qal* and transitive. Most translations render קלתי (*qallôtî*) as "I have become small (or humble)," in its intransitive form.[6] The latter, of course, plays directly to the exegetical view of Job as the "humble servant." Our translation reinforces the notion that Job is standing his ground, maintaining a peer-to-peer posture. This interpretation is reinforced by Num.23[20] where we have already read:

הנה ברך לקחתי וברך ולא אשיבנה
hnh brk lqḥty wbrk wl' 'šybnh
Behold, I took a curse (with me);
But he (Yahweh) blessed and I have no more to say.[7]

The similarity of the idiom is not coincidental, as we have previously demonstrated. Even the interrogative particle מה (*mh*) carries a negative connotation making it synonymous with לא (*l'*).

Chapters 38[1]- 39[30] pertain to the longevity of יהוה (YHWH) and his singular control over the workings of the physical world. In chapters 40[6]-41[26], יהוה (YHWH) continues to describe his superiority over the entire cosmos; however, his tone is more restrained and muted. While his crowning achievement is the act of creation, יהוה (YHWH) has had to deal with the consequences of creation, namely the subjugation of the cosmic monsters בהמות (*bhmwt*) and לויתן (*wytn*).[8] It is almost as if יהוה (YHWH) is looking for some sympathy from Job. Job is hardly overwhelmed by יהוה (YHWH)'s rhetoric, he has already anticipated and conceded the point in 26[12-13]. His final response in 42[1-6] is a masterpiece of diplomacy.

The Code Revealed

The verbal outbursts of יהוה (YHWH) in 38[2-3] and 40[7-8], and Job in 42[2-4] are perhaps the ultimate clues that the author has left regarding both the content of

---

[6] ע'ע verbs such as √סבב, √גלל , √דלל, √חנן, √שנן occur both in transitive and intransitive forms. That this is the only transitive occurrence of √קלל in the *qal* form is not unusual a work replete with *hapax legomena.*

[7] We have referenced this verse in our discussion of "blessing" and "cursing."

[8] See 40[15] and 40[25]. For a discussion of לויתן (*lwytn*) see Wilson (2002).

his *agendum* and the method he has used to articulate it. Here, in the final stage of his investigation, he puts the following words into their respective mouths:

38:2-3 – **יהוה** (YHWH) is the speaker:

מי זה מחשיך עצה במלין בלי דעת
אזר נא כגבר חלציך ואשאלך והודיעני
my zh mḥšyk ʿṣh bmlyn bly dʿt
ʾzr nʾ kgbr ḥlṣyk wʾšʾlk whwdyʿny
Who is this that darkens counsel with ignorant words?
Gird your waist like a man; and I will ask you and you shall inform me.

40:7-8 – **יהוה** (YHWH) is the speaker:

אזר נא כגבר חלציך אשאלך והודיעני
האף תפר משפטי תרשיעני למען תצדק
ʾzr nʾ kgbr ḥlṣyk ʾšʾlk whwdyʿny
hʾp tpr mšpṭy tršyʿny lmʿn tṣdq
Gird your waist like a man; I will ask you and you shall inform me.
Will you indeed frustrate my justice?
Will you vilify me so that you may be whole?

42:2-4 – Job is the speaker:

מי זה מעלים עצה בלי דעת
לכן הגדתי ולא אבין
נפלאות ממני ולא אדע
שמע נא ואנכי אדבר אשאלך והודיעני
my zh mʿlym ʿṣh bly dʿt nplʾwt mmny wlʾ ʾdʿ
šmʿ nʾ wʾnky ʾdbr ʾšʾlk whwdyʿny
Who is this that conceals counsel with ignorance?
So that it is I who speak without understanding;
Things too wondrous for me that I do not know.
Listen now and I will speak; I will ask you and you shall answer.

The common elements of these three passages are the complaint of deliberate obfuscation and the challenge to provide an answer. **יהוה** (YHWH)'s explicit challenge stands in clear contrast with the doubles entendre implied in the Prologue. The author's methodology can be identified as follows:

1. There is no direct *BH* antecedent for **מחשיך עצה** (*mḥšyk ʿṣh*) – "darkens counsel" or **מעלים עצה** (*mʿlym ʿṣh*) – "conceals counsel." We read, however, on point, in Isa.29[15]:

הוי המעמיקים מיהוה לסתר עצה והיה במחשך מעשיהם ויאמרו מי ראנו ומי ידענו
hwy hmʿmyqym myhwh lstr ʿṣh whyh bmḥšk mʿśyhm wyʾmrw my rʾnw wmy ydʿnw
O you who hide deep in order to hide [your] counsel from YHWH,
[You] whose deeds are in the dark; They say; "Who sees us? Who knows us?"

2. The phrase במלין בלי דעת (*bmlyn bly dʿt*) and עצה בלי דעת (*ʿṣh bly dʿt*) are reflected (in a slightly modified inverse form) in the speech of ʾElihu in 35[16], where he accuses Job as follows:

ואיוב הבל יפצה פיהו בבלי דעת מלין יכבר
wʾywb hbl ypṣh pyhw bbly dʿt mlyn ykbr
And Job opens his mouth with emptiness,
And in ignorance keeps on [talking].

Our author is letting us know that he is also the author of the ʾElihu section.

3. The idiom אזר חלציך (*ʾzr ḥlṣyk*) occurs only here and in Isa.11[5], where we read:

והיה צדק אזור מתניו והאמונה אזור חלציו
whyh ṣdq ʾzwr mtnyw whʾmwnh ʾzwr ḥlṣyw
And wholeness shall be the girdle of his hips
And steadfastness the girdle of his waist

After all the denials of the parity of צדק (*ṣdq*) between humanity and יהוה (YHWH), it is this issue that becomes the focal point.

It is essential to understand that none of the words צדק (*ṣdq*), צדיק (*ṣdyq*) and צדקה (*ṣdqh*) are explicitly mentioned in this exchange between יהוה (YHWH) and Job. They are inherently understood with the overtone of a sense of superiority. יהוה (YHWH) expresses his superiority as "prime being" and "creator." Job's counter-thrust of outright rejection is more than adequately up to the task. יהוה (YHWH) retreats into a plea for human sympathy; however, Job will have none of it.

יהוה (YHWH)'s accusation of Job of obfuscation is disingenuous. Our author may cast aspersion on the character of יהוה (YHWH); however, he never ever insinuates that יהוה (YHWH) is ignorant or unknowing. So what can he possibly mean with the words מי זה מחשיך עצה במלין בלי דעת (*my zh mḥšyk ʿṣh bmlyn bly dʿt*) – "Who is this that darkens counsel with ignorant words?"

יהוה (YHWH) can only be referring to himself and his inability to speak openly. If the reader has not already figured this out for himself, then the author feels compelled to enlighten him before the book is closed and the message lost. We can now understand יהוה (YHWH)'s double exhortation of Job[9] with the cryptic instruction אזר נא כגבר חלציך ואשאלך והודיעני (*ʾzr nʾ kgbr ḥlṣyk wʾšʾlk whwdyʿny*) – "Gird your waist like a man; and I will ask you and you shall inform me." יהוה (YHWH) is aware that Job has the answer and he knows that it lies in √צדק (*ṣdq*) when he says תרשיעני למען תצדק (*tršyʿny lmʿn tṣdq*) – "Will you vilify me so that you may be whole?" Our author's use of the coded phrase אזר...חלציך (*ʾzr ḥlṣyk*) underscores this message further.

Job's riposte of מי זה מעלים עצה בלי דעת...אשאלך והודיעני (*my zh mʿlym ʿṣh bly dʿt... ʾšʾlk whwdyʿny*) – "Who is this that conceals counsel with ignorance?...I will ask you and you shall answer" is both sardonic and disingenuous. He knows the answer and it is not the same as יהוה (YHWH)'s. The author has figured out that "divine" צדק (*ṣdq*) and "human" צדק (*ṣdq*) are not the same. Job's final utterance exposes יהוה (YHWH) even further:

42: 1-6

ידעתי כי כל תוכל ולא יבצר ממך מזמה
מי זה מעלים עצה בלי דעת לכן הגדתי ולא אבין נפלאות ממני ולא אדע
שמע נא ואנכי אדבר אשאלך והודיעני
לשמע אזן שמעתיך ועתה עיני ראתך
על כן אמאס ונחמתי על עפר ואפר

ydʿty ky kl twkl wlʾ ybṣr mmk mzmh
my zh mʿlym ʿṣh bly dʿt nplʾwt mmny wlʾ ʾdʿ
šmʿ nʾ wʾnky ʾdbr ʾšʾlk whwdyʿny
lšmʿ ʾzn šmʿtyk wʿth ʿyny rʾtk
lkn ʾmʾs wnḥmty ʿl ʿpr wʾpr

I know that you are capable of all
And that no design is beyond you.[10]
Who is this that conceals counsel with ignorance?
So that I speak without understanding
Things too wondrous for me that I do not know.
Listen now and I will speak; I will ask you and you shall answer.
I have heard report of you and now my eye has seen you.
And so I reject [you] and I feel sorry for all humanity.

---

[9] See 38^3 and 40^2

[10] Lit. "is cut off from you."

With these words, Job hands יהוה (YHWH) the ultimate humiliation and rejection. יהוה (YHWH) is the obfuscator who withholds knowledge from humanity. Job, for his part, has only suspected יהוה (YHWH)'s deeds and motives; Now he has converted suspicion to knowledge, rumor to visual empirical evidence. Since human and divine צדק (*ṣdq*) are equal and equivalent, then the best Job offers is a stand-off. If יהוה (YHWH) fails to understand, then Job claims victory.

עַל כֵּן אמאס ונחמתי עַל עָפָר ואפר (*ʿl kn ʾmʾs wnḥmty ʿl ʿpr wʾpr*)–And so I reject [you] and I feel sorry for all humanity. We achieve our rendition of this difficult verse by moving the Masoretic pause (*ʾetnak*)to **אמאס** (*ʾmʾs*) from **ונחמתי** (*wnḥmty*). One might conjecture that the Masoretes understood this verse well; however, they could not publish such a rejection for the "faithful" reader.

Job has turned the tables and takes the lead. The deity must now listen and follow. Job rejects יהוה (YHWH) on the basis of his knowledge and experience. Humanity must do likewise and reject יהוה (YHWH); if not, Job offers nothing but a cynical pity.

Conclusion

Were the author to have ended his investigation at this point, we would have been forced to conclude that human and divine צדק (*ṣdq*) are equal and equivalent as stated above. That given, it would follow that the universe can be governed by humanity and that humanity is indeed the master of its own fortunes. The deity would have rendered itself obsolete itself the moment it created humanity.

Our author is clearly not satisfied with these conclusions; he believes that, while a tension exists between humanity and deity, the two must somehow co-exist. Thus he provides the final epilogue.

Absolute Relatives: The Third Epilogue

Chapters 42 [7-17]

In the final epilogue, the author returns to the prose style of the Prologue. There is a twofold message in this literary stylistic pattern. First, on a superficial level, the prose epilogue provides a symmetry to the layout of the book. Second, and more important, the author uses this device to indicate his preference of solution to the question that he has posed from the very outset of his investigation.

42:7

ויהי אחר דבר יהוה את הדברים האלה אל איוב
ויאמר יהוה אל אליפז התימני
חרה אפי בך ובשני רעיך כי לא דברתם אלי נכונה כעבדי איוב

wyhy 'ḥr dbr yhwh 't hdbrym h'lh 'l 'ywb
wy'mr yhwh 'l 'lypz htymny
ḥrh 'py bk wbšny r'yk ky l' dbrtm 'ly nkwnh k'bdy 'ywb

And so it was after YHWH had spoken these words to Job
That YHWH said to 'Eliphaz the Temanite,
"I am very angry with you and your two friends,
For you have not spoken the truth to me as has my servant Job."

In the very first colon of the Epilogue, our author continues to propagate his patriarchal portrait of Job, harkening back to Gen.15[1].

אחר הדברים האלה היה דבר יהוה אל אברם במחזה לאמר
אנכי מגן לך שכרך הרבה מאד

'ḥr hdbrym h'lh hyh dbr yhwh 'l 'brm bmḥzh l'mr
'l tyr' 'brm 'nky mgn lk śkrk hrbh m'd

After these events, the word of YHWH [came] to Abram in a vision, saying,
"Fear not, Abram; I am your shield, your reward will be very great."

Of the eight occurrences in *BH*[1] of the phrase אחר הדברים האלה (*ʾḥrhdbrym hʾlh*) – "After these events," it is only Gen.15[1] that focuses on יהוה (YHWH)'s word and our author takes this opportunity to make two points. First, he informs us that יהוה (YHWH) is Job's protector (presumably *vis-à-vis* the three "friends"). Second, Job is to be rewarded after his harrowing experience (as Abram was to be rewarded for rescuing Lot), a subtle concession to השטן (*haśśaṭan*)'s crucial question of 1[9]—החנם ירא איוב אלהים (*hḥnm yrʾ ʾywb ʾlhym*)—"Is it *gratis* that Job reveres *ʾelohîm*?

The verse would also seem to indicate a face-to-face encounter between Job and יהוה (YHWH), a privilege that was not afforded to any of the patriarchs and bestowed only upon Moses.[2] The *BH* antecedent for this verse qualifies the nature of the encounter with the word במחזה (*bmḥzh*) – "in a vision," which we are expected to understand here also.

ויאמר יהוה אל אליפז התימני (*wyʾmr yhwh ʾl ʾlypz htymny*) – "YHWH said to ʾEliphaz the Temanite." This *ad hominem* communication is remarkable. There are other instances of יהוה (YHWH) communicating with "non-devotees" but it is always using the device of either a dream or an intermediary such as a מלאך (*mlʾk*) – "messenger."[3] Even in the case of Bilʿam,[4] the term used is ויקר (*wyqr*) "and (YHWH) happened to meet," for the purpose of putting words in Bilʿam's mouth. Perhaps our author is demonstrating the similarities and contrasts of the failures of Bilʿam and the three "friends." Bilʿam was unwilling and the three "friends" were unwitting. Bilʿam understood יהוה (YHWH)'s message; the three "friends" never got the message.

חרה אפי בך ובשני רעיך (*ḥrh ʾpy bk wbšny rʿyk*)—"I am very angry with you and your two friends." The expression of divine anger by literally the "flaring of the nostrils" is reserved for those who would do other than worship יהוה (YHWH) alone and whose fate is sealed.[5] The implication is that the three "friends" (who were not described in the Prologue as worshippers of יהוה YHWH) have tacitly supported Job in his raging tirade. The unanswered question is: why should they be at all concerned with יהוה (YHWH)'s anger? There is also no indication that their faith had turned away from יהוה (YHWH).

---

[1] Gen.22[1],39[7],40[1]; 1Kings17[17],21[1]; Esther 2[1],3[1].

[2] See Num.12[8], in which the language is circumlocutory.

[3] Num.22[31] in the case of Bilʿam.

[4] Num.23[16]

[5] See particularly Deut.6[14] for context although the expression occurs too frequently to list by individual citation.

We will see in the following verse that our author is expressing humor at the expense of יהוה (YHWH).

כי לא דברתם אלי נכונה (*ky l' dbrtm 'ly nkwnh*) – "For you have not spoken the truth to me." This is another unusual idiom. It is a circumlocution since it does not make an outright accusation of lying. This is in keeping with 1[22] and 2[10] in which the same technique is applied with reference to Job. There is, however, one reference in ψ 5[10] that seems to be the author's source:

אין בפיהו נכונה קרבם הוות קבר פתוח גרונם לשונם יחליקון
'yn bpyhw nkwnh qrbm hwwt qbr ptwḥ grwnm lšwnm yḥlyqwn
There is no truth in their[6] mouth, their innards are vacant;
Their throat is an open grave, they indulge in flattery.[7]

Thus the intent of **נכונה** (*nkwnh*) is not so much "truth"; it signifies something far stronger, which we can discern only from its opposite that appears in these two verses. It would appear to indicate "absolute correctness," any deviation from which carries a penalty that only ritual atonement will avert. We note again that Job is dealing with precisely this issue in 1[5]. יהוה (YHWH) is admitting the veracity and integrity of Job's original indictment of him.

כעבדי איוב (*k'bdy 'ywb*) – "as [has] my servant Job" carries a crucially important message. Our author leads us to Num.12[7-8a]:

לא כן עבדי משה בכל ביתי נאמן הוא
פה אל פה אדבר בו ומראה ולא בחידת...
l' kn 'bdy mšh bkl byty n'mn hw'
ph 'l ph 'dbr bw wmr'h wl' bḥydt
Not so My servant Moses; in all my house he is [the most] faithful.
I speak with him face to face,[8] in vision[s] and without riddles.[9]

This affirmation of Job's fidelity and integrity is accomplished by comparison with Moses. It is a statement that validates Job's faith and way of

---

[6] Lit. "his"
[7] Lit. "they make their tongue smooth."
[8] Lit. "mouth to mouth"
[9] Note the contrast of "straight talk" (**פה אל פה** – *ph 'l ph*) with "riddles" (**חידת** – *ḥydt*). This is important since the untranslatable word **משל** (*mšl*) of 27[1] and 29[1] is compared to (**חידה**) (*ḥydh*) in Prov.1[6] and Hab.2[6]. One might reasonably question whether our author is using the word **משל** (*mšl*) in two diametrically opposite senses as in the case of √ברך (*brk*).

life prior to יהוה (YHWH)'s episode of self-doubt. It also validates the statement at the beginning of the verse:

ויהי אחר דבר יהוה את הדברים האלה אל איוב
wyhy ʾḥr dbr yhwh ʾt hdbrym hʾlh ʾl ʾywb
And so it was after YHWH had spoken these words to Job

42:8

ועתה קחו לכם שבעה פרים ושבעה אילים
ולכו אל עבדי איוב והעליתם עולה בעדכם
ואיוב עבדי יתפלל עליכם כי אם פניו אשא לבלתי עשות עמכם נבלה
כי לא דברתם אלי נכונה כעבדי איוב
wʿth qḥw lkm šbʿh prym wšbʿh ʾylym
wlkw ʾl ʿbdy ʾywb whʿlytm ʿwlh bʿdkm
wʿbdy ʾywb ytpll ʿlykm ky ʾm pnyw ʾśʾ lblty ʿśwt ʿmkm nblh
ky lʾ dbrtm ʾly nkwnh kʿbdy ʾywb
And now, take for yourselves seven bullocks and seven rams
And go to my servant Job and make a burnt offering for yourselves,
And Job, my servant will pray for you
For I will favor him and not make a disgrace of you,
For you have not spoken the truth to me as has my servant Job.

Now our author lets us in on his sarcastic humor. Having thoroughly chastised the three "friends," יהוה (YHWH) prescribes a ritual sacrifice as expiation. The sacrifice is that which Bilʿam prescribed for Balak in Num.23[1,29].[10] Neither Bilʿam nor Balak was a follower of יהוה (YHWH) nor were the three "friends." The sacrifice was of no avail in the case of Bilʿam and it would take the participation of Job to for יהוה (YHWH) to "make an exception" (**כי אם** – *ky ʾm*) and change his mind about killing the three "friends."

While YHWH/*haśśaṭan* and *haśśaṭan*/YHWH appear to have been reintegrated into a single entity, our author cannot resist raising the possibility that this condition is subject to change. יהוה (YHWH) has two natures and the world must recognize them for what they are.

---

[10] **והכן לי בזה שבעה פרים ושבעה אילים** (*whkn ly bzh šbʿh prym wšbʿh ʾylym*)—"and prepare for me seven bullocks and seven rams."

עבדי איוב (*k'bdy 'ywb*) – "My servant Job." The repetition of this phrase three times in this one verse marks the elevation of Job to the status of Abraham and Moses as has been stated before.[11]

יתפלל עליכם (*ytpll 'lykm*) —"[Job] will pray for you." This is a construction that occurs only here and in 1Sam.1[10]:

והיא מרת נפש ותתפלל על יהוה ובכה תבכה
why' mrt npš wttpll 'l yhwh wbkh tbkh
And she was bitter of soul,
And she wept as she prayed to(?) YHWH

These two only usages of **התפלל על** (*htpll 'l*) appear to have completely different if not contradictory meanings. The usual construction is **התפלל אל** (*htpll 'l*) – "to pray to." One is tempted to render **על** (*'l*) as "concerning, with regard to" although this is not entirely satisfactory when applied to the Samuel citation. Perhaps more relevant to our scenario is Gen.20[7], where we find yet another interaction involving Abimelech, this time involving Abraham. The occasion is the resolution of their mutual *peccadilloes.*[12] Abraham has told Abimelech that Sarah is his sister and Abimelech has exercised his right as king to kidnap Sarah and make her part of his harem. Abimelech has received a divine dream-vision telling him of Abraham's deceit, acquitting him of any wrongdoing, and instructing him to return Sarah to her husband with the following admonition:

ועתה השב אשת האיש כי נביא הוא ויתפלל בעדך וחיה
ואם אינך משיב דע כי מות תמות אתה וכל אשר לך
w'th hšb 'št h'yš ky nby' hw' wytpll b'dk wḥyh
w'm 'ynk mšyb d' ky mwt tmwt 'th wkl 'šr lk
And now, return the man's wife, for he is a *nab̲î*,
And he will pray for you and [you shall] live;
But if you do not return [her],
Know that you and all of your [household] shall surely die.

Consistent with the patriarchal portrait of Job painted in the Prologue, our author ascribes to Job the status of a *nab̲î*,[13] who can communicate with the

---

[11] We have remarked on the importance of this epithet in 1[1] above.

[12] As was referred to in n.26 above.

[13] **נביא** (*nby*) is commonly rendered "prophet." The true description and status of **נביא** (*nby*) is a subject for another investigation.

divine and avert the divine wrath that will end in death. We should also recall that Abraham was rewarded for his efforts as is Job.

פניו אשא לבלתי עשות (*pnyw ʾśʾ lblty ʿśwt*) – This idiom (with **בלתי** – *blty*) occurs only in Gen.19[21] where we find **יהוה** (YHWH) speaking to Abraham:

ויאמר אליו הנה נשאתי פניך גם לדבר הזה
לבלתי הפכי את העיר אשר דברת
wyʾmr ʾlyw hnh nśʾty pnyk gm ldbr hzh
lblty hpky ʾt hʿyr ʾšr dbrt
And he [YHWH] said to him [Abraham]:
"I have favored you even in this matter
Of not overthrowing the city about which you spoke."

Our author uses the uniqueness of this expression to compare **יהוה** (YHWH)'s favoring of Job to that of Abraham—in keeping with the patriarchal portrait described in the introduction. Not far from the surface is the inherent contradiction expressed in Deut.10[20]:

כי יהוה אלהיכם הוא אלהי האלהים ואדני האדנים
האל הגדל הגבר והנורא אשר לא ישא פנים ולא יקח שחד
ky yhwh ʾlhykm hwʾ ʾlhy hʾlhym wʾdny hʾdnym
hʾl hgdl hgbr whnwrʾ ʾšr lʾ yśʾ pnym wlʾ yqḥ šḥd
For YHWH your god is the supreme god and master;
the great, powerful, and awesome god, who favors none and takes no bribe.

Of course, in Gen.19[21], we find **יהוה** (YHWH) bestowing favor, and in our own verse he bestows favor and demands the expiation offering as the price of mercy (a bribe). This apparent contradiction is a throwback to **השטן** (*haśśaṭan*)'s crucial question in 1[9]:

החנם ירא איוב אלהים
hḥnm yrʾ ʾywb ʾlhym
"Is it *gratis* that Job reveres *ʾelohîm*?

Job's reverence for **אלהים** (*ʾelohîm*) may be *gratis*; however, **יהוה** (YHWH) does not allow himself to be served *gratis*. He pre-empts any possibility of a show of spontaneous faith on the part of Job.

עשות עמכם נבלה (*ʿśwt ʿmkm nblh*) "make a disgrace of you" takes us back to the Genesis Chapter 34 story of Dinah (to which we have already made reference in 1[15]), particularly to Gen.34[7]:

כי נבלה עשה בישראל לשכב את בת יעקב
ky nblh ʿśh byśrʾl lškb ʾt bt yʿqb
For he [Shechem] had committed a disgrace in Israel
By having sexual relations with the daughter of Jacob

נבלה (*nblh*) – the "disgrace" is clearly defined as a sexual offense.[14] It is difficult to imagine what **יהוה** (YHWH) would actually inflict on the three "friends." Perhaps our author is again expressing sarcasm about **יהוה** (YHWH)'s ability to inflict anything.

42:9

וילכו אליפז התימני ובלדד השוחי וצופר הנעמתי
ויעשו כאשר דבר אליהם יהוה וישא יהוה את פני איוב
wylkw ʾlypz htymny wbldd hšwḥy wṣwpr hnʿmty
wyʿśw kʾšr dbr ʾlyhm yhwh wyśʾ yhwh ʾt pny ʾywb
And ʾEliphaz the Temanite, Bildad the Shuhite, and Zophar the Naʿamathite went
And did as YHWH had spoken to them and YHWH showed favor to Job.

This verse continues to beg the question asked in 42[7], namely, why should the three "friends" recognize **יהוה** (YHWH) and the chastisement that he has meted out and why would they instantly obey the word of **יהוה** (YHWH)? After all, we have no evidence from either the Prologue or the body of the book that theirs was an "Israelite" or "Jewish" theology. It would appear that the answer must lie in their concern for Job's well-being, which they demonstrated in the form of imitation, as we saw in 2[12]. In other words, if Job thought it was the right thing to do, then they would do it for his sake.

42:10

ויהוה שב את שבית איוב בתהפללו בעד רעהו
ויסף יהוה את כל אשר לאיוב למשנה
wyhwh šb ʾt šbyt ʾywb bhtpllw bʿd rʿhw
wysp yhwh ʾt kl ʾšr lʾywb lmšnh
And YHWH returned the captivity of Job
In exchange for his praying on behalf of his friend,
And YHWH increased all Job's possessions twofold.

---

[14] See also Deut.22[21]; Jos.7[15]; Jud.19[23], 20[6,10]; 2Sam.13[12]; Jer29[23]. In Isa.9[16] and 32[6], **נבלה** (*nblh*) appears to take on the meaning of "disgraceful speech" as opposed to action. Isa.24[4], the denominative √**נבל** (*nbl*) occurs in the context of either "practicing" or "being in a state of" **נבלה** (*nblh*) similar to the retort of Job to his wife in 2[10].

שב את שבית איוב (*šb ʾt šbyt ʾywb*) – "returned the captivity of Job." At first blush, this might appear to be a veiled reference to the return from exile in Babylon. However, this idiom only makes sense if we accept our suggested reading of **שביה** (*šbyh*) for **שבא** (*šbʾ*) in 1^{15}.[15] This would imply the return of the oxen and the asses that had been taken away in **השטן** (*haśśaṭan*)'s first strike. That this is in fact the case is spelled out arithmetically in 42^{12}.

בהתפללו בעד רעהו (*bhtpllw bʿd rʿhw*) – "in exchange for his praying on behalf of his friend."[16] The prefix **ב** (*b*) of the first word of this phrase denotes "price." Whether Job prayed for one friend or all of them is not material here. What does grab the reader is that Job received something of value in exchange for his efforts. While **יהוה** (YHWH) has predicted the outcome of Job's intercession, he is not pre-emptive in his payment; he pays for services rendered.

We are back (to **השטן** *haśśaṭan*)'s penetrating and crucial question of 1^9:

החנם ירא איוב אלהים.
hḥnm yrʾ ʾywb ʾlhym
"Is it *gratis* that Job reveres *ʾelohîm*?"

Of course we now know that the answer is "No." Had **יהוה** (YHWH) been honest with himself in answering the question in the first place, there would have been no need to for our author to embark on this endeavor. With his ambivalent exchange with (to **השטן** *haśśaṭan*), **יהוה** (YHWH) has wrought a terrible tragedy on a devotee whose only transgression was to be faithful (to the exclusion of loving) to a fault.

למשנה (*lmšnh*) – "twofold." This usage is quite common in *BH*. We shall see that the "doubling" refers to the quantity of Job's livestock as enumerated in 1^3.

42:11

ויבאו אליו כל אחיו וכל אחיתיו וכל ידעיו לפנים ויאכלו עמו לחם בביתו
וינדו לו וינחמו אתו על כל הרעה אשר הביא יהוה עליו
ויתנו לו איש קשיטה אחת ואיש נזם זהב אחד
wybʾw ʾlyw kl ʾḥyw wkl ʾḥytyw wkl ydʿyw lpnym wyʾklw ʿmw lḥm bbytw
wyndw lw wyḥmw ʾtw ʿl kl hrʿh ʾšr hbyʾ yhwh ʿlyw
wytnw lw ʾyš qśyṭh ʾḥt wnzm zhb ʾḥd

---

[15] The *Qere* **שבות** (*šbyh*) is not material to this discussion. See *BDB* 986.

[16] *GK* §*91k* explains **רעהו** (*rʿhw*) as a plural form with the orthographic letter **י** (*y*) missing, citing 1Sam.30^6 and Prov.29^6 as similar cases. However, neither of these instances is conclusive and *GK* retreats to the suggestion that this is a "collective."

And all of his brothers, sisters and previous acquaintances came
And ate bread with him at his house. And they consoled and comforted him
For all the evil that YHWH had brought upon him.
And each man gave him one qesitah and one gold ring.

This is the one and only occasion where there is any mention of a family that extended beyond Job's wife and children. The terms "brothers" and "sisters" are used discreetly since his children are no longer alive. Where were they and his "previous acquaintances" when he really needed them? We note that they are "acquaintances" as opposed to friends since that term is reserved for the "three friends." Also notably missing is Job's wife, although she must clearly be alive to bear Job's post-ordeal children. Job's pious asceticism in his previous life had rendered him almost hermetic as we have already observed. One can only conclude that these people had not approved of Job's lifestyle and thus avoided him. The only person who had stayed with Job was his wife. She had recognized the consequences of Job's "piety" and had spoken her mind only to be rudely and unkindly rejected. She is now absent, perhaps unable to deal with the fact that her "disgraceful talk" was indeed the reality and that the price of "perfect integrity" was beyond human means.

Our author has very carefully chosen the phrase used to describe the consolation of Job. It has its antecedent in Gen.37[35], which describes the efforts of Jacob's children to comfort him after he had learned the fate of Joseph:

ויקמו כל בניו וכל בנתיו לנחמו וימאן להתנחם
wyqmw kl bnyw wkl bntyw lnḥmw wym'n lhtnḥm
And all of his sons and daughters arose to comfort him,
And he refused to be comforted.

The contrast is quite stark—Jacob refuses any comfort while Job accepts. We have already postulated that our author excluded Jacob from the patriarchal character attributes that he ascribed to Job. We have also shown that he used Jacob specifically for the purpose of describing **יהוה** YHWH. Job did not reject consolation; the "friends," while having ostensibly come for that very purpose, never offered any because they did not know how to offer it. There is the subtle suggestion of reverse psychology that **יהוה** YHWH is inconsolable since he is the explicit agent of Job's misfortune, as is stated in the very next phrase, and he is once again regretting an action that he has errantly taken.

על כל הרעה אשר הביא יהוה (*ʿl kl hrʿh ʾšr hbyʾ yhwh*) – "For all the evil that YHWH had brought upon him" connects us with 2[11] of the Prologue and the citation from 1Kings 9[9]:

על כן הביא יהוה עליהם את כל הרעה הזאת
ʿl kn hbyʾ yhwh ʾlyhm ʾt kl hrʿh hzʾt
And so, YHWH has brought all this evil upon them.

It is interesting to note that all of Job's bearers of comfort and consolation understood that it was יהוה YHWH who was responsible for Job's misfortune. They seem to accept the imperfection and compromise that Job in his *naïveté* would not admit.

קשיטה (*qśyṭh*) – "*q^e^śîṭâh*" is a unit of currency of as yet undetermined value. The word occurs also in Gen.33[19] and derivatively in Jos.24[32]. The context of the Genesis citation is as follows:

ויקן את חלקת השדה אשר נטה שם אהלו מיד בני חמור אבי שכם במאה קשיטה
wyqn ʾt ḥlqt hśdh ʾšr nṭh šm ʾhlw
myd bny ḥmwr ʾby škm bmʾh qśyṭh
And he [Jacob] purchased the portion of the field in which he had pitched his tent,
From the sons of Hamor the father of Shechem, for one hundred qesitah.

Why does our author use the *q^e^śîṭâh* as the currency of choice as opposed to the more recognizable *shekel*? As can be readily ascertained from the passage cited above, he wishes to remind us of יהוה (YHWH)'s ongoing presence through the actions of Jacob. יהוה YHWH is rewarding Job, [17] again validating the skepticism of השטן *haśśaṭan*) in 1[9].

נזם זהב אחד (*nzm zhb ʾḥd*) – "one gold ring." In the same way that our author chose the קשיטה (*qśyṭh*) in order to emphasize its "tainted" nature, he has similarly selected the "gold ring." The *BH* antecedent occurs in Jud.8[23-25,27].

Gideon, enraged by the disloyalty and distrust of the populace of Succoth and Penuʾel during his pursuit of the Midianites, has returned to these towns and destroyed them. The Israelites ask Gideon to be their king but he declines, asserting that the kingship belongs to יהוה YHWH. Gideon, trying to pacify the people, acts as follows:

ויאמר אליהם גדעון אשאלה מכם שאלה ותנו לי איש נזם שללו
כי נזמי זהב להם כי ישמעלים הם
ויאמרו נתון נתן ויפרשו את השמלה וישליכו שמה איש נזם שללו...
ויעש אותו גדעון לאפוד ויצג אותו בעירו בעפרה
ויזנו כל ישראל אחריו שם ויהי לגדעון ולביתו למוקש

---

[17] This is also reminiscent of the ancient Mesopotamian practice of rewarding the winner of a debate or disputation. See *COS* 1.180 (310).

wy'mr 'lyhm gd'wn 'š'lh mkm š'lh wtnw ly 'yš nzm šllw
ky nzmy zhb lhm ky yšm'lym hm
wy'mrw ntwn ntn wyprśw 't hśmlh wyšlykw šmh 'yš nzm šllw...
wy'ś 'wtw gd'wn l'pwd wyṣg 'wtw b'yrw b'rph
wyznw kl yśr'l 'ḥryw šm wyhy lgd'wn wlbytw lmwqš
And Gideon said to them,
"Let me ask a favor of you. [I want] each of you give me the ring of his booty,"
For they had rings of gold, since they were traders.
And they said, "We will surely give."
And they spread out a garment and there each man tossed the ring of his booty...
And he [Gideon] made it into an *ephod* and set it up in his town of Ofrah,
And all Israel worshipped it there
And it became a trap for Gideon and his household.

This lengthy citation[18] is relevant not only for its reference to "gold rings"; it provides us with two additional insights. First, the "gold rings" were the spoils of a war waged in the name of יהוה YHWH. Second, Gideon used them to create an *ephod*, a garment that was to be worn by the High Priest, which was covered by the מעיל (*m'yl*), the coat that Job tore in his rage and grief.[19]

Thus the "presents" that Job received from his family and friends were reminiscent of the scars left by Job's ordeal. Although the ordeal is over, יהוה YHWH leaves a reminder that, while he is omniscient and omnipotent, the aspects of cruelty and unpredictability are real.

42:12

ויהוה ברך את אחרית איוב מראשתו
ויהי לו ארבעה עשר אלף צאן וששת אלפים גמלים ואלף צמד בקר ואלף אתונות
wyhwh brk 't 'ḥryt 'ywb mr'štw
wyhy lw 'rb'h 'śr 'lp ṣ'n wššt 'lpym gmlym w'lp ṣmd bqr w'lp 'twnwt
And YHWH blessed Job's latter days even more than his former [days];
And he owned 14,000 sheep, 6,000 camels, 1,000 yoke of cattle, and 1,000 she-asses.

ויהוה ברך (*wyhwh brk*) – This is the only occasion in the book of Job where the √ברך (*brk*) is attributed to the deity; hence its meaning "And YHWH blessed." ויהוה ברך (*wyhwh brk*) has its *BH* antecedent in Gen.24[1], where we read:

---

[18] This is almost certainly the antecedent for the Pentateuchal story of Aaron and the "Golden Calf" in Ex.32[1-4].
[19] See 1[20] above.

ואברהם זקן בא בימים ויהוה ברך את אברהם בכל
w'brhm zqn b' bymym wyhwh brk 't 'brhm bkl
And Abraham was old, advanced in days,
And YHWH blessed Abraham with everything.

Once again, Job's patriarchal status is aligned with that of Abraham. The quantities of livestock are exactly double the amount that Job possessed prior to his ordeal.[20]

42:13-15

ויהי לו שבענה בנים ושלוש בנות
ויקרא שם האחת ימימה ושם השנית קציעה ושם השלישית קרן הפוך
ולא נמצא נשים יפות כבנות איוב בכל הארץ
ויתן להם אביהם נחלה בתוך אחיהם
wyhy lw šbʿnh bnym wšlwš bnwt
wyqr' šm h'ḥt ymymh wšm hšnyt qṣyʿh wšm hšlyšyt qrn hpwk
wl' nmṣ' nšym ypwt kbnwt 'ywb bkl h'rṣ
wytn lhm 'byhm nḥlh btwk 'ḥyhm
And he had seven sons and three daughters.
And he named the first Yemimah, the second Qeṣiah, and the third Qeren HaPuk.
And there were not found women as beautiful as the daughters of Job in all the land;
And their father gave them an inheritance among their brothers.

These three verses are apparently enigmatic and linguistically difficult.
שבענה (*šbʿnh*) is an unrecognized form in *BH*. It would appear to be clear from the context that it means "seven." Some scholars see this as an Aramaism and justify it based on the frequency of Aramaisms in the poetic body of the book. However, **שבענה** (*šbʿnh*) is not a recognizable Aramaism. The *Targum* interprets it as a dual form,[21] perhaps to fit in with the doubling of Job's wealth; however, that leaves the problem of only three daughters. Smith, describing the composition of the divine family at Ugarit, observes that:

> The different tiers of the divine household are analogous with the four tiers of the pantheon. The top two tiers are occupied by the divine parents and their children, while the bottom two tiers of the pantheon consist of deities working in the divine household. El is the father of deities and humanity. Accordingly, El's capacity as ruler of the pantheon is expressive of his function as patriarch of the family. Correspondingly, his wife Athirat (biblical Asherah) is considered the

---

[20] See 42^{10} above.

[21] *Targum* reads **ארבסר** (*'rbsr*) – "fourteen." *LXX* renders as "seven"

> mother of deities and humanity. El and Athirat are the divine royal parents of the pantheon, and the dominant deities are generally regarded as their royal children...These divine children are called in generic terms 'the seventy sons of Athirat'. This number is well known as a conventional number for a generally large group...The convention for presenting the royal family in terms of this number is evident in the case of Jerubbaal and his 70 sons (Judg.9^5)...The leading members of Emar are called 'the seventy sons of Emar'...One of the two Tel Dan inscriptions refers to the 'seventy kings' faced by the Aramean king...
> The second tier of gods can have their own household as well. Baal...has three 'daughters' (*bt*) called Pidray, 'Arsay and Tallay...[22]

Smith, by the foregoing citation, has perhaps unwittingly stumbled across the meaning of **שבענה** (*šbʿnh*). His description of the family of the pantheon describes seventy sons and three daughters. While having no philological or lexical grounds to render **שבענה** (*šbʿnh*) as "seventy" (we have no solid grounds for rendering **שבענה** (*šbʿnh*) as "seven," or for that matter, "fourteen") we can suppose that our author uses this traditional description from antiquity to set up the scenario for the upcoming climactic conclusion to his work. He is about to use the story of the daughters of Zelophehad (**צלפחד** – *ṣlpḥd*), which is characterized by the absence of sons. Thus he constructs Job's reconstituted family with all the grandeur befitting royalty. With almost a wry humor he draws on a well-known paradigm to provide the male heirs necessary for him to resolve one loose end from the beginning of the Prologue. In 1^4, we read:

והלכו בניו ועשו משתה בית איש יומו
ושלחו וקראו לשלשת אחיתיהם לאכל ולשתות עמהם
whlkw bnyw wʿsw mšth byt ʾyš ywmw
whlkw wqrʾw lšlšt ʾḥytyhm lʾkl wlštwt ʿmhm
And his sons would go and make a feast, each in his home
And they would send invitations to their three sisters to eat and drink with them.

It appears that while Job's sons each had their own houses, his daughters were not afforded the same privilege and lived at home with their parents. Now that Job has survived his ordeal, presumably by dint of his √**צדק** (*ṣdq*), he seizes the opportunity to set right this injustice and inequity. Job may even now perceive this as his own sin—unintentional though it may have been—and the proximate cause of the divine anger that wrought his calamities. Our author uses

---

[22] Smith (2001, 42-43)

the story of the daughters of Zelophehad (**צלפחד** – *ṣlpḥd*)[23] to solve Job's perceived problem with both **אלהים** (*'lhym*) and **יהוה** (YHWH). We read the substantive portion of Num.27[1-7]:

ותקרבנה בנות צלפחד...ואלה שמות בנתיו מחלה נעה וחגלה ומלכה ותרצה
ותעמדנה לפני משה...פתח אהל מועד לאמר
אבינו מת במדבר והוא לא היה בתוך העדה הנועדים על יהוה בעדת קרח
כי בחטאו מת ובנים לא היו לו
למה יגרע שם אבינו מתוך משפחתו כי אין לו בן
תנה לנו אחזה בתוך אחי אבינו ויקרב משה את משפטן לפני יהוה
ויאמר יהוה אל משה לאמר כן בנות צלפחד דברת
נתון תתן להם אחזת נחלה בתוך אחי אביהם
והעברת את נחלת אביהן להן

wtqrbnh bnwt ṣlpḥd... w'lh šmwt bnwty wmḥlh nʿh wḥglh wmlkh wtrṣh
wtʿmdnh lpny mšh... ptḥ 'hl mwʿdl 'mr
'bynw mt bmdbr whw' l' hyh btwk hʿdh hnwʿdym ʿl yhwh bʿdt qrḥ
ky bḥṭ'w mt wbnym l' hyw lw
lmh ygrʿ šm 'bynw mtwk mšpḥtw ky 'yn lw bn
tnh lnw 'ḥzh btwk 'ḥy 'bynw wyqrb mšh 't mšpṭn lpny yhwh
wy'mr yhwh 'l mšh l'mr kn bnwt ṣlpḥd dbrt
ntwn ttn lhm 'ḥzh btwk 'ḥy 'byhm whʿbrt 't nḥlt 'byhn lhn

And the daughters of Zelophehad approached…
And these were the names of his daughters, Mahlah, Noʿah, Haglah, Milkah and Tirzah.
And they stood before Moses…at the door to the "tent of meeting" saying:
"Our father died in the wilderness,
and he was not among Korah's group who banded together against YHWH;
He died on account of his own sin for he had no sons.
Why should our father's name be demeaned in his family because he had no sons?
Give us an inheritance among our father's brothers."
And Moses brought their case[24] before YHWH.
And YHWH said to Moses: "The daughters of Zelophehad are right;
Indeed, give them an inheritance among their father's brothers,
And you shall hand down their father's inheritance to them."[25]

The daughters of Zelophehad (**צלפחד** – *ṣlpḥd*) are analogous to Job's daughters. Just as the daughters of Zelophehad could not inherit their father's

---

[23] See Num.27[1-11]. The story is also recounted, using different language with a clearly more legalistic bent in Num.36. A parallel, albeit briefer account occurs in Josh.17[3,4].
[24] Lit. "their judgment."
[25] The irregularities of gender in the declaration of Num.27[7] (**אביהם** (*'byhm*) and **להם** (*lhm*) are masculine while referring to women) are repeated in 42[15].

real property, neither could Job's daughters. Similarly as the daughters of Zelophehad (צלפחד – *ṣlpḥd*) are identified by name—(מחלה (*mḥlh*), נעה (*n'h*), חגלה (*ḥglh*), מלכה (*mlkh*), and תרצה (*trṣh*), so are Job's daughters—ימימה (*ymymh*), קציעה (*qṣy'h*), and קרן הפוך (*qrn hpwk*).[26] As Moses caused a wrong to be righted in granting inheritance rights to daughters, so does Job. Only Job goes further; Moses tackled the issue of posthumous female inheritance in the absence of male heirs. Job deals with the issue while he is still alive and despite the fact that he had male heirs. Job recognized his own sin (חטא – *ḥṭ'*), unintentional as it may have been,[27] and it was not going to be the cause of his death, as it had been in the case of Zelophehad (צלפחד – *ṣlpḥd*).

Machinist deals with this issue but is entangled in a dating issue that derails his train of thought.[28] He entertains the possibility that:

> the Job author is, in fact, reacting to the Zelophahad story in its Numbers and Joshua versions....On the other hand, perhaps it is better to be more cautious about how exclusive the connections between the two texts are, especially because it is not clear that on other criteria we can date Zelophahad, either in its Numbers and Joshua form, earlier than Job.

Since we know that the Deuteronomist preceded Ezekiel and the Priestly redactor, we can be certain that our author was intimately familiar with the Zelophehad (צלפחד – *ṣlpḥd*) story. Consequently, Machinist cannot advance beyond the social and legal advance represented by the Job story without the

---

[26] See Num.27[1].The literal meanings of the names are not relevant to the matter at hand. Pope (1974, 353) misses the meaning of the entire episode. He mentions the daughters of Zelophehad only in the context of inheritance and concentrates on discerning the literal meanings of their names.

[27] This is the meaning of כי בחטאו מת ובנים לא היו לו (*ky bḥṭ'w mt wbnym l' hyw lw*) – He died on account of his own [unintentional] sin for he had no sons. The unintentional sin of Zelophehad (צלפחד – *ṣlpḥd*) was that he did not have any sons. The lack of a male heir is considered to be a sin; the language used to describe the demise of Zelophehad (צלפחד – *ṣlpḥd*) is identical to that of Deut.24[16], which is accurately reflected in Ezek.18[20,24]. The unintentionality is conveyed through the use of the √חטא (*ḥṭ'*) and its connotation of "missing the mark."

[28] Machinist (1997, 74ff.)

benefit of the Pentateuchal (or Hexateuchal) base account(s). He is never able to understand the substantive value derived by our author.[29]

The direct analogy of these two stories ends here. Our author has stated *ab initio* that Job was ירא אלהים (*yr*ʾ *ʾlhym*) – "reverent of *ʾelohîm*."[30] We have stipulated that אלהים (*ʾlhym*) represents the perpetual institution of justice. For Job in the Prologue, a sin against אלהים (*ʾlhym*), albeit unintentional, would be unconscionable and undermine the basis of his absolute value system. Job of the 3rd Epilogue has learned that, while אלהים (*ʾlhym*) is unchanging, humanity cannot deal with the vagaries of life "in the image of אלהים (*ʾlhym*)." Not all wrongs are absolute; they can be rectified. Perfect wholeness √צדק (*ṣdq*) is not possible; the best humanity has to offer is "the pursuit of wholeness."

In the Prologue, Job could never suspect that אלהים (*ʾlhym*) might be at the root of his troubles. He laid the blame squarely at the feet of יהוה (YHWH). Job was ignorant of the fact that he was the object of יהוה (YHWH)'s fears about his own inadequacies, yet he was intuitively aware that it was the hand of יהוה (YHWH) that was present in all of his travails. Now in the 3rd Epilogue, Job understands the inexactness of "wholeness" and equity. It is יהוה (YHWH)'s "judgment" that the daughters of Zelophehad be treated fairly and he comprehends the pursuit of "wholeness" (√צדק (*ṣdq*). It is just that the "wholeness" of יהוה (YHWH) is different from that of humanity. Job's daughters will receive the "wholeness" of יהוה (YHWH).

Thus our author has manufactured a brilliant resolution to the questions about the natures of god and humanity that he presented to the reader in the Prologue.

יהוה (YHWH) and man share a mutual need for one another and are therefore reciprocally affected each by the action of the other. Unwillingness to voluntarily adapt on the part of either the deity or humanity will inevitably result in catastrophe for both. Neither יהוה (YHWH) nor humanity can exist without change.

Why Zelophehad (צלפחד – *ṣlpḥd*)?

The interpretation that we have just suggested certainly satisfies the author's desire to present a final resolution to the philosophical enterprise. However, the

---

[29] Fishbane (1985,99n.) refers to this passage *en passant* in his discussion of the Zelophehad (צלפחד – *ṣlpḥd*) story. He sees it only as part of the continuum of the development of the legal process.

[30] See 1[1].

Zelophehad (צלפחד – *ṣlpḥd*) story serves a second and perhaps more personal purpose, namely the politico-religious identity of the author.

One of the major differences between the Sadducees and the Pharisees was that the Sadducees followed a traditional practice of their own in granting the daughter the same right of inheritance as the son's daughter in case the son was dead.[31] This went further than the *BH* Zelophehad (צלפחד – *ṣlpḥd*) story, which gave the daughters rights of inheritance only if there was no son and only if they married a member of their tribe.

The author focuses very clearly on Job's granting his daughters their inheritance while their brothers were still alive. This goes even further than the main stream and is an innovation that can only be an outgrowth of Sadducee practices.

Schiffman has suggested that the sect of the Dead Sea Scrolls was a Sadducean splinter from the Sadducee High Priesthood in Jerusalem:

> "The earliest members must have been Sadducees unwilling to accept the *status quo* establishment in the aftermath of the Maccabaean revolt. The Maccabees, by replacing the Zadokite high priesthood with their own, reduced the Zadokites to a subsidiary position for as long as Hasmonaean rule lasted. Even after leaving Jerusalem, the Dead Sea sect continued to refer to its leaders as the 'Sons of Zadok'. These were indeed Sadducees who protested the imposition of Pharisaic views in the Temple under the Hasmonaean priests."[32]

He bases this theory on the similarities of certain recorded Sadducee practices and those articulated in *Miqṣat Maʿaśeh ha-Torah* (*4QMMT*). We have already demonstrated that the author of the Book of Job used language that occurs in the Dead Sea Scrolls to the exclusion of *BH*. While Schiffman's view is not universally accepted,[33] the recording of a daughter's direct right of inheritance in the Book of Job gives more than a measure of support to his hypothesis. If in fact the Book of Job is a Sadducean product, then we will be able to narrow its date to the middle of the 2nd century BCE.

42:16-17

ויחי איוב אחרי זאת מאה וארבעים שנה
ויירא את בניו ואת בני בניו ארבעה דרות
וימת איוב זקן ושבע ימים

---

[31] *Meg. Ta'an.* v.; *Tosefta Yadayim.* ii. 20;BT *Bava Bathra* viii. 1, 115b
[32] Schiffman, (1994, 88).
[33] VanderKam (1994, 93-95).

wyḥy ʾywb ʾḥry zʾt mʾh wʾrbʿym šnh
wyrʾ ʾt bnyw wʾt bny bnyw ʾrbʿh drwt
wymt ʾywb zqn wśbʿ ymym
And Job lived for one hundred and forty years after this
And he saw four generations of his children and grandchildren.
And Job died, old and contented.

מאה וארבעים שנה (*mʾh wʾrbʿym šnh*) – "one hundred and forty years." There is some confusion about the arithmetic of totaling the length of Job's life. Perhaps the number 140 signifies double the length of a man's life as stated in ψ90[10]. Perhaps it simply signifies a number greater than the 110 years of Joseph's life since the hyperbole extends to the second colon of the verse. More likely, though, is the probability that it unambiguously demonstrates that Job's fixing of the inheritance issue enabled him to survive his sin[34] and live to old age.

וירא את בניו ואת בני בניו ארבעה דרות (*wyrʾ ʾt bnyw wʾt bny bnyw ʾrbʿh drwt*) – "And he saw four generations of his children and grandchildren." Up to the very end, our author emphasizes the magnitude of Job's repair of the injustice that he had inflicted on his daughters. This is both a reflection and hyperbole of Gen.50[23]:

וירא יוסף לאפרים בני שלשים
wyrʾ ywsp lʾprym bny šlšym
And Joseph lived to see[35] the third generation of the children of Ephraim

זקן ושבע ימים (*zqn wśbʿ ymym*) – "old and contented" occurs in Gen.35[29] describing the death of Isaac.. Job is a patriarch to the end. The quilt is finished.

---

[34] Which would have been the proximate cause of his death, had the author continued to follow the Zelophehad (**צלפחד** – *ṣlpḥd*) story literally.
[35] Lit. "saw"

"RIGHTEOUSNESS" AND "WHOLENESS" RELIGION, POLITICS AND ETHICS

Having presented a unique intertextual approach to the Book of Job, we must devote some time and space to a discussion of its place in the history of Judaism. This we shall attempt to extract from the literary data that we have compiled. It is fully well realized that this exercise may be speculative.

When we consider the terms צדק (*ṣdq*), צדיק (*ṣdyq*) and צדקה (*ṣdqh*), we tend immediately to focus on qualities such as "goodness" "righteousness," and "piety." Pentateuchal characters such as Abraham, Isaac, Jacob, Moses, Aaron, and a host of post-biblical names of prophets, priests and rabbis come to mind almost at once. It is noteworthy that this list of names is timeless and ageless, spanning generations that saw victory, defeat, wealth, poverty, oppression, and liberation. The circumstances change but צדק (*ṣdq*), צדיק (*ṣdyq*) and צדקה (*ṣdqh*) continue to find relevance.

Cognate Occurrences of √צדק (*ṣdq*)

√צדק (*ṣdq*) is extremely well attested in the ancient Near East. The following are a few examples:[1]

We find *ṣaduq* meaning "right", "just" in the El Amarna letters. Abdi-Heba of Jerusalem writes to the king of Egypt, "See, my Lord, I am right (*ṣa-du-uq*)…"[2]

In Old South Arabic, the verb *ṣdq* means "to be trustful, be just, fulfill an obligation." The noun means "right, due, truth" and the adjective means "proper, appropriate," with the *nuances* of "happy and fortunate."[3]

In the Ugaritic *Keret* epic, *ṣdqh* appears as an abstract noun parallel with *yšrh*.[4] Elsewhere, the king of Ugarit is described as *bʿl ṣdq*.[5].

---

[1] For a full treatment of √צדק (*ṣdq*), see *HALOT* 1001-1007.
[2] 14th century BCE, El Amarna Letters (*EA* 287:32)
[3] *DOSA*, 416–18.
[4] *KTU* 1.14, ll.12-13, *COS*, 1.102. See also Yeḥimilk inscription below.
[5] *UT*, 1007:4

The words *ṣdq* and *yšr* occur together in the Phoenician Yeḥimilk inscription from Byblos describing "the righteous king and just king."[6] *ṣmḥ ṣdq*, "a righteous, lawful branch," occurs in the Phoenician Lapēthos inscription.[7]

In the bilingual inscription from Karatepe, Azatiwadda recounts his good deeds and says that "every king made me as a father because of my righteousness (*bṣdqy*), my wisdom, and the goodness of my heart."[8]

The substantive *ṣdq* occurs in the Zinçirli inscriptions. In the *Barrākib* inscription the incumbent says that he was seated on the throne "because of the loyalty of my father (*bṣdq ʾby*) and because of my own loyalty (*bṣdqy*)."[9]Likewise the *Panamuwa* inscription refers to (*bṣdq ʾby*).[10]

On an Aramaic tomb inscription from Nērāb, SE of Aleppo, Siʾgabbar, priest of Sahar, had inscribed "because of my righteousness (*bṣdqty*) in his presence, he gave me a good name and prolonged my days".[11]

The word *ṣdqh* appears with the definite article *ṣdqtʾ* in a 5th–4th century BCE inscription from Tēmā in Arabia.[12]

A 5th-century Phoenician inscription commemorating the foundation of a temple near Sidon records that the king *ʿBDʿŠTRT* and *bn ṣdq* were its founders.[13].

In light of the many meanings of √צדק (*ṣdq*) just enumerated, it is difficult to understand the practice of Bible scholars of using the umbrella term "righteousness." One simply cannot accept that *BH* language and idiom should remain constant and unchanging simply because *BH* is a single compilation. The collection that forms *BH* covers a significantly large period of time; therefore its vocabulary must be examined in the context of the time period in which it occurs. By the same token, one must beware of the pitfalls of defining usages to fit theologies that are as yet non-existent.[14]

One measure of the importance of the concept of √צדק (*ṣdq*), which we call "wholeness" is the fact that it occurs fifteen (15) times in the Book of Genesis, forty-two (42) times in the Pentateuch (including Genesis), forty six (46) times in the Book of Ezekiel (primarily in chapters 18 and 33), and thirty-six (36) times in the Book of Job. Only Psalms and Proverbs (10-12) in the "wisdom"

---

6 10th-century BCE. *COS* 2.39, *KAI* 4
7 3rd century BCE. *KAI* 43. See also Jer.23[5].
8 8th century BCE. *COS*, 2.31, *KAI* 26
9 8th century BCE. *COS*, 2.38, *KAI* 216
10 8th century BCE. *COS*, 2.37, *KAI* 215
11 7th century BCE. *COS*, 2.59, *KAI* 276
12 *KAI* 226A, *DISO*, 243, *DNSWI*, 964
13 *KAI* 16
14 See the articles on "righteousness" in the *Anchor Bible Dictionary*.

literature can boast a comparable frequency. This is not to say that צדק (*ṣdq*), צדיק (*ṣdyq*) and צדקה (*ṣdqh*) always carry the meaning of "wholeness" throughout *BH*. As we have mentioned before, the Hebrew Bible often allows a triliteral root to include an entire semantic range. This is certainly true of √צדק (*ṣdq*) in the case of Proverbs, Psalms and sections of the Pentateuch that deal with justice and jurisprudence.[15] Other uses of √צדק (*ṣdq*) reflect "piety," "equity," "religiosity," and indeed "righteousness." We have shown that our author is extremely selective in his choice of words; nevertheless, the books of Job, Ezekiel, Psalms, and Genesis may provide us with some clues.

√צדק (*ṣdq*) in the Contexts of the Various Source Texts

Having identified √צדק (*ṣdq*), which we describe as "wholeness" as the central theme in the Book of Job, we must now set about establishing exactly what √צדק (*ṣdq*) meant to the author of Job. We have posited that our author used the Book of Genesis as the archetype for his character portrayals. We similarly state that the √צדק (*ṣdq*) of Genesis in particular and the Pentateuch in general represented a unique moral standard or attribute.

We also know that two of the author's primary substrate sources for the Prologue to Book of Job are Ezek.$14^{13\text{-}20}$ and Ezek.$18^{5\text{-}9}$ in which יהוה (YHWH), through the prophet Ezekiel, divides humanity into four categories of sinners and evildoers. יהוה (YHWH) will deal with these groups by use of four punishments, famine, wild beast, sword, and pestilence. [16] There will be no survivors, save Noah, Daniʾel and Job, who, by dint of their "wholeness" (בצדקתם (*bṣdqtm*)), will survive. [17] Even they will be unable to save their own family members. Newsom suggests that:

> Indeed, the evidence provided by the reference to Job in Ezekiel suggests that the traditional story known by Ezekiel may well have had a different plot. But the author could take a figure such as Job,

---

[15] Tsevat (1966, 29) recognizes the importance of √צדק (*ṣdq*), which he counts among "roots, which express the idea of justice."

[16] See Appendix 3 for the full citations.

[17] Greenberg (1983 257-8) cites Ezek.$14^{13\text{-}23}$ as an example of the doctrine of divine retribution and relates it to the episode of Sodom and Gomorrah in Gen.18. He goes so far as to question whether Ezekiel rejects the Genesis passage since the survivors are non-Israelite. However, he fails to make the crucial connection between Job and צדקה (*ṣdqh*) in Ezek.$14^{13\text{-}20}$, the definition of צדיק (*ṣdyq*) in Ezek.$18^{5\text{-}9}$, and Abraham and צדיקם (*ṣdyqym*) in Gen.18.

> renowned for righteousness, and compose a didactic tale in which our character's righteousness was tested and confirmed. [18]

Newsom seems not to have considered the totality of Ezek.14[13-20] and the supporting definitional material of Ezek.18[5-9]. Having taken her position, she is now forced down the tortuous path of re-inventing her own exegetical, albeit erudite, version of the author's intent. While she reaches a point of focus on √צדק (*ṣdq*), she never understands its centrality.

On the one hand, Job and Daniʾel share in common the deaths of their children. On the other hand, Noah is saved along with his three sons; were it otherwise, their deaths would have assured the annihilation of the humanity. This latter exemption is crucial since the annihilation of the world would necessitate the irrelevance of the deity, and the story would come to an end. Thus in Ezek.14[23], the prophet allows for the survival of a small remnant of survivors, who would begin anew, having learned from the mistakes and guilt of their fellow humans.

This substrate is interwoven into the fabric by the author of the Book of Job. Job is introduced as the "perfect whole man" by the author's attribution to Job of Noah's quality as צדיק תמים (*ṣaddîq tamîm*).[19] He follows the prescribed law to the last detail, both to his own social detriment and that of his children. His children are affected indirectly by their father's over-zealous efforts to maintain their "wholeness" in preemptively expiating any inappropriate thought or deed on their part. The author denigrates this very quality in 12[3], where he refers to the צדיק תמים (*ṣaddîq tamîm*) as a "joker."

יהוה (YHWH) is proud of Job's "perfect wholeness" and brags about it to his *doppelgänger* השטן (*haśśaṭan*). The latter, being a realist, knows only too well that:

כי אדם אין צדיק בארץ אשר יעשה טוב ולא יחטא

ky ʾdm ʾyn ṣdyq bʾrṣ ʾšr yʿśh ṭwb wlʾ yḥṭʾ

For there is no man who is a *ṣaddîq* in the world, who does good and does not sin. [20]

---

[18] Newsom (2003, 17, 266 n.49) is forced into the position that Ezek. 14[14,20] "implies that Job, by means of his righteousness, managed to save his sons and daughters from some danger rather than losing them in an inexplicable catastrophe."

[19] We encounter here the term תמים (*tamîm*) as a modifier for צדיק (*ṣaddîq*). The semantic difference between "wholeness" and "perfection" is once again paradigmatic for the author's logical treatment of words as unique entities. It is only by this method that the true purpose of the book will become apparent. This reading modifies that of the Masoretic text, which separates the words and makes them parts of two discrete phrases.

[20] See Eccles.7[20].

השטן (*haśśaṭan*) recognizes the logical impossibility of the existence of a צדיק תמים (*ṣaddîq tamîm*), a "person who practices perfect wholeness."

Our author understands this well and ventures into *terra incognita* investigating the quality of the life of a surviving צדיק תמים (*ṣaddîq tamîm*). Using the four "disasters" as a vehicle, he describes the (mis)fortunes of the survivor. The picture that he paints is not pretty; the צדיק תמים (*ṣaddîq tamîm*) is reduced to abject misery. Not only does the author describe the devastation and its effects, he focuses on the plight of the survivor, his affliction with incurable disease, his wife's incendiary imprecation to blasphemy, and the very remote sympathies of those who knew his predicament.

The implicit question that the author is asking is "Why bother?" If this is the reward for צדק (*ṣdq*) "wholeness," is it worth achieving? In fact, even if the צדיק תמים (*ṣaddîq tamîm*) has no ulterior motive and practices "wholeness" (צדקה – *ṣdqh*) *gratis* (חנם – *ḥnm*), is this a life worth living? The answer is, of course, a ringing "no," a stinging indictment of the deity. That being the case, who or what is the moral compass for a human being? This is our author's point of departure in his quest for an answer.

As regards the arrival of a "messiah" who will restore the world to pristine perfection, similar implicit questions arise. If the deity is failing as a צדיק תמים (*ṣaddîq tamîm*), then how can a human achieve such a status? Since both the deity and humanity share identical attributes, they are both incapable of being צדיק תמים (*ṣaddîq tamîm*).

Our author cannot accept the futility of human existence; there must be a definition of צדק (*ṣdq*) "wholeness" that recognizes and satisfies these conditions. The ʾElihu Epilogue of asserts the absolute power and "wholeness" of the deity, while the יהוה (YHWH) Epilogue questions divine omnipotence and even admits a suggestion of the absolute power and "wholeness" of humanity.

Neither is satisfactory to our author. It is only in the Final Epilogue that our author realizes the fallacy of his original syllogism. The common descriptor צדק (*ṣdq*) "wholeness" does not mean the same for the deity as it does for humanity.

צדק (*ṣdq*) in the Book of Genesis

All of the occurrences of צדק (*ṣdq*), צדיק (*ṣdyq*) or צדקה (*ṣdqh*) in the Book of Genesis describe or are ascribed to human beings. The classic definition of √צדק (*ṣdq*) in the Book of Genesis occurs in Gen.18[23]ff. where Abraham pleads with יהוה (YHWH) not to destroy the cities of Sodom and Gomorrah if an ever-declining number of צדיקים (*ṣdyqym*)[21] can be found there. We must infer the definition of √צדק (*ṣdq*) as the opposite of the character deficiencies attributed to the people of Sodom and Gomorrah. We read in Gen.13[13]:

ואנשי סדם רעים וחטאים ליהוה מאד
wʾnšy sdm rʿym wḥṭʾym lyhwh mʾd
And the people of S^{e}dom were very evil and very sinful to YHWH.

We are not informed the exact nature of the sins of Sodom. Abraham attempted negotiation on behalf of any inhabitant of Sodom who was not "evil." The "evil" was at least the homosexual behavior as described in Gen.19[4,5]. Our author fully recognizes that Abraham's description of the people of Sodom is subtly different from that of יהוה (YHWH). In Gen.18[20], *BH* restates יהוה (YHWH)'s position as follows:

ויאמר יהוה זעקת סדם ועמרה כי רבה וחטאתם כי כבדה מאד
ארדה נא ואראה הכצעקתה הבאה אלי עשו כלה ואם לא אדעה
wyʾmr yhwh zʿqt sdm wʿmrh ky rbh wḥṭʾtm ky kbdh mʾd
ʾrdh nʾ wʾrʾh hkṣʿqth hbʾh ʾly ʿśw klh wʾm lʾ ʾdʿh
And YHWH said, "The cry of Sodom and Gomorrah is great and their sin is grievous.
Let me go down and see if they have caused the cry that comes to me;
If not, then I will know it.

This is the word of יהוה (YHWH) as reported by *BH*. Abraham's rejoinder to יהוה (YHWH)'s intention reads as follows in Gen.18[23]:

ויגש אברהם ויאמר האף תספה צדיק עם רשע
wygš ʾbrhm wyʾmr hʾp tsph ṣdyq ʿm ršʿ
And Abraham stepped forward and said,
"Will you indeed sweep away the *ṣaddîq* with the wicked man?"

The whole notion of "sin" – חטא (*ḥṭʾ*) with its subtle subtext of unintentionality has been dropped and has been substituted with רשע (*ršʿ*) – "(intentionally) wicked." Abraham presses יהוה (YHWH) even further in Gen.18[25]:

---

[21] צדיקים (*ṣdyqym*) is the masculine plural of צדיק (*ṣdyq*).

חלילה לך מעשת כדבר הזה להמית צדיק עם רשע והיה כצדיק כרשע
חלילה לך השפט כל הארץ לא יעשה משפט
ḥlylh lk mʿśt kdbr hzh lhmyt ṣdyq ʿm ršʿ whyh kṣdyq kršʿ
ḥlylh lk hšpṭ kl hʾrṣ lʾ yʿśh mšpṭ
Far be it from you to do such a thing,
To kill a whole man along with a wicked man,
And the whole would be like the wicked;
Far be it from you! Will he who judges the world not do justice?

One cannot ignore Abraham's turning the issue from one of implicit morality to one of explicit legality.

We have already mentioned Gen.15⁶:

והאמן ביהוה ויחשבה לו צדקה
whʾmn byhwh wyhšbh lw ṣdqh
And he believed in YHWH and he [YHWH] credited him with *ṣdqh.*

This difficult verse has spawned a plethora of literature. The accepted interpretation of Gen 15^6 is that Abraham believed in Yahweh and he (Yahweh) attributed it (the act of believing) to him (Abraham) [as] צדקה (*ṣdqh*). Some scholars have seen the background to this verse in the liturgy of the temple. One who conducts himself properly with reference to an existing communal relationship, is declared by the priest to be "righteous." Man is "righteous" as long as he observes the rules of this communal relationship established by God, i.e. the covenant and the commandments." The Abraham episode is not within the realm of cult; "it is transferred to the realm of God's free and personal relationship to Abraham."[22] According to von Rad, the author of Gen 15^6 has יהוה (YHWH), and not a priest or Levite, make the pronouncement. יהוה (YHWH) pronounces Abraham to have fulfilled "righteousness," to share צדקה (*ṣdqh*), not by an act or a work, ritual or otherwise, but by faith.

This idiom occurs, albeit not in the exact form, in ψ106^{31} with reference to Phineḥas, who "rose up and intervened and the plague was stayed, this [action] was reckoned[23] to him לצדקה (*lṣdqh*):

ותחשב לו לצדקה
wtḥšb lw lṣdqh
And it was counted to him for wholeness

---

[22] von Rad, (1961, 185).

[23] Vocalized in the *nipʿal* conjugation (passive) *watêḥašêb lô liṣdaqâh.*

LXX similarly renders the phrase in the passive mode:

καὶ ἐλογίσθη αὐτῷ εἰς δικαιοσύνην

in both Gen.15[6] and ψ106[31].

Our author would most likely have agreed that Abraham was the possessor of צדקה (*ṣdqh*), especially since the deity is never associated directly with √צדק (*ṣdq*) in the Book of Genesis. √צדק (*ṣdq*)in the Book of Genesis is a purely human attribute.

In a stunning contrast, Jacob ascribes צדקה (*ṣdqh*) to himself in Gen.30[33], when he says to Laban[24]:

וענתה בי צדקתי ביום מחר כי תבוא על שכרי לפניך
w'nth by ṣdqty bywm mḥr ky tbw' 'l śkry lpnyk
And my wholeness will answer for me later,
when you come to look into my wages with you.

If, as we suspect, our author describes the character of יהוה (YHWH) in terms of Jacob, then we must make note of the fact that Jacob is claiming his צדקה (*ṣdqh*) in the context of a ruse that he is planning for Laban; Jacob's צדקה (*ṣdqh*) is not "honest." The divide between "human" and "divine" is deliberately blurred. The implication here is that there is not a clear difference between "human" and "divine" wholeness.

In general, √צדק (*ṣdq*) appears to be the diametric opposite of רשע (*rš'*),[25] which carries the connotation of "wickedness" or "legal guilt." However, we cannot assign an all-inclusive meaning of "innocent" since צדיק (*ṣdyq*) and נקי (*nqy*) seem to be explicitly differentiated in Ex.23[7], where we find:

מדבר שקר תרחק ונקי וצדיק אל תהרג כי לא אצדיק רשע
mdbr šqr trḥq wnq ywṣdyq 'l thrg ky l' 'ṣdyq rš'
You shall keep a distance from a false matter;
You shall not kill one who is *naqî* or *ṣaddîq*,
For I shall not cause the wicked to become *ṣaddîq*

---

[24] In a conversation that we shall cite (see 1[9])as part of the author's use of the character of Jacob as part of his portraiture of יהוה (YHWH).

[25] The author makes this quite clear in 40[8] when he has יהוה (YHWH) say תרשיעני למען תצדק *tršy'ny lm'n tṣdq*– "Will you vilify me so that you may be whole?"

Yet we find נקי (*naqî*) – "innocent" and צדיק (*ṣaddîq*) in parallel in ψ94[21]:

יגודו על נפש צדיק ודם נקי ירשיעו
ygwdw ʿl npš ṣdyq wdm nqy yršyʿw
They gang up against the life of the *ṣaddîq*
And make the blood of the innocent wicked.

and Job 22[19]:

יראו צדיקים וישמחו ונקי ילעג למו
yrʾw ṣdyqym wyśmḥw wnqy ylʿg lmw
Those who are *ṣaddîq* see it and are glad;
The innocent are scornful toward them.

The latter two citations demonstrate the development of the use of language. We might consider a nuanced difference between and נקי (*naqî*) – "innocent" and צדיק (*ṣaddîq*) – "whole" is that the (צדיק *ṣaddîq*) may have blood of others on their hands," whereas the "innocent" (נקי *nqy*) are inherently "guiltless. The only blood that a (נקי *nqy*) has on his hands is his own. We shall see below that our author needs to substitute נקי (*naqî*) for צדיק (*ṣaddîq*)

There is no indication that the words צדק (*ṣdq*), צדיק (*ṣdyq*) and צדקה (*ṣdqh*) represent uniquely divine attributes or qualities. In fact, in the entire Pentateuch, we find only one occasion on which יהוה (YHWH) is described as צדיק (*ṣdyq*),[26] and one occasion on which יהוה (YHWH)'s צדקה (*ṣdqh*) is mentioned.[27]

The author's philosophical *crux* occurs in 22[3], where, through the mouth of ʾEliphaz, he poses the question of whether Job's continuing efforts "to perfect his ways" has any valid purpose. The question implicitly raises the issue of the true nature of √צדק (*ṣdq*). ʾEliphaz's contention that צדקה (*ṣdqh*) is inherent to the divine asserts the Aristotelian axiom of "one word, one meaning." That is to say that each noun or adjective is unique as to its meaning and attributes. Therefore, if צדקה (*ṣdqh*) is a divine attribute, then it cannot be applied to humanity.[28] Uniqueness is absolute and not relative.

We now turn back to 1[8,9], and examine יהוה (YHWH)'s initial observation about Job's unique qualities that constitute "wholeness" and השטן (*haśśaṭan*)'s

---

[26] See Ex.9[27]. In Deut.32[4], it is אל (*ʾl*) who is described as צדיק (*ṣaddîq*).
[27] See Deut.33[21].
[28] As noted in 1[1], this is the position of *1QH[a]* col.12 ll.30-31.

sarcastic response bringing Job's motivation into question. We can now see the irony of the exchange.

√צדק (*ṣdq*) in the Book of Psalms

If one sets the date of the Book of Job at the beginning to the middle of the 2nd century BCE, one must now promote the relevance and currency of the Book of Psalms with respect to the Book of Job. Indeed, if we examine √צדק (*ṣdq*) as it occurs in the Book of Psalms, we find that its permutations occur some one hundred and forty (140) times. The entire *gamut* of the meanings of צדק (*ṣdq*) and צדקה (*ṣdqh*) is represented. This is perhaps not surprising since the content of the Book of Psalms spans almost the entire history of the Jewish-Israelite experience.[29]

Early critical scholarship generally regarded the Psalms as the product of the Maccabaean-Hasmonaean era. This view was based on the premise of the late development of pure monotheism in Israel and that the Book of Psalms therefore postdated the prophets.[30] The numerous traces of Psalms' language in the prophetic literature were explained by the influence of the latter on the former. The individualist consciousness that is mirrored in the psalms was taken as evidence for a highly developed, and hence late, stage in the history of the religion of Israel. Granted these assertions, it was not difficult to interpret allusions to historic events in the Book of Psalms as reflections of internal and external affairs in Judea in the course of the 2nd century BCE.[31]

While this position may not be completely supportable, it does deserve consideration. It is granted that if we accept it at either end of the spectrum (pure Davidic authorship vs. Hasmonaean-Maccabaean authorship) we are forced to make serious concessions in order to accommodate undeniable exceptions to the rule.

It is generally agreed that the Book of Psalms is the collection of a number of different anthologies. The precise identification of these different anthologies is a subject for debate; the Book of Psalms does not easily lend itself to classification in accordance with any one consistent method. We can be relatively certain that the Book of Psalms is not purely Davidic in authorship, even if only by the fact of the inclusion of ψ126 and ψ137.[32] We shall provide

---

[29] See *ABD* on "Righteousness" for an attempt to present the nuanced meanings of צדק (*ṣdq*) and צדקה (*ṣdqh*) ii the Book of Psalms.

[30] This is the position taken by modern day "minimalists."

[31] See Johnson (1951, 162–209) for a complete discussion.

[32] Which specifically reference the return from the 1st Exile c.540 BCE.

some evidence that perhaps suggests the later authorship of at least some of the chapters.

צדיק (*ṣdyq*) and its Meaning in the Book of Psalms

Just as √צדק (*ṣdq*), in the form of צדק (*ṣdq*) and צדקה (*ṣdqh*), has a history of development in *BH*, the same can be said of צדיק (*ṣdyq*). Our investigation has led us down a path whose end is defined by the real politico-religious world of the author of the Book of Job. We have suggested that the date of the author's world was as late as the early 2nd century BCE.

It is at this point in Jewish history that the definition of צדיק (*ṣdyq*) became of such importance that it became literally a matter of life and death. This is the time during which the question of mutually exclusive definitions of צדיק (*ṣdyq*) arose. The Book of Psalms provides some critical clues.

The Book of Psalms contains two (and perhaps three) types of Psalm that have as yet to be described. These are what may be called the "politico-religious psalms." They are identified by the appearance of two key words, namely, צדיקים (*ṣdyqym*), and חסידים (*ḥsydym*).[33] When one these two "labels" occurs, it is almost always to the exclusion of the other one. The process of identifying the "labels" is simpler than identifying which group they represented.

We would like to agree (although with some modification as to dates) with the suggestions that צדיק (*ṣdyq*) represents the orthodox splinter sect of the Sadduceans.[34] Similarly, חסיד (*ḥsyd*) represents the sect known as the *Ḥasidim* or Ασιδαῖοι (*Asidaioi*).[35]

The key to the identification is an occurrence of צדיק (*ṣdyq*), or חסיד (*ḥsyd*) for that matter, in a setting that is not reflective of its literal meaning. For example, $\psi 146^{8-9}$ reads:

יהוה פקח עורים יהוה זקף כפופים יהוה אהב צדיקים
יהוה שמר את גרים יתום ואלמנה יעודד ודרך רשעים יעות
yhwh pqḥ ʿwrymy hwh zqp kpwpym yhwh ʾhb ṣdyqym
yhwh šmr ʾt grym ytwm wʾlmnh yʿwdd wdrk ršʿymyʿwt
YHWH opens the eyes of the blind, YHWH lifts up those who are bowed down,
YHWH loves *ṣdyqym*.
YHWH watches over the strangers; he upholds the orphan and the widow,
And he brings to ruin the way of the wicked.

---

[33] Possibly also חוסים (*ḥwsym*) and other occurrences of √חסה (*ḥṣh*) to denote Essenes.

[34] In agreement with Schiffman's proposal (1994, 88-89).

[35] See 1Macc.2^{42}. 7^{14} and 2Macc.14^{6}. Also Kampen (1988), Collins (1977, 201-5), and Davies (1977, 128).

In this sequence listing YHWH's acts of social justice, the phrase יהוה אהב צדיקים (*yhwh ʾhb ṣdyqym*)–"YHWH loves the righteous" is clearly the "odd man out." Nowhere in *BH* do we find צדיק (*ṣdyq*) as a category of social repression. The only context in which צדיק (*ṣdyq*) takes on any tangible meaning is as the "moniker" of a politico-religious group.

Thus, in ψ118[15,19-20], we read:

קול רנה וישועה באהלי צדיקים...
פתחו לי שערי צדק אבוא בם אודה יה
זה השער ליהוה צדיקים יבאו בו
qwl rnh wyšwʿh bʾhly ṣdyqym...
ptḥw ly šʿry ṣdq ʾbwʾ bm ʾwdh yh
zh hšʿr lyhwh ṣdyqym ybʾw bw
There are glad songs of victory in the tents of *ṣdyqym*...
Open to me the gates of righteousness,
So that I may enter through them and give thanks to YHWH.
This is the gate of YHWH; *ṣdyqym* shall enter through it.

The last verse is redundant. פתחו לי שערי צדק (*ptḥw ly šʿry ṣdq*)–" Open to me the gates of righteousness" stands alone without need of further explanation. The specification of צדיקים (*ṣdyqym*) must signify a distinct group. Otherwise, we should have to understand that none of YHWH's other followers are eligible to enter the gates of *ṣdq*.[36]

In his article on *Hasidim*, Kampen is at best ambiguous:[37]

> While the name is rooted in the use of the term *ḥasîdîm* in the Hebrew Scriptures it is doubtful that Ps 149:1 or other references to *ḥasîdîm* in the Psalms should be used as evidence of the group mentioned in 1 and 2 Maccabees. The appearance of the name in Greek transliteration does suggest that at least the translator of 1 Maccabees and the author of 2 Maccabees understood the term as a proper noun; hence any argument that claims these references merely allude to pious Jews in general must be rejected.

Kampen appears to be trying to have it both ways. The evidence would seem to point to specific groups. While 2 Maccabees identifies the Ασιδαῖοι

[36] These two psalms are linked by another common denominator, namely, the admonition not to put one's trust in נדיבים (*ndybym*)–"princes." This may be a reference to the "establishment" Zadokite priesthood.
[37] *ABD* on "Hasidim."

(*Asidaioi*) as one of the groups that supported Judas Maccabaeus, we know nothing of the group's origins and activities in the fifty or so years prior to the Maccabaean Revolt. Psalm 149, with its three references (*pace* Kampen) to חסידים (*ḥsydym*), is another fine example of a politico-religious group. We read ψ149[1,5a,6,9b]:

שירו ליהוה שיר חדש תהלתו בקהל חסידים...
יעלזו חסידים בכבוד...
רוממות אל בגרונם וחרב פיפיות בידם
לעשות נקמה בגוים תוכחת בלאמים...
הדר הוא לכל חסידיו

šyrw lyhwh šyr ḥdš thltw bqhl ḥsydym...
yʿlzw ḥsydym bkbwd...
rwmmwt ʾl bgrwnm wḥrb pypywt bydm
lʿśwt nqmh bgwym twkḥt blʾmym...
hdr hwʾ lkl ḥsydyw

Sing to YHWH a new song, his praise in the assembly of *ḥsydym*...
Let the *ḥsydym* exult in glory...
Let the high praises of ʾEl be in their throats and two-edged swords in their hands,
To execute vengeance on the nations and punishment on the peoples...
This is glory for all his *ḥsydym*.

The חסידים (*ḥsydym*) of Psalm 149 are militant and represent the quality of חסד (*ḥsd*) –"loyalty" with which YHWH is so often associated. They sound a war cry, brandish swords, and aspire to wreak vengeance on the foreign oppressors. On the other hand, ψ58[11] exhorts:

ישמח צדיק כי חזה נקם ירחץ פעמיו בדם הרשע

yśmḥ ṣdyq ky ḥzh nqm

The *ṣdyq* will rejoice when he sees vengeance done;
He will bathe his feet in the blood of the wicked.

This is literature that sounds far more like propaganda than imprecation or praise. Thus, by the middle of the 2nd century BCE, צדיק (*ṣdyq*) had likely become both a religious and political "hot potato." As we have already remarked, the Samaritans had already early on adapted a "moniker" צדוקי (*ṣadôqy*) that connected their religious and messianic beliefs to the priestly patronym צדוק (*ṣadôq*). It is hardly a "stretch" to suggest that the צדיקים (*ṣdyqym*) acted likewise connecting themselves to the priestly patronym צדוק (*ṣadôq*). However, this connection was to identify themselves as adherents of a

Judaism whose origins lay in the early orthodox Zadokite priesthood. They clearly intended to remain distinct from Zadok and the politico-religious party known as the Sadducees.[38]

צדק (*ṣdq*) in Mid-Second Temple Times

Pryzybylski, in his investigation of the concept of "righteousness" in the Gospel of Matthew, attempts to track the development of √צדק (*ṣdq*) from the time of the Dead Sea Scrolls, through Tannaitic times to the final redaction of the Gospel of Matthew.[39] The target word is δικαιοσύνη (*dikaiosúne*), which occurs seven times in Matthew.[40] Pryzybylski attempts to define δικαιοσύνη (*dikaiosúne*) in terms of contemporary religious beliefs and practices, much as we are attempting to do with צדק (*ṣdq*), צדיק (*ṣdyq*) and צדקה (*ṣdqh*) in the time of the author of the Book of Job. While the results of Pryzybylski's study are not germane to us, his methodology is of interest. His study is based upon statistics, the number of times each of the words צדק (*ṣdq*), צדיק (*ṣdyq*), צדקה (*ṣdqh*), and δικαιοσύνη (*dikaiosúne*) occurs in major works along a time line that ends with the Gospel of Matthew. Pryzybylski's basic premise is that since Matthew contains more Old Testament citations than any of the other Gospels, there should be some line of continuity of meaning and usage that connects the two.[41] In order to try and accomplish this, he uses the works of two German scholars, G. Strecker and M.J. Fiedler[42], whose views are diametrically opposed. Strecker maintains that *Rechtsschaffenheit*, "righteousness," is "always seen as a demand upon man; never as the gift of God." Fiedler, on the other hand, "claims that righteousness is both the eschatological gift and demand of God. The gift, however, precedes the demand."[43]

Within the constraints of his basic premise, Pryzybylski encounters problems related to the sparseness of written evidence for the period between the return from exile in Babylon in the 5th century BCE and the sectarianism of the 3rd

---

[38] This is not to suggest that the patronym צדוק (*ṣadôq*) – Zadok is derived from √צדק (*ṣdq*), rather that √צדק (*ṣdq*) with its contemporary currency was associated with the Zadokite Priesthood.

[39] Pryzybylski (1980, 1-12)

[40] As opposed to once in Luke, twice in John and not at all in Mark.

[41] Pryzybylski (1980, 3).

[42] Strecker, *Der Weg der Gerechtigkeit: Untersuchungen zur Theologie des Matthäus* (*FRLANT* 82: Göttingen, 1971). Fiedler, *Der Begriff* δικαιοσύνη *im Matthäus-Evangelium, auf seine Grundlagen Untersucht* (Ph.D. dissertation Martin Luther-Universität, Halle-Wittenberg, 1957).

[43] Pryzybylski (1980, 1).

through 1st centuries BCE. Had Pryzybylski included the references to צדק (*ṣdq*), צדיק (*ṣdyq*) and צדקה (*ṣdqh*) in the Book of Job in his timeline, he would have been able to avail himself of a crucial stepping stone in his continuum.

√צדק (*ṣdq*), √זכה (*zkh*) and δικαιοσύνη

As stated above, both *BH* and *DSS* usages of צדק (*ṣdq*), צדיק (*ṣdyq*) and צדקה (*ṣdqh*) and the use of δικαιοσύνη (*dikaiosúne*) in Matthew present the question of whether "wholeness" is a gift from the divine or an obligation upon humanity. As is the case with the Arabic cognate of צדיק (*ṣdyq*),[44] the Greek δίκαιος (*díkaios*) has an underlying meaning of "loyalty" along with "cultic ritual correctness" that reaches back into Homeric antiquity.[45] Societal changes and developments of the legal system added the *nuances* of "justice" and "fairness." The word δικαιοσύνη (*dikaiosúne*) is not attested in Classical Greek until after the establishment of the Athenian *polis* in the 5th century BCE. While the usages of צדיק (*ṣdyq*) and δίκαιος (*díkaios*) may have developed along parallel lines in the Near East, the two words have no lexical connection.[46]

There might, however, be a mutual point of contact between the concept of "rightness" or "purity" as expressed through the word δίκαιος (*díkaios*). There is no certain etymological origin to the Greek stem δίκαι- (*díkai-*). The Semitic biliteral stem *זכ (*zk*)[47] meaning "to be pure" or "to be innocent" might easily be transformed to the Greek. We have already seen that √צדק (*ṣdq*) and √זכה (*zkh*) are used in parallel in the Book of Job.[48]

√צדק (*ṣdq*) in the Author's *Agendum*

Using the methods described in the *Introduction*, we have been able to identify a single comprehensive *agendum* from the Prologue alone, one that is supported by the text and bears no relationship to the traditional exegetical explications. The central theme is a series of questions and statements regarding √צדק (*ṣdq*), to which we have referred as "wholeness."

1. What are "faith" and "wholeness?" Are they qualities that are shared by humanity and the Divine? Is man really created "in the image of "the

---

[44] صديق – *ṣdyq AED*, 392

[45] Hence Hesiod's use of the word δικαιότερον (*dikaióteron*) "more righteous" to describe the generation of the "heroes." See above 1[6].

[46] *GEL*, 429; *AED*, 392-3

[47] Expressed in the triliteral roots זכה (*zkh*) and זכך (*zkk*).

[48] See 15[14] and 25[4].

deity?" If so, why can the qualities of "faith" and "wholeness" not be shared? In fact, is it not possible for humanity to outdo the deity in these qualities? How are "faith" and "wholeness" measured?

2. Can there exist a *scenario* whereby the world can be restored to its "wholeness" at the time of its Creation? If so, then what are the mechanics? Under the definition of "wholeness," can the Divine create a mechanism to effect this restoration?
3. Worship by ritual alone is worthless. Ritual fails as an apotropaic device; therefore, each man is responsible for his own deeds and "whole" conscience (צדק (*ṣdq*) and צדקה (*ṣdqh*)). Humanity is not reconciled to this reality.
4. The author posits more than one aspect to the deity. The deity consists of three *personae*, one, יהוה (YHWH), is emotional and idealistic, the other, השטן (*haśśaṭan*), is rational and realistic. These two *personae* are forever battling one another in the struggle for an ultimately unachievable balance in the world. The third *persona* is אלהים (*ʾelohîm*), the institution of justice and equity. The notion that אלהים (*ʾelohîm*) is perpetual and immutable and exists separate from יהוה (YHWH) is an illusion. "Wholeness" consists of the integration of all three *personae*—a logical impossibility.
5. The direction of human life does not consist of a series of accidents; it is shaped by the interaction of יהוה (YHWH) and humanity with respect to √צדק (*ṣdq*) – "wholeness." Since יהוה (YHWH) is uncertain, then there can be no certainty for humanity.
6. The Book of Genesis is not simply a collection of stories designed to relate contemporary society to its most primitive historical origins. Genesis is itself a Prologue that describes a programmatic picture of the social and ethical development of the human and divine *personae*. The patriarchal stories predefine theogony and the fine line that separates the nature(s) of יהוה (YHWH) and humanity.
7. History and time cannot be reversed. In the same way that Job cannot will away that act of "Creation" in 3^3, the Deity cannot restore the universe to the state of "wholeness" that existed prior to the "Creation." There is no possibility of the existence (or for that matter creation) of a mortal being that possesses the "wholeness" of the Deity. Hence, there is a limit to the power of the Deity. "Creation," once conceived and performed, must be recognized as its own entity.

In summary, our author is struggling with the issues of order and disorder in the terrestrial world. The solution of accidents and disorders through the action of "divine" power contradicts the author's central thesis that humanity solves its own problems in its continuing effort to achieve √צדק (*ṣdq*) – "wholeness." The entirety of the Book of Job is an investigation of the inequality of human and divine "wholeness."

AN HISTORICAL CONTEXT

We have some external sources for mid 2nd Temple history and thought, mainly from Josephus, pseudo-Aristeas, Philo of Alexandria, Eusebius, Alexander *Polyhistor* and others; however, they are for the large part reporting events and trends that occurred centuries before their own times. In addition, their reporting bears the unmistakable marks of programmed *agenda* that are not pertinent and indeed distort the realities to varying degrees.

This is a story of religion and politics mutually driven. The setting is a time of civil and religious unrest in the province of Judah, which was under the occupation of the Seleucid Greek Empire. Judah had been a small province in the Achaemenid Empire established by the Persian King Cyrus I. When Alexander the Great conquered the Persian Empire, Judaea and Israel, by default, became a part of the Greek Empire. Alexander died in 323 BCE and the Empire fell apart. The turbulent years from 323 to 301 BCE saw conflicts among the generals of Alexander the Great, which ended with the parceling out of the Alexander's empire and the creation of the first Hellenistic kingdoms. Alexander's generals, known as Diadochs, literally "successors," established their own fiefdoms on the rest of the Alexander's empire.[1]

Two of Alexander's generals, Ptolemy and Seleucus, each began his own dynasty. Ptolemy took the western portion of Alexander's empire, which he ruled from Cairo, while Seleucus appropriated the eastern territories, which he ruled from Antioch in modern day Syria.

For the first one hundred years following the breakup of Alexander's empire, Judaea and Israel were in the Egyptian sphere of the Ptolemies. The Lagides seem to have given Israel and Judaea a wide berth, most likely in the expectation of loyalty in exchange.[2] There is a dearth of information about the populace itself; however, we do know that certain cities were vested with the status of the

---

[1] Ptolemy *Lagus*, Alexander's half bother (Egypt and Palestine); Seleucus *Nicator* (Mesopotamia and Syria); Cassander (Macedonia and Greece); Antigonus (Asia Minor); Lysimachus (Thrace).

[2] Josephus reports the deportation to Alexandria by Ptolemy *Lagus* of a broad cross-section of the population. They were given the privileges of native citizens. (*Ant.* 12.1.1).

Greek *polis*.[3] In 201 BCE, the Seleucid Antiochus III wrested the territory away after defeating the Egyptian Lagides at Banyas in Coele-Syria.

This was a time of Judaism in flux, when the Jewish religion was not yet set into the Rabbinic Judaism of the *Mishnah* and the *Talmud*. Neusner calls this period between the Babylonian exile in 586 BCE and the destruction of the Second Temple in 70 CE "the time of Judaisms."[4]

While occupation by the Seleucids ultimately led to the desecration of the Temple in Jerusalem, the Seleucids themselves did not at first pursue an *agenda* of religious persecution. In fact, Josephus reports a decree permitting the Jews to observe their laws and customs, exempting them from certain taxes and contributing to the restoration and maintenance of the Temple in Jerusalem.[5] They, through the shrine-worship of statues of Zeus and other Greek gods and the propagation of a Hellenist culture, followed their own cultic path. However, the Jews of Judaea were embroiled in their own internal strife, only a part of which could be attributed to the insidious attractiveness of Hellenism.

Judaea was the exception to the rule; the attempts of the Seleucids at a "live and let live" peaceful occupation would ultimately end in failure. The population of Judaea, which might generically be termed Jewish, seems to have gradually spawned heterogeneous sects each of which possessed its own religious or political *agenda*. The most radical of these, the Maccabees, ultimately agitated for complete political and religious independence. The Seleucids, with the support of the influential Tobiad family, countered with draconian measures that forbade the ritual observances of the Jews and were capped by the installation of a statue of Zeus in the Jerusalem Temple. These measures were not simply imposed *e cathedra*, they were militarily enforced in an effort to dilute the indigenous Jewish religion such that it would disappear into the Greek pantheism of the Seleucids. This regimen was to be similarly followed later by the Romans.

In the early-to-mid 2nd century BCE, there arose a political dissatisfaction, albeit muted, with the Zadokite handling of Hellenism and the Seleucids. *Vox populi* was expressed in the form of schisms, the most significant of which may have culminated in the secession of the Sadducean orthodox priesthood from the main Zadokite High Priesthood in Jerusalem.[6] The obscure notion of a ""“messiah”" came in to its own. The concept of an anointed Davidic or Priestly prince who would come to restore Israel was a perfect answer to the religious and political predicament of the time—especially since nobody knew what kind

---

[3] For example Ptolemaïs (Acre) and Scythopolis (Beth She'an).
[4] Neusner (1994, 12ff.)
[5] Josephus *Ant.* 12.3.3
[6] Schiffman (1994, 71)

of restoration was to take place. Would it come in the form of political independence or an end to the Greek cultural influence? The concept was vague and perhaps helped unite an otherwise fragmented populace.

From the 2nd century BCE on, "Messianic" texts from the Prophets were reread from a contemporary perspective. They were regarded as texts announcing the coming of a leader who was to restore the world to its pristine state and defeat the Seleucid enemy along the way. Other biblical texts seemed to fit the same picture, and one of these was the "oracles" of Bilʿam.[7] To the best of our knowledge, these lines had never been considered messianic up to this time; from now on, the "star and the scepter" were to become a Messianic trademark.

There is a possibility that Judah the Maccabee and—after his death in 161 BCE—his brother Jonathan were recognized as "messiahs"; however, the major sources, *1* and *2 Maccabees* do not mention this. Perhaps the reason was that the Maccabaeans were not descendants of David. They were acceptable as kings, but could never be a "messiah." More troublesome was the fact that they did not belong to the Zadokite family that was entitled to the high priesthood. It is possible that the Maccabaean "usurpation" of this office was considered scandalous and it is possible that it caused the "Teacher of Righteousness" to leave Jerusalem and become involved with any of a number of sects whose writings have been found at Qumran.

The notion of an invisible god was very troubling to all the ancient occupiers of this territory. In later times, it became extremely appealing to the servant class of the occupiers who, as they became more educated, used the concept to subvert and undermine their own masters. Eradication of such a belief was therefore probably high on their occupiers' *agenda*.

Full-scale resistance to this occupation would not surface until the time of the Maccabaean "uprising" c.167 BCE; however, that is not to deny the existence of religion-driven political groups and politics-driven religious groups. We know little of the former. On the other hand, the latter was represented mainly by High Priesthood in Jerusalem.

One of the amazing phenomena of Jewish history was the ability of the High Priesthood to survive the turbulent vicissitudes of the times since its institution under Moses as the *élite* clergy under the leadership of Moses' brother Aaron. It weathered the machinations of David and Solomon and the subsequent breakup of the monarchy. The priests managed to roll with the tides of royalty, good and bad, be they kings of Israel in the north or of Judah in the south.

---

[7] See Collins (1995).We have demonstrated the importance of the Bilʿam story as a device used by the author of the Book of Job.

Now, in the early 3rd and late 2nd centuries BCE, the High Priests in effect collaborated with their Seleucid rulers by not opposing the installation of statues of Greek gods for worship in Jerusalem (although not in the Temple).

The early Second Temple period had an undisputed protagonist whose role the sages struggled to downplay—the house of Zadok. Members of this priestly family controlled the Jerusalem temple without interruption up to the eve of the Maccabaean revolt. They were the first keepers and interpreters of that Torah on which the sages would claim to have had exclusive control since its Mosaic inception.

Many centuries before the emergence of the rabbinic movement, the Zadokites had been themselves at the center of a similar revolution that reshaped the past of Israel in order to validate their rise to power. The Zadokite historiography presents the "reconstruction" of the Jerusalem temple after the Babylonian exile as the triumphant restoration of the pre-exilic order that traced its origins to Mt. Sinai. Where ancient sources stress continuity, however, modern scholars see discontinuity and innovation, if not evidence of a *coup d'état*.

The priest Joshua, son of Jehozadak, presided at the dedication of the new temple during the time of Ezra and Nehemiah early in the 5th century BCE. He was not the fortunate descendant of a dynasty of high priests who regained the position his family had been deprived of for some time. He was rather the first high priest to come to power in the history of Israel. His authority was not the natural result of an established tradition but the outcome of a struggle for supremacy that during the Babylonian exile and the early Persian period opposed the house of Zadok to the Davidic monarchy and to the other priestly families of Israel.

The balance of power within the Jewish people was dramatically altered. The returnees imposed their hegemony over the remainees, the peoples of the land and their leaders—the Tobiads of Ammon and the Sanballats of Samaria. With the fall of the last king of Judah, Zerubbabel and the "House of David" lost any political visibility and the Davidic prophets their religious authority. The priesthood of the Zadokites promptly pre-empted the monarchic and prophetic prerogatives. It took a much longer time to find a new balance within the priesthood that would enlarge the foundations of the Zadokite power without diminishing their supremacy. The hierarchy of high priests, priests, and Levites was the result of struggles and ruthless exclusions, behind which the Priestly writing barely hides. The Torah view of a natural genealogical succession of "sons of Levi," "sons of Aaron," and "sons of Pinḥas" became the rallying cry of emerging schisms. Tensions gradually resulted in accommodation and compromise in which the majority of priestly groups found stability and mutual advantage.

Zadokite theology offered a framework of stability and order centered round the temple sacrificial system and the notion of personal responsibility and accountability. The Zadokites saw themselves as the faithful keepers of God's creative order, established through a coherent system of graded purity and maintained under God's omnipotent and unchallenged control.

However, in spite of its accomplishment and undeniable authority, the Zadokite leadership was not without its critics. As we shall see, the Samaritan schism had tremendous and lasting consequences for the definition of Jewish identity. The Tobiads, although temporarily alienated, remained a significant political power. The legacy of the prophets never died off; however, more important for the future developments of Jewish thought is the challenge that internal movements of opposition posed to the Zadokite order.

The Zadokite and later the Hasmonaean priesthoods kept the majority of the population in check while walking the fine line that served both their own interests and the interests of the Seleucids. Of course the interests of the High Priesthood were economic; they needed the income from worshippers who paid to make sacrifices at the Temple. The money went both for Temple upkeep and the personal welfare of the High Priesthood.

The opposition consisted of lesser-known religion-driven political groups. Among these were Essenes, Therapeutai, Sadduceans, Boethusians, Dositheans,[8] the sect(s) of the Dead Sea, and certainly some other splinter groups. These would fall under the heading of "Judaisms" mentioned earlier. Some of these groups were residents of Judaea, others had exiled themselves, especially to Egypt and Babylonia. Our knowledge of most of these groups comes from the writings of Josephus, the apologist Jewish historian of the 1st century CE and Philo of Alexandria who lived at the turn of the millennium from 20 BCE – 50 CE. The sect(s) of the Dead Sea are known to us from their own writings that were discovered in the caves of Qumran, some twenty miles SE of Jerusalem by the Dead Sea.

Aside from the idiosyncratic practices of these groups, the focus of their venom was the Zadokite High Priesthood. This was articulated especially in the Dead Sea Scrolls, where we find an almost slavish adoration of a Zadokite priesthood that practiced the ritual according to the Torah. Of course, the fact that this particular sect felt compelled to leave Jerusalem in order to practice the prescribed ritual accentuates the polemic nature of their writings. These "collaborators" were not legitimate; the failure of the High Priesthood to stand up for its faith in the face of occupation was the very height of treason.

---

[8] Some of these names may be overlapping.

We can presume from those original writings that survive and from the later historians that the ultimate deliverance would come upon the arrival of a "messiah."

To summarize, it would appear that the author could only have lived in Israel at a time when religious schisms were forming and the notion of Messianism was just beginning to be articulated in contemporary terms. Such a time would be during the 2nd Temple Hellenist period at the beginning to middle of the 2nd century BCE.[9] The collaboration, tacit or otherwise, of the Zadokite priests with the Seleucid occupiers and the priestly squabbles and infighting of the period may prove to be the fundamental target of the Dead Sea Scrolls sect and the author of the Book of Job.[10] Equally important, the author appears to have been familiar with Hellenistic philosophy and the teachings of Aristotle. He lived in a time when he was able to ponder religious and philosophical issues but could not present his questions and arguments explicitly.

---

[9] Tsevat (1966, 32).

[10] We have noted Job assuming a "priestly" role in 1^5, when he prepares sacrifices for his children in the manner of the Temple priests.

GLEANINGS

The "Code": An Intertextual Cipher

Perhaps the most exciting aspect of this investigation is the discovery that the author of the Book of Job used a "code." One might have guessed the existence of a "subtext" or *agenda* simply from the lexical and literary problems posed by the text. In fact, scholars have unknowingly been uncovering snippets of this subtext while pursuing theological implications through exegetical or hermeneutical leads.

The "subtext" turns out to be "supertext" and *vice versa*. The author is truly a product of his time, which fostered the kind of repression conducive to literary inventiveness. The large part of Joban scholarship has been devoted to the reading and interpretation of the "superficial" text and pursuing a "politically correct" exegesis. The "intertextual cipher" of the Book of Job is unique in *BH*.

The single most interesting literary discovery is the intertextual relationship between the Book of Job and the Dead Sea Scrolls. *BH* intertextual studies have traditionally been centered on the texts of the Hebrew Bible. Comparisons and contrasts have been drawn from surrounding cultures that antedated *BH* by long periods. It is undeniable that many of the origins of *BH* are to be traced to these cultures; however, *BH* is heterogeneous both synchronically and diachronically. The Dead Sea Scrolls have opened a window into the life of the mid-to-late 2nd Temple period; however, their sectarian nature discourages generalizations about the life of the times. While the literature of the Dead Sea Scrolls generally confirms the antiquity of *BH*, it is only with the Book of Job that we can verify the validity of expressions for which there is no *BH* comparison.

Scholars have traditionally perceived intertextuality as a device intended to evoke an inexact association with a person or an event. Our author takes intertextuality to a new level. In raising the level of intertextuality to a set of exact associations, he is able to use the device "programmatically." Instead of associating odd words and phrases, he applies intertextuality to entire stories in the pursuit of his *agenda*.

Abraham, Isaac and Jacob: Dividing the Patriarch Pie

By referencing the patriarchal stories of the Book of Genesis, the author is able to define the characters of Job, YHWH, and *haśśaṭan*. The resulting character traits vividly portray the different patriarchal personalities. Rather than the homogeneous "righteous" characters of Abraham, Isaac, and Jacob, we are shown individuals in vivid and contrasting colors.

Job is a fortunate curmudgeon who observes ritual in worship of a god whom he does not comprehend. He fears that his good fortune will be adversely affected if he or any of his family offends his god to the point that he makes pre-emptive sacrifices in atonement for any sins that they *might* commit. When he becomes the unwitting pawn in YHWH's internal struggle with his alter ego *haśśaṭan*, he lashes out in anger. The author uses the characters and stories of Abraham and Isaac to create this composite patriarch.

YHWH is Job's object of ritual worship. Using the stories of Jacob, the author describes a God who is insecure, needing constantly to validate his self-image. To this end, YHWH is portrayed as conniving and whimsical, willing to consider almost any measure to achieve his end. He is afraid that if his worst fears become reality, he will lose his relevance to his mortal creations. He will even consider total annihilation to prevent this possibility.

As much as YHWH frets over his insecurities, *haśśaṭan* is a hard realist. As YHWH's *alter ego*, he sees the world as it is and is totally non judgmental about it. He is the foil for YHWH's worries, always at the ready to conduct an empirical test, sometimes for better but usually for worse. *haśśaṭan* takes his character principally from the "messenger of God" stories of Genesis, the Bilʿam story, and the vision of Zechariah 3[1]ff. Although he exists for the large part as an independent of Yahweh, he can operate only within the constraints established by YHWH.

ʾelohîm is revered by Job but not worshipped by him. *ʾelohîm* is the *eminence grise* who casts a shadow over all humanity. He is the unspoken symbol of ethics and correctness, monolithic and unvarying. *ʾelohîm* is incapable of relationship; he neither speaks nor responds. His rectitude is unquestionable.

Job ritually worships YHWH and ethically "reveres" *ʾelohîm*. Although oblivious to the fact, Job also rolls with the punches of *haśśaṭan*. When Job realizes that there is an aspect of YHWH that he has not seen or experienced before, he feels both betrayed and angry all at once. For the first time in his life he has lost his footing; recovering it leads Job on a tortuous path as he investigates previously unimaginable possibilities.

The "Source of All Evil"

In a famous speech from William Shakespeare's *Julius Caesar*, Mark Antony declares, "The evil that men do lives after them; the good is oft interred with their bones." The author makes a statement that goes one step further. Had he been familiar with Shakespeare, he might have said that the same applies to God.

As he does with the Patriarchs, the author uses exact intertextual references to a Biblical theme to make his point. He makes programmatic use of the Genesis and Judges stories of Abimelech as paradigms of evil. Evil deeds are perpetrated by humanity; however, these are only the occasions or "proximate causes." It is the deity who is at the root. The Abimelech stories span the gamut of evil, ranging from peccadillo in Genesis to genocide in Judges.

The Bilʿam Story

The Bilʿam Story seems to be utilized for several purposes throughout the book of Job. First of all, it supplies the connecting strand from the Prologue, through the rubrics that open almost every chapter, on to the 3rd Epilogue with which the book closes. Second, it serves the author in his portrayal of the concept of "blessing without blessing" and "cursing without cursing." By using this device, the author expresses himself behind a veil of *double entendre*. Thirdly, the Bilʿam Story provides the basis, in the contemporary vernacular, for the discussion of the plausibility and nature of a human "messiah."

"Wholeness" and "Righteousness

While √צדק (*ṣdq*) does not appear in either the Prologue or the 3rd Epilogue, it is the keyword (or, to use Clines' term, "nodal" word), in all of its senses, that the author uses to make his philosophical argument. The range of meaning of √צדק (*ṣdq*) includes "wholeness," "righteousness," "legal innocence," "loyalty," and "friendship." Its denominatives, aside from צדק (*ṣdq*) and צדקה (*ṣdqh*), include:

- צדיק (*ṣdyq*) the definitive practitioner of "wholeness" and possibly a member of a putative group referred to as צדיקים (*ṣdyqym*).
- the *onomasticon* צדוק (*ṣdwq*) as assumed by the Zadokite priestly family (as opposed to צדוק (*ṣdwq*) the High Priest at the time of Solomon), the Sadduceans, Samaritans, the Sadducees
- the attribute of the "messiah," צמח צדק (*ṣmḥ ṣdq*)

The Author's Quest

By most accounts, the pervasion of Hellenist thought and custom into Judaism, such as it was, sat well with the Jerusalem Zadokite "establishment." However, the times were already in a state of flux such that sectarian splinter groups were spawned, each touting its own individual version of the nature of "correct" Judaism.

The author of the Book of Job set about the business of applying methods of Greek philosophy to Judaic principles in an effort to reconcile some apparently mutually exclusive premises. He faced the challenge of untangling threads that stretched back into antiquity. The questions that this work would generate were "heretical" enough to require the author to work "undercover" as it were.

The fundamental philosophical contradictions in contemporary Judaism were:

- How could you have separate "human" and "divine" "wholeness" when God supposedly created man in his own image?
- If such a distinction really existed, how was it manifested?
- Did God make a "mistake" with "Creation?" If so, was he trying to "fix" it? Could he "fix" it?
- Could the "mistake" of "Creation" only be "fixed" by divine action through human agency? If so, what would be the character of such a human being?

The author attempts to answer these questions by rewriting the patriarchal literature of the Book of Genesis and the story of Bilʿam in the Book of Numbers to fit his hypothesis. That is to say, he recreates the *dramatis personae* to accommodate the characters of his reconstructed "Creation."

Besides "Creation," the author recognized the tangible reality of the different sectarian needs for salvation and their proposed solutions. In order to solve for the issue of salvation, he constructs a Messianology out of the Bilʿam story and the "צמח (*ṣmḥ*) vision" of the prophet Zechariah.

The Author's Findings

The author pursues his investigation and comes away without a single clear and substantive conclusion. Thus he leaves the reader with not one but three epilogues. First, there is the monologue of the intolerant ʾElihu, a fundamentalist theist, who can brook no criticism of the Divine. The צדק (*ṣdq*) or צדקה (*ṣdqh*) of the Divine are paramount. Second is the reply of יהוה (YHWH) to Job "from the whirlwind" and Job's unrelenting counter-attack and rejection in response. Third is what we refer to as the 3rd Epilogue, in which יהוה (YHWH) and Job come to a compromise of mutual recognition of each other's imperfections and their mutual need for co-existence.

On the subject of "human" and "divine" צדק (*ṣdq*) "wholeness," he finds that the two are mutually exclusive. The attributes of the "image of the Divine" are not identical to those of the "Divine." Absolute "wholeness" is a logical impossibility. While neither god nor man can reach absolute perfection, their maximum potential must be measured by a different yardstick. Thus as the "Divine" cannot hold absolute sway over "humanity," in the same way "humanity" cannot totally disassociate itself from the "Divine." The answer to the survival of "Creation" is an uneasy truce and an eternal tension between the "Divine" and "humanity" that can never be resolved.

With regard to the "messiah" and "salvation," the author finds a similar impossibility. The premise of "salvation" and the restoration of absolute purity and perfection to the universe cannot happen. A "human messiah" cannot achieve the level of "divine" perfection necessary for the total obliteration of the impurity born of the existence of "humanity." By the same token, the "Divine" cannot reverse time and undo "Creation" thereby restoring the universe to its pristine state. Perfection, purity, and "wholeness" can be achieved only by the total obliteration of humanity. The problem with the latter alternative is that there will be no "humanity" to witness the "perfection." It would take until the 16th century CE and the advent of Lurianic *Kabbalah* before these questions were systematically approached.

A Final Word on the Author and His Times

While we cannot even conjecture the name of the author of the Book of Job, we have discovered several significant aspects of his thought and writing. He most likely lived in Israel or Samaria in the early-to-mid 2nd century BCE; hence perhaps the abundance of Aramaisms that occur throughout his writings. Some association with the Samaritans is not to be discounted, given his intense familiarity with Samaritan eschatology and the story of Bilʿam. He was educated in the syllogistic principles of Aristotle, which permeated his reasoning and the "one word-one meaning" structure of his code.

Conclusion

Of course, these concluding statements oversimplify the intellectual wrangling that the author practices throughout this work. One cannot but marvel at the elegance of the code he has devised. The sheer magnitude of the knowledge base required to pull off his investigation is staggering. The articulation of complex questions and arguments, all the while paying attention to minute details, leaves the reader in awe. One cannot help but feel insignificant in the presence of such a "beautiful mind."

THE RECRUITMENT OF BILʿAM
NUM.22[20-35]

ויבא אלהים אל בלעם לילה ויאמר לו אם לקרא לך באו האנשים קום לך אתם ואך את הדבר
אשר אדבר אליך אתו תעשה. ויקם בלעם בבקר ויחבש את אתנו וילך אם שרי מואב. ויחר אף
אלהים כי הולך הוא ויתיצב מלאך יהוה בדרך לשטן לו והוא רכב אתנו ושני נעריו עמו. ותרא
האתון את מלאך יהוה נצב בדרך וחרבו שלופה בידו ותט האתון מן הדרך ותלך בשדה ויך
בלעם את האתון להטתה הדרך. ויעמד מלאך יהוה במשעול הכרמים גדר מזה וגדר מזה. ותרא
האתון את מלאך יהוה ותלחץ אל הקיר ותלחץ את רגל בלעם ויסף להכתה. ויסף מלאך יהוה עבור
ויעמד במקום צר אשר אין דרך לנטות ימין ושמאול. ותרא האתון את מלאך יהוה ותרביץ תחת
בלעם ויחר אף בלעם ויך את האתון במקל. ויפתח יהוה את פי האתון ותאמר לבלעם מה עשיתי
לך כי הכיתני זה שלש רגלים. ויאמר בלעם לאתון כי התעללת בי לו יש חרב בידי כי עתה
הרגתיך. ותאמר האתון אל בלעם כי אנכי אתנך אשר רכבת עלי מעודך עד היום הזה ההסכן
הסכנתי לעשת לך כה . ויגל יהוה את עיני בלעם וירא את מלאך יהוה נצב בדרך וחרבו שלופה
בידו ויקד וישתחו לאפיו. ויאמר אליו מלאך יהוה על מה הכית את אתנך זה שלש רגלים הנה אנכי
יצאתי לשטן כי ירט הדרך לנגדי. ותראני האתון ותט לפני זה שלש רגלים אולי נטתה מפני כי
עתה גם אתכה הרגתי ואותה החייתי. ויאמר בלעם אל מלאך יהוה חטאתי כי לא ידעתי כי אתה
נצב לקראתי בדרך ועתה אם רע בעיניך אשובה לי. ויאמר מלאך יהוה אל בלעם לך עם
האנשים ואפס את הדבר אשר אדבר אליך אתו תדבר וילך בלעם אם שרי בלק.

wybʾ ʾlhym ʾl blʿm lylh wyʾmr lw ʾm lqrʾ lk bʾw hʾnšym qwm lk ʾtm wʾk ʾt hdbr ʾšr ʾdbr ʾlyk ʾtw tʿśh. wyqm blʿm bbqr wyḥbš ʾt ʾtnw wylk ʿm śry mwʾb. wyḥr ʾp ʾlhym ky hwlk hwʾ wytyṣb mlʾk yhwh bdrk lśṭn lw whwʾ rkb ʿl ʾtnw wšny nʿryw ʿmw. wtrʾ hʾtwn ʾt mlʾk yhwh nṣb bdrk wḥrbw šlwph bydw wtṭ hʾtwn wtlk bśdh yk blʿm ʾt hʾtwn lhṭth hdrk. yʿmd mlʾk yhwh bmšʿwl hkrmym gdr mzh wgdr mzh. wtrʾ hʾtwn ʾt mlʾk yhwh wtlḥṣ ʾl hqyr wtlḥṣ ʾt rgl blʿm wysp lhkth. wysp mlʾk yhwh ʿbwr yʿmd bmqwm ṣr ʾšr ʾyn drk lnṭwt ymyn wśmʾwl. wtrʾ hʾtwn ʾt mlʾk yhwh trbṣ tḥt blʿm wyḥr ʾp blʿm wyk ʾt hʾtwn bmql. wypṭḥ yhwh ʾt py hʾtwn wtʾmr lblʿm mh ʿśyty lk ky hkytny zh šlš rglym. wyʾmr blʿm lʾtwn ky htʿllt by lw yš ḥrb bydy ky ʿth hrgtyk. wtʾmr hʾtwn ʾlblʿm ky ʾnky ʾtnk ʾšr rkbt ʿly mʿwdk ʿd hywm hzh hhskn hsknty lʿśt lk kh. wygl yhwh ʾt ʿyny blʿm wyrʾ ʾt mlʾk yhwh nṣb bdrk wḥrbw šlwph bydw wyqd wyštḥw lʾpyw. wyʾmr ʾlyw mlʾk yhwh ʿl mh hkyt ʾt ʾtwnk zh šlš rglym hnh ʾnky yṣʾty lśṭn ky yrṭ hdrk lngdy. wtrʾny hʾtwn ṭṭ lpny zh šlš rglym ʾwly nṭth mpny ky ʿth gm ʾtkh hrgty wʾwth hḥyyty. wyʾmr blʿm ʾl mlʾk yhwh ḥṭʾty ky lʾ ydʿty ky ʾth nṣb lqrhty bdrk wʿth ʾm rʿ bʿynyk ʾšwbh ly. wyʾmr mlʾk yhwh ʾl blʿm lk ʿm hʾnšym wʾps ʾt hdbr ʾšr ʾdbr ʾlyk ʾtw tdbr wylk blʿm ʿm śry mwʾb.

That night *ʾelohîm* came to Bilʿam and said to him, "If the men have come to summon you, get up and go with them; but do only what I tell you to do." So Bilʿam got up in the morning, saddled his she-ass, and went with the officials of Moab. However, *ʾelohîm*'s anger was kindled because he was going, and YHWH's messenger took his stand in the road as his adversary. Now he was riding on the she-ass, and his two servants were with him. The she-ass saw YHWH's messenger standing in the road, with a drawn sword in his hand; so the she-ass turned off the road, and went into the field; and Bilʿam struck the she-ass, to turn it back onto the road. Then YHWH's messenger stood in a narrow path between the vineyards, with a wall on either side. When the she-ass saw YHWH's messenger, it scraped against the wall, and scraped Bilʿam's foot against the wall; so he struck it again. Then YHWH's messenger went ahead, and stood in a narrow place, where there was no way to turn either to the right or to the left. When the she-ass saw YHWH's messenger, it lay down under Bilʿam; and Bilʿam's anger was kindled, and he struck the she-ass with his staff. Then YHWH opened the mouth of the she-ass, and it said to Bilʿam, "What have I done to you, that you have struck me these three times?" Bilʿam said to the she-ass, "Because you have made a fool of me! I wish I had a sword in my hand! I would kill you right now!" But the she-ass said to Bilʿam, "Am I not your she-ass, which you have ridden all your life to this day? Do I take care of you in such a way?" And he said, "No." Then YHWH opened Bilʿam's eyes, and he saw YHWH's messenger standing in the road, with his drawn sword in his hand; and fell prostrate on his face. YHWH's messenger said to him, "Why have you struck your she-ass these three times? I have come out as an adversary, because your way is perverse before me. The she-ass saw me, and turned away from me these three times. If it had not turned away from me, surely just now I would have killed you and let it live." Then Bilʿam said to YHWH's messenger, "I have sinned, for I did not know that you were standing in the road to oppose me. Now therefore, if it is displeasing to you, I will return home." YHWH's messenger said to Bilʿam, "Go with the men; but speak only what I tell you to speak." So Bilʿam went with the officials of Balak.

APPENDIX 2

JOB AND JONAH
A Short Comparison

Thematic compatibility

There is a thematic similarity between the Book of Jonah and the Prologue of the Book of Job. Both works deal with the mutual responsibilities of the divine and the human or the lack thereof.[1] There is perhaps even a similarity even in the literal meanings of the names of the central characters—Jonah as the dove flying upward and Job as the hater striking inward.

The Flight of Jonah

The book recounts the story of the travels and misfortunes of an unwilling individual named יונה בן אמתי (*ywnh bn ʾmty*) – Jonah the son of Amittai,[2] who is selected by יהוה (YHWH) to travel to Nineveh, the capital of Assyria The inhabitants of Nineveh are evil people and Jonah is to spread the word that Nineveh was about to be destroyed.[3]

Job, by comparison, is unwittingly selected by יהוה (YHWH) as the paragon of human "wholeness" and the bearer of ultimate salvation for humanity.

Flight as vertical downward to the bottom of the ocean as opposed to as opposed to horizontal over land

In Jonah 1[3], Jonah "arises" – ויקם (*wyqm*) to flee to Tarshish away from יהוה (YHWH)." He then begins a path of descent. He "descends" – וירד (*wyrd*) to Jaffa, where he boards a ship bound for Tarshish. He pays his fare and "descends" – וירד (*wyrd*) into the ship.

Job does not flee since he is not aware of his predicament until he is in its midst.

The Storm

The ship promptly runs into a violent storm—רוח גדולה (*rwḥ gdwlh*) that יהוה (YHWH) has raised.[4] Jonah once again descends – וירד (*wyrd*) to the very bottom of the ship.

Job experiences the very same רוח גדולה (*rwḥ gdwlh*) as part of his testing.

The captain orders Jonah to pray to his god for intercession; however, the crew cast lots and decides that the "winner" must be the cause of their misfortune. Jonah "wins" the lottery. The crew interrogate Jonah as to his origins:

---

[1] This is the basis for further study and is offered here for informational purposes.

[2] Jonah 1[1]. See also 2Kings 14[25] where יונה בן אמתי (*ywnh bn ʾmty*)—Jonah the son of Amittai is described as "the prophet from Gath Haḥeper." This retrojected attribution of a name is identical to that of Job in Ezek. 14[14.21].

[3] Nineveh actually fell in 612 BC.

[4] See Job 1[19].

ומאין תבוא מה ארצך ואי מזה עם אתה
(*wmʾyn tbwʾ mh ʾrṣk wʾy mzh ʿm ʾth*)
"and whence do you come, what is [the name of] your country,
and to what people do you belong?[5]

Jonah confesses "I am a Hebrew"—עברי אנכי (ʿ*bry ʾnky*)[6] and "I revere YHWH the god of the heavens" – יהוה אלהי השמים אני ירא (*ʾt yhwh ʾlhy hšmym ʾny yrʾ*).[7] The crew asks what they have to do to quiet the sea and Jonah tells them that he is the cause of the problem and that if they throw him overboard, all will be well. The crew invokes the name of יהוה (YHWH), throws Jonah overboard, and the storm abates. The crew then offers sacrifices to יהוה (YHWH) and they are saved. Of course, Jonah never made it to Nineveh.

Deliverance from drowning by the fish and השטן (*haśśaṭan*)

Meanwhile, יהוה (YHWH) causes a large fish to swallow Jonah. He remains in the belly of the fish for three days during which he is introspective, prays, and declares יהוה (YHWH) to be his salvation. יהוה (YHWH) has the fish spit Jonah out on to dry land.

We may well draw a comparison between "the great fish" and השטן (*haśśaṭan*) as יהוה (YHWH)'s tools, the one as rescuer, the other as "prover."

The Second Mission

יהוה (YHWH) now calls upon Jonah a second time to go to Nineveh and deliver his message. This he does and the people of Nineveh immediately believe Jonah, mourn, and promptly reform their ways. God (האלהים – *hʾlhym*)[8] sees their repentance and regrets that he ever thought to destroy them.

In the Prologue to Book of Job, יהוה (YHWH) expresses similar regrets but accuses השטן (*haśśaṭan*) of deceiving him about Job.

Jonah's recognition of YHWH's fickle nature and his displeasure

Jonah is irate and questions why יהוה (YHWH) ever sent him to Nineveh in the first place since יהוה (YHWH) knew that that he would not make good on his plan to destroy the city and its inhabitants. He considers his ordeals to have been a complete waste of time and declares:

ועתה יהוה קח נא את נפשי ממני כי טוב מותי מחיי
wʿth yhwh qḥ nʾ ʾt npšy mmny ky ṭwb mwty mḥyy
"And now, YHWH, take my soul from me, for my being dead is better than my living"

---

[5] Jonah 1[8] and Job 1[6].
[6] Jonah 1[9].
[7] Jonah 1[9].
[8] Jonah 3[10].

APPENDIX 2

יהוה (YHWH) asks Jonah if he really wishes to be that angry. Jonah does not reply. He leaves the city and lives in a hut to await the true outcome of Nineveh.

Job similarly vents his spleen against יהוה (YHWH). His expression in Job 3^3ff. of his wish for the "annihilation of Creation" is far more vehement than Jonah's most irate outburst. Yet there is a comparison of the pathos and desperation and a stark contrast in intensity.

There is no guarantee of salvation

Despite the parable of the gourd[9] that teaches that all divine creations are ephemeral and that divine compassion is eternal, Jonah insists that he prefers "anger until death" and repeats the phrase טוב מותי מחיי (*ṭwb mwty mḥyy*) – "death is better for me than life."[10]

The book ends with a strangely worded sentence:

ואני לא אחוס על נינוה העיר הגדולה
אשר יש בה הרבה משתים עשרה רבו אדם
אשר לא ידע בין ימינו לשמאלו ובהמה רבה
w'ny l' 'ḥws 'l nynwh h'yr hgdwlh
'šr yš bh hrbh mštym 'śrh rbw 'dm
'šr l' yd' byn ymynw lśm'lw wbhmh rbh
And I shall not have pity on the great city of Nineveh
That contains more than 120,000 people
Who cannot distinguish right from left, and much cattle.

This verse is commonly translated as a rhetorical question in explanation of יהוה (YHWH)'s responsibility for his creation. If it were truly a question, we would expect the interrogative הלא (*hl'*) expressing the sense "shall I not take pity?" It is perhaps more cogent to translate the sentence in the absolute as above. Rather than vindicate יהוה (YHWH), it would validate Jonah's disgust at יהוה (YHWH)'s constant ambivalence.

Vawter understands the comparison of the apparent capriciousness of יהוה (YHWH) in the Books of Job and Jonah although perhaps for the wrong reasons.[11] His perspective is that of the Deity and the breadth of its compassion for humanity.

We would submit that human knowledge of divine compassion is presumptuous. The best that humanity can achieve is a profound knowledge of its own condition and a total ignorance of divine intentions. It is the frustration brought about by this ignorance that generates the internal tension of the human condition.

---

[9] Jonah $4^{6\text{-}11}$

[10] Jonah 4 $^{8\text{-}9}$.

[11] Vawter (1983, 109 ff.).

THE DEFINITION OF צדיק (*ṣdyq*) AND THE NOAH CONNECTION EZEKIEL 18[5-9]

ואיש כי יהיה צדיק ועשה משפט וצדקה
אל ההרים לא אכל ואת עיניו לא נשא אל גלולי בית ישראל
ואת אשת רעהו לא טמא ואל אשה נדה לא יקרב
ואיש לא יונה חבלתו חוב ישיב גזלה לא יגזל
לחמו לרעב יתן ועירם יכסה בגד
בנשך לא יתן ותרבית לא יקח מעול ישיב ידו
משפט אמת יעשה בין איש לאיש
בחקותי יהלך ומשפטי שמר לעשות אמת צדיק הוא חיה יחיה

w’yš ky yhyh ṣdyq w‘śh mšpṭ wṣdph
’l hhrym l’ ’kl w’t ‘ynyw l’ nś’ ’l glwly byt yśr’l
w’t ’št r‘hw l’ ṭm’ w’l ’šh ndh l’ yqrb
w’yš l’ ywnh ḥbltw ḥwb yšyb gzlh l’ ygzl
lḥmw lr‘b ytn w‘yrm yksh bgd
bnšk l’ ytn wtrbyt l’ yqḥ m‘wl yśyb ydw
mšpṭ ’mt y‘śh byn ’yš l’yš
bḥqty yhlk wmšpṭy šmr l‘śwt ’mt ṣdyq hw’ ḥyh yḥyh

A man who would be whole would do justice and wholeness.
He does not eat upon the mountains or lift up his eyes to the idols of the house of Israel.
He does not defile his neighbor’s wife or approach a woman during her menstrual period,
He does not oppress anyone, but restores to the debtor his pledge, commits no robbery.
He gives his bread to the hungry and covers the naked with a garment.
He does lend with interest or collect with increase, and withholds his hand from iniquity.
He performs with truth and justice between contending parties.
He follows my statutes, and is careful to observe my ordinances, acting in truth
Such a one is whole; he shall surely live.

NOAH, DAN’EL AND JOB: EZEKIEL 14[13-20]

בן אדם ארץ כי תחטא לי למעל מעל ונטיתי ידי עליה ושברתי לה מטה לחם
והשלחתי בה רעב והכרתי ממנה אדם ובהמה
והיו שלשת האנשים האלה בתוכה נח דנאל ואיוב המה בצדקתם ינצלו נפשם נאם אדני יהוה
לו חיה רעה אעביר בארץ ושכלתה והיתה שממה מבלי עובר מפני החיה
שלשת האנשים האלה בתוכה חי אני נאם אדני יהוה אם בנים ואם בנות יצילו
המה לבדם ינצלו והארץ תהיה שממה
או חרב אביא על הארץ ההיא ואמרתי חרב תעבר בארץ והכרתי ממנה אדם ובהמה
ושלשת האנשים האלה בתוכה חי אני נאם אדני יהוה לא יצילו בנים ובנות כי הם לבדם ינצלו
או דבר אשלח אל הארץ ההיא ושפכתי חמתי עליה בדם להכרית ממנה אדם ובהמה
ונח דנאל ואיוב בתוכה חי אני נאם אדני יהוה אם בן אם בת יצילו המה בצדקתם יצילו נפשם

bn'dm 'rṣ ky tḥṭ' ly lm'l m'l wnṭyty ydy 'lyh wšbrty lhm mṭh lḥm whšlḥty bh r'b
whkrty mmnh 'dm wbhmh
whyw šlšt h'nšym h'lh nḥ dn'l w'ywb hmh bṣdqtm ynṣlw npšm n'm 'dny yhwh
lw ḥyh r'h ''byr b'rṣ wšklth whyth šmmh mbly 'wbr mpny hḥyh
šlšt h'nšym h'lh btwkh ḥy'ny n'm 'dny yhwh 'm bnym w'm bnwt yṣylw
hmh lbd m ynṣlw wh'rṣ thyh šmmh
'w ḥrb 'by' 'l h'rṣ hhy' w'mrty ḥrb t'br b'rṣ whkrty mmnh 'dm wbhmh'
wšlšt h'nšym h'lh btwkh ḥy'ny n'm 'dny yhwh
l' yṣylw bnym 'w bnwt ky hm lbdm ynṣlw
'w dbr 'šlḥ 'l h'rṣ hhy' wšpkty ḥmty 'lyh bdm lhkryt mmnh 'dm wbhmh
wnḥ dn'l w'ywb btwkh ḥy'ny n'm 'dny yhwh
'm bn 'm bt yṣylw hmh bṣdqtm yṣylw npšm

Mortal, when a land sins against me by acting faithlessly,
and I stretch out my hand against it,
and break its staff of bread and send famine upon it,
And cut off from it human beings and animals;
Even if these three men, Noah, Dani'el and Job, were in it,
they would save only their own lives by their wholeness, says Adonai YHWH.
If I send wild animals through the land to ravage it, so that it is made desolate,
And no one may pass through because of the animals;
Even if these three men were in it, as I live, says Adonai YHWH,
they would save neither sons nor daughters;
they alone would be saved, but the land would be desolate.
Or if I bring a sword upon that land and say, 'Let a sword pass through the land,'
And I cut off human beings and animals from it;
Though these three men were in it, as I live, says Adonai YHWH,
They would save neither sons nor daughters, buy they alone would be saved.
Or if I send a pestilence into that land, and pour out my wrath upon it with blood,
to cut off humans and animals from it;
Even if Noah, Dan'el and Job were in it, as I live, says Adonai YHWH,
they would save neither son nor daughter;
They would save only their own lives by their wholeness.

THE OCCURRENCES OF צדק (*ṣdq*), צדיק (*ṣdyq*) AND צדקה (*ṣdqh*) IN THE BOOK OF JOB

4:17

האנוש מאלוה יצדק אם מעשהו יטהר גבר

hʾnwš mʾlwh yṣdq ʾm mʿśhw yṭhr gbr

6:29

שבו נא אל תהי עולה ושבי עוד צדקי בה

šbw nʾ ʾl thy ʿwlh wšby ʿwd ṣdqy bh

8:3

האל יעות משפט ואם שדי יעות צדק

hʾl yʿwt mšpṭ wʾm šdy yʿwt ṣdq

8:6

אם זך וישר אתה כי עתה יעיר עליך ושלם נות צדקך

ʾm zk wyšr ʾth ky ʿth yʿyr ʿlyk wšlm nwt ṣdqk

9:2

אמנם ידעתי כי כן ומה יצדק אנוש עם אל

ʾmnm ydʿty ky kn wmh yṣdq ʾnwš ʿm ʾl

9:15

אשר אם צדקתי לא אענה למשפטי אתחנן

ʾšr ʾm ṣdqty lʾ ʾʿnh lmšpṭy ʾtḥnn

9:20

אם אצדק פי ירשיעני תם אני ויעקשני

ʾm ʾṣdq py yršyʿny tm ʾny wyʿqšny

10:15

אם רשעתי אללי לי וצדקתי לא אשא ראשי שבע קלון וראה עניי

ʾm ršʿty ʾlly ly wṣdqty lʾ ʾśʾ ršy śbʿ qlwn wrʾh ʿnyy

11:2

הרב דברים לא יענה ואם איש שפתים יצדק

hrb dbrym lʾ yʿnh wʾm ʾyš śptym yṣdq

12:4

שחק לרעהו אהיה קורא לאלוה ויענהו שחוק צדיק תמים

śḥq lrʿhw ʾhyh qwrʾ lʾlwh wyʿnhw śḥwq ṣdyq tmym

13:18

הנה נא ערכתי משפט ידעתי כי אני אצדק

hnh nʾ ʿrkty mšpṭ ydʿty ky ʾny ʾṣdq

15:14

מה אנוש כי יזכה וכי יצדק ילוד אשה

mh ʾnwš ky yzkh wky yṣdq ylwd ʾšh

17:9

ויאחז צדיק דרכו וטהר ידים יסיף אמץ

wy'ḥz ṣdyq drkw wṭhr ydym ysyp 'mṣ

22:3

החפץ לשדי כי תצדק ואם בצע כי תתם דרכיך

hḥpṣ lšdy ky tṣdq w'm bṣʿ ky ttm drkyk

22:19

יראו צדיקים וישמחו ונקי ילעג למו

yr'w ṣdyqym wyśmḥw wnqy ylʿg lmw

25:4

ומה יצדק אנוש עם אל ומה יזכה ילוד אשה

wmh yṣdq 'nwš ʿm 'l wmh yzkh ylwd 'šh

27:5,6

חלילה לי אם אצדיק אתכם עד אגוע לא אסיר תמתי ממני
בצדקתי החזקתי ולא ארפה ולא יחרף לבבי מימי

ḥlylh ly 'm 'ṣdyq 'tkm ʿd 'gwʿ l' 'syr tmty mmny
bṣdqty hḥzqty wl' 'rph wl' yḥrp lbby mymy

27:17

יכין וצדיק ילבש וכסף נקי יחלק

ykyn wṣdyq ylbš wksp nqy yḥlq

29:14

צדק לבשתי וילבשני כמעיל וצניף משפטי

ṣdq lbšty wylbšny kmʿyl wṣnyp mšpṭy

31:6

ישקלני במאזני צדק וידע אלוה תמתי

yšqlny bm'zny ṣdp wydʿ 'lwh tmty

32:1,2

וישבתו שלשת האנשים האלה מענות את איוב כי הוא צדיק בעיניו
ויחר אף אליהוא בן ברכאל הבוזי ממשפחת רם באיוב חרה אפו על צדקו נפשו מאלהים

wyšbtw šlšt h'nšym h'lh mʿnwt 't 'ywb ky ṣdyq hw' bʿynyw
wyḥr 'p 'lyhw' bn brk'l hbwzy mmšpḥt rm b'ywb ḥrh 'pw ʿl ṣdqw npšw m'lhym

33:12

הן זאת לא צדקת אענך כי ירבה אלוה מאנוש

hn z't l' ṣdqt 'ʿnk ky yrbh 'lwh m'nwš

33:26

יעתר אל אלוה וירצהו וירא פניו בתרועה וישב לאנוש צדקתו

yʿtr 'l 'lwh wyrṣhw wyr' pnyw btrwʿh wyšb l'nwš ṣdqtw

33:32

אם יש מלין השיבני דבר כי חפצתי צדקך

'm yš mlyn hšybny ky ḥpṣty ṣdqk

34:5

כי אמר איוב צדקתי ואל הסיר משפטי

ky ʾmr ʾywb ṣdqty wʾl hsyr mšpṭy

34:17

האף שונא משפט יחבוש ואם צדיק כביר תרשיע

hʾp śwnʾ mšpṭ yḥbwš wʾm ṣdyq kbyr tršyʿ

35:2

הזאת חשבת למשפט אמרת צדקי מאל

hzʾt ḥšbt lmšpṭ ʾmrt ṣdqy mʾl

35:7,8

אם צדקת מה תתן לו או מה מידך יקח

לאיש כמוך רשעך ולבן אדם צדקתך

ʾm ṣdqt mh ttn lw ʾw mh mydk yqḥ

lʾyš kmwk ršʿk wlbn ʾdm ṣdqtk

36:3

אשא דעי למרחוק ולפעלי אתן צדק

ʾśʾ dʿy lmrḥwq wlpʿly ʾtn ṣdq

36:7

לא יגרע מצדיק עיניו ואת מלכים לכסא וישיבם לנצח ויגבהו

lʾ ygrʿ mṣdyq ʿynyw wmlkym lksʾ wyšybm lnṣḥ wygbhw

37:23

שדי לא מצאנהו שגיא כח ומשפט ורב צדקה לא יענה

šdy lʾmṣʾnhw śgyʾ kḥ wmšpṭ wrb ṣdqh lʾ yʿnh

40:8

האף תפר משפטי תרשיעני למען תצדק

hʾp tpr mšpṭy tršyʿny lmʿn tṣdq

REFERENCES TO NAMES OF DEITIES IN CHAPTERS 3^{4}-42^{6}

Chapter 3 – Job

3^{4}

היום ההוא יהי חשך אל ידרשהו **אלוה** ממעל ואל תופע עליו נהרה

3^{23}

לגבר אשר דרכו נסתרה ויסך **אלוה** בעדו

3^{25}

כי **פחד** פחדתי ויאתיני ואשר יגרתי יבא לי

Chapter 4 – ʾEliphaz

4^{9}

מנשמת **אלוה** יאבדו ומרוח אפו יכלו

4^{17}

האנוש מ**אלוה** יצדק אם מעשהו יטהר גבר

Chapter 5 – ʾEliphaz

5^{8}

אולם אני אדרש אל **אל** ואל **אלהים** אשים דברתי

5^{17}

הנה אשרי אנוש יכחנו **אלוה** ומוסר **שדי** אל תמאס

Chapter 6 – Job

6^{4}

כי חצי **שדי** עמדי אשר חמתם שתה רוחי בעותי **אלוה** יערכוני

$6^{8,9}$

מי יתן תבוא שאלתי ותקותי יתן **אלוה**
ויאל **אלוה** וידכאני יתר ידו ויבצעני

6^{14}

למס מרעהו חסד ויראת **שדי** יעזוב

Chapter 7 – Job

Chapter 8 – Bildad

8^{3}

ה**אל** יעות משפט ואם **שדי** יעות צדק

8^{5}

האם אתה תשחר אל **אל** ואל **שדי** תתחנן

8[13]

כן ארחות כל שכחי **אל** ותקות חנף תאבד

8[20]

הן **אל** לא ימאס תם ולא יחזיק ביד מרעים

Chapter 9 – Job

9[2]

אמנם ידעתי כי כן ומה יצדק אנוש עם **אל**

9[13]

אלוה לא ישיב אפו תחתו שחחו עזרי רהב

Chapter 10 – Job

10[2]

אמר אל **אלוה** לא תרשיעני הודיעני על מה תריבני

Chapter 11 – Zophar

11[5-7]

ואולם מי יתן **אלוה** דבר ויפתח שפתיו עמך

ויגד לך תעלמות כי כפלים לתושיה ודע כי ישה לך **אלוה** מעונך

החקר **אלוה** תמצא אם עד תכלית **שדי** תמצא

Chapter 12 – Job

12[4]

שחק לרעהו אהיה קרא ל**אלוה** ויענהו שחוק צדיק תמים

12[6]

ישליו אהלים לשדדים ובטחות למרגיזי **אל** לאשר הביא **אלוה** בידו

12[9]

מי לא ידע בכל אלה כי יד **יהוה** עשתה זאת

Chapter 13 – Job

13[3]

אולם אני אל **שדי** אדבר והוכח אל **אל** אחפץ

13[7,8]

ה**לאל** תדברו עולה ולו תדברו רמיה

הפניו תשאון אם **לאל** תריבון

Chapter 14 – Job

Chapter 15 – ʾEliphaz

15[4]

אף אתה תפר יראה ותגרע שיחה לפני **אל**

15[8]

הבסוד **אלוה** תשמע ותגרע אליך חכמה

15[11]

המעט ממך תנחמות **אל** ודבר לאט עמך

15[13]

כי תשיב אל **אל** רוחך והצאת מפיך מלין

15[25]

כי נטה אל **אל** ידו ואל **שדי** יתגבר

Chapter 16 – Job

16[11]

יסגירני **אל** אל אויל ועל ידי רשעים ירטני

16[20,21]

מליצי רעי אל **אלוה** דלפה עיני

ויוכח לגבר עם **אלוה** ובן אדם לרעהו

Chapter 17 – Job

Chapter 18 – Bildad

18[21]

אך אלה משכנות עול וזה מקום לא ידע **אל**

Chapter 19 – Job

19[6]

דעו אפו כי **אלוה** עותני ומצודו עלי הקיף

19[21,22]

חנני חנני אתם רעי כי יד **אלוה** נגעה בי

למה תרדפני כמו **אל** ומבשרי לא תשבעו

19[26]

ואחר עורי נקפו זאת ומבשרי אחזה **אלוה**

Chapter 20 – Zophar

20[15]

חיל בלע ויקאנו מבטנו יורישנו **אל**

20[29]

זה חלק אדם רשע מאלהים ונחלת אמרו מאל

Chapter 21 – Job

21[9]

בתיהם שלום מפחד ואין שבט אלוה עליהם

21[14,15]

ויאמרו לאל ממנו ודעת דרכיך לא חפצנו
מה שדי כי נדענו ומה נועיל כי נפגע בו

21[19]

אלוה יצפן לבניו אונו ישלם אליו וידע

21[22]

הלאל ילמד דעת והוא רמים ישפוט

Chapter 22 – ʾEliphaz

22[2,3]

הלאל יסכן גבר כי יסכן עלימו משכיל
החפץ לשדי כי תצדק ואם בצע כי תתם דרכיך

22[12,13]

הלא אלוה גבה שמים וראה ראש כוכבים כי רמו
ואמרת מה ידע אל הבעד ערפל ישפוט

22[17]

האמרים לאל סור ממנו ומה יפעל שדי למו

22[23]

אם תשוב עד שדי תבנה תרחיק עולה מאהלך

22[25,26]

והיה שדי בצריך וכסף תועפות לך
כי או על שדי תתענג ותשא אל אלוה פניך

Chapter 23 – Job

23[16]

ואל הרך לבי ושדי הבהילני

Chapter 24 – Job

24[1]

מדוע משדי לא נצפנו עתים וידעיו לא חצו ימיו

24^{12}

מעיר מתים ינאקו ונפש חללים תשוע ו**אלוה** לא ישים תפלה

24^{25}

ואם לא אפו מי יכזיבני וישם ל**אל** מלתי

Chapter 25 – Bildad

25^{4}

ומה יצדק אנוש עם **אל** ומה יזכה ילוד אשה

Chapter 26 – Job

Chapter 27 – Job

$27^{2,3}$

חי **אל** הסיר משפטי ו**שדי** המר נפשי

כי כל עוד נשמתי בי ורוח **אלוה** באפי

27^{8-11}

כי מה תקות חנף כי יבצע כי ישל **אלוה** נפשו

הצעקתו ישמע **אל** כי תבוא עליו צרה

אם על **שדי** יתענג יקרא **אלוה** בכל עת

אורה אתכם ביד **אל** אשר עם **שדי** לא אכחד

27^{13}

זה חלק אדם רשע עם **אל** ונחלת עריצים מ**שדי** יקחו

Chapter 28 – Job

28^{23}

אלהים הבין דרכה והוא ידע את מקומה

Chapter 29 – Job

29^{2}

מי יתנני כירחי קדם כימי **אלוה** ישמרני

$29^{4,5}$

כאשר הייתי בימי חרפי בסוד **אלוה** עלי אהלי

בעוד **שדי** עמדי סביבותי נערי

Chapter 30 – Job

Chapter 31 – Job

31^{2}

ומה חלק **אלוה** מעל ונחלת **שדי** ממרמים

31[6]

ישקלני במאזני צדק וידע **אלוה** תמתי

31[14]

ומה אעשה כי יקום **אל** וכי יפקד מה אשיבנו

31[23]

כי **פחד** אלי איד **אל** ומשאתו לא אוכל

31[28]

גם הוא עון פלילי כי כחשתי **לאל** ממעל

31[35]

מי יתן לי שמע לי הן תוי **שדי** יענני וספר כתב איש ריבי

Chapter 32 – Elihu

32[2]

על צדקו נפשו **מאלהים**

32[13]

פן תאמרו מצאנו **אל** ידפנו לא איש

Chapter 33 – Elihu

33[4]

רוח **אל** עשתני ונשמת **שדי** תחיני

33[6]

הן אני כפיך **לאל** מחמר קרצתי גם אני

33[12]

הן זאת לא צדקת אענך כי ירבה **אלוה** מאנוש

33[14]

הן באחת ידבר **אל** ובשתים לא ישורנה

33[26]

יעתר אל **אלוה** וירצהו וירא פניו בתרועה וישב לאנוש צדקתו

33[29]

הן כל אלה יפעל **אל** פעמים שלוש עם גבר

Chapter 34 – Elihu

34[5]

כי אמר איוב צדקתי **ואל** הסיר משפטי

34[9]

כי אמר לא יסכן גבר ברצתו עם **אלהים**

34^{10}

חלילה לאל מרשע ושדי מעול

34^{12}

אף אמנם אל לא ירשיע ושדי לא יעות משפט

34^{23}

כי לא על ישים עוד להלך אל אל במשפט

34^{31}

כי אל אל האמר נשאתי לא אחבל

34^{37}

כי יסיף על חטאתו פשע בינינו יספוק וירב אמריו לאל

Chapter 35 – Elihu

35^{2}

הזאת חשבת למשפט אמרת צדקי מאל

35^{10}

ולא אמר איה אלוה עשי נתן זמרת בלילה

35^{13}

אך שוא לא ישמע אל ושדי לא ישורנה

Chapter 36 – Elihu

36^{2}

כתר לי זעיר ואחוך כי עוד לאלוה מלים

36^{5}

הן אל כביר ולא ימאס כביר כח לב

36^{26}

הן אל שגיא ולא נדע מספר שניו ולא חקר

Chapter 37 – Elihu

37^{5}

ירעם אל בקולו נפלאות עשה גדלות ולא נדע

37^{10}

מנשמת אל יתן קרח ורחב מים במוצק

$37^{14,15}$

האזינה זאת איוב עמד והתבונן נפלאות אל
התדע בשום אלוה עליהם והופיע אור עננו

37[22,23]

מצפון זהב יאתה על **אלוה** נורא הוד

שדי לא מצאנהו שגיא כה ומשפט ורב צדקה לא יענה

Chapter 38 – YHWH

38[41]

מי יכין לערב צידו כי ילדיו אל **אל** ישועו יתעו לבלי אכל

Chapter 39 – YHWH

39[17]

כי השה **אלוה** חכמה ולא חלק לה בבינה

Chapter 40 – YHWH

40[2]

הרב אם **שדי** יסור מוכיח **אלוה** יעננה

40[9]

אם זרוע כ**אל** לך ובקול כמהו תרעם

40[19]

הוא ראשית דרכי **אל** העשו יגש חרבו

Chapter 41 – YHWH

Chapter 42[1-6] – Job

APPENDIX 6

A PROPOSED IDENTIFICATION OF "SECTARIAN" PSALMS
A TENTATIVE LIST

Psalms referring exclusively to צדיקים (*ṣdyqym*):
1, 33, 34, 52, 55, 58, 68, 69, 75, 92, 112, 119, 125, 129, 140, 146.

Psalms referring exclusively to חסידים (*ḥsydym*):
4, 12, 16, 18, 43, 50, 79, 85, 88, 89, 97, 132, 148, 149.

Psalms referring exclusively to חוסים (*hwsym*):
2, 16, 17, 18, 25, 31, 34, 36, 37, 46, 57, 61, 62, 71, 73, 91, 104, 144.

Psalms referring both to צדיקים (*ṣdyqym*) and חסידים (*ḥsydym*):
4, 32, 116, 118, 145.

Psalms referring both to צדיקים (*ṣdyqym*) and חוסים (*hwsym*):
7, 11, 14, 64, 72, 94, 141, 142.

Psalms referring to צדיקים (*ṣdyqym*), חסידים (*ḥsydym*), and חוסים (*hwsym*):
31, 37.

This material may be the basis for further study.

ABD	*The Anchor Bible Dictionary*, (ed David Noel Freedman). (New York: Doubleday 1997, 1992).
AED	*Arabic English Dictionary* (ed. J.G. Hava). (Beirut: Catholic Press, 1915)
AHw	*Akkadisches Handwörterbuch* (Wiesbaden, 1959-1975).
BH	*Biblia Hebraica Leningradensia* (ed. A. Dotan). (Peabody, MA: Hendrickson, 2001)
BDB	*Hebrew and English Lexicon of the Old Testament* (eds. Brown, Driver, Briggs). (Oxford: Clarendon Press, 1959)
CAD	*The Assyrian Dictionary of the Oriental Institute of the University of Chicago* (editorial board, Ignace J. Gelb *et al.*) (Chicago, Ill.: The Institute, 1956-1999)
COS	*The Context of Scripture* (ed. W.W. Hallo). Volumes 1-3. 1997, 2000, 2002 (Leiden: Brill)
DNWSI	*Dictionary of Northwest Semitic Inscriptions* (ed. J. Hoftijzer), (Leiden: E.J. Brill, 1994).
DISO	*Dictionnaire des inscriptions sémitiques de l'ouest* (ed. C. Jean and J. Hoftijzer) (Leiden: E.J. Brill, 1965).
DSS	*The Dead Sea Scrolls Study Edition* (ed. and trans. F.G. Martinez and E.J.C. Tigchelaar).2 Vols. (Leiden: E.J. Brill, 1998).
GEL	*A Greek-English Lexicon.* (Liddell, H.G. and Scott, R.) (Oxford: Clarendon Press, 1961).
HALOT	*The Hebrew and Aramaic Lexicon of the Old Testament* Volumes 1-5 1994, 1995, 1996, 1999, 2000 (Leiden: E.J. Brill)
GKC	*Gesenius' Hebrew Grammar* (ed. E. Kautzsch), (rev. A.E. Cowley). (Oxford: Clarendon Press, 1957).
JAS	*Dictionary of the Targumim, Talmud Babli, Yerushalmi and Midrashic Literature.* Compiled by Marcus Jastrow. (New York: Judaica Press, 1971
JSOT	*Journal for the Study of Old Testament.* Sheffield: Sheffield Academic Press.
JSOTS	*Journal for the Study of Old Testament Supplement Series* Sheffield: Sheffield Academic Press.
KAI	*Kanaanäische und aramäische Inschriften* (eds. H. Donner and W. Röllig). (Wiesbaden, O. Harrassowitz, 1962-64)
KJ	*King James Version*

NJPS	*Tanakh: A New Translation of the Holy Scriptures According to the Traditional Hebrew Text.* (Philadelphia: Jewish Publication Society, 1985)
NRSV	*Holy Bible: New Revised Standard Version with Apocrypha.* (New York: Oxford University Press, 1989)
HUCA	*Hebrew Union College Annual*
JSOT	*Journal for the Study of Old Testament*
UT	*Ugaritic Textbook.* C.H. Gordon. AnOr 38 (Rome: Pontifical Biblical Institute, 1965
NRSV	*Holy Bible: New Revised Standard Version with Apocrypha.* (New York: Oxford University Press, 1989)
VT	*Vetus Testamentum*
WBC	*Word Biblical Commentary.* (Word Books: Dallas)

Allegro, John Marco
1958. *The People of the Dead Sea Scrolls*. New York: Doubleday & Co.
Clines, D.J.A.
1985. "False Naivety in the Prologue of Job." *HAR* 9 pp. 127-136
1989. *Job 1-20. WBC* Vol. 17.
Collins, John J.
1977. *The Apocalyptic Vision of the Book of Daniel.* Missoula, MT: Scholars Press.
1995. *The Scepter and the Star: The Messiahs of the Dead Sea Scrolls and Other Ancient Literature*. New York: Doubleday and Co.
Cook, Patton and Watts (Eds.)
2001. *The Whirlwind: Essays on Job, Hermeneutics and Theology in Memory of Jane Morse. JSOTS* 386.
Crown, Alan D. (ed.)
1989. *The Samaritans*. Tübingen: J.C.B. Mohr.
Cooper, Alan
1990. "Reading and Misreading the Prologue to Job." *JSOT* 46 pp. 67-79
Davies, P.
1977. "Ḥasidim in the Maccabean Period." *JJS* 28 pp. 127–40.
Driver, G.R.
1965. *The Judaean Scrolls: The Problem and a Solution*. Oxford: Basil Blackwell.
Fishbane, Michael
1965. Biblical Interpretation in Ancient Israel. Oxford: Clarendon Press
Fulco, William J.
1976. *The Canaanite God Rešep*. New Haven: American Oriental Society.
Gaster, Moses
1927 *The Asatir: The Samaritan Book of the Secrets of Moses.* London: The Royal Asiatic Society.
Ginsburg, C. D.
1966. *Introduction to the Massoretico-Critical Edition of the Hebrew Bible* pp. 1–8, 18, 777. New York: Ktav Publishing House.
Greenberg, Moshe
1983. *Ezekiel 1-20: A New Translation with Introduction and Commentary.* Anchor Bible Vol. 22. New York: Doubleday and Co.
Habel, Norman C.
1985. *The Book of Job: A Commentary*. Philadelphia: The Westminster Press
Hackett, Jo Ann.
1984. *The Bilam Text from Deir 'Alla. HSM* 31 (Chico, Calif.: Scholars Press).
Handy, Lowell, K.
1993. "The Authorization of Divine Power and the Guilt of God in the Book of Job: Useful Ugaritic Parallels." *JSOT* 60 pp.107-118.
Hoffer, Victoria
2001. "Illusion, Allusion and Literary Artifice in the Frame Narrative of Job." *JSOTS* 336, pp.84-99.

Hoffman, Yair
1981. "The Relation between the Prologue and the Speech-Cycles in Job: A Reconsideration." *VT* 31 pp. 160-170
Hurvitz, A.
1966. *The Identification of Post-Exilic Psalms by Means of Linguistic Criteria*
Irwin, W.A.
1962. *Peake's Commentary on the Bible*. (Black and Rowley, eds.). London: Thomas Nelson and Sons
Jaeger, Werner
1967. Aristotle: Fundamentals of the History of His Development. Oxford: Clarendon Press
Johnson, A. R.
1951. "The Psalms" *The Old Testament and Modern Study* (ed. H. H. Rowley), pp. 162–209. London, Oxford University Press.
Josephus, Flavius
1980. *The Works of Josephus* (trans. William Whiston), Peabody, MA: Hendrickson Publishers
Kampen, J.
1988. *The Hasideans and the Origin of Pharisaism.* SCS 24. Atlanta: Scholars Press.
Levin, Saul
1978. *The Father of Joshua/Jesus.* Binghamton: SUNY.
Machinist, Peter
1997. "Job's Daughters and Their Inheritance." *The Echoes of Many Texts: Reflections on Jewish and Christian Traditions.* (ed. W. Dever and J.E. Wright). Brown Judaic Studies 313. Atlanta: Scholars Press.
Neusner, Jacob
1984. *Judaism in the Beginning of Christianity.* Philadelphia: Fortress Press,.
1994. *Rabbinic Judaism: The Documentary History of its Formative Age.* Bethesda, MD: CDL Press.
Newsom, Carol A.
2002. *The Book of Job: A Contest of Moral Imaginations.* New York: Oxford University Press.
2003. "'The Consolation of God': Assessing Job's Friends Across a Cultural Abyss." *JSOTS* 373.
Nodet, Etienne
1997. *A Search for the Origins of Judaism: From* Joshua *to the Mishnah.* (trans. E. Crowley). *JSOTS* 248.
Oppenheim, A. Leo
1964. *Ancient Mesopotamia: Portrait of a Dead Civilization.* Chicago: University of Chicago Press.
Owens, John Joseph
1971. "The Prologue and the Epilogue." *Review and Expositor* 68 457-467.

Pomykala, Kenneth E.
1995. *The Davidic Dynasty Tradition in Early Judaism: Its History and Significance for Messianism.* Atlanta: Scholars Press,.
Pope, Marvin H.
1974. *Job: A New Translation with Introduction and Commentary.* Anchor Bible Vol. 15. 3rd Edition. New York: Doubleday and Co.
Pryzybylski, Benno
1980. *Righteousness in Matthew and his World of Thought.* Cambridge: Cambridge University Press.
Pyeon, Yohan
2003. *You Have not Spoken What Is Right About Me: Intertextuality and the Book of Job. SBL* 54. New York: Lang.
Rabin, Chaim.
1957. *Qumran Studies.* London: Oxford University Press
Rose, Wolter H.
2000. *Zemah and Zerubbabel: Messianic Expectations in the Early Postexilic Period. JSOTS* 304.
Rose, Valentinus
1886. *Aristotelis Fragmenta.* Berlin
Sanders, J. A.
1965. *The Psalms Scroll of Qumran Cave 11 (11QPs^{a}) DJD* IV, Oxford: Clarendon Press
Schiffman, Lawrence H.
1975. *The Halakhah at Qumran.* E. J. Brill Leiden,
1981. "Jewish Sectarianism in Second Temple Times." *Great Schisms in Jewish History* (ed. R. Jospe, and S. Wagner) New York: Ktav
1983. *Sectarian Law in the Dead Sea Scrolls: Courts, Testimony and the Penal Code.* Chico: Scholars Press
1994. *Reclaiming the Dead Sea Scrolls.* Philadelphia,: Jewish Publication Society
Shanks, Hershel.
1993. *Understanding the Dead Sea Scrolls.* New York: Vintage Books
Smith, Mark S.
2001. "The Divine Family at Ugarit and Israelite Monotheism." *JSOTS* 336, 40-68
Strauss, Leo
1952. *Persecution and the Art of Writing.* Glencoe, Illinois: Free Press
Stec, David M.
1994. *The Text of the Targum of Job.* Leiden: E.J. Brill
Stone, Michael E.
1984. *Jewish Writings of the Second Temple Period.* Philadelphia: Fortress Press,
Talmon, Shemaryahu.
1991. *Jewish Civilization in the Hellenistic-Roman Period.* Philadelphia: Trinity Press International
Tsevat, Matitiahu
1980. *The Meaning of the Book of Job and Other Biblical Studies.* New York: Ktav.

VanderKam, James C.
1994 *The Dead Sea Scrolls Today.* Grand Rapids: William B. Eerdmans Publishing Company
von Rad, Gerhard
1961. *Genesis: A Commentary* (trans. J. H. Marks). Philadelphia: Westminster Press.
Weiss, Meir
1983. *The Story of Job's Beginning. Job 1-2: A Literary Analysis.* Jerusalem: Magnes Press.
Wilson, Leslie
2001. *The Serpent Symbol in the Ancient Near East.* Lanham, MD: University Press of America

STUDIES IN JUDAISM
TITLES IN THE SERIES
PUBLISHED BY UNIVERSITY PRESS OF AMERICA

Judith Z. Abrams
The Babylonian Talmud: A Topical Guide, 2002.

Roger David Aus
Matthew 1-2 and the Virginal Conception: In Light of Palestinian and Hellenistic Judaic Traditions on the Birth of Israel's First Redeemer, Moses, 2004.

My Name Is "Legion": Palestinian Judaic Traditions in Mark 5:1-20 and Other Gospel Texts, 2003.

Alan L. Berger, Harry James Cargas, and Susan E. Nowak
The Continuing Agony: From the Carmelite Convent to the Crosses at Auschwitz, 2004.

S. Daniel Breslauer
Creating a Judaism without Religion: A Postmodern Jewish Possibility, 2001.

Bruce Chilton
Targumic Approaches to the Gospels: Essays in the Mutual Definition of Judaism and Christianity, 1986.

David Ellenson
Tradition in Transition: Orthodoxy, Halakhah, and the Boundaries of Modern Jewish Identity, 1989.

Paul V. M. Flesher
New Perspectives on Ancient Judaism, Volume 5: Society and Literature in Analysis, 1990.

Marvin Fox
Collected Essays on Philosophy and on Judaism, Volume One: Greek Philosophy, Maimonides, 2003.

Collected Essays on Philosophy and on Judaism, Volume Two: Some Philosophers, 2003.

Collected Essays on Philosophy and on Judaism, Volume Three: Ethics, Reflections, 2003.

Zev Garber

Methodology in the Academic Teaching of Judaism, 1986.

Zev Garber, Alan L. Berger, and Richard Libowitz

Methodology in the Academic Teaching of the Holocaust, 1988.

Abraham Gross

Spirituality and Law: Courting Martyrdom in Christianity and Judaism, 2005.

Harold S. Himmelfarb and Sergio DellaPergola

Jewish Education Worldwide: Cross-Cultural Perspectives, 1989.

William Kluback

The Idea of Humanity: Hermann Cohen's Legacy to Philosophy and Theology, 1987.

Samuel Morell

Studies in the Judicial Methodology of Rabbi David ibn Abi Zimra, 2004.

Jacob Neusner

Ancient Israel, Judaism, and Christianity in Contemporary Perspective, 2006.

The Aggadic Role in Halakhic Discourses: Volume I, 2001.

The Aggadic Role in Halakhic Discourses: Volume II, 2001.

The Aggadic Role in Halakhic Discourses: Volume III, 2001.

Analysis and Argumentation in Rabbinic Judaism, 2003.

Analytical Templates of the Bavli, 2006.

Ancient Judaism and Modern Category-Formation: "Judaism," "Midrash," "Messianism," and Canon in the Past Quarter Century, 1986.

Canon and Connection: Intertextuality in Judaism, 1987.

Chapters in the Formative History of Judaism. 2006

Dual Discourse, Single Judaism, 2001.

The Emergence of Judaism: Jewish Religion in Response to the Critical Issues of the First Six Centuries, 2000.

First Principles of Systemic Analysis: The Case of Judaism within the History of Religion, 1988.

The Halakhah and the Aggadah, 2001.

Halakhic Hermeneutics, 2003.

Halakhic Theology: A Sourcebook, 2006.

The Hermeneutics of Rabbinic Category Formations, 2001.

How Important Was the Destruction of the Second Temple in the Formation of Rabbinic Judaism? 2006.

How Not to Study Judaism, Examples and Counter-Examples, Volume One: Parables, Rabbinic Narratives, Rabbis' Biographies, Rabbis' Disputes, 2004.

How Not to Study Judaism, Examples and Counter-Examples, Volume Two: Ethnicity and Identity versus Culture and Religion, How Not to Write a Book on Judaism, Point and Counterpoint, 2004.

How the Halakhah Unfolds: Moed Qatan in the Mishnah, ToseftaYerushalmi and Bavli, 2006.

The Implicit Norms of Rabbinic Judaism. 2006.

Intellectual Templates of the Law of Judaism, 2006.

Is Scripture the Origin of the Halakhah? 2005.

Israel and Iran in Talmudic Times: A Political History, 1986.

Israel's Politics in Sasanian Iran: Self-Government in Talmudic Times, 1986.

Judaism in Monologue and Dialogue, 2005.

Major Trends in Formative Judaism, Fourth Series, 2002.

Major Trends in Formative Judaism, Fifth Series, 2002.

Messiah in Context: Israel's History and Destiny in Formative Judaism, 1988.

The Native Category - Formations of the Aggadah: The Later Midrash-Compilations - Volume I, 2000.

The Native Category - Formations of the Aggadah: The Earlier Midrash-Compilations - Volume II, 2000.

Paradigms in Passage: Patterns of Change in the Contemporary Study of Judaism, 1988.

Parsing the Torah, 2005.

Praxis and Parable: The Divergent Discourses of Rabbinic Judaism, 2006.

The Religious Study of Judaism: Description, Analysis and Interpretation, Volume 1, 1986.

The Religious Study of Judaism: Description, Analysis, Interpretation, Volume 2, 1986.

The Religious Study of Judaism: Context, Text, Circumstance, Volume 3, 1987.

The Religious Study of Judaism: Description, Analysis, Interpretation, Volume 4: Ideas of History, Ethics, Ontology, and Religion in Formative Judaism, 1988.

Struggle for the Jewish Mind: Debates and Disputes on Judaism Then and Now, 1988.

The Talmud Law, Theology, Narrative: A Sourcebook, 2005.

Talmud Torah: Ways to God's Presence through Learning: An Exercise in Practical Theology, 2002.

Texts Without Boundaries: Protocols of Non-Documentary Writing in the Rabbinic Canon: Volume I: The Mishnah, Tractate Abot, and the Tosefta, 2002.

Texts Without Boundaries: Protocols of Non-Documentary Writing in the Rabbinic Canon: Volume II: Sifra and Sifré to Numbers, 2002.

Texts Without Boundaries: Protocols of Non-Documentary Writing in the Rabbinic Canon: Volume III: Sifré to Deuteronomy and Mekhilta Attributed to Rabbi Ishmael, 2002.

Texts Without Boundaries: Protocols of Non-Documentary Writing in the Rabbinic Canon: Volume IV: Leviticus Rabbah, 2002.

A Theological Commentary to the Midrash - Volume I: Pesiqta deRab Kahana, 2001.

A Theological Commentary to the Midrash - Volume II: Genesis Raba, 2001.

A Theological Commentary to the Midrash - Volume III: Song of Songs Rabbah, 2001.

A Theological Commentary to the Midrash - Volume IV: Leviticus Rabbah, 2001.

A Theological Commentary to the Midrash - Volume V: Lamentations Rabbati, 2001.

A Theological Commentary to the Midrash - Volume VI: Ruth Rabbah and Esther Rabbah, 2001.

A Theological Commentary to the Midrash - Volume VII: Sifra, 2001.

A Theological Commentary to the Midrash - Volume VIII: Sifré to Numbers and Sifré to Deuteronomy, 2001.

A Theological Commentary to the Midrash - Volume IX: Mekhilta Attributed to Rabbi Ishmael, 2001.

Theological Dictionary of Rabbinic Judaism: Part One: Principal Theological Categories, 2005.

Theological Dictionary of Rabbinic Judaism: Part Two: Making Connections and Building Constructions, 2005.

Theological Dictionary of Rabbinic Judaism: Part Three: Models of Analysis, Explanation, and Anticipation, 2005.

The Theological Foundations of Rabbinic Midrash, 2006.

Theology of Normative Judaism: A Source Book, 2005.

Theology in Action: How the Rabbis of the Talmud Present Theology (Aggadah) in the Medium of the Law (Halakhah). An Anthology, 2006

The Torah and the Halakhah: The Four Relationships, 2003.

The Unity of Rabbinic Discourse: Volume I: Aggadah in the Halakhah, 2001.

The Unity of Rabbinic Discourse: Volume II: Halakhah in the Aggadah, 2001.

The Unity of Rabbinic Discourse: Volume III: Halakhah and Aggadah in Concert, 2001.

The Vitality of Rabbinic Imagination: The Mishnah Against the Bible and Qumran,2005.

Who, Where and What is "Israel?": Zionist Perspectives on Israeli and American Judaism, 1989.

The Wonder-Working Lawyers of Talmudic Babylonia: The Theory and Practice of Judaism in its Formative Age, 1987.

Jacob Neusner and Ernest S. Frerichs

New Perspectives on Ancient Judaism, Volume 2: Judaic and Christian Interpretation of Texts: Contents and Contexts, 1987.

New Perspectives on Ancient Judaism, Volume 3: Judaic and Christian Interpretation of Texts: Contents and Contexts, 1987.

Jacob Neusner and James F. Strange

Religious Texts and Material Contexts, 2001.

David Novak and Norbert M. Samuelson

Creation and the End of Days: Judaism and Scientific Cosmology, 1986.

Proceedings of the Academy for Jewish Philosophy, 1990.

Aaron D. Panken

The Rhetoric of Innovation: Self-Conscious Legal Change in Rabbinic Literature, 2005.

Norbert M. Samuelson

Studies in Jewish Philosophy: Collected Essays of the Academy for Jewish Philosophy, 1980-1985, 1987.

Benjamin Edidin Scolnic

Alcimus, Enemy of the Maccabees, 2004.

If the Egyptians Drowned in the Red Sea Where are Pharaoh's Chariots?: Exploring the Historical Dimension of the Bible, 2005.

Rivka Ulmer

Pesiqta Rabbati: A Synoptic Edition of Pesiqta Rabbati Based upon all Extant Manuscripts and the Editio Princeps, Volume III, 2002.

Manfred H. Vogel

A Quest for a Theology of Judaism: The Divine, the Human and the Ethical Dimensions in the Structure-of-Faith of Judaism Essays in Constructive, 1987.

Anita Weiner

Renewal: Reconnecting Soviet Jewry to the Soviet People: A Decade of American Jewish Joint Distribution Committee (AJJDC) Activities in the Former Soviet Union 1988-1998, 2003.

Eugene Weiner and Anita Weiner

Israel-A Precarious Sanctuary: War, Death and the Jewish People, 1989.

The Martyr's Conviction: A Sociological Analysis, 2002.

Leslie S. Wilson

The Serpent Symbol in the Ancient Near East: Nahash and Asherah: Death, Life, and Healing, 2001.